Boudica Britannia

Boudica Britannia
Rebel, war-leader and Queen

Miranda Aldhouse-Green

Harlow, England • London • New York • Boston • San Francisco • Toronto
Sydney • Tokyo • Singapore • Hong Kong • Seoul • Taipei • New Delhi
Cape Town • Madrid • Mexico City • Amsterdam • Munich • Paris • Milan

PEARSON EDUCATION LIMITED

Edinburgh Gate
Harlow CM20 2JE
United Kingdom
Tel: +44 (0)1279 623623
Fax: +44 (0)1279 431059
Website: www.pearsoned.co.uk

First edition published in Great Britain in 2006

© Pearson Education Limited 2006

The right of Miranda Aldhouse-Green to be identified as author
of this work has been asserted by her in accordance
with the Copyright, Designs and Patents Act 1988.

ISBN-13: 978-1-4058-1100-2
ISBN-10: 1-4058-1100-5

British Library Cataloguing-in-Publication Data
A CIP catalogue record for this book can be obtained from the British Library

Library of Congress Cataloging-in-Publication Data
Aldhouse-Green, Miranda J. (Miranda Jane)
  Boudica Britannia / Miranda Aldhouse-Green. -- 1st ed.
     p. cm.
  Includes bibliographical references (p.   ) and index.
  ISBN-13: 978-1-4058-1100-2
  ISBN-10: 1-4058-1100-5
    1. Boadicea, Queen, d. 62. 2. Great Britain--History--Roman period, 55 B.C.–449 A.D.
  3. Great Britain--History, Military--55 B.C.–449 A.D. 4. Queens--Great
  Britain--Biography. 5. Women soldiers--Great Britain--Biography. 6. Romans--Great
  Britain. 7. Iceni--History. I. Title.

DA145.3.B6A43 2006
936.2'04092--dc22
[B]

2006050665

All rights reserved; no part of this publication may be reproduced, stored
in a retrieval system, or transmitted in any form or by any means, electronic,
mechanical, photocopying, recording, or otherwise without either the prior
written permission of the Publishers or a licence permitting restricted copying
in the United Kingdom issued by the Copyright Licensing Agency Ltd,
Saffron House, 6–10 Kirby Street, London EC1N 8TS. This book may not be lent,
resold, hired out or otherwise disposed of by way of trade in any form
of binding or cover other than that in which it is published, without the
prior consent of the Publishers.

10 9 8 7 6 5 4 3 2 1
10 09 08 07 06

Set by 3
Printed by Henry Ling Ltd, The Dorset Press, Dorchester

The Publisher's policy is to use paper manufactured from sustainable forests.

For my daughter Elisabeth

Boudica Britannia

When the British warrior queen,
Bleeding from the Roman rods,
Sought, with an indignant mien,
Counsel of her country's gods,

Sage beneath a spreading oak
Sat the Druid, hoary chief;
Ev'ry burning word he spoke
Full of rage and full of grief.

'Princess! If our aged eyes
Weep upon thy matchless wrongs,
'Tis because resentment ties
All the terrors of our tongues.

Rome shall perish – write that word
 In the blood that she has spilt;
Perish, hopeless and abhorr'd,
Deep in ruin as in guilt.

Rome, for empire far renown'd,
Tramples on a thousand states;
Soon her pride shall kiss the ground –
Hark! The Gaul is at her gates.

Other Romans shall arise,
Heedless of a soldier's name;
Sounds, not arms, shall win the prize,
Harmony the path to fame.

Then the progeny that springs
From the forests of our land,
Arm'd with thunder, clad with wings,
Shall a wider world command.

Regions Caesar never knew
Thy posterity shall sway,
Where his eagles never flew,
None invincible as they.'

Such the bard's prophetic words,
Pregnant with celestial fire,
Bending, as he swept the chords
Of his sweet but awful lyre.

She, with all a monarch's pride,
Felt them in her bosom glow;
Rush'd to battle, fought and died;
Dying, hurl'd them at the foe.

'Ruffians, pitiless as proud,
Heav'n awards the vengeance due;
Empire is on us bestow'd,
Shame and ruin wait for you.'

('Boadicea' by William Cowper, 1731–1800; from W.A.C. Wilkinson and N.H. Wilkinson eds. 1954. T*he Dragon Book of Verse.* Oxford: Clarendon Press, 25–6.

Contents

List of illustrations	x
List of maps	xi
Author's acknowledgements	xiii
Publisher's acknowledgements	xiv
Preface	xv
1 Boudica's ancestors	1
2 Conquering a myth: Claudius and Britannia	36
3 Client-kingship in the Roman Empire: Prasutagus and Boudica	67
4 Other Boudicas: 'big women' in Iron Age Europe	93
5 *Femmes fatales*: Boudica and Cartimandua	120
6 The role of the Druids in Boudica's Rebellion	144
7 Rape, rebellion and slaughter	172
8 Aftermath: retribution and reconciliation	209
9 The Icenian wolf: legend and legacy	241
Epitaph	252
Bibliography	255
Index	279

Illustrations

Black and white plates

1.1	The early Roman temple at Hayling Island, Hampshire.	16
1.2	Inscribed Icenian coin.	22
1.3	'Norfolk wolf' coin found in 2000, from near Burnham Market, Norfolk.	23
2.1	Bronze head of Claudius, from a monumental statue found in the river Alde, Suffolk.	37
2.2	Gold coin (an *aureus*) of Claudius.	44
2.3	Fragment of Claudius's triumphal arch at Rome.	45
2.4	Britannia and Claudius on the carving from Aphrodisias, Turkey.	46
2.5	The temple inscription from Chichester, mentioning Togidubnus.	49
2.6	Marble head of a youth, mid-first century AD, from Fishbourne.	51
2.7	Reconstruction drawing of the façade of the temple of Claudius at Colchester.	59
3.1	The Crownthorpe hoard, Norfolk.	69
4.1	Bronze statuette of a woman on a cult-wagon from a chieftain's grave at Strettweg, Austria.	101
4.2	Bronze statuette of a female warrior, from Dinéault, Brittany.	103
4.3	Early nineteenth-century statue of the prophetess Veleda.	107
5.1	'Romans go home!' graffito, on display in the Museum of London.	133
5.2	Bronze amulet depicting a bound captive or slave, from Brough-under-Stainmore, Cumbria.	136
6.1	The great ritual enclosure at Fison Way, Thetford.	161
6.2	The male head from the temple pediment at Bath.	167

8.1	The cavalry training ring at the Lunt, Baginton, outside Coventry.	213
8.2	Conquered Britons, on a distance slab at Bridgeness, on the Antonine Wall, Scotland.	214
8.3	The tombstone of Julius Classicianus, found in London.	217
9.1	Modern concrete frieze depicting schematised confrontation between the Romans and Boudica's Britons.	242

Maps

1	Southern England and Wales in the late Iron Age.	5
2	*Civitates* or tribal states in which Roman Britain was administered.	9
3	Possible tribal centres and distribution of terret types within Icenian territory in the late Iron Age.	24
4	Aulus Plautius's initial campaigns during the Claudian invasion of Britain.	40
5	British and Roman forces before the final pitched battle between Boudica and Suetonius Paulinus.	197

Colour plates

1. Hoard of Icenian silver coins, found in a pot at Honingham, Norfolk.
2. The Winchester hoard of gold jewellery.
3. The Sedgeford torc terminal.
4. Potsherd depicting a Trinovantian horseman, from Kelvedon, Essex.
5. The Catuarus ring found at Fishbourne.
6. Aureus of Nero showing a portrait of the emperor as a young man.
7. Portrait of Caratacus, on a stained-glass window in the Moot Hall, Colchester Town Hall.
8. Cleopatra, depicted on the rear external wall of the Dendera temple of Hathor, Egypt.
9. Boudica and her daughters; a marble statue in Cardiff City Hall.
10. Reconstruction of Boudica's chariot in the Castle Museum, Colchester.

11 The body of a middle-aged female from Haraldskaer, Jutland.
12 Chariot-burial of a woman with a facial disfigurement, Wetwang Slack, East Yorkshire.
13 The Gallo-Roman horse-goddess Epona, from Alesia, Burgundy.
14 Antiquarian picture of Boudica/Boadicea.
15 Llyn Cerrig Bach, Anglesey.
16 Druids confront the Romans led by Suetonius Paulinus on Anglesey.
17 Decorated crescentric plaque from Llyn Cerrig Bach, Anglesey.
18 The late Roman jeweller's hoard from Snettisham, Norfolk.
19 Roman cavalry tombstone of Longinus, from Colchester.
20 The burning of the temple of Claudius at Colchester.
21 Glass bead from the Gresham Street site, London.
22 Blackened grain, and burnt coins from the Boudican destruction layer in London.
23 Jeweller's hoard of Roman gemstones stowed away in a pot made in Lyon.
24 Bronze statue of Boudica, erected on the Thames Embankment, 1902.
25 'Boadicea' on a stained-glass window in the Moot Hall, Colchester Town Hall.

Author's acknowledgements

I should like to thank the several individuals and institutions who have helped me with this book, both in terms of information and in the acquisition of illustrations. Dr Paul Sealey (The Castle Museum, Colchester), himself a Boudican specialist, kindly acted as the 'anonymous' external reviewer of the book, and I am immensely grateful to him for pointing out errors and for his generous sharing of ideas. Dr Joann Fletcher, Guy de la Bédoyère, Chris Rudd, Liz Cottam, Dr Philip de Jersey, Dr Iain Ferris, Dr Richard Hingley, Dr Richard Reece and Dr Philip Macdonald all helped provide me with pictures. Stephen Yates (Colchester Museums Resource Centre); Mei Boatman (Castle Museum, Colchester); Philip Crummy (Colchester Archaeological Trust); Dr John Davies and Dr Tim Pestell (Norwich Castle Museum); Tim Thorpe (King's Lynn Museum); David Thorold and Kate Warren (St Albans Museum); David Rudkin (Fishbourne Roman Palace and Museum); Sarah Williams (The Museum of London); Jeff Cook (Cardiff County Council) and Merilyn Baldwin (Mayoral Office, Colchester Borough Council) helped me with illustrations, information or both. I thank Anne Leaver and Paul Jenkins for their drawings. Finally, I would like to express my gratitude to my husband, Professor Stephen Aldhouse-Green, for his unfailing support and encouragement. This book was written within the context of a crossroads in my life, including a house move and job changes; that I was able to complete it amid these turmoils was entirely due to him: thank you, Stephen.

Publisher's acknowledgements

We are grateful to the following for permission to reproduce copyright material:

Plates 2, 3, 12, 18 and Figure 5.2 from The British Museum, © The Trustees of the British Museum; Plates 4, 19 and 20 from Colchester Borough Council; Plate 6 and Figure 2.7 courtesy of Guy de la Bédoyère; Plate 8 courtesy of Joann Fletcher; Plate 11 from the National Museum of Denmark; Plate 13 and Figures 4.1 and 4.3 courtesy of Paul Jenkins; Plates 14 and 16 from Topham Picturepoint; Plate 15 courtesy of Philip Macdonald; Plate 17 from Amgueddfedd ac Orielau Cenedlaethol Cymru, National Museums & Galleries of Wales; Plates 21, 22, 23 and Figure 5.1 © Museum of London; Plate 24 courtesy of Dr Richard Hingley; Figure 1.2 and 1.3 courtesy of Chris Rudd; Figures 2.2, 2.3, 6.2 and 8.2 courtesy of Anne Leaver. Figure 2.4 illustration by Mark Breedon courtesy of Iain Ferris; Maps 1, 2, 4 and Figure 8.3 courtesy of Professor Martin Millett

In some instances we have been unable to trace the owners of copyright material, and we would appreciate any information that would enable us to do so.

Preface

Most of Britain is marshland ... the barbarians usually swim in these swamps or run along in them, submerged up to the waist. Of course, they are practically naked and do not mind the mud because they are unfamiliar with the use of clothing ... They also tattoo their bodies with various patterns and pictures of all sorts of animals. Hence the reason why they do not wear clothing, so as not to cover the pictures on their bodies.

Herodian History[1]

It seems incredible that a Greek historian, writing in the late second or early third century AD, long after Britain had become an integral part of the Roman Empire, should present the province of Britannia as inhabited by naked, painted mud-bathers, almost non-human, dwelling in a land covered by marshes, a kind of 'bongo-bongo land'.[2] Boudica lived much earlier, in the mid-first century AD, when Britain was a fledgling province, not yet subjugated, and which erupted in an incandescence of violent rage and anti-Roman hatred that has been likened to the situation in present-day Iraq. The Romans then made the fatal mistake of underestimating the power of a woman living on the edge of the world. Despite her origins and her gender, Boudica raised an army of over 200,000, caused the death of 70,000 Roman settlers or Romanised Britons, sacked three Roman cities and decimated a Roman legion, before being defeated in pitched battle.

This book is not simply about a person in history, but about the earliest freedom movement recorded from Britain, in AD 60/1. It is therefore a book about Britannia, about British identity and independence, about resistance to oppressive colonialism, and about the attempt, by a tiny minority community in eastern England, to challenge the military might of the Roman Empire. Boudica (or Boadicea) is well known today, but the lack of hard evidence for her existence and legendary struggle against Rome is astonishing. For historical accounts of Boudica, we are reliant on brief passages from the ancient authors Tacitus and Dio

Cassius, neither of whom were contemporaries of the Boudican Rebellion. Each of these historians wrote entirely from a Roman perspective and both had a 'spin' on the episode – an agenda or interpretative prism through which they were seeking to present their account. We tend to speak of *romanitas* in describing the adoption of Roman culture by provincials, but we should, perhaps, substitute another term, *humanitas*, because in spreading Roman ways throughout the empire what the Romans thought they were doing was bringing humanity to lands where the population was not quite as human as they were.

But archaeology is redressing the balance: recent and current investigations in East Anglia are demonstrating that the culture of Boudica's tribe of the Iceni and that of the neighbouring Trinovantes, Boudica's allies in her uprising, was far from primitive but offered a strongly focused alternative cultural identity to that of the Romans. In the first centuries BC and AD, the Iceni boasted highly sophisticated craftspeople and moneyers, producing superb gold jewellery and quantities of gold and silver coins. Whilst they are usually seen as living in scattered farming settlements, new research indicates that certain sites can be identified as 'proto-cities', occupying extensive areas. Some of these sites may even have been visited by Boudica herself, perhaps 'a regular visitor, most likely residing in royal quarters, as she did in a number of prestige sites across the region'.[3] So we should not think in terms of the imposition of Roman customs and culture upon a barren, cultureless Britannia. Instead, in certain regions of the island at least, the indigenous population enjoyed a culturally rich identity. which was fully capable of dealing with Mediterranean values, both material and ideological, that had travelled north-west with Caesar, Claudius and Nero. Boudica's Rebellion serves to demonstrate one manifestation of Britain's struggle for identity in the face of a massive external threat, from what some Britons, at least, regarded as 'bloody foreigners'.[4]

This book constitutes a journey, a quest-tale, for an illusory figure at the beginning of recorded history in Britain. We know so little about Boudica: a few fragments of narrative from two Roman writers, neither of whom possessed particular sympathies with her stand for freedom at the very edges of the known world, where people were different, not quite human and in need of the civilising influence of Rome. We cannot even be certain that Boudica existed at all; she could have been an imaginary figure, invented by classical historians as a means of exploring ideas of barbarism and its antidote. But it is precisely because we know so little that we can imagine so much. Auden's poem *Archaeology* contains surprising insights into the discipline from someone not of the profession:

> *Knowledge may have its purposes,*
> *But guessing is always*
> *More fun than knowing.*[5]

Notes and references

1. Herodian *History* III 14.67; trans. Whittaker 1969, 359.
2. An unhappy phrase used by Alan Clark of Nigeria: Clark 1993, 136.
3. Farrar 2005, 18.
4. The title of a book by Winder about attitudes to immigration into Britain through history: Winder 2004.
5. Auden *Selected Poems*, ed. Mendelson 1979, 302.

CHAPTER 1

Boudica's ancestors

Some dozen Romans of us, and your lord –
The best feather of our wing – have mingled sums
To buy a present for the Emperor;
Which I, the factor for the rest, have done
In France. 'Tis plate of rare device, and jewels
Of rich and exquisite form, their values great

Shakespeare *Cymbeline*[1]

Shakespeare's British king Cymbeline was none other than Cunobelin, the great British king who ruled a huge swathe of south-east England (including Kent, Essex, Hertfordshire and beyond) between about AD 10 and AD 40[2]. According to Shakespeare, Romans were by no means strangers to the court of Cymbeline, a point that has been made by John Creighton before me.[3] Iachimo, the speaker of this passage, is himself an Italian, and he comments on how Romans and Britons are pooling their resources to purchase treasure for the emperor (probably Tiberius). The gift itself, obtained in Gaul, is described as 'of rare device', and therefore is perhaps of Gallic make. The importance of the passage for our investigation of Boudica lies in its presentation of Shakespeare's image of a Britain in which Britons and Romans mingled freely *before* the official invasion and conquest in AD 43, with regular comings and goings between the island and the continent, although, as the play unfolds, tensions between the members of the two countries erupt into violent antagonism. The enmity between the two nations is eventually reconciled at the end of the drama in the words of the soothsayer, whose speech alludes to the uniting of Caesar's favours with 'the radiant Cymbeline', and of Cymbeline, who says:

> ... Set we forward; let
> A Roman and a British ensign wave
> Friendly together. So through Lud's Town march;
> And in the temple of great Jupiter
> Our peace we'll ratify; seal it with feasts.[4]

Archaeological discoveries have lent increasing support to Shakespeare's view of pre-Roman Britain; a Britain that was familiar with Rome and Roman ways long before the apparently cataclysmic events of the Claudian invasion of AD 43 and a Britain – in the south-east of the country at any rate – that, perhaps from the time of Caesar's first visits in 55 and 54 BC, was drawing increasingly closer to the Roman orbit. It is with Caesar, therefore, that it is appropriate to begin our exploration of early linkages between Britain and Rome. Without Caesar, it is arguable that Britain would never have become part of the Roman Empire and that the stage upon which the Boudican Rebellion was enacted would never have been set. Having set that stage, the final part of this chapter examines the archaeological evidence for the Iceni and Trinovantes in the first century BC and earlier first century AD.

Julius Caesar's Britain: a tale of two Britons

> *But his expedition against Britain was peculiarly remarkable for its daring. He was the first to bring a navy into the Western Ocean and to sail through the Atlantic Sea with an army to make war. The reported size of the island had appeared incredible and it had become a great matter of controversy among writers and scholars, many of whom asserted that the place did not exist at all and that both its name and the reports about it were pure inventions. So, in his attempts to occupy it, Caesar was carrying the Roman empire beyond the limits of the known world. He twice crossed to the island from the coast of Gaul opposite and fought a number of battles in which he did more harm to the enemy than good to his own men; the inhabitants were so poor and wretched that there was nothing worth taking from them. With the final result of the war he was not himself wholly satisfied; nevertheless, before he sailed away from the island, he had taken hostages from the King and had imposed a tribute.*
>
> Plutarch Life of Caesar[5]

The Greek writer Plutarch was born in about AD 46 and died around 120, so he was commenting about events taking place 150 years earlier than his work, and thus beyond living memory. Perhaps the most important part of Plutarch's narrative on Caesar's British expeditions concerns attitudes to Britain, a land beyond the world known to the Greeks and Romans, indeed a land that belonged to the realms of myth rather than reality, on the other side of Oceanus (Ocean), the great river perceived by the ancients to encircle the world known to humans.

In introducing the subject of Britain, Caesar himself speaks of it in a manner that, as has been pointed out in recent literature,[6] suggests a certain lack of *humanitas* in terms of its inhabitants:

> *Most of the tribes living in the interior do not grow grain; they live on milk and meat and wear skins. All the Britons dye their bodies with woad, which produces a blue colour and gives them a wild appearance in battle. They wear their hair long; every other part of the body, except for the upper lip, they shave. Wives are shared between groups of ten or twelve men, especially between brothers and between fathers and sons; but the children of such union are counted as belonging to the man with whom the woman first cohabited.*[7]

Caesar, then, is deliberately constructing an image of the Britons for the audience at home that polarised them and rendered them as different as possible from the Romans. Caesar was not the only one to record the painted bodies of the islanders: the Augustan poet Ovid referred to them as 'green-painted';[8] Martial mentions their paint and their blueness,[9] and Propertius 'warns his mistress not to imitate the Britons by painting her face'.[10] Herodian's comment about naked, mud-encrusted and painted Britons[11] endorses a classical viewpoint that remained long after Britannia was incorporated into the Roman Empire. This reputation of the ancient British, covered in woad and dressed in animal pelts, was to remain in the British consciousness right up until our own time. In 1911 a drawing by Henry Ford was used to illustrate a book entitled *A School History of England*, by Fletcher and Kipling, that showed a confrontation between Romans and Britons on the English shore. The Romans are depicted as clean, white, short-haired, fresh-faced young officers, while the Britons are dark with tattoos, with long wild hair. Richard Hingley is right in his surmise that such a picture was probably profoundly influenced by analogies with the British in India, and a perceived resemblance between the Romans/English, on the one hand, and the British/Indians, on the other.[12]

David Braund[13] draws attention to other broadly contemporary literature that similarly treats Britain as a legendary place, notably to a comment by one Philodemus of Gadara (Palestine), writing just before Caesar embarked for the island, an author who doubted the very existence of Britain or the Britons.[14] It was important to Caesar that he was the first to do things; he modelled himself on Alexander, who had so dramatically extended the frontiers of the Greek world,[15] and retained a sense of rivalry with the Macedonian conqueror's memory to the time of his death. By mounting expeditions to Britain, Caesar was sending out a powerful message to Rome: that he was afraid of nothing and that he possessed the ability to conquer even mythical territory, thus presenting himself as more than human himself. Even Caesar's conquest of Gaul was considered by his peers to be a remarkable feat: Cicero was impressed by his contemporary's colonisation work there, among a previously unknown people.[16] So how much more spectacular would be Caesar's adventures even further to the west, beyond Ocean and the world of humans?

In planning his first reconnaissance of Britain in 55 BC, Caesar himself admitted that he left the expedition rather late in the year. But he justified this initial visit on the grounds that: 'I knew that in almost all of our campaigns in Gaul our enemies had received reinforcements from the Britons'.[17] This is an interesting statement for, on the one hand, Caesar was playing on the idea of Britain as a mythical place beyond the edge of the world but, on the other, he acknowledged that the Gauls were fully aware of the Britons and had close liaisons with them.[18] Indeed, two years before the British campaigns, he made the interesting comment that a king of the powerful Gaulish hegemony of the Suessiones (around Soissons, in north-east France) had at one time controlled not only a large part of Gaul but a substantial portion of Britain as well.[19] Caesar clearly had a major problem, in his endeavours to pacify Gaul, in the capacity of Gallic agitators to use neighbouring Britain as a refuge, for he refers to this situation on several occasions: for instance, in Book II of his *de Bello Gallico* he speaks of the rebellious Bellovaci, erstwhile allies of the peaceful Burgundian Aedui, who 'fled to Britain when they realised what a disaster they had brought upon their country'.[20]

1 ◆ Boudica's ancestors

Two individuals are crucial to our understanding of Caesar and Britain: Commius, a Gaul of the tribe of the Atrebates, and Mandubracius, a British prince of the Trinovantes (see Map 1). Both noblemen played a central role in Caesar's Britain, that is the area of south-east England closest to the Gallic mainland, and it is arguably their legacy that served to define the Britain inherited by Claudius in AD 43. We first hear of Commius in Book IV of Caesar's *de Bello Gallico*, in the context of his reception of British ambassadors sent by worried tribes on learning of Caesar's planned invasion. Caesar says that 'I sent them [the envoys] back home and with them Commius, whom I had made king of the Atrebates

MAP 1 ◆ *Southern England and Wales in the late Iron Age (the squares plot the sites of 'urban' centres – oppida).*

Source: Millett 1995.

after I had subdued that tribe'.²¹ The Atrebates were a Belgic tribe occupying territory in northern Gaul, between the rivers Somme and Sambre. Commius was badly treated when he arrived in Britain, being cast into chains before being delivered back to Caesar. The following year, in the much more serious second British campaign, Caesar once again used Commius as a mediator between himself and the British army under the leadership of Cassivellaunus.²² So far, then, Commius had shown himself an ardent and loyal supporter of Rome and of Caesar in particular. But then something happened to overturn this state of affairs, for we next hear of the Atrebatian as an enemy to *romanitas*. In describing the last great uprising of the Gauls under Vercingetorix, Caesar speaks of Commius as having thrown in his lot with the freedom fighters, even though – in his own words – the Roman commander had 'ordered that his tribe should be exempt from taxation and have its independence restored'.²³ In the same passage, Caesar comments, somewhat plaintively, that the desire of the Gauls to shake off the Roman yoke negated all former friendships and that old acts of kindness were forgotten. Commius continued his bid for freedom even after the decisive battle of Alesia in 52 BC (when Gaul finally lost its independence to Rome).

The final book of the Gallic Wars (Book VIII) was written, after Caesar's death, by Aulus Hirtius, a soldier who had fought under the general in several Gallic campaigns. In it, he continues charting the history of Commius's liberation-movement activities, describing the Atrebatian's alliance with the Bellovacan chieftain Correus in his plot to attack the Suessiones who lived under the suzerainty of the more powerful Remi (a tribe occupying the region around Rheims). The Remi appealed to Caesar against this threat, and we learn that Commius took an initiative to seek aid in his planned rebellion from some of the German tribes.²⁴ The Bellovaci were defeated, their leader Correus killed in battle and, when the tribe began negotiations with the Romans, Commius returned as a refugee to the Germans, from whom he had sought help before. Later, Caesar's lieutenant, Labienus, conspired to have Commius murdered, and the Atrebatian 'resolved never again to come into the presence of any Roman'.²⁵ Commius's last entrance on to the Gallic stage is described towards the end of Hirtius's narrative, in which Commius – after more seditious activity – made peace with Rome, on the understanding that he would live where the Romans wanted him to live and do as he was told, as long as he could keep to his oath never again to encounter a Roman.

The reason for Commius's importance to Caesar's Britain is that archaeology testifies to the presence of someone with the same name who, during the Caesarian period, was minting coins in south-east England. Now, for the first time, British moneyers used the Latin language to incorporate the names of rulers into its imagery, and one of these was 'Commios'. This is highly significant both in terms of Commius himself, if it is the same person,[26] and because of the abrupt change in the motifs on British coins to include names. In an innovative recent study,[27] John Manley has suggested that:

> Caesar's sudden appearance in the south-east [of Britain] should not just be perceived as a temporary diversion for a great Roman general in the process of conquering Gaul, but instead a determined effort to establish dynasties in the two most powerful tribes of the south-east who would owe their loyalty to Rome.[28]

It is surely no coincidence that Commius's kingdom was centred on a tribe named the Atrebates, and it is likely, then, that in his desire to get as far from Rome as possible, he had emigrated to Britain and set up a new Atrebatian polity in the Hampshire/Sussex region. However, the use of the Latin language on the coinage suggests that Commius was not entirely divorced from *romanitas*, and Manley has posited that he might even have been established in southern England as a client-king, a local ruler friendly to Rome, whose loyalty bought him a measure of independence from heavy-handed colonial authority. However, Commius's client-ruler status is inherently unlikely, given his undoubted antipathy towards Rome. At any rate, the British coinage indicates that a Commius was the founder of a British dynasty that continued at least until the reign of Verica.[29]

Caesar's (and Hirtius's) narrative makes it look as though Commius retained a hatred of Rome and all things Roman in his new British life. Two issues are important here: first that, in Commius's pro-Roman years, Caesar repeatedly sent him to Britain as a negotiator; this suggests that Commius had some kind of affinity with Britain from early on and that, therefore, he might already have a network of British contacts (and even relatives) when he decided to leave Gaul for good. Indeed, Caesar himself clearly states that the Gallic ruler enjoyed considerable authority in Britain.[30] Second, we learn from Caesar that he established Commius as king of the Gallic Atrebates, a gesture that might have been meaningful or simply, as argued by Creighton,[31] have endorsed a pre-existing regime. But it may be that Caesar played the king-maker in Britain as well as Gaul and that he established Commius on a British throne also. If the Atrebatian was so treated, it hardly speaks of sworn enmity between the two of them. Hirtius, after all, does say that Commius came to terms with Rome, even though he reputedly wished to eschew contact with all Romans. In Creighton's words:

> Since a straightforward reading of Hirtius would suggest rehabilitation, then such a role for him, as a friendly king on the edges of the Roman world, fits reasonably happily with the way we know Rome interfered with the peoples on her frontiers ... Caesar had a perfect right to impose a king [on the Britons].[32]

The story of Commius, then, may have a particular resonance with the Boudica situation a hundred years later, for the Iceni, too, enjoyed client-kingdom status, as we shall see (Chapter 3).

The second individual who played a significant role in Caesar's Britain was a young Trinovantian prince called Mandubracius. He steps on to the stage during Caesar's second British campaign in 54 BC, when the general was engaged in smashing the forces of Cassivellaunus, a chieftain who may have ruled over the Catuvellauni (who occupied a large territory north of the Thames, including Hertfordshire, Buckinghamshire, eastern Oxfordshire and part of Essex) (see Map 2). Caesar tells us that Cassivellaunus had 'by general agreement' been given 'the supreme command and direction of the campaign' against the invading Romans.[33] The British ruler allegedly deployed his force of 4,000 charioteers to harry the legions in guerrilla warfare and it was while these skirmishes were going on that Caesar was asked for help by the Trinovantes, a tribe whose lands lay principally in Essex and who shared a border with the Catuvellauni. Caesar's account is interesting:

> In the meantime the Trinobantes sent a deputation to me. They are perhaps the strongest tribe in the southeast of Britain and it was from them that young Mandubracius had come to me in Gaul to put himself under my protection, having had to flee for his life after his father, the king of the tribe, was killed by Cassivellaunus'.[34]

In this short, terse passage, Caesar provides a great deal of information concerning the political situation in Britain and his own role in its devel-

MAP 2 ◆ *Civitates* or tribal states in which Roman Britain was administered.

Source: Millett 1995.

oping complexity. It seems that, despite Cassivellaunus's supremacy and the pledges of allegiance he had had from neighbouring peoples, a powerful next-door tribe was less than happy with his burgeoning powers and aggressively expansionist policies. They were so worried about the threat to their own royal family and the fear that their young king-designate would, like his father, be deposed and assassinated, that they took the extreme measure of entrusting him to Caesar's protection.

So, as in the case of Commius, Caesar played the role of king-maker and actively interfered in British affairs, at least in the south-east.

Later in the same passage, we are told that the Trinovantian ambassadors promised that the tribe would surrender to Caesar and implored him to save Mandubracius from the rapacity of the Catuvellaunian regime and reinstate him as king. Caesar responded by demanding hostages and corn and, in return, sent the Trinovantian prince back to Britain as king of the Trinovantes. Seeing that this tribe was now protected from Cassivellaunus, others sought similar protection. After a battle in which the British army was worsted, the Catuvellaunian king sent embassies to Caesar offering surrender, 'using Commius the Atrebatian as an intermediary'. Terms were agreed, with a Roman demand for hostages and tribute from Cassivellaunus, together with a strong dictat that he interfered with neither Mandubracius nor his tribe. It would have been highly advantageous to Caesar to leave Britain with a friendly king and people in the south-east, who remained under obligation to him and who, presumably, would contribute to ensuring that the terms were maintained.

With this statement, Mandubracius passes out of history but this is not the case with the Trinovantes for, as we shall see, they were to play a major part in the Boudican drama that was to unfold in the next century. But Caesar had played the king-making game with ingenuity, for he now had two powerful British friends and polities: Mandubracius and the Trinovantes in the east, and Commius and the Atrebates in the south. After Caesar's assassination in 44 BC, other Romans became proactive in British affairs.

Caesar cannot, by any stretch of the imagination, be credited with the subjugation of Britain. He only operated in the south-east, and he did not stay long enough to consolidate or secure the results of his campaigns. Nonetheless, he did achieve two highly significant things: first, he put Britain on Rome's map, bringing it into the realms of possible absorption into the empire; second, he played a major role in sculpting the politics of south-east England, thus leaving behind a legacy that would impinge considerably upon later relationships between Britain and Rome. Indeed, as David Braund has pointed out,[35] the Augustan poet Ovid had claimed that Caesar had 'conquered the water-girt Britons',[36] but Tacitus is more reserved about Caesar's achievements in Britain, saying that 'he can be seen to have shown it to his descendants, not to have handed it down to them'.³⁷

From Caesar to Gaius: plans and hiatuses

> Now, however, some of the dynasts there [in Britain], having arranged friendships with Caesar Augustus by embassies and by paying court, have set up dedications on the Capitol and made all but one with the Romans the whole island. And they tolerate heavy duties on exports from there to Keltike [Gaul] and on imports from Keltike (these are ivory chains and necklaces and amber-goods and glass-ware and other trinkets of such a sort), so that there is no need for a garrison on the island.³⁸

So wrote the Greek geographer Strabo in the reign of Tiberius, in c. AD 18, four years after the death of Augustus. David Braund argues that Strabo's testimony is of particular value, since the author was well-informed about politics, cultural diversity and provincial affairs.³⁹ John Creighton argues that for foreigners to be allowed to make dedications on the Capitol (the holiest place within the city), special permission would have to have been granted by the Senate and, so, was a jealously guarded privilege.⁴⁰ Unlike some Augustan writers, notably the poet Horace, Strabo's account is not a simple eulogy of the emperor but appears – on the surface, at any rate – to contain some historicity. Strabo's comment is in accord with Augustus's own official record of his achievements, the *Res Gestae*, an inscribed monument, originally consisting of two – now lost – bronze pillars outside his mausoleum. However, a copy of the text is preserved in stone at a temple to the imperial cult at Ancyra in Turkey.⁴¹ On the inscription, the emperor states that a number of British kings made supplication to him, notably Dubnobellaunus and Tincomarus.⁴² The *Res Gestae* purports to be a terse list of things done, and ranges from the building or refurbishment of temples, aqueducts and other public amenities to the bringing of the *pax romana* to the known world.

So both Strabo and Augustus allude to a traffic of goodwill between Rome and the Britons in the reign of the first emperor, a traffic facilitated by Caesar's groundwork. Both make the important point that Britons came to Rome, and this means that British aristocrats would have returned home with a taste for Roman goods and a fair inkling of how

Roman custom worked. Strabo came across young Britons in Rome,[43] probably having been sent there by their elders to gain a Roman education because it was perceived that thereby lay the road to prosperity in the Roman Britain of the future. In the above-quoted passage, Strabo is in a sense making excuses for Augustus' non-military intervention in Britain. But Horace sends a rather different message:

> Guard Caesar bound for Britain at the world's end,
> Guard our young swarm of warriors on the wing now
>   To spread the fear of Rome
> Into Arabia and the Red Sea coasts.[44]

and

> Thunder in heaven confirms our faith – Jove rules there;
> But here on earth Augustus shall be hailed as
>   God also, when he makes
> New subjects of the Briton and the dour
> Parthian ...[45]

and

> The Mede, the Indian, the once unsubduable
> Spaniard, the nomad Scythian – thee all nations
>   (O Shield of Italy
> And her imperial metropolis)
>
> Revere; thee Nile, who still conceals her secret
> Springs, and the Danube and the hurrying Tigris
>   And the whale-burdened sea
> That bursts on the exotic British coast.[46]

Horace's *Odes* are unashamed praise-poetry designed to flatter the emperor. Similar sentiments, though presented in a loftier manner, were expressed in Virgil's great Augustan epic poem *The Aeneid*. The juxtaposition of peoples in the poems is interesting, for Britain is still on the edge of the world and is often spoken of in the same breath as the Parthians, an intractable enemy to Rome on the eastern frontiers of the empire. Horace and Virgil were writing as contemporaries of Augustus. But Dio Cassius compiled his *Roman History* between AD 200 and 229, when there was no possible reason to flatter his subject directly. Dio is definite in his statement that a conquered Britain was on Augustus's agenda. The historian makes two references to the emperor's militaristic intentions for the island, the first relating to the year 27 BC, the second to the following year. His first comment is to the effect that Augustus planned a British expedition but was deflected by a longer stay than intended in Gaul. Apparently, he considered it more important to delay in Gaul since affairs there were fairly turbulent, while it seemed to him that Britain was likely to give little trouble but accede to the terms offered without war.[47] However, Dio's next record of the British situation is entirely different, and it appears that Augustus misread the Britons' seeming acquiescence, for now the chronicler says 'Augustus was planning an expedition into Britain, since the people there would not come to terms, but he was detained by the revolt of the Salassi'.[48]

But Strabo's statement (above) indicates that these troubles were transitory, for by the end of Augustus's reign, high-status Britons were being granted special, treaty-driven favours in Rome. The two British kings mentioned by name, on the *Res Gestae*, as having sought asylum with the emperor were presumably acting within a context of close and friendly relations with both Rome and Augustus, and would have been assured of a welcome in Italy. Their flight also indicates that politics in south-east England were unstable and either that their territories were being threatened by neighbouring tribes hungry for extra land and power or by relatives in their own lands wishing to stage coups and usurp their ruling position.

Two British kings, Dubnovellaunus and Tincomarus, are known from Iron Age coinage in south-east Britain. To make the situation still more complicated, there may have been two rulers called Dubnovellaunus, one belonging to the Kentish Cantiaci, the other ruling in Trinovantian territory (or 'they' may have been a single individual minting coins in the two regions, with the implication of political authority in both areas). Tincomarus, probably a son of Commius, reigned in the southern kingdom (Sussex and Hampshire), while Tasciovanus (perhaps a descendant of Cassivellaunus) ruled in the eastern kingdom north of the Thames.[49] The evidence of the coinage is interesting and confusing, for it is difficult to tell to what extent the distribution of named coins reflects demographic movements, perhaps involving expansion (and dispossession of people already living in the contested territory), or diplomatic exchange.

The Winchester hoard[50] and the Hayling Island temple:[51] archaeological evidence for Britain and Augustan Rome

In September 2000 Kevin Halls was out with his metal detector near Winchester in Hampshire when he discovered part of what proved to be a hoard of gold jewellery, consisting of two 'necklace torcs', four brooches (comprising two pairs, of which one was still joined together by a link-chain) and two rough-outs (blanks) for gold bar-bracelets (see Plate 2)[52]. Jeremy Hill rightly surmises that the ornaments form two distinct sets and the smaller size of one torc may indicate that the jewellery once belonged to a male and female.[53] Intrinsically, the hoard is exciting enough, but there is strong evidence, both from the content of the gold and from the design of the necklaces, that the source of the metal may lie in the Mediterranean world and that Greek artists were involved in the production of the objects. Excavation of the hoard's immediate context revealed no other archaeological evidence, but the site itself may have been specially chosen for deposition, for it was on a low hilltop with good views over the surrounding countryside and, what is more, there is convincing evidence of a settlement nearby, inhabited by people who imported material from the classical world and, of course, the Iron Age precursor of Roman Winchester was active in the second and first centuries BC. This brings us to the date of the Winchester hoard and its relevance to our story of Augustan Britain. The gold objects were probably manufactured between *c.* 80 and 30 BC, but may have been deposited considerably later, for there are signs of wear on both the brooches and the neck ornaments.[54] What is interesting about the deposition is its interpretation as a sacred act, in a context of 'ritual events that specifically had to take place "in the landscape" and away from domestic occupation'.[55]

The Winchester jewellery may well have been worn during the reign of Augustus, and either adorned – or was originally owned – by people who had close contacts with the Mediterranean world. Such possession argues for other kinds of kinship with Graeco-Roman society. It is tempting to make links, if necessarily speculative and tentative, between the people involved with the Winchester hoard and Commius or Tincomarus who, we know from classical literature and coinage (see above), ruled the southern kingdom in the later first century BC (Manley suggests that

1 ♦ Boudica's ancestors

Tincomarus took over from Commius in the 20s BC after having – perhaps – been schooled in Roman-style leadership at the imperial court[56]). We have to be careful, though for, as Jeremy Hill and his co-authors rightly say, 'it is just as likely that other, totally unknown, individuals deposited the hoard'.[57] But, even so, the fact that this ritual act occurred at all during this period suggests that high-ranking individuals were present in south-east England, who enjoyed close liaisons with Italy and even Greece; people who, like Commius and his descendants, were sufficiently *au fait* with Graeco-Roman *mores* to call themselves *Rex* (king), a title that appears on the coinage but which would have been more at home in the eastern empire than at Rome itself, given the Roman antipathy to kingship.

At around the time that the Winchester jewellery was being worn and deposited, something else took place in the Atrebatian kingdom that may also be associated with the Commian dynasty, namely the building of the sanctuary on Hayling Island. In the late first century BC, a community on the Hampshire coast erected a rectangular structure inside a trapezoidal enclosure to bound some kind of central focus, maybe a great timber post (analogous to the one in the centre of the great ceremonial structure built in the early first century BC at Navan Fort in County Armagh[58]). Subsequently, this was remodelled, the enclosure squared off and within this a substantial round house was built to enclose the original feature. The sanctity of this structure is suggested not so much because of its architectural form but on account of the large deposits of brooches, coins and other objects, some (apparently deliberately) damaged,[59] as if to transform them into offerings suitable for the otherworld. Such treatment of votive objects has good analogies elsewhere in Britain and western Europe during the later Iron Age and Roman periods, notably at the Middle Iron Age 'war-sanctuary' of Gournay (Oise) in northern Gaul,[60] where thousands of broken weapons were deposited in holy ground.

The other factor in interpreting late Iron Age Hayling Island is its replacement early in the Roman period with a substantial stone temple, with a circular *cella* (inner sanctum) surrounded by a large rectilinear enclosure or *temenos* bounding the sacred area, consisting of a galleried wall, perhaps containing porticos for pilgrims to view images or other votive objects (see Figure 1.1). John Creighton has suggested that the Hayling shrine might have been built to accommodate a 'cult of

FIGURE 1.1 ◆ *The early Roman temple at Hayling Island, Hampshire.*
Source: Henig 2002.

Commius', citing as possible evidence some late Iron Age coinage minted by one of his descendants, Verica.[61] Some of these coins bear imagery that points to the expression of a cult modelled on a Roman ancestral rite, including portraits of ancestors, human figures perhaps depicting gods or heroes, and representation of temples. Creighton (citing Daphne Briggs's study of the coin-assemblages at Hayling[62]) links the primary Iron Age phase at the site with Commius and/or his son Tincomarus and the secondary phase (after a distinct gap in the coin sequence) with Commius's descendant Verica, a prince who, like Mandubracius and others (see below) made supplication to Rome for help against his neighbours. It is to these suppliants and their enemies that we now turn.

British politics and Roman interference: focus on the eastern dynasty

Under Augustus's successors to the imperial purple, Tiberius and Gaius (Caligula), Britain – or at any rate the south-east – continued to feature on Rome's agenda. We know little from classical writers about Tiberius's attitude towards Britain, but we do know that, in general, the new emperor was against imperialist expansion for its own sake, and this accords with his professed republican and somewhat introverted sympathies. David Braund sums up the probable situation in his statement that 'Augustus's preference for diplomacy was maintained by Tiberius: the point is illustrated by the decision of the British king Verica to mint coins bearing the imperial head of that emperor'.[63] Indeed, Tacitus refers to friendly relationships between Britain and Rome some two years into Tiberius's reign, in AD 16, when he describes a misfortune that befell part of Germanicus's fleet which strayed into British waters after campaigning in Germany. The ships were caught in a storm in the North Sea and blown way off course, and a group of them washed up on the British coast:

> Others had been carried to Britain, and were sent back by its chieftains. Men coming from these remote regions told strange stories – of hurricanes, unknown birds, sea-monsters, and shapes, half-human and half-animal, which they had seen or in their terror had imagined.[64]

This comment by Tacitus is interesting not only in so far as it presents a friendly, co-operative Britain, whose rulers are sufficiently anxious to keep in with Rome to return damaged Roman ships (and their contents) unharmed to Germanicus's main force, but in the apparent attitude of these soldiers to a Britain that – despite Caesar's expeditions to the island and the undoubted links between south-east England and the Continent – was still regarded as a place of awe, mystery and freakishness. This is important, for it brings into sharp focus the Claudian conquest of AD 43. What is clear about the episode chronicled by Tacitus is that it was not the chieftains of the south-eastern dynasties that must have been involved: if ships were blown off course in the North Sea, they would have turned up on the shores of territory belonging to eastern tribes that may have been situated to the north of the lands belonging to the Catuvellauni or even the Trinovantes. Indeed, it is more than possible that these friendly chieftains belonged to the Iceni, a polity relatively unknown to the Romans, and this may, in part, explain the land's legendary reputation as an uncharted region, home to monsters and mythic creatures. The involvement of the Iceni with Germanicus's army as an ally accords with their status as a client-kingdom at the time of the Boudican Rebellion more than four decades later (see Chapter 3).

Having looked at the essentially pro-Roman southern British kingdom, ruled by Commius and then Tincomarus, it is time to see what part the eastern dynasty, north of the Thames, played in the unfolding drama that was late Iron Age south-east England. Both southern and eastern dynasties are important in terms of the later Boudican episode since, as we shall see, each played a major role in events leading up to the revolt in AD 60; the south following its traditional path of allegiance to Rome, and the eastern dynasty, or at least an element within it, causing trouble within the fledgling province. But, although the rulers of the Catuvellauni (their name means 'expert warriors'[65]) pursued expansionist policies that sometimes brought them into conflict with Rome, there is little real evidence to suggest that the successors of Caesar's enemy Cassivellaunus were dyed in the wool opponents of Roman imperialism. Indeed, there is evidence that, like Commius and his kind, the eastern dynasts had a great deal to do with Rome and *romanitas* long before the Claudian conquest in AD 43.

One of the first of these rulers who, after Cassivellaunus, is known to us by name was Tasciovanus, a king who minted coins north of the Thames, at Verulamium (or Verlamion, to give the Iron Age town its allegedly more accurate name); some with his name inscribed on them and the word 'RIG' or 'RICON(I)', a British word meaning 'king'. This decision to identify kingship in British rather than in Latin (the Roman word 'REX' was chosen by southern British kings and by Cunobelin) may be significant in terms of his wish to assert his own ethnicity. Tasciovanus reigned in the Essex/Hertfordshire heartlands of the Catuvellauni from 10 BC (or earlier) to *c.* AD 10, when he was succeeded by his son Cunobelinus.[66] John Creighton argues that the distribution of

Tasciovanus's coinage indicates that his territory was already expanding before his son's 'imperialist' policies, which led him to encroach seriously upon the southern kingdom. But the imagery Tasciovanus (and Cunobelinus) chose for their coins shows a desire to emulate Rome, for it contains a range of Romanised motifs and, interestingly, both rulers minted coins with both Roman imperial heads and more 'Celtic'-looking portraits, as if to convey messages associated both with being Catuvellaunian and being Rome's friends.[67] What is particularly interesting about the coinage is the choice of images depicting the monsters of Graeco-Roman myth: fantastic creations like Pegasus, the winged horse. In classical tradition, such weird hybrids occupied the edgy places, on the edge of the world.[68] In the words of Creighton 'our dynasts saw themselves as living in a remote region, beyond Ocean'.[69] Thus, these Britons were perpetuating the Roman perception of Britain as a legendary otherworld and holding a mirror up to themselves as different, strange and exotic, even though they were – of course – at the centre of their own world.

When Tasciovanus died, he was undoubtedly buried with much pomp and ceremony. Indeed, archaeology attests a number of rich cremation graves in south-east Britain during the late first century BC and early first century AD. The Lexden Tumulus, just outside Camulodunum, was probably built for someone whose death and funeral took place about 10 BC,[70] perhaps a king called Addedomarus.[71] The tomb was richly furnished and contained objects foreign to Britain that might well have been gifts from Rome to a friendly barbarian monarch: the most striking of such material comprises a folding chair, or *sella curulis*,[72] a piece of furniture that not only spoke loudly of Roman material culture but of Roman ways of sitting and, quite possibly, of Roman-style authority. Also in the Lexden grave were fragments of chain-mail that closely resemble Roman military equipment.[73] Most of the objects in the tomb were ritually broken before their deposition in the grave. Like Commius and Tincomarus in the southern kingdom, the rulers of the eastern dynasty may have been involved in the traffic in *obsides*, relatives of barbarian chiefs educated at Rome.[74]

Cunobelinus succeeded Tasciovanus, probably in *c.* AD 10, and ruled until AD 40–3. On his coinage he describes himself as 'Son of Tasciovanus', just as Tincomarus styled himself 'Son of Commius'. Other named individuals on the eastern coin issues also called themselves *filius* (son). It is probable that, in some instances, this was a formulaic title designed to place the person within a particular dynasty, but it was also a device that aped the practice of the Roman imperial house during the reigns of Augustus and Tiberius,[75] the former wishing to present himself as the legitimate heir of Julius Caesar, the latter as Augustus's rightful successor. So the British royal houses of south-east England were, by this means, deliberately embracing *romanitas*. We know about Cunobelinus by name not just through the coins he minted[76] but also from Suetonius, who mentions him as the father of Adminius, the exile who asked Gaius for help while the emperor was in the Rhineland.[77] It was probably as late as AD 39 or 40 that Adminius made his bid for help against his father. Like Tasciovanus before him, Cunobelin may well have been friendly to Rome (certainly, some of his coins show images of very Roman-like victories[78]), although the expulsion of his son and the latter's request for Gaius's help suggests that a rift within the dynasty may have polarised the situation and caused Cunobelin to suffer Rome's disfavour. Dio tells us that the British king died just before the Roman invasion.[79]

The writer Suetonius speaks at some length about Gaius Caligula, Britain and Cunobelinus's estranged son Adminius. The emperor's encounter with the Britons occurred in the context of an imperial expedition to Germany, when he was visited by a supplicant from the eastern British kingdom, a son of Cunobelinus (ruler of the Catuvellauni) who had fallen out with his father:

> All that he accomplished in this expedition was to receive the surrender of Adminius, son of the British King Cymbeline, who had been banished by his father and come over to the Romans with a few followers. Caligula, nevertheless, wrote an extravagant despatch, which might have persuaded any reader that the whole island had surrendered to him.[80]

This is interesting for, although we have the precedent of Mandubracius, the Trinovantian, and Caesar, this time the rift was within the dynasty: a family conflict indicating the presence of factions within the tribe. What happened next seems – on the face of it – very odd imperial behaviour indeed:

> In the end, he drew up his army in battle array facing the Channel and moved the siege-engines into position as though he intended to bring the campaign to a close. No one had the least notion what was in his mind when, suddenly, he gave the order: 'Gather sea-shells!' He referred to the shells as

'plunder from the sea, due to the Capitol and to the Palace, and made the troops fill their helmets and tunic-laps with them; commemorating this victory by the erection of a tall lighthouse, not unlike the one at Pharos, in which fires were to be kept going all night as a guide to ships. Then he promised every soldier a bounty of four gold pieces, and told them: 'Go rich, go happy!' as though he had been excessively generous.[81]

This act of Caligula's is generally interpreted as a sign of the emperor's mounting insanity. But David Braund has presented a somewhat kinder and possibly more balanced interpretation, namely that Gaius was expressing his victory over Ocean, a symbolically charged motif that was used both by Julius Caesar and Claudius in self-presentation as conquerors of the unknown 'beyond world' of Britain.[82]

After Cunobelinus's death (which may have been from natural causes, as he would have been quite an age in the early 40s AD) two of his sons, Togodumnus and Caratacus, put up a fierce resistance to Claudius's army. If Cunobelinus had been friendly to Rome, the change of policy adopted by these sons could, indeed, have led to a plot by them to assassinate the old king. At about the same time, Dio Cassius tells us that a certain 'Berikos' (or Verica) fled to Claudius for help during an inter-dynastic struggle in Britain. Their story is the substance of the next chapter.

Before we leave the *dramatis personae* of late Iron Age Britain, we should at this point look at the archaeological evidence for a remarkable burial of a Catuvellaunian chieftain that took place at Folly Lane, St Albans in about AD 50–5,[83] for it is just possible that it was that of Cunobelinus himself. The discrepancy between the date of the king's death and the chronology of the Folly Lane burial need not disturb us unduly, since we know from the archaeological investigation that the body of the person buried lay in state for a considerable time before the final funerary rites, including the construction and burning of a great pyre, were conducted. The burial contained fragments of what may have been an ivory chair of Roman type, and images of similar chairs were depicted on some of Cunobelin's coins.[84] The high status of this tomb is indicated not only by the elaborate ceremonial activity associated with it, but also by the presence of the bodies of three women, placed at the entrance to the burial enclosure, and perhaps attendant sacrifices to accompany the dead man to the afterlife, maybe even as sexual partners.[85] The site of the pyre was marked by a timber post and, about 20 years later, a temple was built on top of the burial mound. The individual interred here, in the heart of what had been Cunobelinus's territory, must have been of paramount importance to his people, so much so that the rare rite of human sacrifice seems to have been enacted at the time the funerary enclosure was constructed. Moreover, the site of the burial remained a *locus sanctus*, an ancestral holy place for many years after his death.

Wolves and horse-lords: the archaeology of the Iceni and the Trinovantes

> *The first to revolt ... were the Iceni. We had not defeated this powerful tribe in battle, since they had voluntarily become our allies.*[86]

At the time of the Claudian Invasion of Britain, the king of the Iceni was Antedios: we know his name because it appears on Icenian coinage. Tacitus's comment (above) confirms that this ruler must have enjoyed a

FIGURE 1.2 ◆ *Inscribed Icenian coin. The drawing is a composite image based on a reconstruction from several specimens of the type, c. AD 10–40.*

Source: Artist Jane Bottomley; © Chris Rudd.

· 22 ·

1 ◆ Boudica's ancestors

treaty relationship with Rome, a situation that Prasutagus, Boudica's husband, inherited and was in place until his death in AD 60. The Iceni are special, in archaeological terms, because they are the only tribe to have identified themselves by name on their coins (see Figure 1.2): inscriptions with the word 'ECEN' beneath the image of a horse on late issues undoubtedly refer to an abbreviated form of 'Iceni'.[87] This tribal name is related to those of certain Gallic peoples, including the Cenomagni of Cisalpine Gaul (the far north of Italy where it borders France) and a tribe called the Aulerci Cenomani (of south Normandy).[88] Caesar records that, on his second visit to Britain in 54 BC, one of the tribes that surrendered to him was one calling itself the Cenimagni, a name that Derek Allen was convinced was that of the Iceni:[89] indeed, the name could be translated as 'the Great Iceni' (*Iceni Magni*).

The coinage tells us that the Iceni inhabited an area of East Anglia bounded in the north by the Wash, beyond which lay the territory of the Corieltavi and, in the south by a frontier with the Trinovantes in Suffolk. A distinctive form of early uninscribed Icenian gold coin is the so-called 'Norfolk wolf' type, made of dark gold and depicting a snapping wolf, its dorsal crest erect in aggression (see Figure 1.3). These coins are generally accepted as having been issued between about 65 and 45 BC, but may have continued in circulation, or even still minted, for some time afterwards.[90]

FIGURE 1.3 ◆ *Obverse and reverse of a 'Norfolk wolf' coin found in 2000, from near Burnham Market, Norfolk.*

Source: © Chris Rudd; supplied by Philip de Jersey.

· 23 ·

The choice of emblem may have a bearing on the self-presentation of this particular tribe: the wolf is both a wild creature, a potential enemy to humans, and also lives and hunts in packs; it therefore may have acted as a symbol of independent solidarity.

Paul Sealey[91] has drawn attention to distinct archaeological differences between the Iceni and their southern neighbours who, we know from classical literature, had direct contact with Rome (in this context we should think of Mandubracius, the Trinovantian refugee suppliant at Caesar's court: see above). Most striking of these differences lay in distinct ways of making and fashioning pots: while the Trinovantes used the arguably more sophisticated technique of wheel-throwing their pots, a custom that emanated from the Continent, many of the the Iceni stuck to the old way of making ceramic vessels by hand, and went on doing this right up until the time of Boudica.[92] The site at Sedgeford in north-west Norfolk has produced high-status tableware that was, nonetheless, handmade.[93] We also think that the Iceni may well have consisted not of a uni-

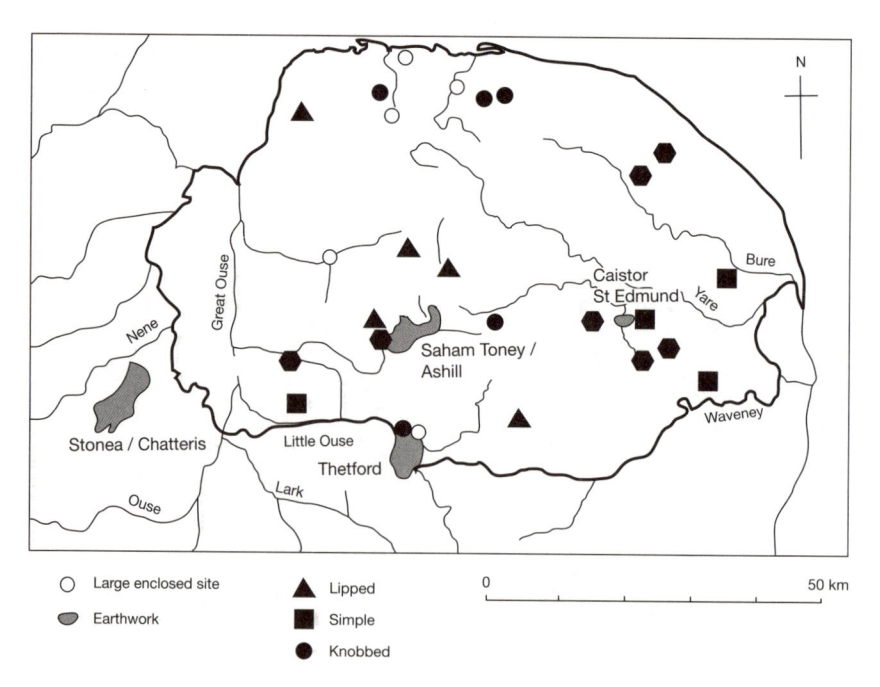

MAP 3 ◆ *Possible tribal centres and distribution of terret types within Icenian territory in the late Iron Age.*

Sources: Hingley & Unwin 2005 and Davies 1999.

1 ♦ Boudica's ancestors

fied political entity but, rather, was decentralised and split up into different groups: their coinage was minted at a number of separate sites,[94] and the evidence from horse-harness, particularly terrets, shows considerable regional diversity of forms (see Map 3).[95]

The rich cremation-burial at Stanway, just outside Colchester, of a high-ranking man who died in about AD 50, exemplifies the way the Trinovantes had early embraced Roman material culture, for Roman medical equipment and a Roman board game and no local ceramics were interred with the remains of the dead man.[96] While the Iceni seem deliberately to have set their faces against innovation from outside their own region (rather as happened in the Soviet Union under communism), the Trinovantes were open to innovation from outside. Such difference in attitudes can also be seen by the apparent lack of commercial exchange with Roman markets among the Iceni, which, again, is in stark contrast to the archaeological evidence from Trinovantian and Catuvellaunian material culture, which is laced with Italian imports, such as amphorae and fine goods (see below). But, despite this kind of evidence, the Iceni did sometimes import precious goods from Rome: the silver cups from Hockwold (Norfolk),[97] among other material, suggest that the upper echelons of East Anglian society did appreciate exotica from the centre of the empire, even if they were less happy with the rest of the Roman package. But even these cups may convey a hidden message of resistance: they were deliberately destroyed in an act that may have been ritually driven, but may also (or instead) have been designed to show contempt for *romanitas*.

Sites in both Trinovantian and Icenian territory have produced chilling reminders of the darker side of life here, in the form of sets of iron manacles that belong to the late Iron Age or early Roman period. The Icenian ones have been found at several sites, including Hockwold[98] (the site of discovery not only of the silver cups but also of a Romano-British sanctuary containing remains of priestly regalia, including six crowns or diadems[99]). Trinovantian manacles have been found at the important 'ancestral' site of Sheepen,[100] near the original tribal capital at Camulodunum. Sheepen had probably been of ceremonial significance for people living in the region for many centuries before the Roman conquest: in 1100 BC a bronze cauldron was deliberately buried in a pit; in the later Iron Age coin minting went on here, and the slave-shackles also fit into a profile of a central place where the nobility congregated on occasions for a range of social activities, perhaps including the making of marriage alliances, the dispensing of justice, and trade of all kinds, including, perhaps, the sale of slaves. The Sheepen restraints have been interpreted as evidence for the enslavement of Trinovantian Britons by Romans in the early years post-conquest,[101] but the high status and clearly ceremonial character of Sheepen (and Hockwold) perhaps make it more likely that the manacles indicate the imprisonment of Britons by other Britons.[102]

Icenian gold

The Iceni were a wealthy tribe, although we do not know the source of their prosperity, particularly in view of their apparently closed-market system; very probably at least some of this wealth came from the production and sale of salt, a valuable commodity in the European Iron Age and Roman periods. When Prasutagus died, he left a fortune jointly to the Emperor Nero and his own two daughters. The then Roman procurator, Decianus Catus, clearly considered the stripping of Icenian assets to be extremely worthwhile,[103] despite the risk to the new province of Britannia. Archaeologically, this wealth is highly visible, both in terms of precious-metal coin-hoards, hastily buried for security at the time of the Boudican Rebellion (one hoard, found in 1982, at Field Baulk, March in Cambridgeshire comprised 872 silver Icenian coins placed for safekeeping in a pot[104]) and in the evidence for fabulous riches from Snettisham (Norfolk), in the form of gold, silver and electrum jewellery, whose deposition dates to the mid-first century BC. There, more than 100 torcs (and more than 200 pieces altogether) were discovered in the 1950s and 1990s in no less than eight hoards.[105] Many were placed together in 'nests' within pits, of which some had false bases concealing the most precious ornaments from looters. The precise purpose of burying these hoards is uncertain: the jewellery may constitute a ritual deposit, an offering to the local gods (similar to what Strabo describes as occurring among the Volcae Tectosages of south-western Gaul in 106 BC[106]) or a tribal treasury. But some of the Snettisham material was unfinished, broken or unworn, and some of it consisted of ingots and metalworking debris, perhaps representing smithing, an activity not inconsistent with the concept of ritual deposition. While some of the torcs were heavy and difficult to imagine being worn except for ceremonial occasions, others were large and showy, but hollow and made of light sheet-gold, giving them the appearance of solid gold while being light in weight.[107] Archaeological investigations are still being carried out at Snettisham and, interestingly, Bronze Age material has now come to light here. While these earlier findings may simply reflect repeated occupation of the location, it is possible that the Bronze Age metalwork was deliberately curated by later people, in acts of respect and veneration of their ancestors.

The group of six gold torcs from Ipswich, Suffolk indicates that Snettisham by no means represents the sole wealth of the Iceni in the first century BC.[108] What is intensely interesting about the discovery of such a mass of gold ring-ornaments in Icenian territory is the description of Boudica by Dio, who claims that she wore a great golden torc around her neck.[109] While Boudica lived perhaps a hundred years later than the deposition of the Snettisham and Ipswich hoards, it is nonetheless significant that Dio identifies this feature of Boudica's regalia. But we must remember that the Romans would have been familiar with British and Gallic torcs, and that they may – to Roman eyes – have been an iconic badge of barbarian splendour.[110] References from classical literature show that torcs were an important mark of nobility and status for Gallic society.[111] Thus, one author, Quintilian, refers to a gift of a massive gold torc presented to the Emperor Augustus by supplicants from Gaul.[112] Torcs are known archaeologically in Europe from the Middle Bronze Age (*c.* 1200 BC), so it is not at all surprising that the Iceni were hoarding these objects in the first century BC and their chieftains still wearing them in AD 60. We should remember, too, that some torcs would have been heirlooms, kept and handed down for generations. So it is not impossible that Boudica actually wore one of the Snettisham torcs.

One of the Icenian sites producing gold is Sedgeford, near King's Lynn. The archaeological evidence for high-status activity comes from two distinct areas, one on the floor of the valley, the other on a low hill top, 200 feet (60 metres) above sea level and, consequentially, providing a locally high point in a flat landscape. In 1965 a gold torc was found on the 'Polar Break Field', on the hill; it had been badly mauled by a harrow and was missing one of its terminals. In the course of an intensive archaeological survey in 2004, the second terminal was miraculously recovered (see Plate 3). The torc dates to about the same time as the Snettisham finds, the mid first century BC. The same field has also yielded deposits of pots that were apparently deliberately broken in some kind of ritual feasting events, along with the remains of sacrificed sheep. Palisades were erected to enclose special areas of the hill top, perhaps as sacred boundaries. In the valley below, two horses were buried entire, probably again in a ceremonial act; and in a cow bone had been placed a hoard of 39 gold coins[113]. So Sedgeford was a site of particular significance for the Iceni; a special place that belonged to the highest echelons of Icenian society. It has been suggested that here was a 'proto-city' covering as much as 8 miles (13 kilometres) and 'haunted by the Iceni's aristocratic warrior caste', who buried their riches in the ground. It is a site which represents 'a focus of civilisation oozing confidence' and, in its final years, may even have been visited by Boudica herself.[114] What is striking about the site is the way that activity apparently came to an abrupt stop there in the years immediately after the Boudican Rebellion. We can only surmise that the people fled in advance of the Roman army, were massacred or forcibly removed. The remains of a burned roundhouse on the hill may speak volumes.[115] The lack of domestic debris suggests that this may have been a non-residential building, maybe used for ceremonial occasions associated with the Icenian priestly ruling classes. If so, it would have been targeted by Suetonius's army for a special act of annihilation.

So, the archaeology of the Iceni is beginning to enable us to build up a picture (albeit a shadowy one) of this enigmatic people. They had wealth in precious metal (jewellery and coinage), and special centres of political or ceremonial significance. They may have turned their faces away from external influences, unlike their close neighbours to the south. They may have pursued a deliberate policy of independence, not only from ideas from outside Britain but even from elsewhere in eastern Britain itself. Notwithstanding this insular attitude, the Iceni seem to have had a friendly relationship with Rome, at least until AD 47, and, in consequence, Boudica was able to call upon her tribal neighbours, the Trinovantes, to join in the rebellion against Rome.

Trinovantian knights

The Trinovantes, too, had had their friendships with the Roman state, but their grievances against Roman greed and insensitivity caused them, too, as we shall see, to change from allies to enemies in Boudica's Britain. The Trinovantes had already suffered partial dispossession before Claudius, in that – so the coinage tells us – their tribal capital at Camulodunum had been taken over by Cunobelinus of the Catuvellauni. The name of this tribal centre means 'Fortress of Camulos' (probably so called after the name of a local war-god), and it must have been galling indeed for such a proud people to see other Britons in power here, and we have seen that a response to such local expansionism led to a plea for help from Caesar. It is thought that Cunobelinus, 'Rex Britannorum', moved his capital from Verlamion to Camulodunum in about AD 10.[116] We have seen (above) that soon after the Claudian Invasion of AD 43, a noble Trinovantian was buried with great ceremony, surrounded by Roman imported goods at Stanway, just outside Camulodunum. So at this time, we can assume that the tribal nobility, or at least some of them, were enjoying the fruits of close contact with Rome. Indeed, a Trinovantian warrior was buried at Kelvedon (Essex) between c. 75 and 25 BC, with accoutrements showing his affinity with both his local area and with Continental Europe, including Rome.[117] All that was to change (see Chapter 7), and the Trinovantes were to prove stalwart in the resistance to colonial imperialism that was whipped up by Boudica.

Like the Iceni, the Trinovantes were horse-lords.[118] The Colchester Castle Museum displays are full of wonderfully ornate horse-harness, including huge terrets set with chunks of coloured glass, clearly designed to make an impressive display. Kelvedon has produced a sherd of black pottery that, though modest in ceramic terms, is highly significant, for it allows us to come face to face with a Trinovantian. Depicted on the fragment is the image of a British warrior, with spiky hair, reminiscent of the lime-washed locks described by Diodorus Siculus as being worn by Gaulish opponents of the Romans in the first century BC,[119] and a beard. He holds a diamond-shaped shield in his left hand and in his right he carries a curious object, a long stave terminating in a crook (see Plate 4). This may be a weapon but is more likely to be some kind of ceremonial staff.[120] This piece of iconography is exciting, for it may be that we are looking at an image of someone very similar to one of the warrior-knights who joined Boudica against the Romans in AD 60. The identity of the image on the Kelvedon potsherd raises interesting questions, for there is other evidence from the site to suggest that special things were going on here in the late Iron Age. Another sherd bears a crude inscription that mentions a god named 'Toutatis', a Gallo-British god associated with the guardianship of the tribe.[121] Could the horseman on the other piece represent this god? It is also worth noting that, at around the time of Caesar's visits to Britain, a high-status warrior – or at least someone interred with the accoutrements of a fighting knight – was buried here at Kelvedon. Such were the fighting men (and women?) who, with their champion, Boudica, faced the regimented troops of the Emperor Nero a century later. The potsherd with its image of a proud warrior[122] speaks volumes, for it is testament to a society where the individual nobleman was the focus of warfare, while for the Romans, each soldier was simply an anonymous element in a unified force. It was to be this individualism which, in the end, was to tell against Boudica's Britons, while the Romans' corporate identity won the day.

Notes and references

1. Act I, Scene vi, lines 184–90; Harper Collins 1994 edition, 1263.
2. Creighton 2000, 76; Sealey 1997, 15; Henig 2002, 33; Manley 2002, 44.
3. Creighton 2000, xii; Creighton 2006, 2–13.
4. *Cymbeline* Act V Scene v, lines 476–81.
5. Plutarch *Life of Caesar* 23, 2–4; trans. Warner 1958, 237.
6. Stewart 1995, 3.
7. Caesar *de Bello Gallico* V,14; trans. Wiseman & Wiseman 1980, 94.
8. Ovid *Amores* 2.16.39.
9. Martial *Epigrams* 11.53.1; 14.99.
10. Propertius *Elegies* 2.18(b). 23f; Stewart 1995, 5.
11. See Preface.
12. Hingley 2000, 66, fig. 5.1 and caption.
13. Braund 1996, 41–2.
14. *De Signis* 5.29–36: 'Since living creatures in our experience are mortal, if there are any living creatures in Britain, they are mortal'; Braund 1996, 42.
15. Worthington 2004.
16. Cicero *de Prov. Cons.* 33.
17. Caesar *de Bello Gallico* IV, 20.

18 See, for example, Caesar *de Bello Gallico* III, 8, where he describes the activities of the maritime Veneti of north-west Brittany, who regularly sailed to Britain.
19 Op. cit. II, 4.
20 Op. cit. II, 14; trans. Wiseman & Wiseman 1980, 49.
21 Op. cit. IV, 21; trans. Wiseman & Wiseman 1980, 81.
22 Op. cit. V, 22; trans. Wiseman & Wiseman 1980, 97.
23 Op. cit. VII, 76; trans. Wiseman & Wiseman 1980, 170.
24 Op. cit. VIII, 6–7; trans. Wiseman & Wiseman 1980, 180–1.
25 Op. cit. VIII, 23; trans. Wiseman & Wiseman 1980, 188.
26 J.D. Hill *et al.* remind us that equation between Caesar's erstwhile ally and the Commius on the southern British coinage is 'not without its problems': Hill *et al.* 2004, 17.
27 Manley 2002.
28 Op. cit., 43–4.
29 Creighton 2000, 69, fig. 3.4; Manley 2002, 44, fig. 7.
30 Caesar *de Bello Gallico* IV, 21; Braund 1996, 60.
31 Creighton 2000, 59–60.
32 Op. cit. 64.
33 Caesar *De Bello Gallico* V, 11   Paul Sealey (pers. com.) has rightly pointed out that Caesar does not attribute Cassivallaunus suzeraignty over the Catuvellauni and thus the connection between ruler and tribe is inferred rather than specifically indicated.
34 Op. cit. V, 20.
35 Braund 1996, 78.
36 Ovid *Metamorphoses* 15.752; trans. Braund 1996, 78.
37 Tacitus *Agricola* XIII, 1; trans. Braund 1996, 78.
38 Strabo *Geographia* IV, 5, 1; trans. Braund 1996, 83.
39 Braund 1996, 81.
40 Creighton 2000, 91.
41 Moore 1954, 128; Chisholm & Ferguson 1981, 10.
42 *Res Gestae* VI, 32; Moore 1954, 40; see Cheesman 1998 for a discussion of the etymology of Tincomarus's name.
43 Braund 1993, 53–5; 1996, 81, 85.

44 Horace *Odes* I, 35: the poem takes the form of a prayer to Fortuna, goddess of Chance, to whom a great temple was dedicated at Antium in Latium; trans. Michie 1964, 81.
45 Op. cit. III, 5; trans. Michie 1964, 151, 153.
46 Op. cit. IV, 14; trans. Michie 1964, 249.
47 Dio Cassius *Roman History* 53.22; after Creighton 2000, 91.
48 Op. cit., 53.25; after Creighton 2000, 91.
49 Creighton 2000, 72–3; Manley 2002, 44–5; Braund 1996, 74.
50 Hill *et al.* 2004.
51 King & Soffe 1991; 1999.
52 Hill *et al.* 2004, 3 and fig. 1.
53 British Museum.
54 Hill *et al.* 2004, 14.
55 Op. cit. 15; Stead 1991.
56 Manley 2002, 46.
57 Hill *et al.* 2004, 17–18.
58 Lynn 1992.
59 Creighton 2000, 192.
60 Brunaux 1988; 1996
61 Creighton 2000, 192–3
62 Op. cit. 195; Briggs *et al.* 1992, 1–62.
63 Braund 1996, 85; Allen & Haselgrove 1979, 2, no. 28.
64 Tacitus *Annals* II, 23; trans. Grant 1956, 86.
65 According to a display panel at the Verulamium Museum; Rivet & Smith 1979, 305.
66 Braund 1996, 70, 74.
67 Op. cit. 1996, 69.
68 King 1995.
69 Creighton 2000, 131.
70 Foster 1986.
71 The name is known from coinage: Creighton 2000, 68–9, 224.
72 Creighton 2000, 181–3.
73 Op. cit. 187.

74 Manley 2002, 143–4; Creighton 2000, 92–4.
75 Creighton 2000, 171.
76 Allen 1975, 1–19.
77 Suetonius *Gaius* 44.2.
78 Creighton 2000, 109.
79 Dio Cassius *Roman History* 60, 20.1
80 Suetonius *Gaius Caligula* 44; trans. Graves 1962, 152.
81 Op. cit. 46; trans. Graves 1962, 152–153.
82 Braund 1996, 95.
83 Niblett 1999, xxv, 20.
84 Creighton 2000, 181–3.
85 Aldhouse-Green 2001a, 165. This idea of sexual partnership in death is suggested for some of the Nubian burials of the Kerma Period *c.* 1600 BC: O'Connor 1993, 52–5; Kendall 1997, 60.
86 Tacitus *Annals* XII, 31–2; trans. Grant 1956, 256.
87 Sealey 1997, 10.
88 Allen 1970, 1.
89 Op. cit.
90 John Davies pers. com.; Van Arsdell 1989, 185–6.
91 Sealey 1997, 5.
92 Op. cit.
93 Neil Faulker pers. com.
94 Sealey 1997, 10.
95 Davies 1999, 19.
96 Crummy 1997, 337–41.
97 Henig 2002, 45.
98 Norwich Castle Museum; John Davies pers. com.
99 Green 1976, 212.
100 Castle Museum, Colchester.
101 Castle Museum, Colchester display boards.
102 Iron Age manacles have been found at Verlamion also: Verulamium Museum.
103 Tacitus *Annals* XIV, 30.

104 Potter 1997, 38.

105 Stead 1991; Creen 1996, 18 9; Wells 1995, 222; Raftery 1991, 566–7.

106 Strabo *Geographia* VI, 17.

107 Norwich Castle Museum.

108 Megaw & Megaw 1989, 216.

109 Dio Cassius *Roman History* 62.2. Sealey (pers. com.) doubts whether Dio's mention of Boudica's 'necklace' was actually a torc, because Boudican metalwork hoards are free of gold jewellery, and torcs ceased to be manufactured in the region long before, although it is perfectly possible that Boudica did wear a torc that had been kept and treasured as an ancestral heirloom: Sealey 1979.

110 Polybius *Histories* II, 29, draws attention to the torcs worn by the Gauls fighting the Battle of Telamon against Rome in 225 BC; and Strabo *Geographica* IV, 4, 5 makes a point of describing the showiness of the Gauls, who loved jewellery and display, torcs and brightly coloured clothes. Virgil (*Aeneid* VIII, line 655) refers to the Gauls who sacked Rome in 387/6 BC as having 'milk-white necks encircled with gold', again a reference to an iconicity of barbarism.

111 Aldhouse-Green 2004a, 42.

112 Quintilian *Institutio Oratoria* VI, 79.

113 Neil Faulkner pers. com.

114 Farrar 2005, 18–19.

115 Neil Faulkner pers. com.

116 Sealey 1997, 15.

117 I am grateful to Paul Sealey for information on the Kelvedon warrior in advance of publication.

118 The large numbers of terrets (horse-harness rings) coming up as metal-detector finds from Icenian territory indicate the importance of horsemanship for this tribe as well as the Trinovantes: Sealey (pers. com.) and Hutcheson (2004) suggests that these terrets might reflect the retention of chariot-warfare here, perhaps, while such outmoded tactics were declining in Essex and Hertfordshire.

119 Diodorus Siculus *Library of History* V, 28.

120 Ross (1986, 79, fig. 36) draws attention to curved 'hockey-stick' like objects held in the hands of images on a Romano-British pottery mould from Northamptonshire and on one of the diadems from the Romano-Celtic temple at Hockwold, Norfolk. The object carried by the Kelvedon horseman also resembles the *lituus* (curved staff) of the Roman *Augur* (a priest who

interpreted the omens of the gods by studying the flight of birds: Adkins & Adkins 1996, 133).

121 Lucan *Pharsalia* I, 444–6; Ross 1967, 171.

122 The image on the potsherd is part of a stamped frieze of such figures, the remainder of which are incomplete (Paul Sealey pers. com.). So it could be argued that the 'individual' to whom I refer is one of many warriors represented or, perhaps, the same person whose depiction is repeated around the vessel.

CHAPTER 2

Conquering a myth: Claudius and Britannia

Claudius's mother often called him 'a monster: a man whom Mother Nature had begun to work upon but then flung aside'; and, if she ever accused anyone of stupidity, would exclaim: 'He is a bigger fool even than my son Claudius!'

Finally, to show what his great-uncle, Augustus, thought of him, I quote the following extracts from the Imperial correspondence:

'My dear Livia,
As you suggested, I have now discussed with Tiberius what we should do about your grandson Claudius at the coming Festival of Mars the Avenger. We both agreed that an immediate decision ought to be taken. The question is whether he has – shall I say? – full command of his five senses ...'

Suetonius *Claudius* [1]

This passage, from Suetonius's life of Claudius, indicates that the future conqueror of Britain had an unpromising start. Probably a sufferer from cerebral palsy, with severe physical incapacity, including both mobility impairment and a stammer, he fell far short of Roman ideals of perfect manhood, and he was an unlikely choice as ruler of the Roman world (see Figure 2.1). But when the young emperor Gaius Caligula was assassinated in AD 41, Claudius – if we believe Suetonius's account[2] – was found hiding behind a curtain, fearing for his life, and chosen by the Praetorian Guard to be emperor of Rome. So, at the age of 50, Claudius badly needed to project himself as a strong, powerful

2 ◆ Conquering a myth: Claudius and Britannia

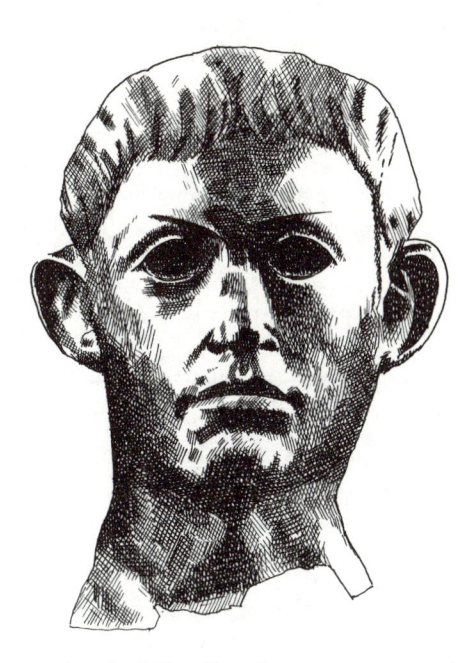

FIGURE 2.1 ◆ *Bronze head of Claudius, from a monumental statue (almost certainly from outside the temple at Colchester), found in the river Alde, Suffolk.*
Source: Artist P.J. Lopeman; © Miranda Aldhouse-Green.

ruler, not least because his survival on the throne depended on the loyalty of the army.

Claudius's persona and background are vital to the understanding both of his decision to conquer Britain (or, at least, part of it) and of subsequent events that led up to and encompassed the Boudican Rebellion. The factors that governed the placement of Britain on Rome's active agenda are complex and intricate, but Claudius's need to prove himself as an emperor worthy of his divine forebear Augustus (and better than Tiberius and Gaius) and Britain's continued symbolism as being on the edge or beyond the edge of the human-controlled world are both crucial to the island's future as a Roman province.

Claudius and Britain: the classical literature

Britain – what sort of a place it is and what sort of inhabitants it produces – will soon be described more precisely and on the basis of greater exploration.

For, behold, the greatest of emperors is opening it up after it has been closed so long, the conqueror of peoples not only unconquered but unknown to boot![3]

Pomponius Mela *Chorographia*

Claudius waged war on the Britons, (a country) where no Roman had set foot since the days of C. Caesar, and when it had been vanquished by Cn. Sentius and A. Plautius, distinguished members of noble families, he held a magnificent triumph

Eutropius Brevarium[4]

Mela's eulogy succinctly sums up what a British conquest meant for Claudius's image, both at Rome and abroad. Claudius is presented here as conqueror of a legendary place, a land of myth shut away until now by its remoteness beyond the north-western edge of the world: the *Ultima Thule* of classical writers.[5] The fourth-century author Eutropius makes a similar point, but he emphasises the significance of Claudius's action in taking up Caesar's mantle and finishing the business begun by his illustrious ancestor.

Two of the most important classical literary sources for Claudius's British campaigns are the narratives of Dio Cassius and Suetonius. While Dio was writing *c.* AD 200–29 and thus nearly two hundred years after the events he described, Suetonius was born in about AD 69 and became chief secretary to the Emperor Hadrian (who reigned between 117 and 138).[6] 'Suetonius was fortunate in having ready access to the imperial and senatorial archives and to a great body of contemporary memoirs and public documents, and in having himself lived nearly 30 years under the Caesars. Much of his information about Tiberius, Caligula, Claudius and Nero comes from eyewitnesses of the events described.'[7] So Suetonius should have the potential for being a reliable source.[8] But the author's work shows a keen ear for sleaze and scandal, and it is sometimes difficult to separate an objective viewpoint from a love of gossip, anecdote and rumour-mongering (traits used to wonderful effect in Robert Graves's books *I Claudius* and *Claudius the God* and in the 1980s television drama adaptation).[9]

What is interesting about Suetonius's treatment of Claudius's invasion of Britain is the lack of importance he accords the campaign itself; indeed he speaks of it in quite dismissive tones, although it is clear from his writing that the resultant triumphal ceremonies played a large part in securing the emperor's standing.

2 ◆ Conquering a myth: Claudius and Britannia

> *Claudius's sole campaign was of no great importance. The Senate had already voted him triumphal regalia, but he thought it beneath his dignity to accept these, and decided that Britain was the country where a real triumph could most readily be earned. Its conquest had not been attempted since Julius Caesar's day; and the Britons were now threatening vengeance because the Senate refused to extradite certain deserters who had landed in Gaul during Caligula's reign.*[10]

It may be that the comment 'of no great importance' relates to a statement later on in the passage, in which the historian says of the emperor's sojourn on the island 'he had fought no battles and suffered no casualties' although he 'reduced a large part of the island to submission'. Suetonius also makes a key remark about Claudius's triumphal procession in Rome, saying that 'the emblems of his victory included the naval crown – ornamented with the beaks of ships and representing the crossing and conquest, so to speak, of the Ocean – which he set on the Palace gable beside a civic crown of oak-leaves'. So, according to Suetonius (and Pomponius Mela), what mattered for Claudius was not so much the annexation of Britain but the conquest of the Ocean, the legendary river that encircled the world. This epic, mythic act put Claudius on a par with the gods.

One further comment by Suetonius confirms Britain's importance for the emperor, the naming of his son by Messalina. The boy had been called Germanicus, after Claudius's much-loved soldier-brother, but he was renamed Britannicus to commemorate his father's British victory. The child was clearly the apple of the emperor's eye, for 'Claudius would often pick little Britannicus up and show him to the troops, or to the audience at the Games, either seated on his lap or held at arms' length. His cry: "Good luck to you, my boy!" was loudly echoed on all sides.'[11]

The testimony of Dio Cassius is somewhat more informative about the Claudian invasion of Britain (see Map 4) Although a Greek, he served Rome as consul in AD 222, and he wrote an enormous 80-volume history of Rome from its foundation in 753 BC to AD 229.[12] We are fortunate indeed that, although only fragments of his *Roman History* survive, one extant passage relates to AD 43, and is the most complete and detailed record of events in Britain at that time. Dio has been credited as a historian who endeavoured to contextualise his narrative by asking questions about why things happened as they did and, at the same time, took a critical approach to his own sources of material.[13] Later in this chapter

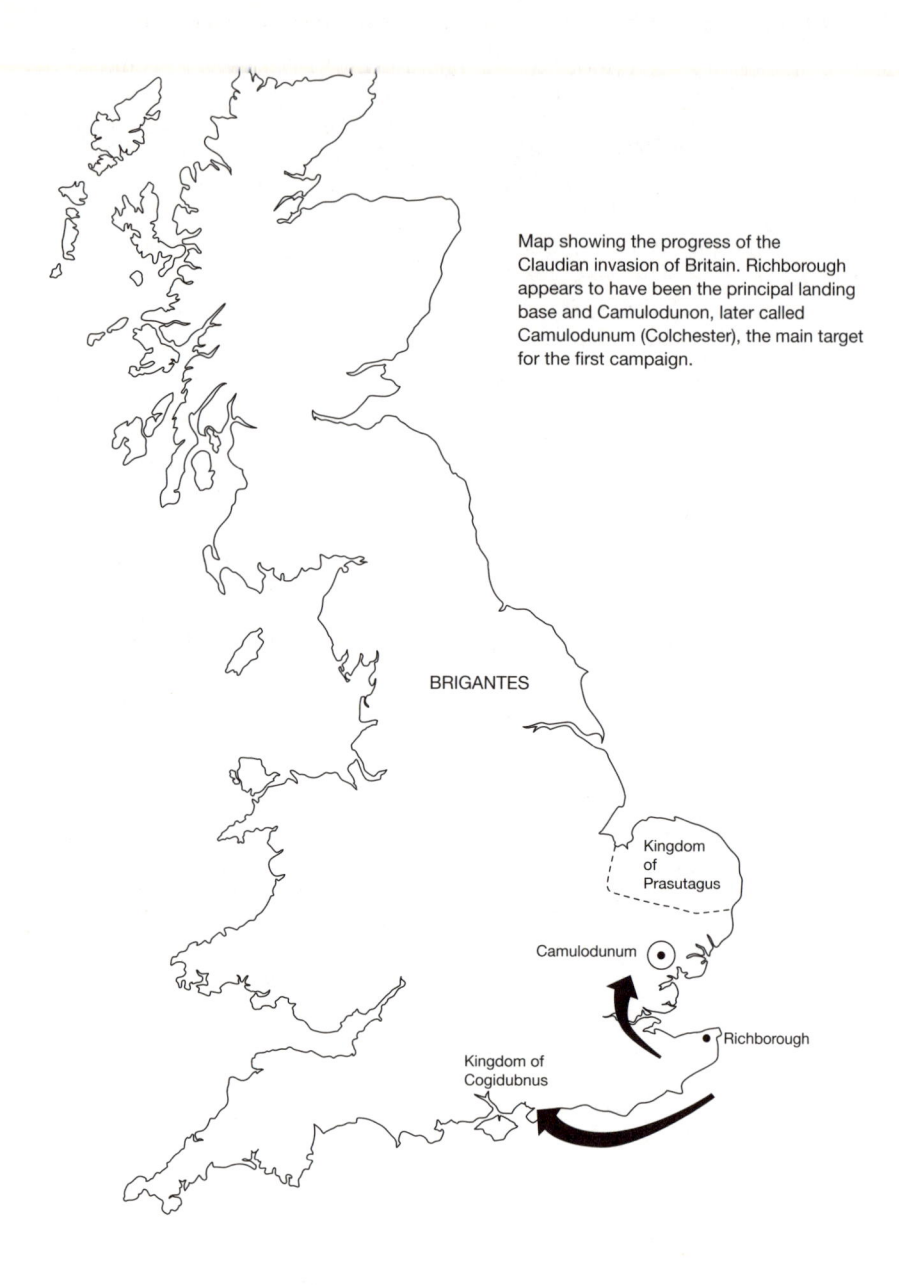

Map showing the progress of the Claudian invasion of Britain. Richborough appears to have been the principal landing base and Camulodunon, later called Camulodunum (Colchester), the main target for the first campaign.

MAP 4 ◆ *Aulus Plautius's initial campaigns during the Claudian invasion of Britain.*

Source: Millett 1995.

2 ♦ Conquering a myth: Claudius and Britannia

we will scrutinise his account carefully, since it contains a great deal of information about the *dramatis personae* of the invasion episode, especially on the British side. While the spotlight is on Claudius himself, two issues concern us with Dio's account: the alleged reason for Roman interference with Britain at this particular time in Claudius's reign, and the behaviour of the emperor himself when Aulus Plautius, commander of the Roman army that formed the invading force, thought that south-east Britain was ready to receive the ruler of the Roman world in person.

The immediate excuse given by Dio for sending an army to Britain was the request for aid by a British nobleman called Berikos, who had apparently been banished from Britain as the result of internecine strife in the south-east. Berikos is almost certainly to be identified with Verica, a ruler of the southern, Atrebatic kingdom and part of the Commian dynasty. Between about AD 30 and 45, Verica minted coins in southern Britain (Hampshire, Surrey and Sussex)[14] that were heavily influenced by Roman themes[15] and, as a son or self-styled son of Commius, was friendly to Rome and may have been one of the *obsides* (young princes who went to Rome to be educated in Roman ways), like Tincomarus (see Chapter 1). Certainly the plea for Roman support by a supplanted or exiled member of the British ruling class was not the first of its kind. Indeed, we have already seen the appearance of the Trinovantian Mandubracius and the Catuvellaunian Adminius before Julius Caesar and Gaius, both of whom were the victims of intra- or inter-dynastic struggles for power. Verica's appeal to Claudius gave him a pretext for war against the Britons, as did the aggressive and unstable condition of the Catuvellaunian kingdom;[16] another was the unfinished business inherited from Caesar (as stressed by Eutropius – see above). Claudius was to gain considerable kudos from the fact that not Caesar, nor Augustus, nor Tiberius nor Gaius had been able to achieve what was accomplished by their disabled and, allegedly, half-witted successor.

Aulus Plautius, who was to become the first governor of Britain, had his work cut out for him in AD 43, for he and his army met with fierce and vigorous resistance from some of the tribes, particularly from the eastern dynasty of the Catuvellauni, where Caratacus and Togodumnus, sons of Cunobelin, were in the forefront of the freedom fighters. One highly significant piece of information given by Dio in this context is that, by this time, Cunobelinus himself was dead (either of natural causes, since he would have been quite elderly in AD 43, or, perhaps, as the result of an anti-Roman coup by his less Romanophile offspring). While Plautius did the real work of conquest, Claudius's presence in Britain, 'at the climax of the campaign'[17] was essential if he were to be seen by the world as an active military ruler. Dio narrates the imperial visit with quiet diplomacy:

> He [Plautius] proceeded to guard what had already been won and sent for Claudius; this is what he had been ordered to do, if there was any particularly stubborn resistance. Indeed extensive preparations had already been made in advance by way of gathering together various types of equipment, including elephants, to back up the invasion force.[18]

The presence of elephants is particularly interesting, for these creatures were charged with symbolism from the past. We should remember not only Hannibal's elephants and their epic Alpine crossing but, more importantly, Julius Caesar's triumphal procession at Rome in 46 BC after the Gallic Wars culminated in the appearance of the general himself 'through an avenue of forty lamp-bearing elephants, arrayed on either side of him'.[19] When Claudius entered Camulodunum (Colchester) with these exotic creatures, he was making a powerful statement both to the Roman army and to the Britons: to the Romans he harked back to his heroic ancestry; to the Britons, the elephants reflected Roman might and the huge, far-flung empire.

Dio is careful to record the emperor's entry into Britain not simply as the act of an armchair ruler, who appeared in triumph in a conquered land only when it was safe to do so. Instead, the Greek chronicler stresses the persona of Claudius the soldier, describing his personal command of the troops by the Thames, his river crossing, his defeat of the enemy in battle and his capture of the main stronghold of Camulodunum, tribal capital of the old king Cunobelinus.[20]

> When the Senate learned of his achievement they hailed him with the title Britannicus and granted him the celebration of a triumph. They also voted that there should be an annual festival in commemoration and that two triumphal arches should be erected, one in the city and the other in Gaul at the point where he had crossed over into Britain. They granted his son the same title.[21]

Suetonius picks up this theme, in describing Claudius's activities at his gladiatorial games, many of which he hosted and paid for. On one of these occasions where – says Suetonius – the emperor sometimes behaved in a relaxed, informal manner, joking with the people and exchanging badinage with the participators, Claudius brought Britain into the performance. He rigged up a theatre on the Campus Martius (the Field of Mars) and, dressed in his purple campaigning cloak, presented a staged performance in which a mock-up of a British fortified settlement was attacked and sacked, and the emperor accepted the 'surrender' of a British king:[22] the stronghold must surely have been intended to be Camulodunum, and it is clear that this event was writ large in Claudius's consciousness.

Inventing outcomes

In the spring of 2005, the prominent Tory politician Michael Portillo presented a BBC Radio series entitled *Things we Forgot to Remember*, a critical discussion of key events in British history and the biased way in which they have been reported. In his programme on the Spanish Armada, Portillo used the term 'inventing outcomes' to describe such creative historical recording.[23] Such a term may usefully be applied to the version of the Claudian invasion of Britain handed down to us by classical and subsequent historians and, indeed, to the accounts of the Boudican Rebellion itself, as given to us by Tacitus and Dio. Every historian works within a context and, generally speaking, most who operated within the Roman Empire would have presented history from a Roman perspective even if, like Tacitus, they had reservations about that imperial milieu. It is quite likely that, like Portillo's Armada, at least some of the 'battles won' recorded for Britain by Rome in the first century AD were by no means the out-and-out successes they were claimed to be. We need always to bear 'invention', or at least hyperbole, in mind when assessing the chronicles of Graeco-Roman authors on military events in Britannia.

Claudius's Britannia: archaeological evidence

> *In fulfilment of a vow, for the safety and the return and the British victory of Tiberius Claudius Caesar Augustus Germanicus, Pontifex Maximus, in his fifth year of tribunician power, imperator ten times, father of his country, consul designate for the fourth time; Aulus Vicirius Proculus, priest of Augustus, military tribune, fulfilled his Vow for the British victory.*[24]

This inscription, from Rusellae in Etruria (Tuscany) was cut in AD 45, two years after the invasion of Britain. Proculus – unusually, perhaps – combined the office of a high-ranking army officer and *sevir Augustalis*, a priest of the imperial cult. Clearly the dedicant was a man of means; setting up public inscriptions (and statues) was an expensive business, and he may, at one and the same time, have commissioned the monument in genuine thanksgiving for the British victory and Claudius's personal safety, while hoping to ensure that his career flourished by making sure he very publicly honoured his emperor. Prayers to the Roman gods often worked in two stages: the first was the *nuncupatio*, the asking part; the second, the *solutio*, the fulfilment of the vow as expressed in material terms, through the setting up of an altar, a statue or a lesser thank-offering. This inscription represents the second and final part of a dialogue with the divine and, particularly, with the goddess of victory in battle.

The Rusellae dedication was by no means the only monument to Claudius's British triumph. We have already noted Dio's statement about the senatorial decree that two commemorative arches be built to mark his great conquest of the Britons. Two pieces of relevant archaeological evidence survive: coins (see Figure 2.2) depicting such an arch, bearing the words 'De Britannis'[25] and part of the actual arch at Rome.[26] Coins were a time-honoured way of spreading good-news propaganda, imperial exploits and army victories and, in their way, were more powerful instruments of 'spin' than public monuments because they had a much wider circulation. The arch-fragment (see Figure 2.3) is interesting but the reading of its main inscription, itself only partially surviving, is controversial and open to a range of interpretations, although it certainly alludes to the submission of several British kings to the emperor and to his subjugation of Ocean.[27] The positioning of the arch in Rome was itself highly-charged: Claudius chose a spot for its erection over the main road leading south out of the city, mirroring the arch set up by the emperor's father Drusus, whose monument to his German victories was placed over the main road leading north.[28] What is clear from all this is the store Claudius set by the conquest of Britain in the propagation of his image as a great and quasi-divine ruler of the world.

So far, this chapter has made precious little reference – directly or indirectly – to the heroine of this book. But one piece of archaeological evidence sheds some light on imperial attitudes to a conquered Britain

2 ◆ Conquering a myth: Claudius and Britannia

FIGURE 2.2 ◆ *Gold coin (an aureus) of Claudius, depicting the emperor's victory over Britannia.*

Source: © Anne Leaver; after Henig 2002.

that resonate with Roman attitudes to Boudica less than two decades later. This is a stone carving from Aphrodisias in south-west Turkey, part of a complex of sculptures from a shrine 'dedicated to Aphrodite and the Julio-Claudian emperors'.[29] Iain Ferris has termed the iconography of this monument a 'pornography of conquest'[30] and rightly so, for it presents Claudius in the act of violating Britannia, personified as a helpless woman (see Figure 2.4).[31] The protagonists in the iconography have been securely identified by the accompanying basal inscription, which mentions the two by name. Both figures face the spectator but otherwise their treatment could not be more different one from the other. The emperor is depicted as a young hero, naked but for a helmet and a *chlamys* or short cloak pinned at the right shoulder and flying outward from his body as if to represent violent action; his right arm is now missing from just below the shoulder but enough remains to allow its once upraised threatening

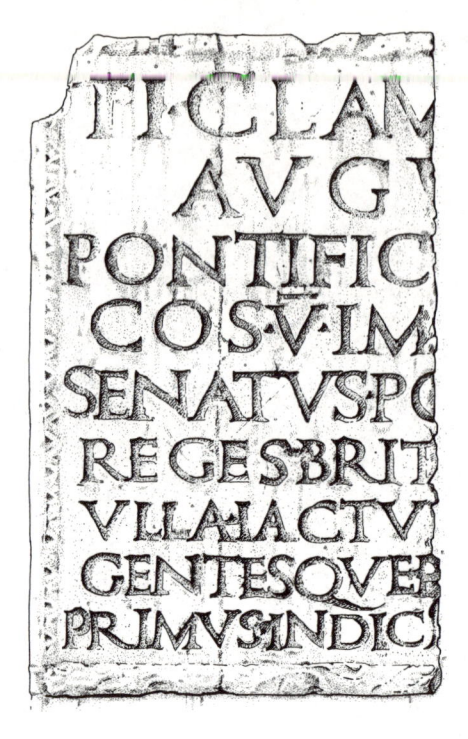

FIGURE 2.3 ◆ *Fragment of Claudius's triumphal arch at Rome, alluding to his conquest of the Britons.*

Source: © Anne Leaver; after Henig 2002.

position to be identified, his left hand grasps Britannia by the hair at the top of her head; his legs straddle the woman's body and his right knee pins down her right thigh. The image of Britannia, by contrast, is utterly subdued by her male aggressor: her thin robe has slipped in the struggle, exposing her right breast, her legs sprawl and her arms are raised as if to try and defend herself. Britannia's back is to Claudius and one has the disturbing feeling that he is about to bugger her. (In his novel, *The Return of Eva Perón*, the author V. S. Naipaul discusses Argentinian machismo in the 1970s, and the sexual attitudes of the macho male: 'His conquest of a woman is complete only when he has buggered her'.[32])

Britannia's bared breast may contain meaning not just in terms of sexual violence but also in her intended image as a barbarian, in particular an Amazon, one of the legendary band of warrior-women from Greek myth who personified ideas of otherness, wildness and lack of control so

2 ◆ Conquering a myth: Claudius and Britannia

FIGURE 2.4 ◆ *Britannia and Claudius on the carving from Aphrodisias, Turkey.*
Source: Illustrator Mark Breedon © Iain Ferris.

abhorrent to the ordered moderation prided especially by the Greek world. We need to think of the entire sculpture not simply as a piece of Roman imperial propaganda but to look at its context within a Hellenised area of the empire, where Greek artistic modes of expression pertained. Britannia at Aphrodisias is depicted as an other being, a barbarian, not quite human and certainly ripe for rape and conquest.[33] Britannia's bared breast may have other symbolism, too, that of nourishment: Britain may be presented as an image of abundance, a land worthy of annexation and a source of future prosperity for the Roman Empire, a land that could be milked of its assets. But those who wish to see Britain as peacefully accepting of *romanitas* and Rome as a graceful benefactor, ushering in the new province as a valued and equal partner, need only to look at the Aphrodisias monument to see another dimension to the relationship between Britain and Rome in the Claudian years. This image of Claudius and Britannia is not so very different from that of Boudica and the Romans in AD 60 only, unlike the submissive woman in the carving, the Icenian queen hit back, at first with devastating effect as we shall see.[34]

Hawks and doves in Claudian Britain
Togidubnus: friend of Rome and Great King of the Britons

> *Aulus Plautius was the first ex-consul to be appointed governor, and soon after him came Ostorius Scapula – both of them fine soldiers. The nearest parts of Britain were gradually shaped into a province, and to crown all came a colony of veterans. Certain states were presented to King Cogidumnus, who maintained his unswerving loyalty down to our own times – an example of the long- established Roman custom of employing even kings to make others slaves.*
>
> Tacitus *Agricola*[35]

Opinions differ as to whether this British king's name was Cogidumnus, Cogidubnus or Togidubnus, but most scholars now call him Togidubnus, so we will refer to him thus in this volume.[36] In the above-quoted passage, Tacitus gives with one hand and takes with another: he acknowledges the Briton's contribution to the peace effort but at the same time he sneers at his collaboration with the conquerors, and there is a not-so-subtle hint that the Roman writer scorns him as a quisling. In dealing with Tacitus as a historian, we have to be aware of his scepticism and the subtlety with which he revealed hidden truths, giving rise to his continual interplays between hidden and overt images of 'actuality'. In the words of Ellen O'Gorman, Tacitus does not 'replace falsehood with truth, thereby erasing the façade, but rather sets the two in conjunction'.[37] This ambiguity probably arises from two factors: first, Tacitus was a republican, and so disapproved of imperial policy in general; second, this client-king probably had a greater and more lasting influence on British affairs in the later first century AD than the author's own father-in-law Agricola,[38] whom he clearly idolised, who served in Britain first as military tribune (during the Boudican Rebellion), then later on as legionary commander and finally governor of Britain in the 70s.

Togidubnus played an important role in the establishment of Britannia as a Roman province. The time about which Tacitus was writing, the governorship of Ostorius Scapula, was in the later 40s AD, a period when the Britons were causing trouble, particularly in East Anglia, northern England and Wales.[39] Rome (and Claudius himself) might have been glad of Togidubnus as an ally and might have shown gratitude not only by giving him lands (perhaps confiscated from other tribes or merely confirming his limited dominion over his own former territory that had been officially annexed by Rome), but also by supporting his rule within a potentially hostile environment. So, according to Tacitus, this British king was operational from just after the invasion until 'our own times' (he wrote the *Agricola* in AD 97–8); if the British nobleman really did live until then, he must have been young when he first played a part in Britain's fortunes. Martin Henig,[40] among others, has made links between Togidubnus's prosperity under the aegis of Rome and the archaeological record for mid-later first-century Britain. The area of Togidubnus's autonomy can be firmly situated in southern England, for he is mentioned on a grand Purbeck marble inscription found in April 1723 at Chichester in West Sussex (see Figure 2.5).[41] According to a reinterpretation of the lettering,[42] the inscription reads:

NEPTVNO.ET.MINERVAE
    TEMPLVM
PRO.SALVTE.DOMVS. DIVINAE
EX.AVCTORITATE.TI.CLAVD.
TOGIDVBNI.REG.MAGN.BRIT.
COLEGIVM.FABROR.ETQVI.IN EO
SVNT D.S.D.DONANTE.AREAM
    ENTE PVDENTINI.FIL

The epigraphy here is highly revealing: Chichester was almost certainly Togidubnus's tribal capital; significantly, its Roman name *Noviomagus Regnensium* means 'the new market of the people of the kingdom[43]'), and here we have a Briton setting up a temple to two Roman gods in honour of the Roman Divine House (that is, the imperial family). More important is the manner in which this pro-Roman ruler chose to style himself: first, he has adopted the name Tiberius Claudius, after the Julio-Claudian imperial house. Anthony Barrett has drawn attention to another official Chichester dedication-slab, sadly now lost, found in 1740.[44] This one is

```
EPTVNO·ET·MINERVAE
   TEMPLVM·
 ·SALVTE·D      ·DIVINAE
 VCTORITA         CLAVD·
 IDVBNI·RL       GN·BRIT·
 GIVM·FABRORE·  QVI·IN·EO·
  D·S·D·DONANTE·AREAM
 ENTE·PVDENTINI·FIL·
```

A Scale of Six Foot.

FIGURE 2.5 ♦ *The temple inscription from Chichester, mentioning Togidubnus.*

Source: Henig 2002.

dedicated to the Emperor Nero, was set up in AD 58 and probably accompanied a grandiose statue. It is likely that the Togidubnus Neptune and Minerva inscription is of similar date. But the most telling part of the temple dedication is the phrase 'by the authority of Tiberius Claudius Togidubnus *Great King of the Britons*' This title has an oriental air to it; it is certainly not the style of a western ruler and would fit better with some of the eastern potentates associated with Rome, such as the Judaean Herod Agrippa. Henig is of the view that Togidubnus, like Verica before him, spent a period of time in the imperial city and here may have learned to call himself *Rex Magnus Britannorum*.[45] That he was permitted to do so by Roman authority suggests that he was a valued and trusted ally in the province.

If Togidubnus was as important to Rome as he seems to have been, then he would probably have been richly rewarded in material terms as well as in indulgence of his taste for grand titles. It is quite possible that the impressive Neronian residence at Fishbourne in Sussex, and its timber precursor, first belonged to someone of Togidubnus's stature. There is no unequivocal evidence for his presence at Fishbourne, but someone called Tiberius Claudius Catuarus lost a gold signet ring there

2 ◆ Conquering a myth: Claudius and Britannia

(found in excavations east of the palace in 1995) inscribed with his name (see Plate 5).[46] His first two names are identical to those of Togidubnus and, similarly, his last name shows he was a Briton. Both received Roman citizenship, probably under Claudius, and proudly adopted his names to indicate the emperor's patronage. The early history of Fishbourne, as elucidated by excavations in the late twentieth century, shows that the site began life as some kind of military installation but that it quickly developed into a 'large, comfortable and well-appointed timber house', in use during the period *c.* AD 45–65. During the reign of Nero, this dwelling was replaced by a substantial and complex stone residence, termed a 'proto-palace' and was later, around AD 75-80, incorporated into a still grander establishment.[47]

In the mid-later first century AD, then, Fishbourne appears to have been the residence of an upwardly mobile individual who derived considerable benefit from *romanitas*. That it might have been inhabited by Britons rather than Roman officials is suggested by the Catuarus ring. If Togidubnus were the house-owner, he might have lived there well into Flavian times: Barry Cunliffe has argued convincingly that he could have been a young man – of about 25 – when he first had dealings with Rome as her ally, and could have lived into his late seventies or eighties.[48] Tombstones from Roman Britain show that some people did attain great age: witness the town-councillor from Gloucester who died at Bath aged 80, Calpurnius Receptus, a priest of Sulis who died, perhaps in office, also at Aquae Sulis at 75;[49] and a remarkable man commemorated on a tombstone from the Bulmore Road cemetery, Caerleon, who reached the grand age of 100.[50] It is just possible that Fishbourne has provided us with actual sight of its owner's face, whether or not this was Togidubnus: the marble head of a youth, probably carved in the mid-first century AD (see Figure 2.6), was found in the rubble of the north wing and it may have been a portrait of the British ruler or of one of the house-owner's children.[51]

There are other signs, too, that the old Atrebatian kingdom expanded under Togidubnus's rule, probably westward towards (and perhaps including) the great temple and spa at Bath. But was there a single action by this British king that would have caused Nero to lavish favours upon him? The answer is that Togidubnus may well have been instrumental in, if not crucial, to Rome's final victory against Boudica. Henig[52] has pointed out that, while the Roman cities of London, Colchester and

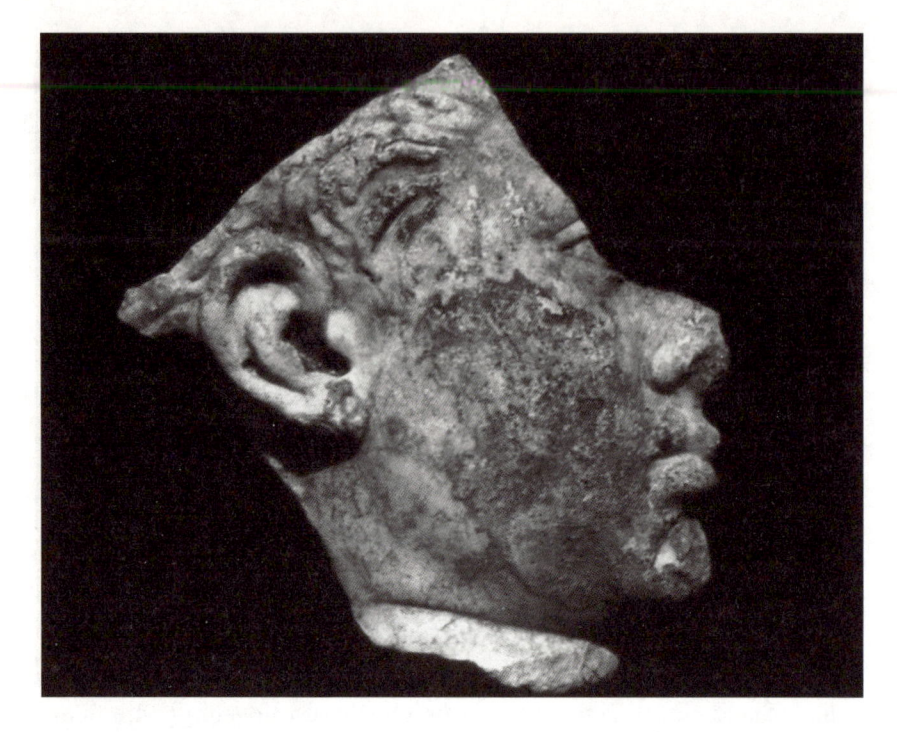

FIGURE 2.6 ◆ *Marble head of a youth, mid-first century AD, from Fishbourne.*
Source: © Fishbourne Roman Palace and Museum.

Verulamium were attacked and sacked by Boudica's forces, neither Silchester nor Chichester were affected and 'the reason probably lies in the resolute action of Togidubnus and his followers. The survival of these towns suggests Boudica's final stand may have been in the Thames valley, against a mixed force of Romans and Togidubnus's Britons'.[53]

Warlike sons: Togodumnus and Caratacus

> Plautius experienced a deal of trouble in searching out their [the Britons'] forces, but when he did find them he defeated first Caratacus and then Togodumnus, both of them sons of Cunobelinus, who was himself by this time dead.
>
> Dio Cassius *Roman History*[54]

The old Catuvellaunian king Cunobelin had many sons: beside Togodumnus and Caratacus, we must remember Adminius, expelled from his lands by his own family and turning up as a suppliant to Gaius on campaign in Germany. Moreover, Tacitus refers to Caratacus's brothers, who were paraded in Rome in chains after their final defeat and then magnanimously pardoned by Claudius.[55] Graham Webster[56] states that the eldest brother, Togodumnus, was Cunobelin's heir and took over leadership of the expanded Catuvellaunian hegemony, while Caratacus began to invade the southern, Atrebatic kingdom, as indicated by the distribution of coinage bearing the word CARA,[57] thus causing Verica to flee for help to the emperor. Dio mentions that the two brothers were also threatening the territory of the Dobunni, a tribe whose lands bordered those of the Catuvellauni, the frontier (according to coin distribution) being somewhere in Oxfordshire. Part of this tribe entered into an alliance with Plautius, who had left a detachment of troops there in order to ensure its safety.

Some time in AD 43, at about the time of the Roman push across the Thames, Togodumnus met his death. We are not told how, but we can infer from Dio's mention of vengeance that he was killed in battle: 'Togodumnus had died about this time, but the Britons, far from yielding, joined together all the more firmly to avenge his death.[58]

So the one brother exits the stage, leaving it clear for the dramatic guerrilla campaigns of Caratacus. But before we follow him on his journey across England to Wales, in his bid for freedom, it is useful to dwell for a moment upon the reasons why Cunobelin's pro-Roman policy had been overturned by his sons. One of the factors has to be the supplication of Verica to Claudius, who was clearly itching for an excuse to annex Britain. Guy de la Bédoyère suggests that it was the Catuvellauni (of all peoples) who would suffer the most from a successful Roman invasion for, at best, this tribe's own predatory policy towards their neighbours would be severely curtailed while, at worst, it too would fall under the Roman yoke, and the aggressive attitude of Togodumnus and Caratacus was unlikely to foster their status as client-kings of Rome.[59]

If Togodumnus has made comparatively little mark on the history of Britannia, the same cannot be said of his brother Caratacus (see Plate 7) who survived to remain a thorn in Rome's flesh for some time. De la Bédoyère draws attention to the fact that, in continuing to oppose the Roman invasion force, Caratacus was swimming against the tide: Cunobelin and Togidubnus knuckled under, seeing advantage to themselves and their territories in so doing, while other princes mentioned in the Roman histories – like Verica – owed their continued free status to the colonisers.[60] The several British kings mentioned on the Arch of Claudius[61] also attest to the compliance of the majority of the indigenous rulers with whom Rome came into contact in the first century AD.

In its way, the continued resistance offered to Roman domination by Caratacus was just as heroic as that of Boudica, although perhaps less romantic. Like the Gallic leader Vercingetorix, who opposed Julius Caesar to the last in 52 BC, Caratacus emerges as Claudius's *bête noir* in Britain, only to end up – as did Vercingetorix, in chains at a Roman triumph. The Catuvellaunian leader did not stay to argue the case with the Claudian army in his own territory but, instead, moved west to the wild Welsh lands that knew little of Rome and had not been seduced by the luxuries of Roman material goods. 'In other words, the Coca-Cola culture of the Roman world simply did not impinge on Silurian consciousness'.[62]

> *The natural ferocity of the inhabitants [of Silurian territory] was intensified by their belief in the prowess of Caratacus, whose many undefeated battles – and even many victories – had made him pre-eminent among British chieftains. His deficiency in strength was compensated by superior cunning and topographical knowledge. Transferring the war to the country of the Ordovices, he was joined by everyone who feared a Roman peace.*[63]

The association between Caratacus and the Silures is well documented. What is less well established is the part that other tribes in south Wales may have played in his freedom movement. Recent work in what was the territory of the Demetae, in south-west Wales, has revealed a chain of Roman forts, in an area usually thought of as having offered little or no resistance to Rome, at such locations as Carmarthen and Llandeilo, where two Roman military establishments have been discovered, one on top of the other.[64] The later of the two Llandeilo forts may be Boudican or immediately post-Boudican, but the earlier one may relate to the activities of the renegade Catuvellaunian prince, and the construction by the Roman army of forts in this region during the mid-first century AD suggests that the forts were employed in the subjugation and control of the Silures to the east. Caratacus must have been a charismatic man, who naturally attracted loyalty. He had a fanatical attitude to freedom, for he won no great pitched battles with Rome but, instead, flitted from place to

2 ♦ Conquering a myth: Claudius and Britannia

place, harrying Roman forces wherever he went and retreating progressively for ever more remote parts of Britain. Silurian territory was wild enough, but the lands of the Ordovices, of mid- and north-Wales were even more impenetrable and the topography was even more difficult. But at last Caratacus faced the Roman legions at a carefully selected site somewhere in Ordovician country.

What is interesting is that it is clear from Tacitus that the Catuvellaunian, operating hundreds of miles away from his power base, was able to whip up some kind of unified support in the west. One reason for this is given in a comment by the Roman writer just before his description of Caratacus's last stand, namely that Ostorius Scapula, the governor who had succeeded Aulus Plautius in AD 47, attacked the lands of the Deceangli, a tribe occupying the far north of Wales, the neighbours of the Ordovices. It is not known to what extent tribes in the area known now as Wales thought of themselves as belonging to a unified entity but, whatever the situation, Caratacus persuaded peoples inhabiting a large swathe of western Britain to rally behind him. Tacitus talks of 'the British chieftains' and describes how Caratacus 'hastened to one point and another'[65] encouraging the men in a manner highly reminiscent of Henry V the night before Agincourt, as portrayed by Shakespeare.

Tacitus employs his favourite device of indirect speech, telling his audience of Caratacus's rallying exhortation to the British forces:

> He invoked their ancestors, who by routing Julius Caesar had valorously preserved their present descendants from Roman officials and taxes, and saved for them, undefiled, their wives and children. These exhortations were applauded. Then every man swore by his tribal oath that no enemy weapons would make them yield – and no wounds either.[66]

Such enthusiasm for battle apparently caused Ostorius Scapula to blench, but his forces were ready to engage the enemy and, after an initial setback, routed Caratacus's army. Tacitus tells us that Caratacus's wife and daughter were taken prisoner and that his brothers (we don't know their names) surrendered. Despite heroic appearances, Caratacus himself was neither captured nor killed in battle but escaped north to the great federal polity of the Brigantes (in Yorkshire and surrounding areas) and their queen Cartimandua. She was no fool – she had already had an unsuccessful brush with Scapula three years before in AD 47 – and she promptly handed him over to the Romans (see Chapter 5). The

Catuvellaunian freedom fighter seems to have blundered badly in throwing himself on the Brigantian ruler's mercy, given that he must have known where her sympathies lay but, as we will see in chapter 3, the tribe was split into pro and anti-Roman factions, and Caratacus may have been seeking help from the latter when he fell into Cartimandua's grasp.[67]

If Caratacus behaved less than nobly after his defeat in battle, by apparently abandoning his family to their capture, he redeemed himself at Claudius's triumph in Rome. Before putting words into his mouth, Tacitus describes the fame of the British resistance fighter:

> *The war in Britain was in its ninth year. The reputation of Caratacus had spread beyond the islands and through the neighbouring provinces to Italy itself. These people were curious to see the man who had defied our power for so many years. Even at Rome his name meant something. Besides, the emperor's attempts to glorify himself conferred additional glory on Caratacus' defeat. For the people were summoned as though for a fine spectacle, while the Guard stood in arms on the parade ground before their camp. Then there was a march past with Caratacus' petty vassals, and the decorations and neck-chains and spoils of his foreign wars. Next were displayed his brothers, wife and daughter. Last came the king himself. The others, frightened, degraded themselves by entreaties. But there were no downcast looks or appeals for mercy from Caratacus.*[68]

Caratacus and Vercingetorix

According to the classical literature, the career of Caratacus has strong analogies to that of his Gaulish counterpart Vercingetorix, who rallied many of the Gallic tribes in a last vain push against the Romans under Julius Caesar in the late 50s BC. In his description of the Arvernian leader's surrender and subsequent fate, Caesar is characteristically laconic, saying only that he 'was surrendered, and the weapons were laid down before me'.[69] But the Greek historian Plutarch, who was born in about AD 46 and died around 120, provides a far more dramatic account of the Gaulish freedom fighter's last act as a free leader:

> *Vergentorix, the supreme leader in the whole [Gallic] war, put on his most beautiful armour, had his horse carefully groomed, and rode out through the gates [of Alesia]. Caesar was sitting down and Vergentorix, after riding round him in a circle, leaped down from his horse, stripped off his armour, and sat at Caesar's feet silent and motionless until he was taken away under arrest, a prisoner reserved for his triumph.*[70]

2 ◆ Conquering a myth: Claudius and Britannia

The Romans were not, in general, magnanimous adversaries: they revelled not only in subjugation of their enemies but in crowing about it afterwards, and the victorious general seized every opportunity to use his success in order to bolster his image at Rome and to ensure the prosperity of his future. Both Vercingetorix and Caratacus suffered the ignominious fate of being taken to the city in chains, paraded through the streets in utter shame and destined for the ultimate humiliation of public execution like common criminals. But while Vercingetorix did indeed suffer this fate (although not before he had languished in prison for five years), Tacitus relates a different end for Caratacus, and puts into the British leader's mouth the words that were to save his life and that of his family:

> *Had my lineage and rank been accompanied by only moderate success, I should have come to this city as friend rather than prisoner, and you would not have disdained to ally yourself peacefully with one so nobly born, the ruler of so many nations. As it is, humiliation is my lot, glory yours. I had horses, men, arms, wealth. Are you surprised I am sorry to lose them? If you want to rule the world, does it follow that everyone else welcomes enslavement? If I had surrendered without a blow before being brought before you, neither my downfall nor your triumph would have become famous. If you execute me, they will be forgotten. Spare me, and I shall be an everlasting token of your mercy!*[71]

Claudius was so impressed by Caratacus's dignity and wise words, both of which served to foster his own image with the Senate and people, that he pardoned the Catuvellaunian and his relatives. As in so many instances, including the Boudican episode itself, Tacitus is using his favourite literary device of *oratio obliqua* (reported speech) in order to explore issues with which he was himself concerned: colonialism, 'civilisation' versus 'the noble savage', and the contrast between the trappings of empire and the simple dignity of the barbarian. Both Plutarch and Tacitus allude to the abrupt change in status undergone by the noble prisoner of war: from leadership to enslavement; from active warrior to chained captive. But the Gallic and British leaders are each portrayed as having ownership of the situation: it is Vercingetorix who draws the attention at the time of his surrender, not Caesar, and it is Caratacus who is centre stage, not Claudius. Had the outcome of the final Boudican battle been different and had the Icenian queen survived to grace Nero's triumph, she may well have earned a similar speech from Tacitus, although her annihilation of three Roman cities in south-east England is unlikely to have earned her a pardon, particularly at the hands of one of Rome's most capricious emperors.

The temple of Claudius at Colchester

> *Moreover, the temple erected to the divine Claudius was a blatant stronghold of alien rule, and its observances were a pretext to make the natives appointed as its priests drain the whole country dry.*
>
> Tacitus *Annals*[72]

Tacitus lists the establishment of the temple to the deified Claudius at Camulodunum (Colchester) as one reason for the disaffection, and ultimate rebellion, of the Trinovantes, a tribe previously amicable to Rome and whose capital had been first overrun by the marauding Catuvellauni and then by the Romans themselves, who created a *colonia* (a garrison town for army veterans) there and parcelled out Trinovantian lands in its environs as allotments for retired soldiers to farm. Although Tacitus mentions the construction of the temple within the context of the Boudican Rebellion of AD 60, it is clear that the temple was at least partly built during the reign of Claudius, even though it was almost certainly not given its official dedication until after his death (emperors were only deified post mortem).[73] It is certain that the appropriation of Trinovantian lands, the takeover of Camulodunum and the building of the temple, right in the town centre, were enough to turn the Trinovantes from firm allies to sworn enemies.

The land issue was not merely one of livelihood but of spiritual disjunction. Archaeological analysis of Britain in the later Iron Age (and indeed earlier) indicates that people's identity and sense of belonging were strongly bound up in the physical environment, the landscape and the perception of belonging within an ancestral context. Our limited understanding of Gallo-British religion during this period based, as it is, partly upon evidence from the Iron Age itself and back-projection from the Roman period,[74] seems to suggest the acknowledgement of an essentially numinous world, where each element in the natural environment – be it a tree, a pool, a mountain or a spring – was imbued with sanctity.[75] If this were the case, then to be pushed off one's land, away from one's ancestors (as manifest both in their perceived continuance as guardians over the living and in the form of their interred remains) struck at the fundamentals of one's very existence. If this is what happened to the Trinovantes, it is no surprise that they bucked beneath the weight of colonisation and threw in their lot with Boudica.

In particular, we should examine the phenomenon of the temple of Claudius at Colchester (see Figure 2.7), for this was a major source of grievance for the Trinovantes, an economic drain, and an ever-visible affront to their independence. According to various studies, Tacitus's statement, which implies that the temple was dedicated to the deified Claudius in his lifetime, is misleading. It is almost unthinkable that the Senate would have agreed to such a precedent in the Roman west and, in any case, Claudius himself would have been totally against such a dedication.[76] In a sense, such subtlety is a red herring, as far as this study is concerned; what is important, however, is the question of when work began on the temple and to what extent it existed as a monument to the

FIGURE 2.7 ◆ *Reconstruction drawing of the façade of the temple of Claudius at Colchester.*

Source: De la Bédoyère 2003b. Drawing: Guy de la Bédoyère

imperial cult while Claudius was alive and when the troubles leading to the Boudican Rebellion were beginning actively to foment. In trying to establish the existence of the temple to Claudius during his lifetime, we need to look at a comment by the Stoic philosopher and financier Lucius Annaeus Seneca. The latter was born in about 4 BC in southern Spain, and was sentenced to death (but not executed) by both Gaius and Claudius, lived in exile in Corsica for eight years (for sexual dalliance with Gaius's sister) and was eventually recalled to the imperial court in AD 49.[77] He was made tutor to the adolescent Nero and, when the new emperor came to power, remained at court as a chief adviser, only to commit suicide in AD 65 after a conspiracy against Nero was uncovered. Seneca's importance to the story of first-century Roman Britain lies in a work entitled the *Apocolocyntosis* ('Pumpkinification'), a satirical piece of fiction in which the dead Claudius attempts to gain admission to Heaven as a god and receives various rebuffs as the gods argue for and against his application. In this work, Seneca makes a telling reference to what must be the temple of Claudius at Colchester:

> He [Claudius] wants to become a god? Is it not enough that he has a temple in Britain, that savages now worship him and, as if he were a god, pray to 'happen on the fool when well-disposed'.[78]

It is Tacitus's allusion to the temple that has caused a measure of debate about the date of its foundation and dedication. In the *Annals* as we have seen, he comments that: 'the temple erected to the divine Claudius was a blatant stronghold of alien rule'.[79] In order to understand the nature of the controversy, it is necessary also to quote the original Latin: '*Ad hoc templum divo Claudio constitutum quasi ara aeternae dominationis aspiciebatur, dilectique sacerdotes specie religionis omnis fortunas effundebant*'. It is the word *constitutum* that is the centre of the problem. According to Duncan Fishwick[80] the use of this term is unequivocal evidence for the construction and dedication of the temple by senatorial decree, something that can only have occurred after the death of the emperor, while Simpson[81] is of the view that, though the official 'constitution' (or dedication) may have taken place after Claudius's death, there is no reason not to assume that the foundation of the temple was in his lifetime.[82]

Even if the temple itself had not been built, it is highly likely that the imperial cult was represented at Camulodunum very soon after the

2 ◆ Conquering a myth: Claudius and Britannia

emperor's visit and perhaps took the form of an open-air altar. The early physical manifestation of such a cult is inherently probable, given that 'it aroused friction between the Roman authorities and the local tribal landowners, which was a contributory cause to the rebellion headed by Boudica'.[83] But there is no reason why a temple could not have been raised to the imperial cult at the time when the *colonia* was being built and, indeed, it would be natural for this to happen at the same time that other public buildings were being raised at Colchester. The whole idea of the imperial cult is that it was less a religious cult than a political statement of *romanitas*, providing a focus of being Roman and declaring the presence of Rome in alien lands. It was the imperial cult that was such a stumbling block for the monotheistic Judaeans (and, indeed, for Roman Christians). While Rome was often tolerant of other belief systems in the territories it conquered, the imperial cult had to be observed because to deny it was also to deny *romanitas* and thus lay the way open to sedition.

If the temple to Claudius were erected, or at least started during his reign, which seems inherently likely, then it would have been an irritant to the Trinovantes from as early as the foundation of the *colonia* itself in AD 49. Unfortunately, archaeological corroboration of an early foundation for the temple is lacking (although, to quote a well-worn archaeological maxim, absence of evidence is not evidence of absence). But it is useful to take a broad look at how the imperial cult, the worship of the emperor (or the idea of the emperor) worked in the Roman world from its inception under Augustus. First, there was a difference between how such a cult was interpreted and used in the western and eastern empires. In the east, the concept of sacral kingship was embedded in ruler-hood. So, for example, the Egyptian Pharoahs were divinities in their lifetimes and Augustus, as heir to the Egyptian throne, had to be divine also. But for the most part, Augustus was meticulous in allowing only worship of the notion of the emperor, or the imperial family,[84] coupled with Roma (the personification of the city-state itself) or with other deities.[85] What he did do, with some adroitness, was to deify his adopted father Julius Caesar, thereby allowing himself to be called 'Son of the Divine Julius' a short step to being divine himself.[86] What is more, there is evidence that the spirit of the Emperor Augustus was venerated in the west, notably at Narbonne, where an inscription from an altar, dedicated a year or so before his death, twice refers to the 'divine spirit of Augustus'.[87]

Only after his death could Augustus be properly admitted into the company of deities, and this pattern was generally to be followed by the other first-century emperors (with exceptions, such as Gaius and Nero).[88] But would such nuances of language and ideology have meant anything to the Britons? Surely, if a temple to Claudius and Roma or to the spirit of the emperor were set up at Camulodunum in the years immediately following the *colonia*'s foundation, the distinction between this and the worship of Claudius as a god might well have been lost on the Trinovantes and their neighbours. So, whatever the rights and wrongs of the way Tacitus's word *constitutum* was used, it is likely that the Trinovantes had to put up with a large, arrogantly classical temple to their conqueror set up in the heart of their tribal centre from some time before Claudius's death. We know that the Neronian temple, at least, was of massive construction, a building very different from anything the Britons would ever have known, and probably offensive in the extreme.[89]

There is one other dimension to the temple of Claudius at Camulodunum, as a source of tension and potential rebellion, and that is the financial support demanded by the Romans of the Britons in whose territory the sanctuary was built. According to Tacitus, this was effected by the appointment of Trinovantians as priests of the cult and levying tribute through them for its upkeep. This was adding insult to injury. Not only was the temple a perpetual visible insult to the autonomy of the Britons, but they had to pay for its construction, upkeep and staff as well. Thus the Romans had divided the Trinovantian community by setting up local priests to milk their fellows dry. The archaeological evidence for this monumental sanctuary indicates that its construction and maintenance would have been colossally expensive. Small wonder that this, coupled with the confiscation of their lands, led the formerly peaceful Trinovantes to join Boudica and, as we shall see (Chapter 7), one of the main foci of attack on Colchester was the hated temple and all it stood for.

Some Claudian Trinovantians

The rich cremation-burial at Stanway, just outside Colchester, of a high-ranking man who died in about AD 50 (see also Chapter 1) and was interred with a Roman-style medical toolkit (albeit with local variation) and board game, exemplifies the way some Trinovantes embraced Roman material culture soon after the Claudian conquest. Other broadly contemporary tombs, probably belonging to members of the highest echelons of local society, include an earlier Stanway grave (c. AD 40) containing 24 imported Roman pots and the unique grave from Colchester that has long been dubbed 'the child's grave' because of the large numbers of clay figurines, formerly thought to be toys, placed in it.[90] Far from being the tomb of a child, the grave is that of a wealthy adult and most of the 'funerary package' of grave-goods are very classical indeed. Some of the 'toys' even depict characters from Greek drama.[91] But despite the *romanitas* of this tomb, one clay image perhaps tells a different story: it depicts a bull with three horns, a common iconographic motif in Roman Gaul, but with its roots in an Iron Age imagery that may contain hidden messages of resistance or, at least, of appropriation and adaptation of Mediterranean ideas to local taste.[92] Another, earlier grave (dating to around AD 43 itself), from St Clare's Drive, Colchester, included ten brooches whose forms reflect links with Romanised Gaul.[93] Broadly contemporary is the tomb at Mount Bures,[94] which contained eating and drinking equipment, but also a splendid iron fire-dog that, with its bull-headed terminals, makes an entirely British statement of the feasting chieftain. Even if Trinovantians living in or around Colchester a few years before the Boudican uprising elected to be buried with Roman accoutrements, it is significant that, notwithstanding their chosen material culture, these same people turned their back on the foreigners from whom they obtained it, to throw in their lot with the freedom fighters.

Notes and references

1 Suetonius *Claudius* 3–4; trans. Graves 1962, 163.
2 Op. cit. 10.
3 Pomponius Mela *Chorographia* 3.6.49; after Braund 1996, 102.
4 Eutropius *Breviarum* 7.13.2; after Black 2000, 1.
5 Such as Pliny *Natural History* 2.187, and Virgil *Georgics* I, line 30. For full discussion of the ancients' view of the northern edges of the world see Kavenna 2005, 3–4.
6 Graves 1962, vii
7 Op. cit.

8   For the 'rehabilitation' of Suetonius as a reliable source (Paul Sealey's word in quotation marks, pers. com.), see Hurley 2001.
9   Graves 1941a, 1941b.
10 Suetonius *Claudius* 17; trans. Graves 1962, 171.
11 Op. cit. 27; trans. Graves 1962, 178.
12 Moore 1954, 10.
13 Op. cit.
14 Allen & Haselgrove 1979, 1–17.
15 Creighton 2000, 76, 192.
16 Frere & Fulford 2001, 45.
17 Black 2000, 4.
18 Dio Cassius *Roman History* 60.22; after Manley 2002, 55.
19 Suetonius *Caesar* 37.2; Braund 1996, 54.
20 Dio Cassius *Roman History* 60.23; after Manley 2002, 55.
21 Op. cit.; after Manley 2002, 56.
22 Suetonius *Claudius* 21.
23 The programme was entitled *Events following the Spanish Armada*: BBC Radio 4, 23 May 2005.
24 An inscription from Rusellae in Etruria (Tuscany), probably on the base of a lost statue of Victory: Braund 1996, 103.
25 Barrett 1991, fig. 1
26 Braund 1996, 102–3; Barrett 1991, 1–19.
27 Barrett 1991, 12, fig. 3.
28 Op. cit. 2.
29 Ferris 1994, 26; 2000, 55–60; Smith 1987, 88 (the quotation is taken from the last author).
30 Ferris 2000, 55.
31 Braund 1996, fig. 28.
32 Naipaul 1980, 155.
33 Aldhouse-Green 2004a, 75; Cohen 1997, 66–92.
34 It is worth alluding to another of the Aphrodisias sculptures that shows a similar scene of violent Roman masculinity and helpless femininity – that of Nero (the reigning emperor at the time of the Boudican Rebellion) in the act of subduing a bare-breasted woman, personification of Armenia: Ferris

(2000, 59) has interpreted this image as depictive of the aftermath of conquest, whereas the carvings of Claudius and Britannia show the struggle in process.

35 Tacitus *Agricola* 14; trans. Mattingly 1948, 64.
36 For a recent re-evaluation of the name of this British king, see Coates 2005, 359–66.
37 O'Gorman 2000, 3.
38 Henig 1998, 9.
39 Tacitus *Annals* 31–2.
40 Henig 1998, 8–9.
41 Bogaers 1979, 243.
42 Op. cit. 245, fig. 2.
43 Cunliffe 1998, 22.
44 Barrett 1979, 239.
45 Henig 1998, 8.
46 Henig 1998, 9; Manley 2002, 121, fig. 25; Cunliffe 1998, 108.
47 Cunliffe 1998, 107.
48 Op. cit. 109.
49 Cunliffe 1995, 107, 102 respectively.
50 Knight 2003, 41.
51 Cunliffe 1998, fig. 53; Henig 1998, 8.
52 Henig 1998, 9.
53 Op. cit.
54 Dio Cassius *Roman History* 60.20; after Manley 2002, 54.
55 Tacitus *Annals* 12.35.
56 Webster 1981, 14.
57 De la Bédoyère 2003a, 34.
58 Deo Cassius *Roman History* 60.22.
59 De la Bédoyère 2003a, 34–5.
60 Op. cit. 36
61 Henig 2002, fig. 12.
62 De la Bédoyère 2003, 38.
63 Tacitus *Annals* 12.33.

64 Jones & Cook 2005.
65 Tacitus *Annals* 12.34; trans. Grant 1956, 257.
66 Op. cit. 12.34.
67 This has been suggested by de la Bédoyère 2003a, 40.
68 Tacitus *Annals* 12.36.
69 Caesar *de Bello Gallico* VII, 89; trans. Wiseman & Wiseman 1980, 176.
70 Plutarch *Life of Caesar*; trans. Warner 1958, 241.
71 Tacitus *Annals* 12.37.
72 Op. cit. 14.31.
73 Fishwick 1972; 1995.
74 Green 1998c.
75 Aldhouse-Green 2000.
76 Fishwick 1972; 1973.
77 Campbell 1969, 7–28.
78 Seneca *Apocolocyntosis* 8.3; after Simpson 1993, 1.
79 Tacitus *Annals* 14.31.
80 Fishwick 1972, 1995.
81 Simpson 1993.
82 For the debate on the dedication of temples to emperors during their lifetimes, see Fishwick 1991 and Simpson 1993.
83 Shotter 2004, 4.
84 A good example is the temple dedicated in AD 2–3 to Augustus's grandsons Gaius and Lucius at Nemausus (Nîmes): Rivet 1988, 164.
85 Ferguson 1970, 90–1.
86 Ferguson 1980, 70–1.
87 *CIL* 12.4333; Chisholm & Ferguson 1981, 165.
88 Warmington 1969, 120–1.
89 Fishwick 1997.
90 Paul Sealey pers. com., Crummy 1992; 1993; 1995; 2002.
91 Eckardt 1999.
92 Green 1998d; Aldhouse-Green 2004a, 209–10.
93 Castle Museum, Colchester.
94 Paul Sealey pers. com. for dating of the Mount Bures grave.

CHAPTER 3

Client-kingship in the Roman Empire: Prasutagus and Boudica

'He nearly always restored the kingdoms which he had conquered to their defeated dynasties, rarely combined them with others, and followed a policy of linking together his royal allies by mutual ties of friendship or intermarriage, which he was never slow to propose. Nor did he treat them otherwise than as imperial functionaries, showing them all consideration.'[1]

Suetonius *Augustus*

In describing the attitude to *externi* (foreigners) taken by Augustus, Suetonius presents him as a magnanimous and expedient emperor who took advantage of connections of obligation and loyalty between Rome and conquered royal families in some of the least troublesome parts of the empire and reinstated their rulers as 'client-kings'. In the same passage, Suetonius also says of Augustus that 'he brought up many of their children as his own, and gave them the same education'. An example of such patronage is that of King Herod of Judaea, whose family was educated in Rome.[2] Such individuals occupied an ambivalent position for, on the one hand, they belonged to the cultural and political milieu of their own indigenous communities yet, on the other, they were vassals of Rome, tied to Roman fortune and obliged to aid Rome in its maintenance of peace within and beyond the boundaries of the client-ruler's territory. These vassal kings 'cushioned' the frontiers of the empire 'by restraining their own people' as well as 'repelling attacks from beyond their own borders.'[3] It is likely, therefore, that these rulers were treated with a fair degree of opprobrium by freedom-loving groups at home, and with condescension by the Roman government. It was a potentially difficult position to sustain; prone to threats from anti-Roman factions and from the changing whim of the reigning emperor. In any case – and this is important for our understanding of the run-up to the Boudican Rebellion – the treaty of friendship between the emperor and any given client-ruler only held good for the lifetime of that particular monarch; at his or her death, the whole situation would be reviewed and, as likely as not, the client-territory would be absorbed into the empire proper.

The whole reason for the use of client-kingdoms by Augustus and his successors, as earlier in the later Republic, was that it provided an economically attractive alternative to full annexation. The latter entailed a standing army of legionaries and auxiliaries, and all the support mechanisms that went to sustain large forces in a foreign land. It could only work, moreover, if the area in question were relatively stable and peaceful and if there was little danger of sedition. Many client-kings in the early Roman empire were almost more Roman than the Romans themselves: they – or their sons – were often educated at Rome and their affiliations were strongly towards *romanitas*. This alone could be a cause of tension in their own domains because they would perhaps go home with attitudes out of kilter with the ethos and mindset of their own community.

Prasutagus, a client-king of the Britons

> *Prasutagus, king of the Iceni, after a life of long and renowned prosperity, had made the emperor co-heir with his own two daughters. Prasutagus hoped by this submissiveness to preserve his kingdom and household from attack. But it turned out otherwise.*
>
> Tacitus *Annals*[4]

In Chapter 2 we encountered King Togidubnus, a British client-king *par excellence*. Archaeology provides a window through which we may view the way of life enjoyed by local Icenian nobility who collaborated with Rome at the time of Prasutagus. Allusion has already been made (Chapter

3 ◆ Client-kingship in the Roman Empire: Prasutagus and Boudica

1) to the Hockwold (Norfolk) hoard of fine Roman silver tableware, some of whose items may have been broken by 'nationalists' as a signal of resistance to the imposition of Roman culture or, more mundanely, have simply been prepared for melting down to make local coins.[5] At about the time of Prasutagus's death, in AD 60, someone deliberately buried a complete drinking set at Crownthorpe, also in Norfolk, comprising a straining bowl, inside which had been placed two cups, a ladle, a skillet[6] and two silvered bowls (see Figure 3.1). The set had belonged to a wealthy Icenian, almost certainly a Briton who had benefited from the Roman alliance and, maybe, even the king himself. Unlike the Hockwold material, this tableware was made of bronze, and although, to some degree, exhibiting Roman taste for wine-drinking, seems also to have been modified to a British palate and aesthetic sense. Thus it included a strainer that could as easily have been used for British beer as Roman wine, and the two drinking cups, of Roman design and similar in form to those from Hockwold, but fitted with duck-ornamented handles that testify to a local taste for animal decoration.[7]

FIGURE 3.1 ◆ *The Crownthorpe hoard, Norfolk.*

Source: © Miranda Aldhouse-Green.

One of the purposes of this chapter is to examine the case of the Icenian client-monarch Prasutagus within the context of other client-kings at around the same period of the Roman Empire. It is possible to argue that the Boudican Rebellion, the nexus of this book, hinges upon the status of the Iceni, in relation to the Roman state and, in particular, on that of its ruling house at the time the revolt took place. Prasutagus was the king of the Iceni, and Tacitus's comment, that the East Anglian king 'was famous for his longstanding prosperity'[8] suggests that, at the time of the rebellion in AD 60, he had ruled over his tribe for a long time. This means that it is more than likely that he was king of the Iceni at the time of the Icenian revolt under the governor Ostorius Scapula in AD 47.[9] It may well be significant that neither Prasutagus nor Boudica are mentioned in Tacitus's *Annals* by name in his account of this early Icenian rebellion, and it has been suggested that this revolt was perhaps as much an uprising against the pro-Roman ruling house as against the Romans themselves.[10]

In anticipation of complexities arising from his death, Prasutagus made a will naming the Emperor Nero as co-heir with his two daughters. Why did he do this? What was the nature of that kingship within the context of Roman provincial administration in Britain, and what was his wife Boudica's position in all this, given that she was not named as one of her husband's heirs? Of one thing we can be reasonably certain, that Prasutagus enjoyed the coveted status of Roman citizenship. This has two important sequiturs: first, that his wife Boudica would also have been granted this badge of Roman affiliation (Tacitus himself alludes to her royal rank[11]); and, second, that the king's will would have legal validity.[12] The very act of making this kind of formal will is testament to Prasutagus's Roman-ness and, in linking Rome with his own family in this manner, he was following a precedent that stretched back at least as far as the second century BC, particularly in cases where the king had no sons or other male heirs.[13] Even so, if – as Tacitus states[14] – Boudica was herself of royal descent, one wonders at her omission from the will (we return to this issue at the end of the chapter). The naming of Nero (see Plate 6) as co-beneficiary perhaps says something about the emperor's cupidity: 'It is only under bad emperors that parents find it necessary to include the emperors in their wills'.[15] But this was not always the reason for so doing: Herod of Judaea left Augustus a fortune in his will: 'To

3 ◆ Client-kingship in the Roman Empire: Prasutagus and Boudica

Caesar he left ten million pieces of coined silver beside vessels of gold and silver and some very valuable garments'.[16]

Literary testimony tells us that Prasutagus was regarded as a king both by Britons and Romans. 'While Suetonius was thus occupied [in smashing the Druids on Anglesey], he learnt of a sudden rebellion in the province. Prasutagus, king of the Iceni ... had made the emperor co-heir with his own two daughters.[17] In this brief passage, delivered in typical laconic Taciteau style, we learn a great deal. First, Tacitus calls Prasutagus *Rex Icenorum*, a deceptively straightforward title using the Latin word for king. If Tacitus is calling Prasutagus 'king', we might fairly conclude that this is how he was perceived by the Roman administration in Britain and by the emperor in Rome. This is, in itself, interesting because the Romans were intensely sensitive about kingship (a phobia that dated back to the time of the tyrant kings of the city-state's early history). But, particularly in their dealings with eastern power systems, as the empire spread into Egypt and the Near East, the Romans had become increasingly familiar with oriental kingship, a form of rule that – rather like the English 'divine right of kings' – acknowledged the status of the monarch as a god. Tacitus may have been calling Prasutagus 'king' partly to exhibit his 'otherness', his difference from being Roman, but we should remember other kings, like Togidubnus (Chapter 2), who used the term on a dedication to Roman deities at Chichester.

Although Tacitus called Prasutagus *Rex*, in the Roman manner, the archaeological evidence for this East Anglian ruler (in the form of inscribed Icenian coinage) tells a slightly different story, in so far as some coin issues indicate that at least one Icenian ruler, Esuprastus, called himself by the native British word for king: 'Rig' or 'Ricon'.[18] Coins are a vital element in the archaeological record for the Iceni in the mid-first century AD.[19] It is interesting that this Icenian chief was almost certainly still minting coins after the Claudian conquest and perhaps he was using part of Seneca's vast loan to the Britons[20] in order to finance such issues, for two sites in Norfolk, Needham and Thetford, have produced clay moulds for coins dating early in the Roman period. Derek Allen suggests that the coins bearing the legend 'ECEN' or 'ECE' should be linked directly with Prasutagus, and that these issues were probably produced after the Roman conquest 'in direct continuity with a pre-existing series',[21] but the direct link with Prasutagus is no longer tenable.²² One coin type bears the legend 'SVBRIPRASTO', which consists of the three elided words *sub ri Prasto* which, up until recently have been translated as 'under King Prasutagus'. But it has been suggested that the coins were minted under the rulership of another, previously unrecorded king called Esuprastus.²³ The choice of words is probably highly significant, in terms of self-projection. Language is important, words are powerful tools (particularly in an almost entirely non-literate context, such as pertained to most Britons in the first century AD), and the coins this ruler issued may have been deliberately used to 'badge' himself as British rather than Roman. The reverse of the coins carries the phrase *Esico fecit* (Esico made it). Esico is a British name, but both 'fecit' and 'sub' are forms of legend that appear specifically to demonstrate the influence of Roman culture.²⁴ On the evidence for the identification of four Icenian minting sites, Paul Sealey has suggested that the 'tribe' was organised according to a decentralised, federated political structure.²⁵ This model would accord with a factionalised situation in AD 47, and tensions between pro- and anti-Roman groups within the Iceni.

The coins are revealing, too, in terms of their iconographical content, for they are imitations of early Neronian issues and the obverse depicts a high-relief profile-portrait that closely resembles Nero himself, while the reverse redresses the cultural balance and bears a very un-Roman design of a fantastic horse, a motif common to a range of tribal rulers' coinage. We can assume that, as rulers of the Iceni, Esuprastus and Prasutagus would have been very directly involved in the minting of their coins, which were themselves symbols of their power, and the tribal leader responsible for minting the coins seems to have wished to project a double message: that of *romanitas* and *britannitas*. One could speculate as to whether, in so doing, the generator of the coins was treading a fine line between presenting his allegiance to the emperor and, at the same time, reassuring the Icenians of his continued identification with his own people. David Braund has drawn attention to the probable playing out of such tensions in AD 47, when the Icenians rebelled against the Roman government.²⁶ One of Prasutagus's legacies (or that of his predecessors) to archaeology is the evidence for a frenzy of coin minting (and of coin-hoard burying²⁷) just before or at the time of the Boudican Rebellion. Allen suggests that the increased production may have been

3 ◆ Client-kingship in the Roman Empire: Prasutagus and Boudica

either in response to Seneca's recall of his loans or to pay for Boudica's war.[28]

The distribution of late Icenian coins is concentrated in the Brecklands of south Norfolk and this has been the basis of suggestions that it is in this region that any kind of Boudican 'palace' was located.[29] But we know of several other late Iron Age Icenian centres of power, including both Sedgeford[30] and Fison Way, Thetford[31] in north-west Norfolk and Stonea Camp in Cambridgeshire (see Map 3). At Stonea there was a large earthwork that has been identified as one of 'Icenian' character[32] and producing mainly Icenian coins. The settlement's economy – in common with the rest of the central fenlands at this period – was based on salt production, a commodity that made the region prosperous before and during the client-king phase. While the lands of the Iceni were friendly to Rome, the locals would have been able to operate this industry without external interference, but archaeological evidence bears witness to a shift in production to the area further west, to the territory of the Corieltavi, at about the time of the Boudican Rebellion: this suggests that, once the Roman authorities considered the Iceni to be unstable, they intervened and shifted the responsibility (and prosperity) of the salt industry from Icenian control, thus marking a dramatic change in the economic status of the region.[33]

Client-kingship in action: the vassal rulers of the south and east

> Next Claudius restored Commagene to Antiochus, since Gaius, though he had himself given him the district, had taken it away again; and Mithridates the Iberian, whom Gaius had summoned and imprisoned, was sent home again to resume his throne. To another Mithridates, a descendant of Mithridates the Great, he granted the kingdom of Bosporus, giving to Polemo some land in Cilicia in place of it. He enlarged the domain of Agrippa in Palestine, who, happening to be in Rome, had helped him to become emperor, and he bestowed on him the rank of consul; and to his brother Herod he gave the rank of praetor and a principality. And he permitted them to enter the senate and to express thanks to him in Greek.
>
> Dio Cassius, *Roman History*[34]

As the Roman Empire physically expanded, during the later Republic and early Principate,[35] so choices were made by the Roman government as to whether particular regions lent themselves to the creation of buffer-states or whether they were so unstable or inherently hostile as to require a constant Roman military or administrative presence, as true provinces. Sometimes, as indicated by the passage quoted above, provinces could be given back to their former rulers. As Dio's comment makes clear, the status of such vassal kings depended, at least in part, upon the particular attitude of the current Roman emperor. Claudius had an especially 'open' policy towards *externi*. Thus, Commagene (southern Turkey), like many of the eastern provinces, had a well-developed monarchical system, and the same was true of Pontus (western Turkey), the kingdom of Mithridates. Initially, at any rate, such eastern client kings were extremely useful to Rome, particularly in defending the empire from the Parthians,[36] and their value is demonstrated by the regular subsidies they received from the centre. But the general trend was towards the eventual absorption of these territories into the empire and, by the end of the first century AD, the majority of the client kingdoms in the Near East, North Africa and Thrace had had their special relationship with Rome changed to full provincial status. In many instances, this happened as a result of bequests made to Rome by such kings in their wills. Bithynia and neighbouring Pontus were bequeathed to Rome by Nicomedes IV, and first administered as a province by Pompey in the mid-first century BC; the province of Asia was left to Rome by King Attalus III of Pergamum (a city in western Turkey) in 133 BC; Pamphylia in south-west Asia Minor was ceded to Rome as early as 189 BC by the Seleucid king Antiochus III[37] (a descendant of Alexander's comrade-in-arms, Seleucus, who established the kingdom there after the general's death). Thrace remained under the rulership of client-kings until AD 46, when the reigning monarch was murdered by his wife, thus giving Claudius an excuse to turn it into a province.[38]

From the later first century AD, however, puppet rulers were still present in the lands around the Euphrates (like Armenia in the far east of Turkey) and along the Rhine and Danube frontiers.[39] One thing is clear: once the buffer of a client-state was removed by full annexation, Rome very often had to police that region with a standing frontier army.[40] (One sees the USA and Britain in much the same situation in present-day Iraq). This is what happened not only in the east but on the Rhine, Danube and – of course – in Britain. The expediency for Rome of establishing buffer states is aptly described by Strabo, in speaking of Cilicia (part of modern Turkey) in Augustan times:

> The region was naturally well adapted to the business of piracy both by land and by sea ... With all this in view, the Romans deemed it better for the region to be ruled by kings than to be under Roman prefects sent to administer justice, who were not likely always to be present or to have armed forces with them.[41]

North Africa and King Juba

There were two King Jubas. Juba I, son of Hiempsal, ruled over Numidia (an area corresponding to the western part of Tunisia and eastern Algeria) in the first century BC. In the civil war between Julius Caesar and Pompey in the 40s BC, Juba made the mistake of siding with Pompey. This was a natural thing to do since, in the carving up of territory between the triumvirs (Pompey, Caesar and Crassus), Pompey had been given Africa. King Juba's army was vanquished and virtually destroyed by Caesar's forces. The defeated king engaged in a fight to the death with a Roman legionary and the survivor was killed by a slave. We do not know whether the legionary or the slave despatched Juba, but his young son (also named Juba) was taken to Rome by Caesar to participate in his victor's triumph.[42] Interestingly, though, the boy was not executed as an enemy of the state but brought up and educated at Rome in the household of the young Octavian (the future Augustus). Juba II, thoroughly steeped in Roman culture and tradition by his upbringing in the capital, became a scholar and an author. His marriage is significant, for his wife was Cleopatra Selene, the daughter of Octavian's bitter enemies Antony and Cleopatra, and it is testament to Roman faith in Juba's loyalty that he was allowed (or even encouraged) to make this marriage-alliance. Susan Raven comments: 'Although his tastes were Greek and his lineage African, Juba's loyalty was to Rome and to his protector Augustus. It never wavered during his fifty-year reign'.[43]

In 33 BC the Mauretanian King Bocchus bequeathed his kingdom (a region approximating to western Algeria and northern Morocco) to Rome. Unlike his Numidian neighbour, Bocchus had supported Caesar in his struggle for power with Pompey and, after his death, his land was placed under direct Roman rule for a time. But Augustus deemed it expedient to hand Mauretania over to the Romanised Juba II, 'as a gift from the Roman state'[44] and he reigned in North Africa from 25 BC until AD 23. Juba presented himself as a Roman ruler; his coins replicated those of Rome and his portrait on them showed a distinct resemblance to Augustus. Like some of the British kings, the legend on his coin issues proclaimed him by the Roman title 'Rex [Iuba]',[45] and this African monarch has been compared with the British Atrebatian ruler Tincomarus,[46] whom we met in Chapter 1. Juba's kingdom was annexed by Gaius in AD 40.[47] One of the reasons for its absorption into the empire was that it was a politically turbulent region, and Rome had had to step in to quell uprisings and sedition that the Mauretanian kings clearly could not control by themselves.[48] It is interesting to note that Suetonius Paulinus, governor of Britain at the time of the Boudican Rebellion, had held high military office in northwest Africa, where he led campaigns against the region's population during the chaos resulting from Gaius's murder of Juba II's son, King Ptolemy.[49]

Egypt: the Ptolemies and Cleopatra

> In victory Octavian could afford to be generous, maintaining an ambivalent attitude towards Cleopatra. She was Rome's enemy, to be feared and abhorred, but there was a nobility about her, and a strength of mind and determination that Romans could not fail to admire.[50]

In 32 BC, a silver denarius was struck in Egypt, depicting the heads of Antony and Cleopatra. The coin-legend on the side bearing the queen's portrait reads 'To Cleopatra, Queen of kings and of her sons who are kings'.[51] A year later, Octavian (later Augustus) defeated Antony and Cleopatra at the battle of Actium and, after centuries of client-kingship, Egypt became fully part of the Roman Empire. In the emperor's own words: 'I added Egypt to the empire of the Roman people'.[52]

This terse statement in Augustus's *Res Gestae* masks the sensitivity with which Egypt was regarded by the emperor after Actium. Egypt's importance to Rome was not simply strategic but economic; from here came a large proportion of Rome's grain supplies. The events leading up to Actium, the bitter war between Octavian and Antony, during which Egypt's granary was unavailable, influenced Augustus in setting up the administration of his Principate. He made sure that Egypt remained under his personal control, setting it apart from all other

3 ◆ Client-kingship in the Roman Empire: Prasutagus and Boudica

provinces and forbidding senators and other high-ranking officials to enter the country without special permission.[53] An equestrian[54] prefect was put in as governor, and the emperor kept a strict eye on his conduct. But Strabo has an interesting comment about the Egyptian situation:

> Egypt is now a province; and it not only pays considerable tribute, but is also governed by prudent men – the prefects who are sent there from time to time. Now he who is sent has the rank of the king; and subordinate to him is the administrator of justice, who has supreme authority over most of the lawsuits.[55]

Since the empire of Alexander broke up at his early death in June 323,[56] Egypt had been ruled by the Macedonian Ptolemaic dynasty founded by Ptolemy Soter, who instituted a kind of hybrid royalty, part Pharoah, part Greek kingship. In 80 BC one of his descendants, Ptolemy XII, who acquired the sobriquet 'Auletes' from his skill as a flute player, had to be bailed out of economic ruin by Roman aid. This kept him going until 58 BC, when he was ousted, following an internal *coup d'état* led by his daughter Berenice, and fled to Rome. During the First Triumvirate, when the three most powerful military Roman leaders (Caesar, Pompey and Crassus) carved up control of the empire between them, Pompey held the east and he reinstated Ptolemy on the Egyptian throne in 56 BC, after Berenice married Archelaus, king of Pontus, and the Romans grew nervous at the development of too strong a power base in that region. So Auletes was installed 'as a friendly ruler in his rich country with every reason to be grateful and compliant not just to Rome in general but to Pompey the Great in particular'.[57]

Ptolemy Auletes died in 51 BC, leaving his throne jointly to his daughter Cleopatra and her younger brother Ptolemy. It was clear from the outset that Cleopatra was in the driving seat, and she appears to have been remarkably astute, for she paid particular attention to the fostering of Egyptianness, especially religion,[58] and thus aligned herself firmly with the divine dynasties of the ancient Pharoahs. An example of this deliberate image projection can be seen on the temple-wall at Dendera, where Cleopatra is depicted in full Egyptian divine regalia (see Plate 8).[59] What is interesting for our story is the analogy that can be drawn between Auletes's will and that of Prasutagus: both named their children as their joint heirs; in neither of their wills is there any mention of their wives (in fact we do not know who was Cleopatra's mother, or even whether she was still alive when her daughter came to power). Cleopatra certainly did not behave like a subservient vassal queen, but seems to have been an independently minded individual; it was this that impressed first Julius Caesar and then Mark Antony. Both men were to become ensnared by the Egyptian queen and to have their heads turned by their assumption of joint rulership with her over a country of immense wealth and antiquity of tradition.

It is interesting to note that the system of client-kingship continued in some parts of the Nile Valley even after the establishment of the Principate. In 29 BC Cornelius Gallus, the first prefect of Egypt appointed by Augustus, set up an inscription, in Greek and Latin, on the island of Philae in the Nile, in which he boasts of his victories in the lands south of the province of Egypt:

> *Gaius Cornelius Gallus son of Gnaeus, Roman eques, first prefect of Alexandria and Egypt after the overthrow of the kings by Caesar [Augustus], son of a god – having been victorious in two pitched battles in the fifteen days within which he suppressed the revolt of the Thebaid, capturing five cities ... and seizing the leaders of these revolts; having led his army beyond the Nile cataract, a region into which arms had not previously been carried either by the Roman people or by the kings of Egypt; having subjugated the Thebaid, the common terror of all the kings; and having given audience at Philae to envoys of the king of the Ethiopians, received that king under [Roman] protection, and installed a prince over the Triacontaschoenus, a district of Ethiopia – dedicated this thank offering to his ancestral gods and to the Nile his helpmate.*[60]

Armenia and Tiridates

> *Although I might have made Greater Armenia into a province when its king Artaxes was assassinated, I preferred, following the precedent of our ancestors, to hand over this kingdom, acting through Tiberius Nero, who was then my stepson, to Tigranes, son of King Artavasdes and grandson of King Tigranes. And afterwards, when this same people revolted and rebelled, after I subdued it through my son Gaius, I handed it over to the rule of King Ariobarzanes, son of Artabazus, king of the Medes.*
>
> Augustus *Res Gestae*[61]

Under the Emperor Nero, trouble erupted in the client-state of Armenia in the extreme eastern part of what is now Turkey. Since republican

3 ◆ Client-kingship in the Roman Empire: Prasutagus and Boudica

times, there had been tensions and outright warfare between Rome and Parthia, just beyond the eastern edge of the empire. (In Roman eyes, the Parthians in the east were regarded not dissimilarly to Britain in the far west: both were examples of extreme barbarism. Indeed, in this context, the term 'parting shot' derives from the Parthians' habit of loosing off arrows when retreating from the battlefield.) The present problem was the result of sabre-rattling by Vologeses, the Parthian king who, without reference to Roman overlordship of Armenia, placed his brother Tiridates on the Armenian throne. Nero's reaction is interesting: rather than challenge the might of Parthia and risk destabilising the whole of that difficult region (with the consonant heavy deployment of armed forces there), he permitted Tiridates to remain in place, so long as he acknowledged Rome's ultimate authority over him and his people, and demonstrated that client relationship by being crowned by Nero. The king duly presented himself in to the emperor in Rome in AD 66, along with an enormous retinue, and was crowned.[62] Dio Cassius recorded the incident with dramatic skill:

> *Tiridates: Master, I am the descendant of Arsaces, brother of the kings Vologeses and Pacorus, and thy slave. And I have come to thee, my god, to worship thee as I do Mithras. Whatever destiny thou spinnest for me shall be mine; for thou art my fate and my fortune.*
> *Nero: Well hast thou done to come hither in person, that meeting me face to face thou mayest enjoy my grace. For what neither my father left thee nor thy brothers gave and preserved for thee, this do I grant thee, that both thou and they may understand that I have the power to take away kingdoms and to bestow them.*[63]

It is difficult to decide which of the two exhibited the greater pride and pomposity, and the power games played by both are clearly detectable. Dio tells us that he refused to obey the command to unbuckle his sword when he came before Nero, 'but fastened it to the scabbard with nails. Yet he knelt upon the ground, and with arms crossed called him master, and did obeisance.' To put aside his weapon would have caused Tiridates to lose face in front of his watching family and entourage, and his behaviour is full of theatrical performance on a grand scale. Dio paints a picture of the flamboyant eastern potentate contrasting with the restrained dignity of the emperor who, nonetheless, indicates his own superior position by making the Armenian ruler sit beneath his feet, in the attitude of a conquered vassal (those readers contemporary with Dio would have been well aware of the irony with which the historian described Nero's image of 'restrained dignity').

Judaea and the Herods

> Claudius sent [Herod] Agrippa to take over his kingdom with more splendid honours than before, giving written instructions to the governors of the provinces and to the procurators to treat him as a special favourite.
> Josephus *Antiquitates Judaicae*[64]

The Palestinian situation in antiquity (as now) was a difficult one. To understand Rome's relationship with this troubled part of the east, and the way that client-kingship worked in the region, it is necessary to refer back to the period between the death of Alexander in the early fourth century BC and the first direct contact between Rome and Palestine in the mid-first century BC. Alexander died without naming his heir, and his generals carved up his world between them, each founding their own dynasty. Palestine initially fell to the Ptolemies (whose main region was Egypt) and, in 200 BC, it was transferred to the control of the Seleucids of Syria.[65] The land was ruled by a series of hereditary kings, in the tradition of other eastern regions, and one dynasty, the Hasmoneans, was responsible for Rome's intervention in Palestine, a relationship that would lead ultimately to its inclusion in the empire. The first Hasmonean king died in 76 BC and, unlike the British client-king Prasutagus, he left his kingdom not to either of his two children (boys) but to his widow Alexandra Salome. 'Her reign led to a situation which, by coinciding with Pompey's eastern campaigns, gave Rome her first foothold in Palestine'.[66]

It is possible to identify several analogies between the Palestinian situation in the 60s BC and the dynastic struggles that took place in Britain in the first centuries BC and AD, and not least between Salome and Boudica, the one a queen by inherited right, the other self-appointed, though also of royal descent. Alexandra's primary difficulty lay in her gender: generally, the Palestinian monarch combined his role as secular ruler with that of high priest, but only men could hold the latter office. Salome circumvented the problem by installing her elder son Hyrcanus as high priest but, when the queen died in 67 BC, the younger son Aristobulus challenged his brother for the monarchy, forcing him to abdicate. The family power struggle continued for some time and, in 63 BC,

3 ◆ Client-kingship in the Roman Empire: Prasutagus and Boudica

Hyrcanus was back on the throne, largely through the efforts of a powerful supporter, an Idumaean named Antipater (father of Herod the Great).

In much the same way that deposed princes in Britain and Gaul appealed to Rome for help, so did both Salome's sons, who each made supplication to Pompey for confirmation of their status as sole ruler. The Roman general could have taken this opportunity to annex Palestine and turn it into a province but chose instead to exercise indirect control, via the client-kingship route, rather than commit heavy military resources to 'that small but turbulent state with its religious peculiarities'.[67] This way, Rome had the final say as to who ruled in Palestine: Hyrcanus was considered the less troublesome of the brothers and so was set up as puppet king of Palestine, with Rome holding the strings. However, Herod's role as a client-king was 'not merely to keep his country peaceful in Rome's interest but also to prepare it for eventual annexation'.[68] This is important for, unlike imperial systems where the ultimate goal was independence from the colonial parent, Rome groomed its buffer states not for autonomy but for full-scale incorporation as Roman provinces. This policy has a direct bearing on the Boudican situation in Britain, for the death of Prasutagus gave Rome the opportunity to re-evaluate the status of Icenian territory and to decide whether or not to keep the status quo or to claim the region for full imperial territory. This Nero decided to do, with dire consequences.

After the defeat and death of Pompey by Caesar, the victor granted Palestine certain concessions (despite its backing of Pompey in the civil war between the two warlords) and, most importantly, granted Jerusalem the right to rebuild its walls following the rebellion against Rome led by Aristobulus and the consequential sacking of the city. After a great deal of further wheeling and dealing, and in the aftermath of Julius Caesar's murder, Antony, who had suzerainty over the east, made Herod, son of Hyrcanus's erstwhile supporter Antipater, client-king of the region and Octavian (before he became Augustus) ceded him more territory. Herod the Great, as he became known, reigned over Judaea from 30 to 4 BC. The Jewish chronicler Flavius Josephus, our fullest source of information about the region, proclaimed the close relationship that developed between Herod and his patron Augustus: 'Herod ... resolved to send his sons Alexander and Aristobulus to Rome, to enjoy the company of Caesar'.[69] Josephus is giving us yet another example of the way client-kings sought to educate their children in the Roman way, by being present at the seat of power, something we have already seen happening in Britain and elsewhere. The purpose would be multifarious: at one and the same time, these princelings would learn how to be Romans; their allegiance – perhaps – would primarily lie with Rome; they would take back the best of *romanitas* to their own lands; and these strongly forged links between centre and periphery would be seen as a guarantee of continuing loyalty and good behaviour between patron and client.

The second Herod whose career is of particular concern for those interested in client-kingship within the Roman empire is Herod Agrippa, who became king of Judaea in AD 40 or 41 and reigned until 44. Agrippa, named for Augustus's great lieutenant and military campaigner, spent much of his childhood at the imperial court with the young Claudius, and the two remained friends into adulthood. Indeed, when he became emperor, Claudius gave Herod Agrippa his full support in maintaining his kingdom.[70] Agrippa was the nephew of Antipas, Herod the Great's successor (after a great deal of intra-dynastic squabbling, betrayal and bloodshed, following Herod's death in 4 BC, in all of which Rome was involved). Antipas did not last long and the continued internecine strife made the region's continued independence untenable: in AD 6 Judaea was made into a Roman province. But Claudius's regard for Agrippa was such that he revoked Judaea's provincial status and returned it to a client-kingdom. But, despite his friendship with the emperor, Agrippa showed himself to be dangerously ambitious, as indicated by the following passage from Josephus:

> Now he was evidently admired by the other kings. At any rate, he was visited by Antiochus king of Commagene, Sampsigeramus king of Emesa, and Cotys king of Armenia Minor, as well as by Polemo, who held sway over Pontus, and Herod his brother who was ruler of Calchis ... When Marsus, governor of Syria arrived at Tiberias (where he had gathered the other kings), the governor was suspicious of all these eastern kings together and sent them all off home.[71]

Client-kingship in Gaul and Germany

To the Emperor Caesar Augustus, son of a god, pontifex maximus, *holding the tribunician power for the fifteenth year, acclaimed* imperator *thirteen times, by Marcus Julius Cottius, son of King Donnus, prefect of the following*

> tribes – the Segovii, Segusini, Belacori, Caturiges, Medulli, Tebavii, Adanates, Savincates, Ecdinii, Veaminii, Iemerii, Vesubianii, and Quadates – and by the tribes which are under his command.
>
> CIL⁷²

This inscription was cut into an arch at Segusio (Susa) in the Cottian Alps of Cisalpine Gaul,⁷³ a Roman province, in the reign of Augustus. *Gallia Cisalpina* had long been part of the Roman Empire by this time, and was largely Italian, in terms of culture and custom.⁷⁴ But the dedication by Julius Cottius, made in 9/8 BC, speaks of a strange and intricate relationship between this region and the emperor, for he describes himself as holding the Roman governor title of prefect and, at the same time, as the son of a local king, Donnus. We know that later in his career Rome permitted him to use the title of king,⁷⁵ so Cottius enjoyed a dual role, as Roman official, representative of the emperor himself, and client-king. His name is interesting, for it is shared with the mountains – the Cottian Alps – over which he held sway, and thus he is firmly identified with his own people, although he has a Roman *praenomen* and *nomen*, the latter perhaps in memory of Julius Caesar.⁷⁶ Cottius is a good example of the Cisalpine Gallic equivalent of the British king Togidubnus and, perhaps, also of the Icenian Prasutagus.

Caesar and Ariovistus

> The Marcomannians and the Quadians down to our time still had native kings, of the noble line of Maroboduus and Tudrus; now they accept even foreign kings, but the power and sovereignty of the kings stem from Roman authority. On occasions they are aided by our armed forces, more often by subsidies, but their domestic power is not thereby reduced.
>
> <div align="right">Tacitus <i>Germania</i>⁷⁷</div>

Tacitus is describing a particular relationship that existed between Rome and some Germanic tribes, a relationship that sought to retain the indigenous monarchic structure while, at the same time, exerting influence over the behaviour of these indigenous kings and their communities. It seems that their loyalty was, to an extent, encouraged by both military aid (to protect against rival factions or takeover bids from neighbouring peoples) and by actual monetary subsidies (in other words, bribes). In the same passage of the *Germania*, the Roman writer speaks of the difference between loyal tribes, such as the Danubian people known as the

Hermundurians, who enjoyed the benefaction of Roman friendship in being able to move and trade without hindrance, and others whose activities were under a greater degree of policing by Rome. The great German leader Ariovistus was one such ruler, but one who jibbed at Roman control, no matter how devolved or indirect. In such instances, a client-king could very quickly become an arch enemy, to be smashed into annihilation; any previous cordiality, of whatever longevity, could be wiped out in a moment of defiance.

In 58 BC, soon after Julius Caesar began the conquest of Gaul, he had to deal with Ariovistus, a German king, who was threatening Gallic territory in the east. Diviciacus, ruler of the Burgundian Aedui, and an ally of Caesar, told the Roman general that there had been two factions among the Gauls, one led by his own tribe and the other by the powerful Arverni, who inhabited the central Gallic area of the Auvergne.[78] After a long struggle for overlordship of the whole country, the Arverni and another powerful tribe, the Sequani (who lived to the north-east of the Aedui) called in mercenaries from across the Rhine to help them. At first, only 15,000 came, but they enjoyed the comparative prosperity of Gaul, sent word back home and were eventually joined by a large contingent of more than 120,000. The Germans and the Sequani had destroyed most of the ruling class of the Aedui and their cavalry, demanding hostages of the surviving aristocrats. In 63 BC, the Aeduan ruler fled to Rome for help,[79] in much the same way as British monarchs, such as Mandubracius, Adminius and Verica, who came in supplication to Caesar, Gaius and Claudius respectively, in search of aid against their own, or neighbouring, peoples (see Chapters 1 and 2) and, thus, incidentally, providing the Romans with a legitimate foothold in those countries.

The alliance between the Germans and the Sequani had backfired on the latter, for King Ariovistus settled his Germans on a third of their land, 'the best in the whole of Gaul',[80] and issued orders that the Gallic tribe vacate another third 'because a few months before, 24,000 of the Harudes had come over to him and he had to find land for them to settle in'.[81] Diviciacus went on to beg Caesar's help against this huge tide of Germans, who would effectively displace a large Gallic population and destabilise the entire region. Caesar sent envoys to Ariovistus requesting talks, but his overtures were repulsed by the German leader. The Roman commander then sent more envoys, with a warning message:

3 ♦ Client-kingship in the Roman Empire: Prasutagus and Boudica

> *Although you enjoy the great privilege, conferred by me personally and by the Roman people, of being given the title of 'King and Friend' by the Senate during my consulship, you show your gratitude to me and the Roman people for this by refusing my invitation to a conference and by making out that matters that affect us both need be no concern to you.*[82]

Ariovistus remained unrepentant and pugnacious, refusing to accede to Caesar's demands that he make peace with the Aedui, cancel the tribute he had imposed on them and return the hostages. The aggression and determination of the German king and the number of his forces began to unsettle Caesar's army and he called a meeting of all his centurions, at which he both admonished them for their faintheartedness and encouraged them by denouncing Ariovistus, saying 'During my consulship ... Ariovistus was very eager in his desire to have the friendship of the Roman people'.[83] Later on, Caesar developed his narrative on how the king's power had come about:

> *When we came to the spot [between the Roman and German camps, where Ariovistus had finally agreed to meet Caesar], I started my speech by recalling my own and the Senate's acts of kindness towards him. The Senate had given him the titles 'King' and 'Friend', and he had received most generous presents. I told him that few people had enjoyed such privileges, which were usually granted only in return for important services to Rome; he on the other hand had no proper right to enter the Senate and no reasonable grounds for making any request, but had gained those benefits only because of goodwill and generosity on the part of me and the Senate.*[84]

These interchanges between Caesar and Ariovistus, and especially Caesar's own words, provide a great deal of information about the German king's relationship with Rome. Caesar was again presenting himself as a king-maker, in the same way as is argued for his activities in Britain, where he may have founded dynasties in the south-east (see Chapter 1). In Rome's eyes, Ariovistus was a client-king, emplaced and supported by Caesar but, as far as the German was concerned, he was a ruler by both right and might, and he was certainly not going to let Caesar dictate his behaviour towards the Aedui and Sequani. What is of particular note is Caesar's comment about the past relationship between Rome and the German ruler: that Ariovistus had visited Rome and had even entered the Senate house. For a foreigner to be honoured in this way was almost unheard of, and signifies the high regard with which he was treated by the Roman government, which presumably found it expedient to have a powerful friend on the Rhine border. But Ariovistus was to prove himself a Caratacus rather than a Togidubnus, and confrontation was inevitable: the Germans were routed in pitched battle, Ariovistus's two wives were killed and he himself had an ignominious escape in a small boat.[85]

Germanicus and Segestes

Segestes himself was also present, a stately sight, unafraid, secure in the knowledge that he had been a good ally. His speech was to this effect: 'This is not the first day of my steadfast loyalty toward the Roman people. From the time I was granted citizenship by the deified Augustus, I have chosen my friends and enemies in accordance with your interests, not from hatred of my fatherland ... but because it was my conviction that the Romans and Germans have the same interests and that peace is better than war ....'

Tacitus *Annals*[86]

In AD 15 Claudius's elder brother Germanicus was deeply engaged in wars against the German tribes on the east bank of the Rhine, and he planned a major campaign during the summer against the powerful Cherusci. Here, as we have already seen in Gaul and Britain, there were both pro- and anti-Roman factions and the people were split in their fealty to Segestes, an ally of Rome, and Arminius, 'Germany's trouble-maker';[87] it was this individual who was responsible for the appalling loss of three legions under general Varus in AD 9, when Augustus was emperor. The situation among the Cherusci was complicated in so far as Arminius was married to Segestes's daughter Thusnelda, and therefore there was a tension within a close-knit kinship group, just as was the case among the Aedui when Caesar was engaged in the conquest of Gaul in the 50s BC. Then, Caesar had conducted negotiations with the pro-Roman Diviciacus, while his brother Dumnorix was fanatically opposed to *romanitas* in any form. Interestingly, Tacitus makes the comment that Thusnelda was 'temperamentally closer to her husband than to her father',[88] an attitude very probably influenced by her pregnancy. The most revealing element in the passage quoted above is the information that Segestes was a Roman citizen.

Following Segestes's appeal, Germanicus received his submission with grace, and promised his family safety in Gaul. We are told that the son born to Thusnelda and Arminius was brought up in Ravenna.

3 ♦ Client-kingship in the Roman Empire: Prasutagus and Boudica

Arminius was maddened by these events and engaged the Romans in bitter combat, initially in the Teutoberg Forest, where the Varian massacre had taken place a few years earlier. Although the German forces were superior in dense woodland, where guerrilla tactics could be deployed, eventually the Romans prevailed in pitched battle. There is an aside to this episode that exhibits Tacitus's admiration of brave women, an attitude we see in his descriptions of Boudica herself, for he comments on a rumour that was circulating at the time of these savage German campaigns, namely that the barbarians had won and were threatening Gaul, instilling panic into the army behind the Rhine who had the wild notion that the river-bridge should be destroyed. It was Germanicus's wife Agrippina who rescued the situation: 'In those days this great-hearted woman acted as commander'.[89]

Boudica: legitimate client queen or illegal pretender?

Tacitus's remark about Agrippina reminds us of Boudica and her situation within the phenomenon of Roman imperial client-kingship, and it is time to return to Britain, to Prasutagus and to Boudica herself (see Plate 9) within this context of Roman rule by proxy. This is an important issue for upon it hangs the whole question of whether or not this woman had a legitimate role as a client-monarch in her own right. From our perusal of vassal kings throughout the eastern and western empire, it is clear that – simply as Prasutagus's widow – Boudica had no claim on the special relationship that had existed between her husband and Rome. She was not a joint ruler, as far as we know and, furthermore, she was not named as heir in Prasutagus's will. This has nothing to do with gender, since their daughters *were* so named. We have also seen that other client-monarchs, notably Cleopatra of Egypt, could be female. It may be that Prasutagus was keen to leave his kingdom to his own blood-kin rather than to his marriage partner (and in so doing he may have thought that Nero was the more likely to continue the client relationship after his death). Or could it be that the reason why Boudica was left out of the bequest was that, like Cartimandua of the Brigantes (see Chapter 5), there was some kind of rift between husband and wife? If this were so, a likely reason was a differing perspective on attitudes to *romanitas*.

While Prasutagus may have been a staunch ally of Rome, Boudica may have entertained just as vehement anti-Roman sympathies. Indeed, such a situation might serve to explain her savage treatment (and that of her daughters and people) by the Romans on her assumption of power and – if more excuse were needed than such treatment – her own aggression towards the colonial power that oppressed the Iceni after the dissolution of the client-Rome relationship at Prasutagus's death. We should not underestimate the role that an anti-Roman faction may have played among the Iceni: it manifested itself in the revolt that took place under Scapula's governorship and may have been influential in the decision of certain Icenian kings to name themselves on their coins by the British term 'Rig' rather than the Roman title 'Rex'. Most crucially, Boudica herself might have belonged to such a faction and may have sought to make a bid for Icenian independence as soon as her husband's death made her free to do so. Not least in seeking to defend her people's freedom was the question of wealth. We know from Tacitus that Prasutagus was rich (and the archaeology of East Anglia in the late Iron Age supports this). But Dio informs us that the Britons were burdened by a crippling loan from Seneca, one of the wealthiest men in Rome, and that this was one of the main causes of the Boudican Rebellion.[90] So Boudica was arguably acting from pragmatism as well as principle. In the next two chapters, we explore the nature of this enigmatic woman, both within the context of women in Iron Age Europe, and in comparison with a powerful female contemporary, Cartimandua.

Notes and references

1 Suetonius *Augustus* 48.

2 Josephus *Antiquitates Judaicae* 15.187–95.

3 Lewis & Reinhold 1966, 109.

4 Tacitus *Annals* 14.31; trans. Grant 1956, 317.

5 Paul Sealey pers. comm.

6 A handled pan.

7 Information from Norwich Castle Museum; Paul Sealey pers. Com.; Sealey 1997, 49–50.

8 Tacitus *Annals* 14.31; after Braund 1996, 133.

9 Op. cit. 12.31.

10 Braund 1996, 132–3.
11 Tacitus *Agricola* 16.
12 Braund 1996, 133.
13 Op. cit.
14 Tacitus *Agricola* 16.
15 Champlin 1991, 66.
16 Josephus *Antiquitates Judaicae* 17.188–91.
17 Tacitus *Annals* 14.31; trans. Grant 1956, 317.
18 Sealey 1997, 12; Braund 1996, 70; Allen 1970.
19 Allen 1970, 3.
20 Dio Cassius *Roman History* 62.2.
21 Allen 1970, 16.
22 See Williams 2000 and Paul Sealey pers. com. for refutation of the connection between Prasutagus and inscribed Icenian coins.
23 Hingley 2005, 40.
24 Sealey 1997, 12; Braund 1996, 69.
25 Sealey 1997, 10.
26 Tacitus *Annals* 12.31; Braund 1996, 132.
27 One such hoard is that from Honingham in Norfolk: a group of Icenian coins deposited and buried in a pot for safekeeping (Norwich Castle Museum) (see Plate 1).
28 Allen 1970, 16–18.
29 Op. cit. 15.
30 Neil Faulkner pers. com.
31 Gregory 1992.
32 Sealey 1997, 10; Todd 2004, 50.
33 Fincham 2004.
34 Dio Cassius *Roman History* 60.8.1–3; after Chisholm & Ferguson 1981, 410.
35 We have to remember that the phrase 'Roman Empire' means two different things: on the one hand, it refers to the area of the world that was conquered and administered by Rome, a phenomenon begun long before the reign of the first emperor, Augustus; on the other, the term is used to refer to the period of Roman political history whose inception was the work of Augustus himself and survived for over 400 years.

36 The Parthians had long been a thorn in Rome's side; virtually unconquerable, they had caused trouble and instability on the Empire's eastern frontier for centuries, and Crassus suffered a catastrophic defeat by this eastern power at the battle of Carrhae in 53 BC: Plutarch *Crassus* 19.

37 Wacher 1987a, 203–13.

38 Op. cit.

39 Lewis & Reinhold 1966, 109–12.

40 Freeman 1996, 388.

41 Strabo *Geography* 14.5.6.

42 Thompson & Ferguson 1969, 20, 132; Raven 1969, 37–8.

43 Raven 1969, 40.

44 Grant 1956, 155, fn 3.

45 De la Bédoyère 2003a, 30.

46 Creighton 2000, 93.

47 Thompson & Ferguson 1969, 132.

48 Raven 1969, 40–1; Tacitus *Annals* 2.52.

49 De la Bédoyère 2003a, 47.

50 Southern 1999, 147.

51 Op. cit. 114–15, fig. 23.

52 Augustus *Res Gestae* 27; trans. Lewis & Reinhold 1966, 17.

53 Augustus organised the empire such that he retained control over troublesome or special provinces. Those that were peaceful and non-contentious he delegated to senatorial control; others were ruled by legates through him. This was a shrewd move, designed to render impossible the kind of warlordship, with army backing, that had pertained under the late Republic (and through which he himself had gained ultimate power after Actium).

54 The rank below that of senator.

55 Strabo *Geography* 17.1.12–13.

56 Worthington 2004, 194.

57 1999, 16.

58 Op. cit. 20–1.

59 Joann Fletcher pers. com.; Kleiner 2005; Riggs 2006.

60 *CIL* III, no. 14, 147; Lewis & Reinhold 1966, 45.

61 Augustus *Res Gestae* 27; trans. Lewis & Reinhold 1966, 17–18.

3 ♦ Client-kingship in the Roman Empire: Prasutagus and Boudica

62 Lewis & Reinhold 1966, 110–12.
63 Dio Cassius *Roman History* 63.1.2–5.4; after Chisholm & Ferguson 1981, 411–12.
64 Josephus *Antiquitates Judaicae* 19.6.1; after Chisholm & Ferguson 1981, 649.
65 Smallwood 1982, 8.
66 Op. cit. 9.
67 Op. cit. 11.
68 Op. cit. 20.
69 Josephus *Antiquitates Judaicae* 15.10.1; trans. Whiston 1886, 426.
70 See Josephus quotation at the beginning of this section.
71 Josephus *Antiquitates Judaicae* 19.8.1; after Chisholm & Ferguson 1981, 651.
72 *CIL* 5, 7231; Lewis & Reinhold 1966, 47; Chisholm & Ferguson 1981, 123.
73 Cisalpine Gaul (literally 'Gaul on this/our side of the Alps') is the name given by the Romans to the part of north Italy that adjoins alpine south-east France; Pascal 1964, 7. Pascal defines it thus. 'It extends from the French Riviera and the Maritime and Cottian Alps eastwards to the border of Yugoslavia, where the boundary of Cisalpine Gaul bisects the peninsula of Istria. Its southern boundary is described by the Gulf of La Spezia, the northern slopes of the Apennines, and the Po, while that on the North is the crest of the Alps, beyond which lie Switzerland and Austria.'
74 Drinkwater 1983, 1.
75 Lewis & Reinhold 1966, 47, fn 149.
76 The *tria nomina* that Cottius possessed (*praenomen, nomen* and *cognomen*) indicate that he held Roman citizenship.
77 Tacitus *Germania* 41–2; trans. Lewis & Reinhold 1966, 110.
78 The Auvergne region takes its name from the tribe of the Arverni, a people who – under their chief Vercingetorix – was to lead the great rebellion against Caesar in 52 BC.
79 Where he encountered the famous Roman orator Cicero, who remarked that Diviciacus was particularly skilled at using augury to predict the future: Cicero *de Divinatione* I, 90.
80 Caesar *de Bello Gallico* I, 31; trans. Wiseman & Wiseman 1980, 30.
81 Op. cit.
82 Op. Cit. I, 35; trans. Wiseman & Wiseman 1980, 31–2.
83 Op. cit. I, 40; trans Wiseman & Wiseman 1980, 34.
84 Op. cit. I, 43; trans Wiseman & Wiseman 1980, 36.

85 Op. cit. I, 53; trans. Wiseman & Wiseman 1980, 40.
86 Tacitus *Annals* I, 57; trans. Lewis & Reinhold 1966, 108–9.
87 Op. cit. I, 54; trans. Grant 1956, 62.
88 Op. cit. I, 57; trans. Grant 1956, 63.
89 Op. cit. I, 59, trans. Grant 1956, 64–5.
90 Dio Cassius *Roman History* 62.2; trans. Ireland 1996, 63–70.

CHAPTER 4

Other Boudicas: 'big women' in Iron Age Europe

Most belligerent nations are much influenced by their women.
Aristotle *Politics*[1]

Boudica drove round all the tribes in a chariot with her daughters in front of her. 'We British are used to women commanders in war', she cried.
Tacitus *Annals*[2]

By any standards, Boudica was a woman 'writ large'. For her to rise to the kind of power she enjoyed and, irrespective of how that status had been achieved, her own community must have acknowledged the possibility of independent female empowerment. Indeed, if we are to believe the words put into Boudica's mouth by Tacitus, the Britons of East Anglia, at least, were thoroughly familiar with female war leaders. The Roman chronicler paints a picture of a woman who not only directed military operations (like the female 'M' played by Dame Judi Dench in the most recent Bond films) but was an active participant, who used her chariot (like an army jeep) to muster and exhort her troops to action (see Plate 10).

Like any ancient historian (and probably like many writing today), Tacitus not only recorded events but could not resist the temptation to embroider, exaggerate and even, perhaps, to interpret beyond the bounds of the evidence. Classical historians were writers of literature first and 'objective' history second[3] and, in her treatise on Tacitus as an author, Ellen O' Gorman comments that Tacitus's works constituted 'an amalgam of history and representation through style'. She also introduces the concept of the 'Iconic woman', as depicted in Tacitus's treatment of the emperor Nero's mother Agrippina[4]. Although Tacitus himself does not make a direct connection between the imperial matriarch and the British freedom fighter, it is clear that he was creating the character of Boudica within the framework of empowered females with whom he was familiar at Rome.

This chapter explores notions of Boudica as an iconic woman within a context of evidence from Iron Age and Roman Britain and Europe. In this quest to find other Boudicas, we look beyond the Graeco-Roman literature and explore, as well, the archaeological evidence for women of high rank in the centuries leading up to Boudica's Rebellion. The purpose behind such an enquiry is to ascertain to what extent Boudica represents a one-off or whether she is part of a legacy of ancestral 'hegemonic femininity'.[5] It is worth posing the question as to whether or not Britain was different from her continental neighbours or whether her position on the edge of the world caused her – like the evolutionary 'deviance', or so-called 'allopatric speciation' of the wildlife in Madagascar, Australia or the Galapagos Islands – to diverge from mainstream androcentric political ideologies, that were so central to the rulership and even citizenship of the classical world. Such themes are best explored through a range of case studies that appear to demonstrate a social environment in which women could and did achieve high – and arguably independently high – status and who might represent the backdrop against which Boudica could become one of the greatest threats the Roman political and military machine ever encountered.

The whole issue of empowered and high-status females, on a par with Boudica, is enlivened by new research into a Romano-British community who lived and died at Brougham in Cumbria between about AD 220 and 300. Brougham was a Roman fort and attached to it was a civilian settlement, a *vicus*; when they died, the inhabitants were cremated and placed in a communal cemetery. The garrison stationed here in the third century AD was a cavalry *numerus*: an irregular type of unit that, from the second century onwards, was recruited to supplement the normal auxiliary troops. What is especially interesting about Brougham is the presence in the cemetery of two women whose pyres contained the remains of horses and military equipment. What does this tell us about the soldiers gar-

4 ◆ Other Boudicas: 'big women' in Iron Age Europe

risoned here? Did the unit contain women? Epigraphic evidence suggests that the *numerus* was created in one of the Danubian provinces, and Hilary Cool has pointed out that this area was the one whence, according to ancient Greek legend, came the Amazons, formidable female warriors.[6] Certainly, if the material culture at Brougham is anything to go by, women might have been fighting, on horseback, alongside men. Even if the equipment and the animals signified status rather than actual military prowess, that in itself indicates that in third-century Roman Britain, there were high-ranking women who were given funerals with full military honours.

The Haraldskaer 'queen'

In 1834 a body was discovered in a peatbog at Haraldskaer near Vejle, a small town in central Jutland. It was that of a woman who had been pinned down into the marsh bed with hurdles made from the branches of local trees. The anaerobic conditions and the bog acids ensured that the body was remarkably preserved, with most of the skin and much of the soft tissue intact. When she was found by local peat-cutters, she was thought to be a medieval Viking queen named Gunhild, and the then king of Denmark instructed that she be given a royal Christian burial and that her remains be interred in a specially made oak coffin in the twelfth-century Church of Saint Nicolai at Vejle, where she still rests today. At the time of her discovery, a post-mortem was conducted on the remains and the results (one knee joint, pierced by a wooden stake, had swelled after penetration) suggested that she had been pinned down in the water while still alive, a horrific death that accounted for the apparent look of terror on her face.

In the year 2000 I became involved (in partnership with the Department of Forensic Science at the University of Århus and Dr Lone Hvass of the Elsinor Museum) in a re-examination of the Haraldskaer woman's remains for a television documentary,[7] and had the good fortune to be able to examine the body at first hand (see Plate 11). New radiocarbon analysis had confirmed that, far from being a medieval Christian queen, this woman had met her death early in the fifth century BC. A faint groove around her throat, missed by the nineteenth-century forensic team, indicated that she had been strangled (like a number of north European Iron Age bog victims), and she was then placed naked in the marsh, her clothes deposited nearby. The Århus pathologists concluded that the bog acids probably accounted for the swelling in her knee joint and so she may have been already dead before the branches pinned her down. But most remarkable of all were her age and her state of health, for she was about 50 years old when she died, itself a rare age to achieve in the Iron Age, and more unusual still she was well nourished, indeed plump, and apparently in perfect health, with none of the signs of degenerative conditions (such as arthritis) that are so common in human remains of this period. The good condition of the Haraldskaer woman's body leads us to speculate as to her social position within her community, for she clearly did no manual work (the bodies of many Iron Age women, for instance, show signs of spinal wear and tear resulting from hours spent kneeling down grinding corn) and she was sufficiently well-fed to enable her to reach such an age. Although we have no evidence as to the woman's identity or rank, it is reasonable to suppose that she enjoyed high status and lived a privileged life until her untimely end.

There is also the question of her violent death by strangulation and her placement naked in a remote marsh-pool, far away from any contemporary settlements. The normal burial rite of the time and region was cremation so she, like the other north European Iron Age bog bodies (a tiny percentage of the population) was singled out for special treatment. I have suggested elsewhere that she may have been the victim of human sacrifice, thus:

> She may have lived a special life and certainly was interred in a special way. Between her life and her burial, she met a death that may, itself, have been special, a death that may have been influenced by who she was in life. Noblewoman, hostage or priestess, she was consigned to the local marsh as a gift to the spirits.[8]

The Haraldskaer woman might well have been the queen of her local community or tribe. She may have been selected as a sacrificial victim, perhaps at a time of great crisis (war, famine or epidemic) that necessitated propitiation by the gods by means of the most precious of sacrificial gifts, the chieftain herself. Her interment, with neither clothes nor grave-goods, but with her clothes beside her, suggests that she was buried with some care and ceremony, and the pinning down of her body, at a precise spot, contributes to the idea of performance, at an event in which the whole

4 ◆ Other Boudicas: 'big women' in Iron Age Europe

community may have taken part. She may even have volunteered herself as a supreme offering in order to safeguard the future of her people.

Boudica's ancestors? British female chariot burials

Boudouica, with an army of up to 230,000 men, rode in a chariot herself and arranged the others in their various positions.

Dio Cassius *Roman History*[9]

Both Tacitus and Dio, the two main chroniclers of the Boudican Rebellion, allude to the Icenian ruler's appearance in a war-chariot. When Julius Caesar invaded south-east Britain in 55 and 54 BC, he was astonished to find that the Britons in this area were still using chariots, which had fallen into obsolescence by the mid-first century BC in Gaul.[10] How much more odd it must have seemed to the Romans that Suetonius Paulinus and his army confronted a *woman* driving such a vehicle? By Caesar's own reckoning,[11] charioteers exhibited incredible skill in battle-contexts. So do we have any archaeological evidence to suggest that women in Britain used chariots before the Roman conquest?

The issue of *PAST*[12] for August 2001 has, on its front page, an article entitled 'A New Cart/Chariot Burial from Wetwang, East Yorkshire'.[13] The grave was that of a woman, about 35 years old, and she had been buried in a barrow beneath the body of the vehicle, the wheels taken off and placed over the chariot-pole (see plate 12). This mid-Iron Age burial (perhaps *c.* 300–200 BC) forms part of a group of some 15 such graves in the area, attesting to a particularly local funeral rite. Two features make this grave special, apart from the gender of the dead person (most of the East Yorkshire vehicle burials – and a new one found in 2004 – were those of men[14]): the richness of the tomb furniture, and a physical attribute of the woman herself. This person was accompanied by an iron mirror, itself a rare commodity, and there is evidence that the handle once had a horse-hair tassel decorated with small blue beads. Apart from this unique find, the horse-harness in the grave appears to have been extensively decorated with coral: if so, 'there is probably more coral present in this one grave than from any other site in Iron Age Britain'.[15] A further article in *PAST* not only confirms that the horse-gear is decorated with pink coral (a Mediterranean import) but that tar made from birch bark (involving a relatively sophisticated technological process) was used as a decorative adhesive on the chariot fittings.[16] The woman's body was also accompanied by joints of pork, food for the journey to the afterlife and generally associated with high-status burials. So we already have a picture of an Iron Age woman, who lived and died two or three centuries before Boudica was causing trouble, and who, in death at least, was treated with considerable respect and veneration. But what is more, there is evidence from her physical remains that she had a facial peculiarity: a large purple growth had disfigured her from childhood. We have, then, to envisage a mature woman of high status, who may have ridden a chariot during her life and who, despite (or perhaps because of) a highly visible facial abnormality commanded great respect in her community. It may even be that she was a religious leader or shaman, a role that may have been combined with rulership. Mirrors are often associated with shamans, with the ability to see into different worlds and to identify oneself as a 'two-spirit' person, able to operate in the worlds of living humans and the spirits.[17] Moreover, there is persistent evidence for the deliberate selection of physically deformed or disabled people for ritual killing in Iron Age Europe.[18] This Wetwang woman was not alone; in 1984 a series of three chariot burials was found, consisting of a woman flanked by two male warriors. Hers was the earliest (fourth century BC), largest, richest and most elaborately furnished and she, too, had a joint of pork and a mirror, together with a curious sealed bronze casket suspended from her belt by a short chain. It may be that this little box, highly decorated with abstract La Tène designs, contained healing substances or consecrated oil.[19]

The lady of Vix and her 'sisters'

A glance at the sepulchral evidence from the European Iron Age illuminates a range of rich female tombs, at least some of which suggest that they were the remains of women who enjoyed considerable power during their lifetimes. Most striking of all is the very early Iron Age burial of a woman from Vix in Burgundy, a lady who died in the sixth century BC and may well have been the ruler of a community governed from the nearby fortified hill-top settlement of Mont Lassois, near Châtillon-sur-Seine.[20] Like the Wetwang woman with her coral and iron mirror, she was in her mid-thirties when she died and, like her, she was buried with a wheeled vehicle but, this time, it was a four-wheeled hearse or bier on which the body lay, similar to other funerary carts found under barrows in contemporary tombs in central Europe. The Vix woman had clearly been an important person in life,[21] for she was interred beneath a towering burial mound 20 feet (6 metres) high and 138 feet (42 metres) in diameter, a monument that would have been visible for miles. The body was adorned with rich jewellery, including a solid gold torc, but most spectacular of all the grave-goods was an enormous bronze *krater* or wine-mixing flagon of Greek design, 5¼ feet (1.64 metres) high, which had travelled all the way from Mediterranean Italy for the funeral of this individual.[22] In the centre of the vessel was the figure of a standing woman, perhaps an image of the 'Lady of Vix' herself. The frieze around the neck of the *krater* depicts a dignified procession of people and wheeled vehicles, perhaps a funeral procession; again it may reflect the ceremonial rituals that accompanied the Vix woman to her grave.

Many wealthy tombs of this period contain equipment for sumptuous feasting but the Vix *krater* stands out for its sheer size, flamboyant decoration and the amount of liquor that it had the capacity to contain. There is no other grave, whether male or female, of comparable richness in the vicinity of Mont Lassois, and it is difficult to escape the conclusion that here lay the most dominant person in the region, buried within sight of the citadel over which she may have ruled.[23] Jean-Louis Coudrot is of the opinion that the grave-goods are particularly significant for, although many were made locally, a range of exotic materials was deliberately chosen in their production: Mediterranean coral, Egyptian minerals, Baltic amber, tin from Cornwall, copper from southern France and lignite from Germany, as if to symbolise the Vix woman's far-flung connections and networks over a huge region of Europe.[24] In his book *La Femme dans la société gallo-romaine*, André Pelletier suggests that the lady from Vix was, perhaps, a priestess or prophetess who could have enjoyed both secular and religious rank in her community,[25] a notion that finds a voice with other continental burials, with the British Iron Age chariot-women already discussed and, indeed, with the persona of Boudica herself, as we shall see.

Looking beyond Vix to cognate western or central European female burials, it is worth noting, particularly, those of the woman buried with a cart and adorned with a bronze coral-decorated torc from Bucy-le-Long (Aisne);[26] a female of fourth century BC date from Waldalgesheim, who was interred with her 'trousseau' of gold torc and armlets;[27] and a coeval tomb at Reinheim also in Germany, wherein a woman was accompanied in her grave by rich accoutrements, including the entire contents of her jewellery casket.[28] The Waldalgesheim 'princess' was brought to her tomb on a chariot that was buried with her, itself a mark of high rank; her jewellery is of especial interest, for the style of its decoration suggests that it was not made locally but was either brought to the region by its owner or imported from further east, perhaps Hungary. This may mean that the Waldalgesheim lady was a foreigner who came to the Bonn area as the result of an exogamous marriage (rather in the manner of later historical women such as Catherine of Aragon, who travelled from Spain to England to marry Henry VIII). The lady of Reinheim was laid in an oak-lined chamber under a mound overlooking the river Blies; she wore gold ring-jewellery – two bracelets and a neck ring – decorated with iconography that may be significant for the identification of the deceased, for one arm ring and the torc bear imagery that may portray the woman herself. Moreover, the figure of the woman depicted is laid out as if for burial, surmounted by a great bird of prey, an image that I have interpreted as, perhaps, reflective of the dead person's apotheosis or of her ability to shape-shift between human and bird form, like a traditional shaman.[29] If the imagery on her jewellery can be interpreted as a portrait of the dead, she was clearly a woman of considerable importance within her community: a person whose ornaments marked her out as special, perhaps with particular powers to go between worlds. In many traditional societies, birds are used as symbols of the supernatural world, and of the escaped soul after death.

From Strettweg to Lemington: images of empowered women

Comparatively few female images survive from Iron Age Europe. Indeed, the Reinheim iconography is exceptional. A unique find from the earliest Austrian Iron Age is that of the grave of a chieftain buried in about 600 BC at Strettweg in Austria who had died, therefore, not very long before the lady of Vix.[30] It consists of a wheeled platform upon which a ritual assemblage of people and animals is depicted as figures in the round. Men and women (and some whose gender is not marked), on foot and on

4 ♦ Other Boudicas: 'big women' in Iron Age Europe

horseback, are grouped around two stags, held by the antlers as if in preparation for sacrifice. Towering over them all, in the very centre of the platform, is the image of a tall, slender and naked woman, her breasts and genitalia emphasised, bearing aloft a great cauldron (see Figure 4.1). Her great size, relative to her companions, her hooped earrings and girdle, which also set her apart from her fellows and, above all, her cauldron mark her as a special person, the central character in the tableau. Perhaps she was either the individual in charge of the ritual depicted or its object: maybe a queen, a high priestess or a goddess. Whatever her precise role, the way she is presented displays her unequivocal power relative to the smaller beings that surround her. It is not entirely fanciful to compare her status with that of the woman buried at Vix.

The lady from Strettweg belongs to the earliest Iron Age in Central Europe. But there is a group of female images from Gaul and Britain,

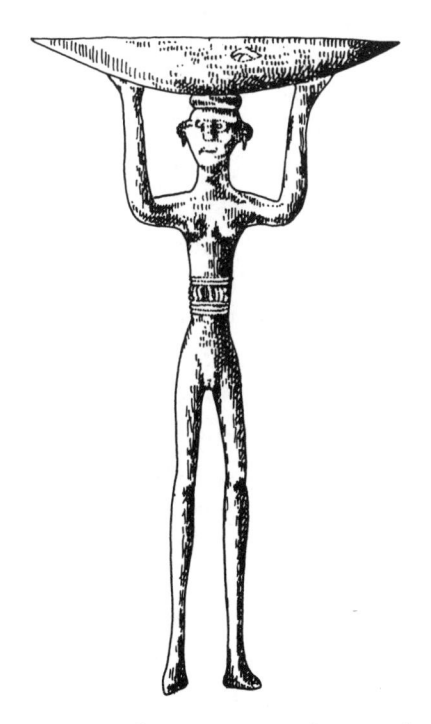

FIGURE 4.1 ♦ *Bronze statuette of a woman on a cult-wagon from a chieftain's grave at Strettweg, Austria, c. 600 BC. On top of the bowl shown was a large cauldron.*

Source: © Paul Jenkins.

belonging to the late Iron Age or Roman period, that also exhibits the 'empowered woman': these are particularly significant since they are shown bearing weapons. This is interesting, particularly in the light of a comment made by Ammianus Marcellinus about the behaviour of Gallic women in battle:

> A whole troop of foreigners would not be able to withstand a single Gaul if he called his wife to his assistance who is usually very strong and with blue eyes; especially when, swelling her neck, gnashing her teeth, and brandishing her sallow arms of enormous size, she begins to strike blows mingled with kicks, as if they were so many missiles sent from the string of a catapult.[31]

Ammianus, it is true, does not speak of women fighting battles with conventional weapons, and it is fair to assume that he is contributing to a picture of barbarism wherein, unlike the ordered masculine world of Roman custom, Gallic women are not really women at all but viragos, bigger and more frightening than their menfolk and who, what is more, break the rules of combat by using feet and teeth and bare fists. But what Ammianus is saying to us is that Gallic women behaved differently and with far more freedom than their sisters in the relatively sequestered life of the Graeco-Roman world.

The notion of women bearing arms is supported by certain pieces of iconography from late Iron Age Gaul that depict females with spears, daggers or swords. Most interesting of these are the images on coins: one image, on coins minted by the tribe of the Remi (around Rheims), is that of a naked woman in profile, running, her plaited hair streaming behind her, brandishing a spear in one hand and a large torc in the other.[32] A variation on this theme shows itself in issues of the Redones, a Breton tribe centred on Rennes: some of their coins depict a frenzied horsewoman or female charioteer waving swords, shields, torcs or branches in each hand.[33] The link between women, weapons and torcs should be pointed out, for the two attributes recur on stone iconography.[34] Torcs were symbols of honour and status in the European Iron Age, often related to warfare, chieftainhood and the flamboyant display associated with an heroic society. Thus the high-ranking ladies from Vix, Reinheim and other wealthy central European Iron Age tombs, together with their male counterparts, were traditionally interred with 'ring-jewellery', while depictions of male warriors, such as those from Hirschlanden in Germany and Lesenho in Portugal, show prominent torcs.[35] The distribution of the

4 ♦ Other Boudicas: 'big women' in Iron Age Europe

Breton coins is especially interesting, for also from the Rennes area comes a large bronze statuette of a woman wearing an elaborate crested helmet, surmounted by the figure of a goose, its neck thrust out in an attitude of extreme aggression (see Figure 4.2).[36] For the Romans (and undoubtedly for Gallo-Britons, too), the character and observed behaviour of geese endowed them with symbolism associated with pugnacity, guardianship and alertness, all necessary appurtenances for warriors.[37]

FIGURE 4.2 ♦ *Bronze statuette of a female warrior, with goose-crested helmet, from Dinéault, Brittany.*

Source: © Musée de Bretagne, Rennes.

There is a link between the late Iron Age coin imagery of Gaul and a Romano-British stone carving from the Cotswolds, at Lomington in Gloucestershire,[38] and thereby the issue of female empowerment is perhaps brought much closer to the Boudican arena. The image is that of a long-robed, wild-haired figure, which grasps a spear in its left hand; its right rests on a cylindrical object, probably some kind of bucket or vat. A roughly scratched inscription, beneath the figure's feet, identifies it as female, for it reads '*Dea Riigina*' ('the Queen Goddess'). While the other female warrior images discussed are anonymous, this British image depicts a divinity, and so we need to be careful in making connections between her and the empowerment of real women, for goddesses cannot be expected to behave like humans. We have only to take a sideways glance at the classical world to acknowledge the fallacy of equating female power with war goddesses: Athene was a warrior deity, and is depicted, in both Greek and Roman (as Minerva) contexts as a young woman armed and wearing helmet and body armour, but Athenian women enjoyed virtually no power or autonomy, and were generally confined to the *oikos* (the household). But notwithstanding this caveat, the Lemington image is potentially significant for, like some of the Gallic coin images, it shows a woman with a weapon in the *left* hand. Bearing in mind that the proportion of left- to right-handed people would have been similar in antiquity to the present day (about 10 per cent), it may be that particular statements are being made by these female images, in terms of difference from the norm, just as the idea of women as warriors was probably counter to general custom. Since the Lemington figure almost certainly came from the sophisticated Roman villa at Chedworth, it might be that, in making or commissioning the image, someone other than the villa owner, perhaps a servant, was using iconography to make a comment about *romanitas*, maybe even in the context of some form of protest or resistance. Although the carving was probably made considerably later than AD 60, when Boudica's Rebellion took place, the image nonetheless resonates, albeit anachronistically, with a notion of Britishness – of 'rule Britannia' – that Boudica would have found deeply satisfying.

The females of Gundestrup: women or goddesses?

She [Boudica] was very tall and grim in appearance, with a piercing gaze and a harsh voice. She had a mass of very fair hair which she grew down to her

4 ◆ Other Boudicas: 'big women' in Iron Age Europe

hips and she wore a great gold torque and a multi-coloured tunic folded round her, over which was a thick cloak fastened with a brooch. This is how she always dressed.

Dio Cassius *Roman History*[39]

The high status of such females as the ladies of Vix, Reinheim and Waldalgesheim is demonstrated – at least in part – by their possession of torcs (decorative metal necklets). Classical writers speak of these adornments as indicative of rank although, significantly, they rarely allude to their use as female apparel (the description of Boudica by Dio Cassius is the exception). On 28 May 1891 a great gilded silver cauldron was found deliberately buried on a small dry island within the Raevemose Bog in Jutland, after having been dismantled into its 13 constituent sheet-metal plates.[40] The cauldron was probably made in about 100 BC, though it may have seen some use prior to its interment. The act of burial was clearly the result of ritual behaviour and best interpreted as a special offering to the gods residing in the marsh.[41] The vessel is unique in its iconography, for both its inner and outer plates have been used to depict a mythic narrative peopled with gods, humans and strange beasts. On certain of the outer plates, the heads and shoulders of males and females are portrayed, the men with elaborate beards, the women invariably with long hair, small but distinct breasts and buffer torcs round their necks, and attended by people or beasts.[42] While two of the men also have torcs, many do not, whereas the women always have them. On one of these outer plates, a woman is depicted apparently engaged in personal grooming: she is attended by two diminutive female servants (their size relative to hers suggesting her divinity or, at least, her ruler status), of whom one is engaged in plaiting her hair.[43] The inner plates contain the most elaborate imagery and on one of these a woman is depicted, her hair also in plaits,[44] and a headband round her forehead. She is attended by a range of animals, real and fantastic, including two peculiar 'elephants', a wolf and two gryphons.[45] But most significantly of all, the woman appears to be riding in a chariot, for flanking her body are two wheels.

It is tempting to see some kind of generic connection, then, between the lady of Gundestrup, female chariot-burials and Boudica herself. The imagery on the Gundestrup cauldron is complex and opaque, and it would be futile to try and reconstruct the storylines behind the images. But it is possible to point to the presence of empowered women, in the repertoire of the artists.⁴⁶ Most interesting of all is the identification of several 'signifiers' that relate the female images of Gundestrup to Dio's description of Boudica: the long hair, the chariot and the torc. While it would be folly indeed to try and establish direct links between the two pieces of evidence, their recurrence in two very different spatial contexts, with a chronological separation of over a hundred years, may hint at some kind of broad connection within north-west Europe in the later Iron Age and early Roman periods.

Women, power and the sacred: spotlight on Veleda

Women have their uses for historians
                    Ronald Syme: The Augustan Aristocracy[47]

It is more than likely that Boudica exercised religious as well as secular authority over her people (Chapter 6). This is suggested by Dio Cassius's description of an event that took place in the sacred grove of Andraste prior to the pitched battle between the forces of the British queen and the Roman governor Suetonius Paulinus. He recounts how, after haranguing her troops, she released a hare secreted in the folds of her clothes and interpreted the omens according to which way it ran: it went in the auspicious direction, 'the whole mass of people shouted for joy',[48] and Boudica addressed the goddess in triumphant prayer. The combination of religious and political leadership was well known in the ancient world (the Pharoahs of Egypt constitute an immediate example). The combination of high secular and religious office was familiar in late Iron Age Gaul, too. During his conquest of the province in the mid-first century BC, Julius Caesar encountered a pair of noble brothers, Diviciacus and Dumnorix, who led the powerful tribe of the Aedui. The former was an ally of Rome; the latter an anti-Roman freedom fighter, who sought to unseat both his brother and Caesar. Two pieces of contemporary literature throw light on the multiple roles of these siblings: although Caesar does not mention it himself, Cicero alludes to a meeting between himself and Diviciacus in Rome in 60 BC and refers to him as a Druid, a holy man with special skills in soothsaying.[49] Caesar himself refers to an incident relating to Dumnorix that indicates he, too, was a religious leader: worried

4 ◆ Other Boudicas: 'big women' in Iron Age Europe

about the possibility of rebellion when away on his second British expedition, the Roman governor issued an order that certain powerful (and potentially troublesome) Gauls should accompany him to the island as hostages for the good behaviour of the Gallic province. Among these was Dumnorix, who protested violently, on the grounds that 'he was not used to sailing and afraid of the sea, and also that religious considerations prevented him'.[50]

If we are seeking an example of an empowered holy woman in later Iron Age Europe, the individual that springs immediately to mind is Veleda, a Germanic prophetess (see Figure 4.3) described in Tacitus's *Histories*. His treatment of this female ritualist is interesting, for it highlights the author's ambivalent attitude to 'barbarians' and the 'civilised'

FIGURE 4.3 ◆ *Early nineteenth-century statue of the prophetess Veleda, by Etienne-Hippolyte Maindron, in the Luxembourg Gardens, Paris.*

Source: © Paul Jenkins.

world of the Roman Empire. In his narratives about Gaul and Britain, we find, at first glance a somewhat puzzling and recurrent feature of Tacitus's writing, namely a sympathy and admiration for the 'noble savage' compared with his less than flattering presentation of the Roman political machine. We see this in his descriptions of anti-Roman British heroes such as Caratacus, Calgacus and, of course, Boudica herself. This curious tension was brought about by Tacitus's republican sympathies.[51] He did not agree with the imperial establishment and took the view that its inception heralded an ever-increasing decadence, tyranny and consonant lack of probity. Indeed, he frequently uses tableaux of rebellion to explore issues concerning colonialism and governance, thereby revealing his thoughts through the veil of biographical description. In Ellen O'Gorman's treatise on Tacitus,[52] she refers to him as a sceptical historian who continually employs a subtle 'interplay between hidden and overt images of actuality'.[53]

We can, perhaps, apply such a model of Tacitean thinking to his treatment of Veleda who is a woman not dissimilar to Boudica, although her power base was different. The character of Veleda is introduced in the author's account of the spectacular rebellion of the Rhenish tribes against Roman colonialism in AD 69–70, which was led by the Batavian Julius Civilis.[54] It is best to let Tacitus have a direct voice:

> *The legionary commander Munius Lupercus was sent along with other presents to Veleda, an unmarried woman who enjoyed wide influence over the tribe of the Bructeri. The Germans traditionally regard many of the female sex as prophetic, and indeed, by an excess of superstition, as divine. This was a case in point. Veleda's prestige stood high, for she had foretold the German successes and the extermination of the legion.*[55]

In the introduction to his translation, Kenneth Wellesley describes this kind of episode as 'wilful digression' on the part of the author, a device to spice up the narrative and add texture to the storyline.[56] So we need to pose the question (which we will later apply to the persona of Boudica herself) as to whether Veleda is nothing more than a literary diversion or whether she actually existed. The foregoing discussion suggests that Iron Age European society was likely to have included empowered women like Veleda, so it is not intrinsically fanciful to acknowledge her as a genuine individual. But we also have to recognise that a specific ancient Roman literary *topos* was the appearance of strange persons at times of crisis, almost

4 ◆ Other Boudicas: 'big women' in Iron Age Europe

as if they are portents or omens of disaster. The Tacitean episode, in which he introduces Veleda to his audience, is interesting for it provides a great deal of information in a few terse comments. Despite her gender and her identity as a barbarian, Veleda is perceived as possessing sufficient 'clout' for her to merit a gift-giving visit from one of the top-ranking generals in the Roman army.[57] Tacitus tells us that Veleda 'enjoyed wide influence' over one of the German tribes and that her reputation was built, at least in large part, from her ability as a seer, a fortune-teller and, in particular, her prophetic utterances foretelling German victory over their Roman oppressors. Two throw-away statements in the passage need following up: Veleda's unmarried status, on the one hand and, on the other, Tacitus's comment about attitudes to female seers among the Germans.

We are given no clues as to Veleda's age: her 'unmarried' state is perhaps more likely to suggest virginity than widowhood, although either is possible. Given Tacitus's statement elsewhere about female chastity,[58] it is unlikely that Veleda was a sexually active single woman. Veleda's marital status should probably be interpreted as in accordance with her special role in her community, as a holy woman whose power must neither be dissipated by sex nor controlled by one man. There are numerous instances of virginal holy women in the ancient literature. Thus Pomponius Mela, a Roman writer of the early first century AD, records the presence of nine virgin priestesses who presided over a sacred island called Sena, one of the Cassiterides (the Isles of Scilly). Mela describes these women as all-powerful, able to predict the future, cure disease, shape-shift and even control the weather.[59] Strabo refers to Cimbrian priestesses who were responsible for the sacrifice of prisoners of war.[60] Early Welsh mythic literature refers to virgin holy women, notably Goewin in the Fourth Branch of the Mabinogi[61] and a group of nine virgin keepers of the sacred Otherworld cauldron in a thirteenth-century Welsh mythic poem *Preiddeu Annwfn* (the Spoils of Annwn).[62]

An important element in assessing the status of these virgin holy women is their treatment as other than real women. Their power is, in part, based upon both their denial of gender and their behaviour as outside the parameters of 'normal' female sexuality. In this way, it becomes acceptable to androcentric societies that such women enjoy extraordinary rank that is at variance with the gender-roles of 'proper' women. The attitude of the Germans to prophetic women thus springs into sharp focus, for again these women are portrayed as 'other': they are empowered precisely because they stand apart, and earn their high status from their ability to communicate with the spirit world. Strabo's female sacrificers were 'grey with age' and this in itself removes them from the intense femaleness associated with reproductive capacity. The final part of Tacitus's passage contains a certain grim irony: Veleda's popularity rested on her ability to deliver good news; one can only imagine how long that popularity would have lasted had she predicted doom and gloom and, more so, if the Germans were defeated.

Later on in Tacitus' account of the Civilis Rebellion, we hear more about Veleda and her treatment by the community; there is irony here, too, in that she is presented as both empowered and sequestered:

> A deputation sent to Civilis and Veleda with gifts secured a decision fully satisfactory to Cologne. But any personal approach to Veleda or speech with her was forbidden. This refusal to permit the envoys to see her was intended to enhance the aura of veneration that surrounded the prophetess. She remained immured in a high tower, one of her relatives being deputed to transmit questions and answers as if he were mediating between a god and his worshippers.[63]

Once again, Tacitus shows himself the master of understatement; contained within this spare passage is a provision of multilayered information and a whole range of issues are raised, though not followed through. During the progress of the Civilis Rebellion, attempts were made by one of the rebel tribes, the Tencteri, to suborn the loyal city of Cologne, a town inhabited mainly by Roman citizens, and to persuade its people to join the revolt. Veleda is presented in an ambiguous light, for she was venerated, as if a goddess; yet, at the same time, her freedom was severely curtailed, albeit – perhaps – voluntarily. Her eyrie may have been designed both as a means of separating her from the profane and as a way of placing her as close as possible to the gods.[64] The role of her male guardian relative seems also to be twofold: on the one hand, he is behaving rather like a brother or father in a Roman family, where the *paterfamilias* had total control over the females in his household;[65] on the other, he seems to be acting as a kind of interpreter, as if Veleda herself is under the influence of the spirits and thus maybe neither hears nor speaks normally. Many of the oracles in Graeco-Roman sanctuaries, such as the Cumaean Sibyl or the Delphic Oracle, spoke 'in tongues' or in riddles that

4 ♦ Other Boudicas: 'big women' in Iron Age Europe

had to be translated by temple officials. Indeed there is a strong link between Veleda and holy women in the ancient Mediterranean world, for these, too, were confined to their sacred precincts, just as ordinary women were kept within the bounds of the household. The Delphic priestess, known as the Pythia, revealed and brought forth prophecy (in ways analogous to females giving birth), but only under the control of men, who interpreted and channelled her spirit-utterances.[66]

The most striking feature of the Tacitean description of Veleda is the level of her influence and power, which rivalled Boudica's own. The citizens of Cologne decided to let Veleda make the final decision as to whether or not to back Civilis and, having heard her arbitration, joined the rebellion. Civilis and Veleda clearly enjoyed almost equal power and Tacitus shows Veleda considerable respect. Indeed the only cynical comment he makes is his reference to the 'excess of superstition' among the Germans generally. Tacitus was interested in the German tribes: indeed, he wrote a treatise called the *Germania* ('On the Origin and Geography of Germany'), in which he describes their customs and social organisation at length. We should remember that his study concerns peoples on the right bank and east of the Rhine: tribes that were never fully conquered and thus never absorbed into the Roman Empire. The *Germania* provides a context for Veleda, for Tacitus takes a long look at the position of women in German society and thereby embeds the persona of the German prophetess within a broader arena. He does not say of Germany what he says of Britain,[67] that the sexes were accorded equal treatment but rather that women were perceived as having a special status. It is worthwhile to quote him at length here:

> It stands on record that armies wavering on the point of collapse have been restored by the women. They have pleaded heroically with their men, thrusting their bosoms before them and forcing them to realize the imminent prospect of their enslavement – a fate which they fear more desperately for their women than for themselves. It is even found that you can secure a surer hold on a state if you demand among the hostages girls of noble family. More than this, they believe that there resides in women an element of holiness and prophecy, and so they do not scorn to ask their advice or lightly disregard their replies. In the reign of the deified Vespasian we saw Veleda long honoured by many Germans as a Divinity, whilst even earlier they showed a similar reverence for Aurinia and others, a reverence untouched by flattery or any pretence of turning women into goddesses.[68]

'Madame Gladiator':[69] gender roles, women and 'otherness' in classical eyes

> Who doesn't know women who use the athlete's rubdown oils
> And wear fine purple sweatcoats?
> Who hasn't seen one with foils,
> Stabbing away at a post, lunging with shields and shrieks,
> And piercing it to the heart, all
> With proper techniques?
> She's well-qualified to blow a trumpet in Flora's games,
> Unless in her heart she considers something beyond and trains
> For the real arena. What modesty can a woman show
> Who wears a helmet and disowns her sex?
>
> Juvenal *Satires*[70]

So wrote the Roman satirist Juvenal in his lampooning of Roman society and its 'manly' women in the earlier first century AD. Juvenal was sickened by the corruption and lack of morality he witnessed in the city, much of which he blamed on the evils of empire, not least the contaminating influence of the east, the rise of the *nouveau riche* and the breakdown in family values at home. In Satire VI, 'A Gallery of Women', he wreaks his savagery on the reversal of gender roles and attempts by women to out-perform men in public life. Juvenal's attitude has a bearing on our quest for Boudica, for it is clear that Roman authors belonged to their social context and that, since in Roman eyes, women should know their place and have little public profile, empowered women outside the Roman world would have been regarded by them with awe, suspicion and disapproval.

Juvenal raises an interesting issue in Satire VI: that of female warriors and, specifically, women gladiators. This is a theme picked up upon by other writers, notably Suetonius, Tacitus and Dio Cassius. In his *Life* of Domitian, Suetonius comments that the emperor staged 'gladiatorial shows by torchlight in which women as well as men took part'.[71] In his *Annals*, Tacitus – writing in the context of the gross moral decline in the Emperor Nero's behaviour just prior to his torching of Rome – describes the way in which the gladiatorial games in the city were debased by 'the number of distinguished women and senators disgracing themselves in the arena'.[72] The writer here gives vent to his contempt for the evils of empire and the utter moral collapse of the Roman aristocracy, led by the emperor himself. His republican sympathies shine through the page in his remarks about the way in which the nobility, male and female, behaved in totally inappropriate ways. It is as though the British prime minister, the Cabinet and the Queen all went into the boxing ring, or enjoyed a bout of mud-wrestling, in front of thousands of spectators!

The question of whether such Roman authors as Suetonius and Tacitus were exaggerating or accurately reporting true events is, of course, open to doubt. What better way to present an imperial regime in the most vicious light possible than to use poetic licence to demonstrate how social norms had been subverted and inverted: senators behaving like slaves and women like men? According to both writers, the emperor himself behaved more like a woman than a man and, what is more, committed the grossest of crimes, that of matricide, thus putting himself totally outside the bounds of human conduct. But were there female gladiators in the Roman Empire? Do we have any independent evidence to suggest that this might have been so? The answer is a tentative yes. *The Times* for 13 September, 2000 published a new archaeological find in London, at a Roman cemetery in Southwark,[73] which seemed to be a burial of a woman who may have been a professional gladiator. Only her pelvis survives, but one of the grave-goods interred with her was a small clay oil lamp on whose surface is a depiction of a fallen gladiator. Another significant discovery with the remains of the dead woman was a group of three other lamps, one of which depicted Anubis, Egyptian god of the dead who was equated, in the Roman world, with Mercury, a deity closely associated with gladiators.[74] Although the evidence is circumstantial and the interpretation necessarily speculative, it is at least possible that here, at Southwark in south London, a woman who had fought in the local amphitheatre (and quite possibly died there in combat) had her tomb. Her mourners gave her a flamboyant send-off: there was a funeral feast at the graveside and the smells of the ceremonial meal would have been mingled with the resinous odour of incense from burning pine cones.

Despite the care taken with her burial, if the lady of Southwark was a female gladiator, she was doubly beyond the pale, for gladiators belonged to a kind of 'untouchable caste' known as *infamis*.[75] They occupied an ambiguous social position in so far as they were glamorised as the darlings of the Roman mobs: physically (and sexually) potent champions who were regarded somewhat in the same light as professional footballers in much of the world today. Even so, they were unfree, fought for their owners and were usually drawn from the ranks of prisoners-of-war, criminals or other marginal groups. The idea of a female gladiator then, was that much more shocking for, in addition to the already long list of unacceptable characteristics, there was the disturbing notion of women behaving like men, strutting about semi-naked in the full glare of publicity and fighting in armed combat. Juvenal's attitude (above) would not have been his alone.

In the summer of 2005 the Prado in Madrid put on a temporary exhibition of Roman paintings, mainly sixteenth and seventeenth-century works with Roman themes. One of these, by Jusepe de Ribera, entitled *Combate de mujeres* ('Fight of the women') depicts a scene in ancient Rome of two fully clothed and noble-looking young women incongruously battling it out with (sixteenth-century) swords and shields. They by no means resemble 'conventional' gladiators but accord rather with Juvenal's picture of high-born women indulging in the sport of combat; nonetheless, there is genuine violence in Ribera's painting, and the fighting women are watched by bands of men armed to the teeth with spears and halbards.[76] Ribera is almost certainly depicting women gladiators, albeit decorously clad in early modern dress.

Medusas of the mind

The idea of the female gladiator as 'beyond the pale', outside the edges of society, takes us back to attitudes towards women in Graeco-Roman society and, in particular, to the treatment of Boudica in the literature. For the Romans, as for the Greeks, women belonged in the household, not in public life. Behind this perceived need to sequester women lay deep-seated notions of the dangerous female, the need to control her immoderacy, and to prevent her threatening to subvert the ordered world of the human male. One of the lurking fears that men entertained about women in ancient Greece was grounded in their physicality, their open interior spaces that could be invaded by spirits and possessed, in a manner contrary to male interests.[77] For the Greeks, man (not woman) was the measure of all things and woman a pale (but perilous) shadow of the male ideal. Curiously, the only acceptable public roles for women, in both Greek and Roman society, were those associated with the sacred, and this was partly because their bodies made them enterable by supernatural

4 ◆ Other Boudicas: 'big women' in Iron Age Europe

forces. But closely connected with the sacred was the idea of women's link with impurity: 'In Greek as in some other cultures, concepts of the sacred are interwoven with concepts of pollution'.[78] So women were inherently dangerous and had to be contained, restrained and controlled by men. We see this perception vividly played out in Euripides's play *The Bacchae*, where the women – the antithesis of culture, order, moderation and control – become mad and behave like wild beasts when possessed by the god Dionysus who, himself, flouts gender roles by oscillating between male and female forms.[79] The female gladiators described with such horror by Roman writers, and the possibility of archaeological evidence for just such a woman in London, would thus have been regarded as dangerous to the ordered world of *romanitas*. Indeed, the lavish, exotic nature of the Southwark burial may have been the result of the need to enact special purification ceremonies for a death of someone regarded as 'out of order'.

The treatment of Boudica, especially by Dio Cassius, may be read within just such a context of women as perilous 'others', who threatened the Roman Empire, the *Pax Romana* and the authority of men. There is another aspect of Boudica as an unnatural woman that we ought to consider, namely her marital status. She was a widow: she had been married and had two daughters. She was thus in a liminal position as married but without a husband. Following ancient Greek models, as a married woman Boudica would have been brought from the wild outside to the ordered male world of her husband. Children and unmarried Greek girls were regarded as untamed, wild and undisciplined, a potential threat to society. The *parthenos* (the nubile virgin girl) was groomed from babyhood for her role as a mature, married woman: the *gyne* who, under the control of her husband, could fulfil her 'safe' function as child-bearer and reproducer of men.[80] Boudica was perhaps perceived as doubly dangerous: through the death of Prasutagus, she had been released from her married state and the control of her husband. What is more, she possessed two marriageable virgin daughters whom their father had made joint heirs with the Emperor Nero. Seen in this perspective, the rape of these daughters takes on new meaning: their deflowering represented a negation of their threatening position as free, untamed women, full of undissipated sexual energy, and the insult made to the royal Icenian household by means both of this rape and the flogging of Boudica herself could be perceived as striking a blow for the order of *romanitas*, the empire and men. In any case, since the women were outside this magic circle, they were not, in the Roman sense, fully human.

Classical mythology abounds with ideas of the edge, the end of the 'civilised' world and the monsters that inhabit the world beyond that of humans. We see it in all the major mythic stories concerning heroes, such as Jason, Odysseus and Aeneas. Some of those monsters were female and they belonged to the stuff of which nightmares are made: the single-breasted Amazon; the half-bird, half-human Harpy; the fish-tailed Siren; and, above all, the Gorgon Medusa.[81] In a sense, Boudica belonged in this category of 'edgy monsters'. She was a woman, yet she flouted the rules that governed gender, in Roman eyes at least. She was dangerous and presented such a threat to *romanitas* that Nero seriously considered letting go the province of Britannia altogether; she was larger than life and portrayed as much fiercer than ordinary men: bigger, harsher-voiced and more commanding. More than all this, she was British; she represented Britannia, a shadowy island lurking beyond the boundaries of the world.

Notes and references

1 Aristotle *Politics* 1296b, 26–7; Rankin 1996, 55.

2 Tacitus *Annals* XIV, 35; trans. Grant 1956, 320.

3 Braund 1996.

4 O'Gorman 2000, 1–3, 69.

5 Foxhall 1994, 133–46; Aldhouse-Green 2004a, 70. I have here deliberately inverted Foxhall's definition of 'hegemonic masculinity'.

6 Cool 2005, 34.

7 For the TV company then called Electric Sky, now Brighton Films, for a series entitled *Tales of the Living Dead*, screened by Channel 4 in February 2001.

8 Aldhouse-Green 2001a, 203.

9 Dio Cassius *Roman History* 62, 8; trans. Ireland 1996, 63–70. Note the particular spelling Dio gives to Boudica's name. The figure Dio attributes to Boudica's army is questionable to say the least and must surely be grossly exaggerated.

10 Caesar *De Bello Gallico* IV, 24.

11 Op. cit. IV, 33.

12 The newsletter of the Prehistoric Society.
13 Hill 2001, 2–3.
14 Boyle 2004, 22–6.
15 Hill 2001, 2.
16 Stacey 2004, 1–2.
17 Aldhouse-Green & Aldhouse-Green 2005.
18 Aldhouse-Green 2001a, 157–60.
19 Dent 1985. 85–92; Green 1995, 18–19.
20 Rolley 2003.
21 Arnold 1995, 153–68; Arnold 1991, 366–74.
22 Until recently, it had been thought that the origin of this vessel was either Corinth or Etruria, but recent research has identified southern Italy, probably Metapontum, as the likely home for the craftspeople who made it: Jean-Louis Coudrot pers. com.; Musée Archéologique, Châtillon-sur-Seine.
23 Green 1995, op. cit., 146–7; Pelletier 1984, 13; Mohen 1991, 102–7; Olivier 2003, 12–14.
24 Jean-Louis Coudrot pers. com.
25 Pelletier 1984 13.
26 Olivier 2003, 14.
27 Megaw & Megaw 1989, 113–14.
28 Megaw 1970, no. 73.
29 Aldhouse-Green, 2004a, 160–1.
30 Bonenfant & Guillaumet 1998, 59–64, figs. 32–6; Aldhouse-Green 2004a, figs. 3.9, 5.7; Green 1989, 137, fig. 56; Mohen *et al.* 1987, no. 27.
31 Ammianus Marcellinus *Histories* XV, 12; after Caldecott 1988, 4.
32 Deyts 1992, 19; Aldhouse-Green 2004a, fig. 3.2.
33 Duval 1987, 49, 51, 53, 57 and *passim.*
34 Notably on a late Iron Age female image from Bozouls, Aveyron (southern France): Deyts 1992, 19.
35 Aldhouse-Green 2004a, figs. 2.6, 3.7.
36 Abbaye de Daoulas 1986, no. 80.01; Green 1995, 34.
37 When the Gauls sacked Rome in 387/6 BC, the Capitol (the sacred centre of the city) was saved because the Romans were alerted to the attack by the sacred geese of Juno whose cackling sounded the alarm: Cary 1965, 70; Livy *History of Rome from its Foundations* 5.51.4; Ogilvie 1970, 734.

38 Aldhouse-Green 2001b, 25, fig. 11; 2004a, fig. 1.11.
39 Dio Cassius *Roman History* LXII, 2.
40 Kaul 1991, 8.
41 For discussion of watery deposition see especially Bradley 1990.
42 Kaul 1991, 28–35, pls. 22–9.
43 Op. cit. 35, pl. 29 (right).
44 For the significance of plaiting, see Aldhouse-Green 2004b, 299–325.
45 Kail 1991, 25, pl .19.
46 It is reckoned that at least five silversmiths were involved in the manufacture of the cauldron. It was probably made in south-east Europe but perhaps commissioned by a Gallic community. Its provenance, in a Danish peatbog, may have come about through looting by a Germanic warband, for classical writers such as Livy chronicle the raiding parties conducted by the Cimbri (inhabitants of what is now North Germany and Denmark): Taylor 1992; Olmsted 1979; Kaul 1991; Kaul *et al.* 1991.
47 Syme 1986, quoted in O'Gorman 2000, 122.
48 Dio Cassius *Roman History* LXII, 6; trans. Ireland 1996, 63–70.
49 Cicero *de Divinatione* I, 90.
50 Caesar *de Bello Gallico* V, 6: trans. Wiseman & Wiseman 1980, 90.
51 Rankin 1996, 148.
52 O'Gorman, 2000.
53 Op. cit. 3.
54 The Batavian tribe occupied what is now part of the modern Netherlands.
55 Tacitus *The Histories* IV, 61; trans. Wellesley 1964, 247.
56 Wellesley 1964, 17.
57 Indeed, the passage seems to imply that Lupercus himself was regarded as a gift to Veleda.
58 Tacitus *Germania* 19: 'Thus it is that German women live in a chastity that is impregnable, uncorrupted by the temptations of public shows or the excitements of banquets'; trans. Mattingly 1948, 116.
59 Pomponius Mela *de Chorographia* III, 6.
60 The Cimbri occupied territory in north Germany and southern Denmark: for reference to the priestesses, see Strabo *Geography* VII, 2, 3.
61 Goewin had a curious role, that of footholder to the king: his power derived from placing his feet in her lap, and loss of the footholder's virginity

compromised both her power and that of the ruler: see Jones & Jones 1976, 55.

62 Jones & Jones 1976, xxiii.
63 Tacitus *Histories* IV; trans. Wellesley 1964, 250.
64 One is reminded of Orthanc, the tower of Saruman, the White Wizard, in Tolkein's *The Lord of the Rings*, an edifice that both separated him from his landscape and enclosed him with spiritual energy.
65 There are, of course, parallels in many Middle Eastern or South Asian societies today.
66 Padel 1993, 6.
67 'Britons make no distinction of sex in their leaders': *Agricola* 16; trans. Mattingly 1948, 66.
68 Tacitus *Germania* 8; trans. Mattingly 1948, 107–8.
69 A term borrowed from Creekmore's translation of Juvenal (Creekmore 1963, 88).
70 Juvenal *Satires* VI, lines 246–53; trans. Creekmore 1963, 96.
71 Suetonius *Domitian* 4; trans. Graves 1962, 273.
72 Tacitus *Annals* XV, 32; trans. Grant 1966, 349.
73 Alberge 2000, 3.
74 In the Roman arena, slaves dressed up in the guise of Mercury were employed to drag away the corpses of slain gladiators: Alberge 2000.
75 Howard 2000
76 Jusepe Ribera's *Combate de mujeres* dates to 1636. M.P. 1124, Museo Nacional del Prado, Madrid.
77 Padel 1993, 3–4.
78 Op. cit. 5.
79 Aldhouse-Green 2003, 99.
80 King 1993, 111–13.
81 King 1995, 141, 148–52; Cherry 1995, 10.

CHAPTER 5

Femmes fatales: Boudica and Cartimandua

While this child's play was going on in Rome, a dreadful disaster occurred in Britain: two cities were sacked, 80,000 Romans and provincials were slaughtered, and the island fell into the hands of the enemy. All this, moreover, the Romans sustained at the hands of a woman, something that in fact caused them the greatest of shame.

Dio Cassius, *Roman History*[1]

Her [Cartimandua's] enemies were incensed, stimulated by disgrace, lest they be subject to the rule of a woman; warriors strong and picked for prowess, invaded her kingdom.

Tacitus *Annals*[2]

This is a tale of two women who lived at roughly the same time in early Roman Britain and each of whom is immortalised by the chronicles of Greek or Roman authors. Both were of royal blood; both exercised authority over and beyond a single tribal territory, and each had a special relationship with the Roman government in Britain. But there their paths diverge, for while Boudica of the Iceni set herself fervently and violently against Rome, Cartimandua, of the northern queendom of the Brigantes, was a collaborator, a client-queen who relied on Roman support and reciprocated by delivering freedom fighters to Roman justice. This chapter is a fitting sequel to the two preceding it for, among other things, it focuses upon issues associated with client-relationships with Rome – those that worked and those that broke down – and upon attitudes to females in power, both from a Roman and a British perspective.

5 ♦ *Femmes fatales*: Boudica and Cartimandua

Our knowledge of Cartimandua is entirely due to historical references; the same is broadly true of Boudica, but we do have coins that mention her royal kindred, and there is plenty of indirect archaeological evidence, in the form of destruction layers in parts of the three cities sacked by her rebel forces in AD 60 (*see* Chapter 7). More indirect still, but nonetheless providing interest, are the small portable objects that late Iron Age Icenians left behind: some of the most striking comprise cosmetic preparation kits, each consisting of a small bowl and grinder, used to pound make-up into powder for facial and body-painting;[3] some are elaborately ornamented with bulls' heads, perhaps used by the female elite, maybe even those at the top, like Boudica. The focus of the current chapter is not the Boudican Rebellion itself but rather an interrogation of the evidence for these two women, unique in the history of Roman Britain in being named and described with detail in contemporary records.

A monstrous regiment of women

Chapter 4 discusses the evidence for the presence of independently powerful women in Iron Age Europe, evidence that draws upon material culture and (for the later period) classical texts. There seems to be no doubt that women could, on occasion, achieve high status; one that was not necessarily contingent upon the rank of fathers, husbands, brothers or sons. In assessing attitudes towards our two current *dramatis personae*, Boudica and Cartimandua, it is quite impossible to disentangle any kind of reality from the bias of ancient historians, such as Tacitus. His writing is full of prejudice, both against women in positions of power and – especially – queenship. However, it is not as simple as that, for Tacitus was a deeply moralistic thinker and writer, and it is clear from comparisons of his treatment of the two British women that he had far more sympathy with Boudica than with Cartimandua, despite the fact that Boudica was a fanatical and extremely dangerous enemy of Roman Britain, while Cartimandua was a staunch ally. Tacitus did not like adulterous women, nor did he accept perfidy, even between barbarians and even if such treachery benefited the Roman cause.

The two quotations at the beginning of this chapter, one from Dio, the other from Tacitus, have in common the peculiar horror felt at destruction and warfare as conducted by women. Dio's testimony is concerned with the sack of a Roman *colonia*, Colchester, and two Roman towns, Verulamium and London, by Boudica's forces.[4] Tacitus is recounting the internecine strife occurring among the Brigantes, where the ruling family was tearing itself and the tribe apart in what was in effect a gigantic marital row, underpinned by fundamental political differences between Cartimandua and her husband Venutius. It is time to look closely at Boudica and Cartimandua, although the actual Boudican campaign and what led to its eruption, is the subject of Chapter 7. First, we should look at 'the woman question',[5] and the deeply entrenched attitude to women in the classical world generally. A good example of how such gender treatment is manifest in Athenian society of the fifth century BC is demonstrated by Euripides' drama *The Bacchae*, in which women (and animals) were perceived as wild, disordered, uncontrolled and 'other', in contrast to the reasoned, intellectually based order represented by men.[6] In ancient Athens women belonged in the *oikos*, the household, and rarely had a chance to participate in public life, except in the religious arena. Rome's women were not so restricted, but they still did not enjoy full emancipation; they could not vote or undertake business independently (except for the Vestal Virgins, who occupied a position outside gender anyway[7]). Considerable discussion in the literature has focused upon how women were depicted in Greek and Roman art, and the way that female imagery often echoed ideas of 'otherness'.[8]

It is interesting that, during the late Republic and early empire, high-ranking Roman women were steadily gaining some autonomy and independent status, and nowhere was this more obvious than in the case of Augustus's wife Livia. Indeed, she set a trend in establishing a context wherein female members of the imperial family enjoyed considerable influence,[9] albeit – nominally at least – by proxy. By the time about which Tacitus and Dio were writing, some of these powerful royal females were attracting notoriety as well as approval: Claudius's wife Messalina dabbled dangerously in treasonable sedition and was executed; another of his wives, Agrippina, mother of Nero, was admired but feared, just as Livia had been.

Tacitus, at least, would have been highly influenced by what was going on in Rome when he painted his portraits of barbarian women of power. In AD 65 a conspiracy was hatched among certain members of the aristocracy, to overthrow Nero and replace him with Calpurnius Piso.[10]

5 ◆ *Femmes fatales*: Boudica and Cartimandua

One of the foremost of these was a woman named Epicharis, a freedwoman (an ex-slave), who tirelessly urged on the conspirators. When the plot was discovered, many were arrested and thrown in chains to await interrogation and torture; in particular, Nero was convinced that Epicharis's gender would render her an especially easy person to break, but she committed suicide rather than betray her fellow revolutionaries:

> Thinking no female body could stand the pain, he [Nero] ordered her to be tortured. But lashes did not weaken her denials, nor did branding – nor the fury of the torturers at being defied by a woman. So the first day's examination was frustrated. Next day her racked limbs could not support her, so she was taken for further torments in a chair. But on the way she tore off her breast-band, fastened it in a noose to the chair's canopy, and placed her neck inside it. Then, straining with all her weight, she throttled the little life that was still in her. So, shielding in direst agony men unconnected with her and almost strangers, this ex-slavewoman set an example which particularly shone when free men, Roman gentlemen and senators, were betraying, untouched, their nearest and dearest.[11]

This passage is revealing, for although Tacitus clearly disapproves of empowered women, such as Cartimandua (see above), he has sympathy and admiration for Epicharis, a woman of lowly birth who, despite her ex-slave status, displayed far more courage and moral fibre than the male nobility involved in the plot against Nero. In the words of David Braund, 'Tacitus's Boudica has more in common with his Epicharis than his Cartimandua'.[12] The irony with which Tacitean narrative is woven demonstrates the author's stance as an admirer of the underclass when pitted against the decadence of imperial Rome, whether that underclass was represented by the servile Epicharis or a British barbarian called Boudica.

Cartimandua the collaborator: the 'sleek pony' of the north

> He [Claudius] ordered the Britons,
> beyond the shores of the known sea,
> and the Brigantes, blue with their shields,
> to give their necks to Roman chains
> and Ocean himself to tremble at
> the new laws of the Roman axe.
>
> Seneca *Apocolocyntosis*[13]

So wrote Seneca, imperial philosopher, writer and usurer, in his *Apocolocyntosis* (or 'The Pumpkinification' of Claudius, a skit on his deification) compiled in the reign of Nero, when the author – at first – enjoyed considerable influence over the young emperor. Much of this work of satire is shot through with personal malice and spite, and this passage is no exception, with its reference to the trembling of Ocean at Claudius's new dominion over Britain. Interestingly, though, Seneca makes a distinction between the Britons and the Brigantes, which may simply be poetic, alliterative licence but may allude to a genuinely perceived difference between northern and southern parts of the island. At any rate, the Brigantes, occupying the far north, are portrayed – like the Druidic occupants of Anglesey (Chapter 6) – as beyond the edge of the world, and all the more barbaric because of their outlandish geographical position.[14] Certainly Rome had cause to encounter the Brigantes before AD 51, when Cartimandua first appears in the preserved works of Tacitus, for this powerful hegemony led a revolt against the Roman governor Ostorius Scapula in about AD 48, just after the uprising of the Iceni. According to Tacitus, this happened when Ostorius was engaged in subduing the north Welsh tribe of the Deceangli, 'ravaging their territory and collecting extensive booty'. The governor had penetrated their lands almost to the western shore when the Brigantes rose up in arms, forcing him to deflect from his subjugation of the north-west and turn east to deal with this new threat. The Brigantian campaign does not seem to have amounted to much: 'The Brigantes subsided; their few peace-breakers were killed, and the rest were pardoned'.[15] The weakness of their bid to halt the Roman occupation suggests that the greater part of their people were not engaged with the process, probably because Cartimandua, staunch ally of Rome, was already in power and in receipt of financial (and maybe other) support from the emperor.

We first hear of Cartimandua in AD 51 when she committed the infamous act of delivering the British freedom-fighter Caratacus to the Romans in chains (see Plate 7). Cartimandua was the queen of the Brigantes, a loosely federated group of tribes and sub-tribes in northern Britain who had, perhaps, only been brought together under Cartimandua's authority in the early–mid-first century AD. In his *The Roman Invasion of Britain* Graham Webster suggested that Cartimandua is likely to have been among the British monarchs who presented them-

5 ◆ Femmes fatales: Boudica and Cartimandua

selves in supplication to Claudius at Camulodunum, after its occupation by Aulus Plautius, and who are immortalised on the emperor's triumphal arches at Rome (dedicated in AD 52) and at Cyzicus in Asia Minor.[16] Tacitus's description of the queen and family discord is redolent of a soap-opera (or the activities of some members of the British royal family), and is worth quoting in full, for it is packed with drama and characterisation, and serves as a striking contrast to the Boudica situation described later in this chapter. But first, we hear of the events of AD 51, when Cartimandua handed over Caratacus to the Romans, after his leadership of the Silures against the Romans had failed, Ostorius had triumphed over the western Britons and Caratacus himself was forced to flee.

> It was a great victory. Caratacus' wife and daughter were captured: his brother surrendered. He himself sought sanctuary with Cartimandua, queen of the Brigantes. But the defeated have no refuge. He was arrested, and handed over to the conquerors.[17]

Another translation,[18] has it that Cartimandua delivered the British war-leader to the Romans in chains and, indeed, the original Latin reads *vinctus ac victoribus traditus est* ('he was handed to the victors bound').[19] Tacitus himself speaks of the queen's treachery in handing over a fellow British aristocrat to almost certain slavery or execution, but perhaps we need to ponder this situation before judging her. Yes, she was a Briton in collaboration with the Roman government, but we have no means of estimating how close were the ties between the Brigantes and other parts of Britain, nor whether the Britons perceived themselves as sharing a distinct and single identity. It may be that the Brigantes felt they were as distinct from other tribes as from Rome and thus Cartimandua might have felt few ties of loyalty with Caratacus. It is something to think about anyway.

The other odd thing about this episode is the behaviour of Caratacus himself and his choice of refuge. For he must have been well aware of Cartimandua's Roman sympathies, and the fact that she had not joined forces with the Silures in attempting to repel the invaders. A large number of potential bolt-holes would have been available to him in the hilly terrain of central or northern Wales, yet he chose to flee to a queen who would not dare to harbour him for fear of compromising her position of client-monarch. The reasons for Caratacus's action may lie in the factionalised nature of the Brigantes, and this is where the dynastic quarrels inside the Brigantian royal house come into play. For Caratacus may have had cause to hope that the anti-Roman lobby there would help him.

After the uncomfortable events of AD 51, Tacitus moves the scene more than a decade onwards to AD 68. The historian gives us two accounts of Cartimandua and the internal dynastic feuds that threatened the region's stability. One is in his *Annals*, the other in the *Histories*. We should peruse the account in the *Annals* in some detail, since it clarifies the Brigantian situation in a way that enables better understanding of the more complex text in the *Histories*. But we need first to refer to the *Histories* since it is there that Tacitus begins by setting the historical context: Rome had been turned upside down by civil strife after Nero's death in AD 68, with no fewer than four claimants to the purple; indeed, the year 68/9 has been termed the year of the four emperors. The writer introduces his account of the Brigantian queen and the enmity between her and her consort, Venutius, by citing Rome's political and military instability as an excuse for Brigantian unrest among the anti-Roman factions in north Britain.

The *Annals*, compiled later than the *Histories*, nonetheless give a more introductory account of the Brigantian situation and the falling-out between Cartimandua and Venutius, a personalisation of the growing tension between pro- and anti-Roman factions in this huge conglomeration of tribes and clanships. It is clear from a cross-reference in Book 12 of the *Annals* that a lost part of the work had already mentioned Venutius.[20] For us, however, this is the first time Cartimandua's consort is mentioned, and the author makes clear the scale of the schism that was rending the Brigantes apart. While Cartimandua, the client-queen, had the might of Rome behind her, Venutius had support, on the ground, as it were, from a large part of the tribe and its federated allies.

> *But after Caratacus had been captured, a man outstanding in his knowledge of military affairs, Venutius, from the tribe of the Brigantes, as I mentioned above, and long faithful and defended by Roman arms when he held Cartimandua the queen in marriage, having fallen out with her and immediately gone to war, had entered hostilities even against us. But at first fighting was between themselves, and Cartimandua, with cunning arts, seized the brothers and relations of Venutius. By that her enemies were incensed, stimulated by disgrace, lest they be subject to the rule of a woman; warriors strong and picked for prowess, invaded her kingdom. The affair had been foreseen by us, and cohorts sent to help fought a fierce battle, which had an*

PLATE 1 ◆ *Hoard of (341) Icenian silver coins, found in a pot at Honingham, Norfolk; Norwich Castle Museum.*

Source: © Miranda Aldhouse-Green.

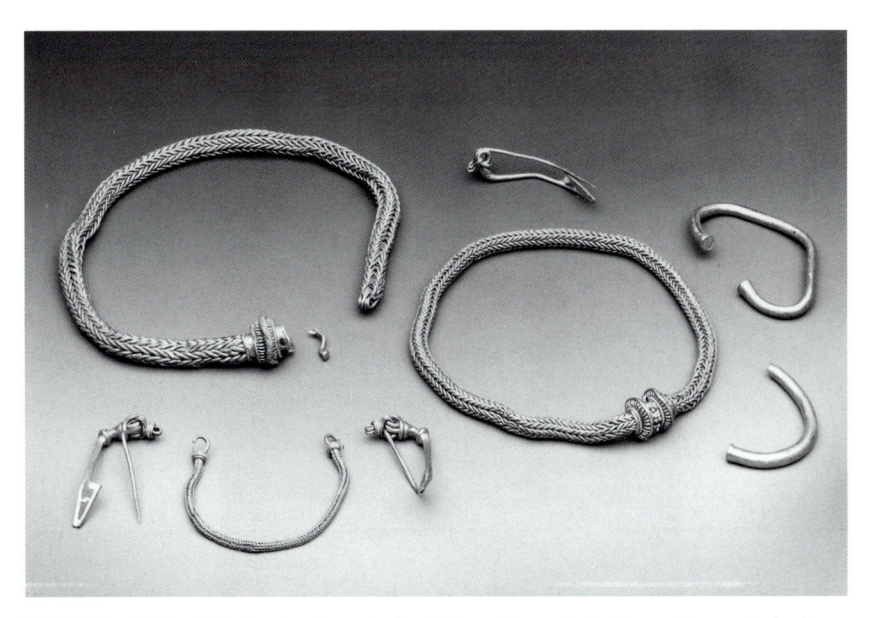

PLATE 2 ◆ *The Winchester hoard of gold jewellery, dated to c. the period of Caesar's 'invasions' of Britain.*

Source: © Copyright the Trustees of The British Museum.

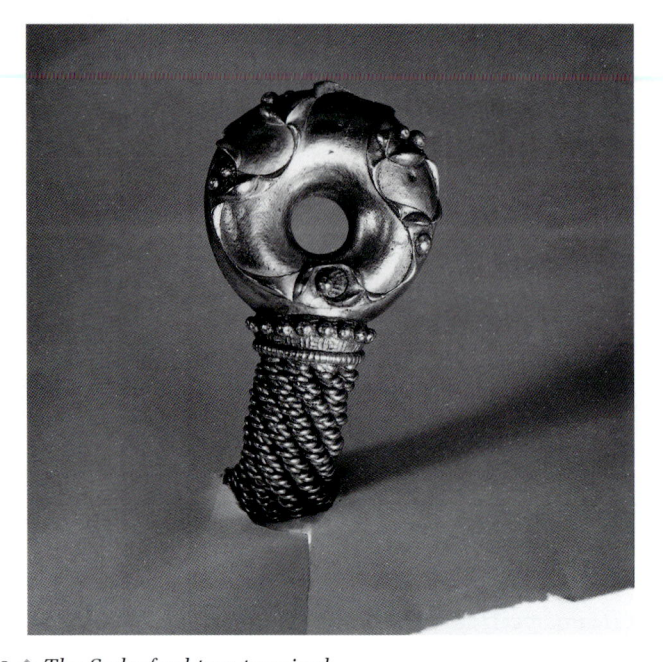

PLATE 3 ◆ *The Sedgeford torc terminal.*

Source: © Copyright the Trustees of The British Museum.

PLATE 4 ◆ *Potsherd depicting a Trinovantian horseman, from Kelvedon, Essex.*

Source: © The Castle Museum, Colchester.

PLATE 5 ◆ *The Catuarus ring found at Fishbourne.*

Source: © Fishbourne Roman Palace and Museum.

PLATE 6 ◆ *Aureus of Nero, showing a portrait of the emperor as a young man.*

Source: © Guy de la Bédoyère.

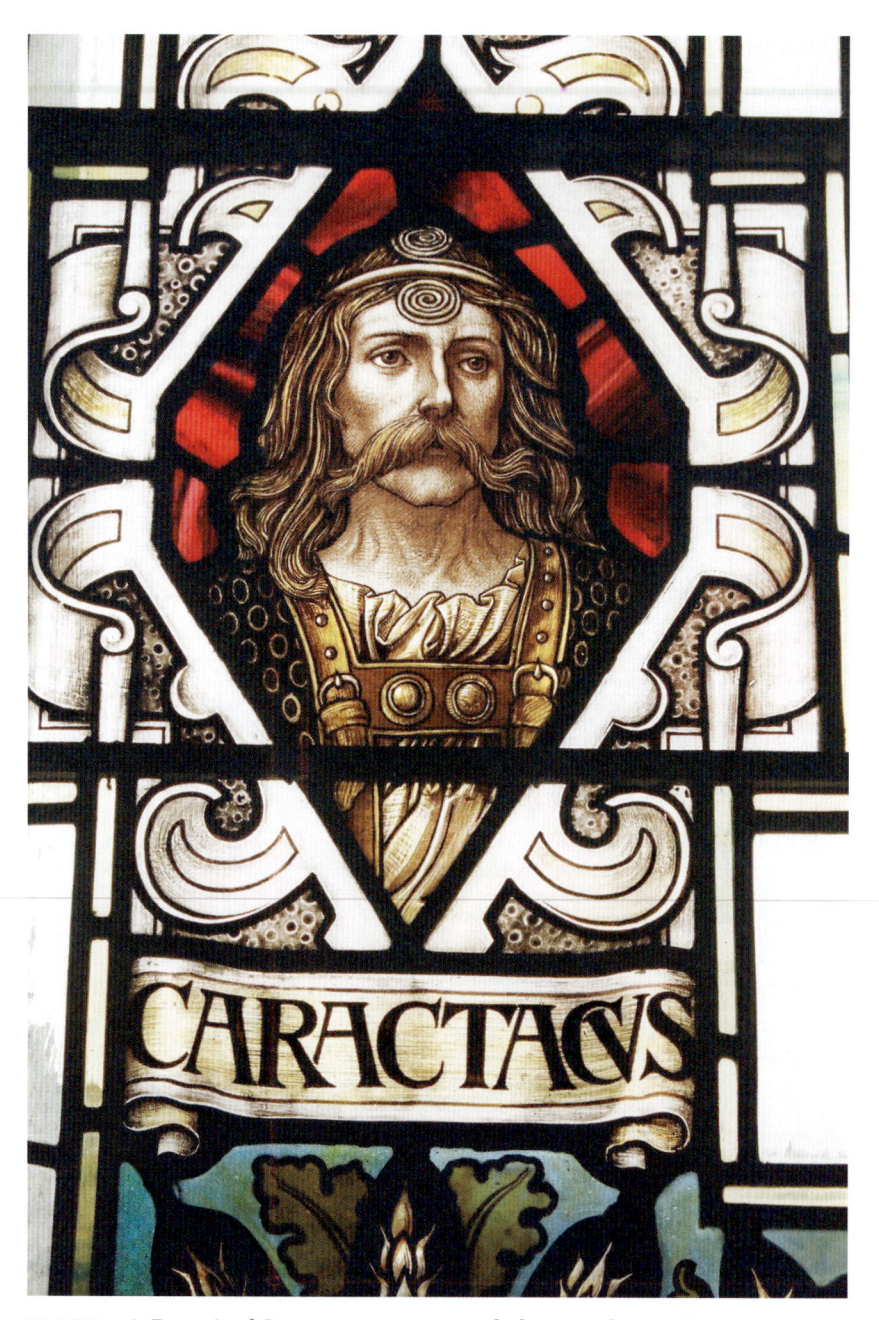

PLATE 7 ◆ *Portrait of Caratacus, on a stained-glass window in the Moot Hall, Colchester Town Hall.*

Source: © Miranda Aldhouse-Green; by kind permission of Colchester Borough Council.

PLATE 8 ◆ *Cleopatra, depicted on the rear external wall of the Dendera temple of Hathor, Egypt; dated to just after 44 BC, when Cleopatra returned to Egypt from Rome after the assassination of Julius Caesar.*

Source: © Dr Joann Fletcher.

PLATE 9 ◆ *Boudica and her daughters; a marble statue by J. Havard Thomas, installed in Cardiff City Hall in October 1916.*

Source: © Miranda Aldhouse-Green; by kind permission of Cardiff County Council.

PLATE 10 ◆ *Reconstruction of Boudica's chariot (complete with war-trumpet or carnyx), as ridden by Alex Kingston in the TV film Boudica; in the Castle Museum, Colchester.*

Source: © Miranda Aldhouse-Green.

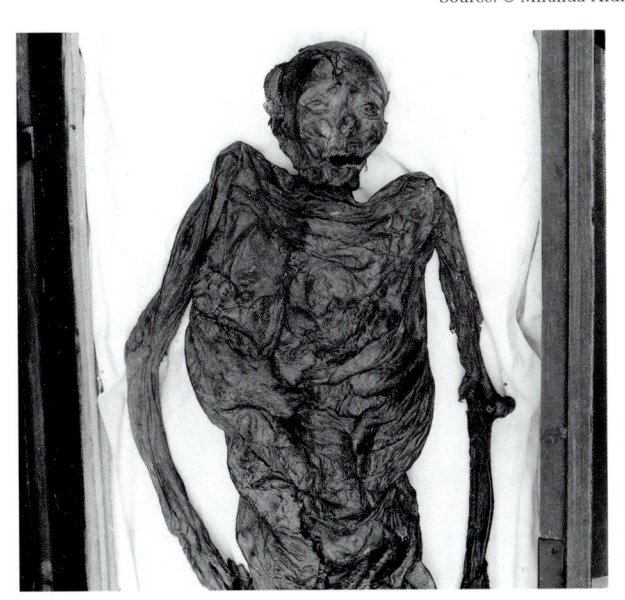

PLATE 11 ◆ *The body of a middle-aged female from Haraldskaer, Jutland, ritually hanged in the fifth century BC.*

Source: © Nationalmuseet, Copenhagen.

PLATE 12 ◆ *Chariot-burial of a woman with a facial disfigurement, interred with a large amount of coral-decorated grave-goods; Wetwang Slack, East Yorkshire.*

Source: © Copyright the Trustees of The British Museum.

PLATE 13 ◆ *The Gallo-Roman horse-goddess Epona, from Alesia, Burgundy.*

Source: © Paul Jenkins.

PLATE 14 ◆ *Antiquarian picture of Boudica/Boadicea.*
Source: Aylett Sammes Britannia Antiqua Illustrata, 1676. Photo: Topham Picturepoint

PLATE 15 ◆ *Llyn Cerrig Bach, Anglesey.*
Source: © Philip Macdonald.

PLATE 16 ◆ *Druids confront the Romans led by Suetonius Paulinus on Anglesey.*

Source: Dudley Wright Druidism. The Ancient Faith of Britain, 1924. Photo: Topham Picturepoint

PLATE 17 ◆ *Decorated crescentric plaque, probably horse-gear; a votive object from Llyn Cerrig Bach, Anglesey.*

Source: © National Museums & Galleries of Wales.

PLATE 18 ◆ *The late Roman jeweller's hoard from Snettisham, Norfolk.*

Source: © Copyright the Trustees of The British Museum.

PLATE 19 ◆ *Roman cavalry tombstone of Longinus, from Colchester.*
Source: © The Castle Museum, Colchester.

PLATE 20 ◆ *The burning of the temple of Claudius at Colchester; a painting by Peter Froste.*

Source: © The Castle Museum, Colchester.

PLATE 21 ◆ *Glass bead from the Gresham Street site, London.*

Source: © Museum of London.

PLATE 22 ◆ *Blackened grain, and burnt coins with samian dish, from the Boudican destruction layer in London.*

Source: © Museum of London.

PLATE 23 ◆ *Jeweller's hoard of Roman gemstones, stowed away in a pot made in Lyon for safekeeping; from Boudican London.*

Source: © Museum of London.

PLATE 24 ◆ *Bronze statue of Boudica, erected on the Thames Embankment, 1902.*

Source: © Richard Hingley and Christina Unwin.

PLATE 25 ◆ *'Boadicea' on a stained-glass window in the Moot Hall, Colchester Town Hall.*

Source: © Miranda Aldhouse-Green; by kind permission of Colchester Borough Council.

5 ◆ Femmes fatales: Boudica and Cartimandua

> *uncertain start but a happier ending. A similar result was fought out by the legion which was commanded by Caesius Nasica.*[21]

Tacitus's terse prose (worthy of Julius Caesar's laconic military style) provides a wealth of overt and half-hidden information, albeit overlaid with a Roman mindset. Taken at face value, it seems from the *Annals* that Venutius conducted himself as an ally of Rome until, as the *Histories* relate, his marriage fell apart. Reading between the lines, the relationship between Venutius and Rome must have been a fragile one, since the Brigantian was willing to throw it all away when he quarrelled with the queen. He appears to have been wooed by the vicarious power, status and Roman friendship emanating from his wife, but underneath he chafed both at his own inferior rank and at Cartimandua's position as the real authority. One interesting element in this account is Tacitus's phrase 'with cunning arts', which refers to the mechanism by which Cartimandua suborned her estranged husband's relatives. One can but wonder at the nature of these 'arts' and we could perhaps imagine that she was employing magical rituals to ensnare them. Chapter 6 explores the link between the Boudican Rebellion and the Druids, and puts forward the notion that Boudica herself might have been trained in religious craft, just as some Gallic political leaders were also religious practitioners. Could it be that Cartimandua, too, had ritual powers that set her apart and made her feared by her peers?

In this context, we should remember Cartimandua's name, 'the sleek pony'[22] perhaps merely an epithet given to her because of some physical characteristic associated with youth, beauty and a spirited nature, or her name could have been a derisory title, given to her because her unbridled sexual appetite earned her an animal sobriquet. But, again, her horse-title might constitute a reference to her shamanic powers as a shape-shifter, a woman-ritualist who could take on the persona of a spirit-animal in order to communicate with the supernatural world.[23] Horses were significant creatures in Gallo-British religion (see Plate 13), both in the Iron Age and Roman periods, and seem to have been important boundary symbols then and in early historical Welsh and Irish mythology[24]. We should also remember (Chapter 4) the cluster of high-status horse-drawn chariot-burials in Iron Age Yorkshire, of which some are female.

It is in the *Histories* that we learn more about the queen herself, the reason for the marital breakdown – and Venutius's anger – and the part played by Rome in the ensuing drama. If the Brigantes were a tribe in factional schism, then these internal disputes can only have been exacerbated by Cartimandua's behaviour; first in handing over Caratacus (who probably enjoyed support from at least certain of the northern clans) and, second, in her adulterous activities. Not only was she unfaithful to Venutius but she insulted him by rejecting him in favour of his body servant, thereby dishonouring him and the entire royal family. She may have misjudged her personal situation, confident in her Roman support and her increased riches, and perhaps did not realise that she had overplayed her hand and had underestimated Venutius's own powers and the anti-Roman feeling that was just waiting for an excuse to erupt. Cartimandua's perfidy – to Caratacus and to Venutius – may have been perceived as intimately associated with contamination of the Brigantian dynasty with Roman corruption. This is certainly how Tacitus presents the story, and here we must remember the writer's own prejudices against empire, kingship and especially queenship. In the passage quoted below, Tacitus comments on the far-reaching influence enjoyed by Venutius, who was able not only to whip up Brigantian insurgence but also to call upon external aid, probably because of complicated kinship links or treaty relationships with neighbouring tribes. It may be, too, that Cartimandua's own hold on the throne was more tenuous than she (or the Romans) thought, although she had been in power for a considerable time before these events. It has been said of her: 'heiress of a royal house whose male line was extinct, she sat on an uneasy throne'.[25] It may be true that her position was weak, but there is sufficient evidence for women in political power in Iron Age Britain (Chapter 4) for us to hesitate before jumping to the conclusion that she held authority only because there was no male to do so, even though Tacitus (in the above passage) mentions anti-female feeling among Venutius's warriors (a remark that may say more about Tacitus than about the Brigantes).[26] In the *Histories* Tacitus paints the queen with a much blacker brush than in the *Annals*. She was cruel, treacherous, scheming and immoral, all vices that Tacitus perceived as present in Rome and all part of the corrupting cancer of supreme power. The historian may well have been making tacit comparisons between this British woman and Messalina, Claudius's consort who, by all accounts combined immoderate use of power with insatiable and treasonable extra-marital sex.[27] Surprisingly, however, the two Tacitean commentaries present a strange

5 ◆ Femmes fatales: Boudica and Cartimandua

discrepancy between them in their portrayal of Venutius's attitude: in the *Annals* he began as a fervent ally of Rome, while in the *Histories* he is depicted as an anti-Roman fanatic. Thus in the *Histories* we read:

> These differences, and the spate of rumours about the civil war, emboldened the Britons to pluck up their courage and follow a man called Venutius, who, quite apart from a violent character and a hatred of all things Roman, was goaded to fury by a personal feud with Queen Cartimandua. She had been for some time ruler of the Brigantes, and was a princess of high birth and hence influence. This she had increased thanks to her treacherous capture of King Caratacus, an action by which she was generally thought to have set the seal upon Claudius' triumph. Hence came wealth and the self-indulgence of prosperity. She tired of Venutius, who was her consort, and gave her hand and kingdom to his armour-bearer, one Vellocatus. This scandal immediately shook the royal house to its foundations. The discarded husband could rely on the support of the Brigantian people, the lover upon the infatuation of the queen and her ruthless cruelty. So Venutius summoned help from outside, and a simultaneous revolt on the part of the Brigantes themselves reduced Cartimandua to a position of acute danger, in which she appealed for Roman assistance. In the event, our cohorts and cavalry regiments did succeed, at the cost of desperate fighting, in rescuing the queen from a tight corner. Venutius inherited the throne, and we the fighting.[28]

The two Tacitean narratives are united, however, in their presentation of the acutely serious situation the Romans faced in combating the Brigantian uprising: first, auxiliary troops and then the legions (the élite of the Roman army) were deployed in quelling Venutius's bid for power (Tacitus stresses his outstanding military capabilities) and in protecting Cartimandua and her buffer-state. The realities of the Brigantian crisis are hinted at in the material culture of the region: Almondsbury, near Huddersfield, has been identified as a significant Brigantian political centre, but Venutius's last stand against the Roman army might well have taken place at the huge fortified stronghold at Stanwick.[29] It is perhaps significant that a large hoard of burnt metalwork, much of it consisting of martial gear, was deposited at Melsonby, very close to Stanwick, tentatively identified as the remains of a high-status cremation-grave,[30] presumably that of a member of the first-century Brigantian warrior-elite Large Roman forts identified in the southern Pennines (such as Osmanthorpe and Rossington Bridge) may have been connected with campaigns against the rebels.[31]

For our knowledge of Queen Cartimandua we are reliant upon a single source, Tacitus, who undoubtedly recorded actual events and individuals in first-century northern Britain. But 'his evident intention to moralise'[32] biases his character sketches and Cartimandua is presented as devious, promiscuous and unreliable, while Venutius gains sympathy because of his faithless wife and because he (quite naturally in Roman eyes) chafed under female authority. Relevant, here, is the patriotic harangue put into the mouth of the Caledonian freedom fighter Calgacus, who defied the Romans under their governor Agricola more than 20 years after Cartimandua betrayed Caratacus. Tacitus refers to a later Brigantian rebellion, in which the tribe, 'with only a woman to lead them, burned the colony, stormed the camp and, if success had not made them grossly careless, might have cast off the yoke'.[33] It is clear that Tacitus is here confusing the Brigantes with the Iceni, and Cartimandua with Boudica, for it was the Icenian who burned Colchester and nearly put paid to Britannia as a Roman province.

When we come to examine the textual evidence for an Icenian noblewoman named Boudica, however, the situation is quite different from the record for Cartimandua. For one thing, we have two sources: Tacitus and Dio. For another, Tacitus has no platform to express either his moral perceptions or his anti-royalist sentiments, for Boudica is loyal, courageous and straightforward, despite her enmity towards Rome, and there is no reason to doubt her chastity. Tacitus, at any rate, appreciated these qualities. Furthermore, she was not a queen but the widow of a king. Nevertheless, the savagery of her revenge caused her actions to be treated with opprobrium by both writers.

Boudica the 'victorious'

> However, the one person who most roused them to anger and persuaded them to go to war against the Romans, the one person thought worthy of leading them and who directed the course of the whole war was Boudouica, a woman of the British royal family who possessed more spirit than is usual among women. Having collected an army of 120,000, she mounted a tribunal made in the Roman fashion out of earth. In stature she was very tall and grim in appearance, with a piercing gaze and a harsh voice. She had a mass of very fair hair which she grew down to her hips, and wore a great gold torque and a multi-coloured tunic folded round her, over which was a thick cloak

5 ◆ Femmes fatales: Boudica and Cartimandua

fastened with a brooch. This was how she always dressed. And now, taking a spear in her hand so as to present an impressive sight, she spoke.

Dio Cassius *Roman History*[34]

Thus, Dio Cassius has immortalised the British freedom-fighter of the Iceni, with her bright flowing hair (see Plate 14), piercing eyes, massive build and brightly coloured garments.[35] Cassius Dio Cocceianus was born in about AD 163, a Greek from Nicaea in Bithynia (Asia Minor), and came to Rome in about AD 180, in his late teens.[36] Dio's perspective is somewhat different from that of Tacitus. In addition to living and writing over a century after the events in Britain he recorded took place, the later historian came from a hybrid Greek and Roman socio-political milieu: born a Greek, he became a Roman senator and a consul. His gargantuan *Roman History* was 80 books long and he wrote in his native language. Although Dio was to all intents and purposes a member of the Roman aristocracy, he never ceased to think of himself as Bithynian, and spoke of going home to his home city of Nicaea. An interesting aspect of Dio's life was his liking and respect for the Roman empress Julia Domna, an able woman who combined a penchant for philosophy with a flair for politics. Indeed, she apparently did a great deal of the Emperor Caracalla's work for him.[37] So, in the course of his career at Rome, Dio had contact with powerful women, albeit that none was of the same calibre as Boudica.

In assessing the value of Dio's comments on Boudica, as a historical account, we should bear in mind that not only was the author far removed in time from events in first-century Britain, but he almost certainly did not go to the province himself, so all his descriptions of the country are second-hand.[38] He spent ten years assembling data from the work of earlier writers but, like most ancient historians, he does not make a habit of naming his sources.[39] One of his favourite genres within the *Roman History* is what Fergus Millar has termed 'tragic history': accounts of human disasters, such as earthquakes and massacres, in order to play on the emotional impact on his audience of these events.[40] His account of the Boudican Rebellion and, in particular, of the atrocities committed by Boudica in cities like London,[41] fall neatly into this category. We ought also to take into account the elements of fiction that form portions of Dio's work, and we can assume that he would have been unable to resist embellishing the drama of episodes like the Boudican campaign.

As in the case of Tacitus, then, we must read Dio with caution and with an understanding of the background and context that caused him to compose his particular brand of historical record. We should not assume that his physical description of the British war-leader owes any more to fact than to literary licence. His creation of a huge, manlike woman, with arresting features and bright hair – all physical characteristics completely alien to those Mediterranean women of whom Dio would have had most experience – may be entirely or partially fictitious, but it certainly adds to the storyline. Dio's Boudica is strange, outlandish and barbaric (like Britain itself); her gender is ambiguous and her clothing and adornments are all stereotypic *topoi* of 'otherness'.

Both Tacitus and Dio call the Icenian freedom fighter by the name of Boudica or Boudouica, a title or epithet deriving from a Celtic word 'bouda', meaning 'victory'.[42] She only appears in the literature in the context of conflict, so we have no means of knowing whether this was the name she was born with or whether it was an honorific title bestowed upon her by her followers or adopted by the woman herself as a propaganda exercise. But Boudica seems to have identified herself with victory: it was to the goddess of this virtue to whom she prayed at the sacred grove in London, after committing unspeakable acts of bestiality towards Roman Londoners. Dio tells us that she conducted sacrificial rites and orgiastic feasting 'in the grove of Andate … the name they gave to Victory'.[43] In this way, Boudica the woman identified herself with the invincibility of Victory the goddess, and thus presented herself to Britons and Romans alike as being above mere humanity, in the same way as she is depicted as beyond gender. There is, moreover, a subtle irony here in the differing treatments of British and Roman 'victory'. While Boudica ('the victorious one') and Andraste, goddess of victory were, for the present, in the ascendant, in the run-up to the rebellion the Roman statue of Victory at Colchester apparently fell with 'its back turned as though it were fleeing the enemy'.[44] This proved to be a sinister omen of what was to befall the Romans at Boudica's hands.

A hatred of all things Roman

Indeed the gods gave them advance warning of the disaster: during the night a clamour of foreign voices mingled with laughter had been heard in the

5 ♦ Femmes fatales: Boudica and Cartimandua

council chamber and in the theatre uproar and lamentation, but it was no mortal who uttered those words and groans; houses were seen underwater in the river Thames, and the Ocean between the island of Britain and Gaul on one Occasion turned blood-red at high tide.

Tacitus *Histories*[45]

It was Venutius, husband and consort of Queen Cartimandua, who was described by Tacitus as harbouring 'a hatred of all things Roman' (see Figure 5.1). But such a phrase applied equally, if not more so, to Boudica. We should examine how and why she was turned from the consort of a pro-Roman client-king to an implacable foe who almost brought down the Roman government in Britain and nearly caused the emperor to abandon Britain altogether. The key to her attitude or, more strictly, her attitude as interpreted through the prism of authors from the classical world, may lie in her alleged speech to the Britons before she led her forces first against three Roman cities and then against Suetonius Paulinus's army. The 'speech' belongs to the well-known genre of fictional harangues created by writers for dramatic effect and, perhaps unwittingly, to express their own perceptions and attitudes. Boudica's speech, written

FIGURE 5.1 ♦ *'Romans go home!' graffito, on display in the Museum of London.*

Source: © The Museum of London.

by Dio,[46] has its counterpart in a monologue put into the mouth of Paulinus as he prepared to engage Boudica's forces in the final pitched battle.

We deal in the next chapter with the events immediately leading to the Boudican Rebellion and the course of the British war itself. But, in the context of examining the persona of Boudica herself, it is worth taking a close look at parts of her harangue of the British army, since it is used by Dio as a mouthpiece for expressing the downside of Roman imperialism, rather in the manner of Tacitus, and for presenting Boudica as a free and noble spirit, to be admired rather than despised. This is interesting, for there is a stark contrast between the historian's sympathetic treatment of her motives and his utter condemnation of her behaviour in Roman London, where she is presented in terms of total barbarity and inhuman cruelty. Dio compiles the speech in three sections, two referring to the past, the third to the future.[47] The first part is worth quoting in full, for it clearly presents the rationale behind the rebellion and allows us to understand the attitudes of some conquered provincials for whom the Roman way was far from the 'American Dream', albeit attitudes imposed upon the protesting Britons by a Graeco-Roman writer seeking to write as dramatically as possible and using old sources as his raw material. But it is worth pointing to the close resemblances between this Boudican 'speech' and Tacitus's creation of another British resistance-harangue, that of Calgacus at the time of Agricola's governorship of Britain.[48] The stock phrases concerning freedom, Roman oppression and British defiance against slavery are all present in both reported speeches.

Boudica allegedly began her harangue thus:

> *You have learned from actual experience what a difference there is between freedom and slavery. As a result, though some of you through your ignorance of which is better were previously deceived by the Romans' tempting promises, now at least you have tried them both and understand how great a mistake you made in preferring an imported tyranny to your ancestral way of life. You have realised how much better is poverty with no master than riches accompanied by slavery. For what great dishonour, what extreme of grief have we not suffered from the moment these Romans arrived in Britain? Have we not been entirely deprived of our most important possessions, and pay taxes on what is left? In addition to pasturing and tilling all our other property for them, do we not also pay an annual tax on our very bodies? How much better would it have been to be sold to masters once and for all, rather*

5 ♦ *Femmes fatales*: Boudica and Cartimandua

than to ransom ourselves every year and retain the empty name of freedom! How much better to have been slaughtered and perish than to go around with a tax on our heads! But why do I mention this? Not even death is free with them; you know how much we pay even for the dead. Among the rest of humanity death frees even those who are slaves; only among the Romans do the dead live for profit. Why is it that though we have no money – how could we have any, from what source? – we are stripped and despoiled like murder-victims? And why should they moderate their behaviour with the passage of time when they have treated us like this from the outset, a time when all men show some consideration even for the animals they have newly caught?[49]

Boudica here compares past with present, the blandishments of the occupying Romans when they first arrived in Britain and the surreptitious creep of oppression and, in particular, the crippling burden of taxation, presumably in both money and kind (corn and meat). There is a keen detestation of servitude in any form: that is the driving force of Boudica's hatred. We know from archaeological evidence, in the form of slave gang-chains,[50] that some late Iron Age Britons practised slavery (probably, for the most part, prisoners of war) (see Figure 5.2). We also have literary testimony: the first-century Greek geographer Strabo[51] refers to British exports of slaves to the classical world, along with hunting dogs and grain, while his contemporary, Diodorus Siculus, commented that the Gauls adored Mediterranean wine and would trade a slave for a single amphora-full.[52]

Tacitus records how, after the Boudican Rebellion, an imperial freedman, Polyclitus, was despatched from Rome to assess the damage done to Britain by the rebels themselves and by Paulinus's reprisals, both of which left the province in political and economic ruin. While Polyclitus, with his enormous retinue and the power of his close association with Nero, succeeded in overawing the Roman army, the Britons were unimpressed by his status as an ex-slave and scoffed that such a person should hold high office in the Roman government: 'The British marvelled that a general and an army who had completed such a mighty war should obey a slave'.[53] Clearly the nuances of freedman status were lost on a people for whom men and women were either free or unfree. Caesar, writing a century earlier, commented on the Gallic social hierarchy, stating that 'the common people are regarded almost as slaves'.[54]

The Britons' contempt for Polyclitus resonates strongly with an episode recorded by Dio at the time of the Claudian invasion in AD 43.

FIGURE 5.2 ◆ *Bronze amulet depicting a bound captive or slave, from Brough-under-Stainmore, Cumbria.*

Source: © Copyright the Trustees of The British Museum.

When Aulus Plautius, the first commander of the occupying force, assembled his army on the north-west coast of Gaul, the soldiers demurred at embarking for Britain, for they were reluctant to sail off the edge of the world, as they saw it. So Claudius sent his representative, an imperial freedman named Narcissus, to speak to the troops, who were so incensed at being addressed by one of slave status that they refused to allow him to open his mouth. But then their sense of the ridiculous restored their good humour: shouting 'Io Saturnalia', they agreed to follow Plautius's command.[55] This phrase refers to a winter festival in the Roman calendar, the Saturnalia, held in honour of Saturn, an ancient Italian god of agriculture, when slaves and their owners changed places for a day, masters waited on their servants and slaves wore the clothing of the free.

5 ♦ Femmes fatales: Boudica and Cartimandua

In her speech, Boudica makes much of the burdens of taxation visited upon the Iceni and the Trinovantes under Roman occupation. The taxes were imposed in order to maintain the army, the new Roman towns, like Verulamium and London, and such 'amenities' as the great temple of Claudius at Colchester, built and financed by Britons with loans from Romans like Seneca, the irony being that the British taxes were buying the symbols and realities of foreign domination. But we need to view such sentiments, as expressed in the speech, in the context of how internal British politics were conducted prior to the Roman invasion. In speaking of neighbouring Gaul, Julius Caesar makes the telling comment that the common people were crushed beneath tax burdens: 'Most of them, crushed by debt or heavy taxes or the oppression of more powerful men, pledge themselves to serve the nobles, who exercise over them the same rights as masters have over slaves'.[56] So the Gauls, and probably the Britons also, were already burdened with taxes as part of their indigenous class-system economy. Indeed, if we can believe Caesar's testimony and apply it to the British situation a hundred years later, Prasutagus and Boudica herself were involved in grinding the faces of the poor in their own tribe before the events of AD 60.

The second section of Boudica's speech analyses the reasons for British oppression by Rome. Here, Dio attributes to Boudica a nationalism that embraces the entire island of Britain:

> We allowed them [the Romans] to set foot upon our island in the first place, and did not immediately drive them out as once we did the famous Julius Caesar. We did not make even the attempt to set sail, a frightful prospect for them while they were still far away, as we did in the case of Augustus and Gaius Caligula. For this reason, though we inhabit so large an island, or rather a continent as it were, surrounded by the sea, and though we have a world of our own and are separated from all the rest of mankind by the Ocean to such an extent that people believe we live in another world under another sky, and some of them – the most erudite included – have hitherto not known for certain what we are called, yet we have been despised and trampled under foot by men who understand nothing except giving vent to their greed. But if we have not done so in the past, let us do our duty now, my countrymen, friends and kinsmen – for I consider you all my kinsmen inasmuch as you inhabit a single island and are called by one common name – now while we remember freedom, so may we bequeath it to our children both as a term and a reality. For if we forget altogether that happy state in which we grew up, what will they do who are reared on slavery?[57]

In reality, there is little evidence to suppose that Boudica was operating on a national scale. There is no mention, in either Dio or Tacitus, that the Iceni and Trinovantes teamed up with the discomfited Silures nor with disaffected elements among the Brigantes, and it seems to have been an exceptional circumstance that led even to collaboration between two neighbouring tribes, let alone any strong alliances further afield. Dio puts into the mouth of Boudica an awareness of a national identity, based on Britain's island status, because it makes a good story and enhances the tale of British rebellion to a grand scale, as though the whole of the province had risen up in arms against their colonial oppressors. The reality is that much of southern Britain, including the lands belonging to Togidubnus (see Chapter 3), remained loyal to the Romans, and we know that Cartimandua's kingdom also stood firm, despite the anti-Roman sympathies of Venutius.

The remainder of Boudica's speech, as invented by Dio, says a great deal about the supposed polarity between the 'noble savages', as represented by Boudica and her people on the one hand and the decadent Romans on the other. Thus the Britons were seen as tough, used to enduring hardship and living off the land, whereas the Romans were soft, too accustomed to easy living and could not cope if they were cold, hungry or deprived of their wine and olive oil. Britain itself is depicted as a world of rugged terrain totally alien to the intruders: mountainous, boggy and full of icy, swift-flowing rivers. Dio makes the Icenian leader allude to the Romans scornfully as hares, while her Britons were dogs and wolves.[58] The reference to hares as timid, hunted animals[59] is the more interesting since, in the next passage, the author describes a divinatory rite enacted by Boudica that involved the release of a hare in honour of Andraste, goddess of victory.[60] (We will see in following chapters that both hares and wolves were significant creatures for the Britons.)

The other striking element in Boudica's alleged harangue is her persistent reference to gender, and particularly to inverted gender. We have an intimation of this in her scornful allusion to the softness (and implied effeminacy) of Roman soldiers, who needed to eat kneaded bread, who sought shelter from the sun and wore copious protective body armour.[61] In the following passage, she (or rather Dio) is more forthright in voicing contempt for effete Roman customs and especially that of the imperial house:

5 ◆ Femmes fatales: Boudica and Cartimandua

I thank you, Andraste, and I call upon you woman to woman, not as one who rules over Egyptians with their burdens as Nitoctis did, nor over Assyrian traders as did Semiramis – this much we have learned from the Romans – nor yet indeed as one ruling over the Romans themselves, as once Messalina did, then Agrippina and now Nero – for though he has the title of man, he is in fact a woman, as his singing and playing the lyre and painted face declare – but as one who rules over Britons who have no knowledge of tilling the earth or working with their hands, but are experts in the art of war and hold all things in common, even their wives and children. Through this the women too possess the same valour as the men. As queen, then, of such men and women, I pray to you and ask for victory, safety and freedom from men who are insolent, unjust, insatiable and impious – if indeed we ought to call them men when they bathe in warm water, eat fancy food, drink unmixed wine, smear themselves with myrrh, sleep on soft beds with boys – boys past their prime at that – and are slaves to a lyre-player – and a bad one at that. May this woman, Domitia Nero, reign no longer over me or you men; rather let her lord it over the Romans with her singing; for they deserve to be slaves to such a woman, whose tyranny they have put up with for so long. For us on the other hand may you alone, Lady, for ever be our leader.[62]

So for Boudica/Dio, British women are as good as men, but the Romans are to be derided because they are ruled by a man/woman and the Romans themselves behave like pampered females, while Boudica and her sisters act like men. There is a mixed message there, or is there? What seems to be revealed is that male attributes were valued. Boudica does not extol the virtue of women as women but of women as men.

Red queen, white queen

In the council chamber, known as the Moot Hall, at the top of the splendid town hall building in the centre of Colchester, there are three large Edwardian stained-glass windows commemorating British monarchs who had a special impact upon the history of the town (see also Chapter 9:and Plate 25). The middle window is dedicated to the queens and was presented by the Ladies of the Borough under the aegis of Emily Sanders, Mayoress 1898–9 and President of the Committee in 1900. The large central roundel depicts Queen Victoria and around the edges of the window are smaller portraits of other powerful female monarchs, all with their names inscribed beneath them, including Eleanor of Aquitaine and Queen Elizabeth I. The portrait at bottom right depicts 'Boadicea':

Boudica is shown as a young warrior-queen, with flowing reddish-gold tresses, a diadem around her head, a gold necklace around her throat, a purplish-red mantle swathes her shoulders and her spear is at the ready, waiting to attack the Roman *colonia* of Colchester. There is no picture of Cartimandua, the other earliest known British queen in the Moot Hall at Colchester, because she was associated with dishonour and trickery rather than courage and patriotic pride. Boudica bequeathed to posterity qualities of freedom, courage and fierce independence, the very essence of being British; conversely, Cartimandua, portrayed by Tacitus as a treacherous adulteress, utterly dependent on Rome and held in contempt even by her subjects, has faded from memory and never had a chance of becoming an immortal icon like her sister-queen.

Boudica was a red queen, described as red-headed or golden-haired by Dio. She wore a blazing gold torc and a brightly coloured cloak, her name was linked with battle, she wrought carnage in the new Roman towns of Britain, she conducted bloody rituals in sacred groves and sought honour by the sword. But Cartimandua is depicted as a contrasting pale shadow, a 'shining pony', sleek with prosperity and sexual gratification, a beast of a woman who played out her conquests in bed rather than on the battlefield, who presented a lily-livered slavishness in choosing Roman patronage rather than British independence and captured the great British freedom-fighter Caratacus by deception.[63] Although Cartimandua was a Roman ally, Tacitus presents her in a far less favourable light than Boudica, and it is clear that he despised her, despite the fact that, had she supported the great rebellion of AD 60, Rome indeed might have lost Britain altogether. Boudica died in action, Cartimandua in a comfortable retirement, perhaps in Rome. Boudica's imagery is that of a wild but honest enemy, Cartimandua as tamed, but capricious. Our sympathies (and, interestingly, those of her Roman enemies) are with the red queen, fighting for freedom against slavery under Rome and thus gaining immortality, rather than with the white queen who chose the easy way and has been erased from British memory.

Notes and references

1 Dio Cassius *Roman History* 62.1; trans. Ireland 1996, 63

2 Tacitus *Annals* 12.40; after Braund 1996, 129

5 ♦ *Femmes fatales*: Boudica and Cartimandua

3 Norwich Castle Museum; Carr 2001, 112–24; Carr 2005.

4 It is interesting, however, that archaeological evidence from the three cities (see Chapter 7) suggests not wholesale destruction but a much more patchy picture, in which certain buildings or areas seem to have been targeted, others left alone.

5 A term taken from a series of articles in Victorian newspapers attacking a new women's movement, which sought to breach the traditional bastions of male preserves in public life, including art: Nunn 1995; Aldhouse-Green 2003, 115.

6 Vellacott 1973, 191–244.

7 Green 1997b, 898–911. For privileges enjoyed by Vestals, see Plutarch, *Life of Numa* 9–10; Ferguson 1980, 57–58.

8 Kampen 1994; 1996; Lyons & Koloski-Ostrow 1997; Rodgers 2003.

9 Bartman 1999, xxi.

10 Tacitus *Annals* 15.51–7.

11 Op. cit. 15.57.

12 Braund 1996, 132.

13 Seneca *Apocolocyntosis* 12.13–18; after Braund 1996, 125.

14 It is worth noting that long after the eventual Roman subjugation of the Brigantes, an eponymous goddess, Brigantia, personification of the region, was venerated in the North. She appears, for instance on an inscribed monument at Birrens in Dumfriesshire, looking remarkably like Britannia on Victorian pennies, with spear and shield: Green 1995, pl. on p. 197.

15 Tacitus *Annals* 12.32; trans. Grant 1956, 256.

16 Webster 1980, 113.

17 Tacitus *Annals* 12.36; trans Grant 1956, 258.

18 Braund 1996, 127.

19 Moore 1954, 46.

20 Tacitus *Annals* 12.40.

21 Op. cit. 12.40; after Braund 1996, 129.

22 Ross 1967, 356. For a discussion of various early Celtic-language words for horses and ponies, see Kelly 1997, 43–63, especially 52–3, which refer specifically to 'mandu' as a term used for young animals in ancient Gaulish.

23 Aldhouse-Green & Aldhouse-Green 2005.

24 Green 1997c; Davies 1997; Wood 1997.

25 Webster & Dudley 1966, 160.

26 Tacitus *Annals* 12.40
27 E.g. Suetonius *Life of Claudius* 36; Tacitus *Annals* 11.25.
28 Tacitus *Histories* 3.45; trans. Wellesley 1964, 172.
29 Haselgrove 2002; 2004, 23.
30 Niblett 2004, 36; Fitts *et al.* 1999.
31 Todd 2004, 53.
32 Haselgrove 2004, 13.
33 Tacitus *Agricola* 31; trans. Mattingly 1948, 81.
34 Dio Cassius *Roman History* 62.2; trans. Ireland 1996, 63–70.
35 See Watts 2005, 92, 95 for archaeological evidence for Boudica's appearance and clothing.
36 Millar 1964, 4–27.
37 Op. cit. 19.
38 Op. cit. 149.
39 Op. cit., 35.
40 Op. cit. 43.
41 Dio Cassius *Roman History* 62.7.
42 Webster 1978, 15; Ross 1967, 360.
43 Dio Cassius *Roman History* 62.7.
44 Tacitus *Annals* 14.31; trans. Grant 1956, 318.
45 Tacitus *Histories* 3.45.
46 Dio Cassius *Roman History* 62.3–5.
47 Op. cit. 62.3–5.
48 Tacitus *Agricola* 30–3.
49 Dio Cassius *Roman History* 62.3; trans. Ireland 1996, 63–70.
50 Aldhouse-Green 2004c.
51 Strabo *Geography* 4.5.2.
52 Diodorus *Library of History* 5.26.3.
53 Tacitus *Annals* 14.39.
54 Caesar *De Bello Gallico* 6. 13; trans. Wiseman & Wiseman 1980, 120.
55 Dio Cassius *Roman History* 60.19.
56 Caesar *De Bello Gallico* 6.13.
57 Dio Cassius *Roman History* 62.4.

5 ◆ Femmes fatales: Boudica and Cartimandua

58 Op. cit. 62.5.
59 For a new discussion on the symbolism of hares, particularly in spring time, see Mason 2005; Page 2005.
60 Dio *Roman History* 62.6.
61 Op. cit. Dio 62.5.
62 Op. cit. 62.6; trans. Ireland 1996, 63–70.
63 Webster 1981, 32. Incidentally, Caratacus is depicted on another of the Edwardian stained-glass windows at Colchester Town Hall as a British king of whom the town could be proud: plate 7.

CHAPTER 6

The role of the Druids in Boudica's Rebellion

The enemy lined the shore in a dense armed mass. Among them were black-robed women with dishevelled hair like Furies, brandishing torches. Close by stood Druids, raising their hands to heaven and screaming dreadful curses. This weird spectacle awed the Roman soldiers into a sort of paralysis. They stood still – and presented themselves as a target. But then they urged each other (and were urged by the general) not to fear a horde of fanatical women. Onward pressed their standards and they bore down on their opponents, enveloping them in the flames of their own torches. Suetonius garrisoned the conquered island. The groves devoted to Mona's barbarous superstitions he demolished. For it was their religion to drench their altars in the blood of prisoners and consult their gods by means of human entrails.

Tacitus Annals[1]

Tacitus's *Annals* presents this vivid account of the reception committee awaiting Suetonius Paulinus's Roman army, massed on the coast of North Wales and preparing to cross to the sacred British island of Mona (Anglesey) to destroy the Druids and their *locus sanctissimus* (holiest of holy places) there. It is my contention that the island, its Druids and its Roman enemies played a crucial role in the unfolding drama of the Boudican Rebellion.

In Book VI of his *de Bello Gallico* ('about the Gallic War'), written while on campaign in Gaul in the 50s BC, Julius Caesar digressed from war news and mused upon the political structure, customs and religious practices of the peoples whose lands he was busy adding to the Roman

Empire. One social group that clearly impressed him were the Druids whom, he says, enjoyed virtually the same status as those he called *Equites* (Knights), the noblemen who were close to the chief himself. Caesar describes with considerable respect the wide-ranging responsibilities of the Druids, their complete control over religious matters, the esteem they enjoyed, and their role as instructors of young upper-class men. He goes on to comment on their judicial powers, their exemption from war-service and taxation and the secrecy of their doctrine.[2] He remarks that their influence was so great that if, because of disobedience to their rule, they banned a particular individual from attendance at sacrificial rituals, that miscreant became a total outcast, an 'unperson' condemned to exist outside his community. This is not the place to describe the Druids in detail: they are not the main protagonists in this drama although, as we shall see, they may have played a crucial part in fomenting the rebellion led by Boudica in AD 60.[3] But one comment by Caesar is of especial significance for our story, a casual reference to the origins of the Druids: 'It is said that the doctrine of the Druids was invented in Britain and was brought from there into Gaul; even today those who want to study the doctrine in greater detail usually go to Britain to learn there'.[4]

Caesar's claim for a British *fons et origo* for the Druids is important, because it firmly situates the Druids in Britain in the mid-first century BC, and thus contributes a backdrop to Tacitus's description of the Druids on Anglesey at the time of the Boudican Rebellion. A further observation by Caesar serves to place the Druids in the sphere of military action and, by implication, at the very heart of freedom movements. For he says 'The Druids attach particular importance to the belief that the soul does not perish but passes after death from one body to another; they think that this belief is the most effective way to encourage bravery because it removes the fear of death'.[5] This is blatant Druidic spin-doctoring: a cynical manipulation of the population by preaching everlasting life to the noble warrior who died in battle. It was also a highly dangerous form of propaganda, for it encouraged a selfless bravado, an eagerness to sacrifice oneself for the cause, an attitude of mind that resonates uneasily with some of the world's present-day troublespots.[6] The issues raised in this chapter concern the Druids as agitators, foci for resistance and perpetrators of rebellion. Such discussion provides a context for one of the greatest uprisings in the history of the Roman Empire, that led by Boudica. It is my belief that the Druids were at least partly responsible for the orchestration of disaffection that led to this cataclysmic event.

The Druids as *agents provocateurs* in the western Roman provinces

The Druids, too, took advantage of the armistice to resume the barbarous rites of their wicked religion.

Lucan *Pharsala*[7]

For the principate of Tiberius Caesar did away with Their Druids and that class of seers and doctors.

Pliny *Natural History*[8]

The introduction of *romanitas*[9] to western Europe did more harm to Druidism than any concerted Roman campaign designed to annihilate them, for it struck at the very roots of their power base, by replacing the old social order with a new one based less on ancestral aristocracies than on values associated with becoming Roman, particularly in the 'power houses' of south-east England. There, tribal structures were being altered from the time of Caesar and were severely damaged during the ensuing Claudian campaigns. In the second place, *romanitas* brought with it a package of religious belief and expression that presented a serious challenge to the status quo of Druidic supremacy in the first centuries BC and AD in Gaul and Britain. The Druids rightly felt that their *locus* within society, even their continued existence, were being threatened. So we have a situation in which a priesthood, under pressure, was being edged out, both physically (towards the far west) and metaphorically. Once the Roman way had a firm footing in Gaul and Britain, we hear much less about the Druids from classical writers: indeed, they get the most air-time – from authors such as Tacitus and Pliny – during the period of direct clashes between the indigenous populations and the Roman army or government. In the literature at least, they became a spent force once *romanitas* had embedded itself in the western world. However, when rebellion in the Gallic provinces sporadically broke out during the first century AD, native religious functionaries were clearly involved.[10]

Let us initially scrutinise the Gallic revolt that took place in AD 21, in the reign of Tiberius, led by Julius Florus and Julius Sacrovir, chieftains

6 ◆ The role of the Druids in Boudica's Rebellion

of the Treveri (in the Moselle Valley) and the Aedui (Burgundy) respectively;[11] they were Gallic aristocrats whose ancestors, as Roman allies, had earned them and their descendants the coveted prize of Roman citizenship. Tacitus gives the reason for the rebellion as being the crippling burden of debt laid on them by the Roman government.[12] This is precisely the scenario that contributed in major part to the decision of the Trinovantes to join Boudica's rebel army 40 years later: we are specifically told that the business tycoon Seneca suddenly called in his high-interest-rate loans to the Britons (we don't know why) and, what was more, this tribe had to shoulder the burden of maintaining the imperial cult, its temple and its priests at Colchester, their own tribal capital.[13] Although Tacitus does not spell out the involvement of the Druids per se, it is highly significant that one of the rebel leaders was named Sacrovir, for the name literally means 'holy man'. It may therefore be that this individual was a priest, perhaps a Druid, or that he adopted this name in order to make a statement concerning the linkages between the secular and the sacred, in the context of what might have been perceived as some kind of holy war, in other words what, for the Muslim world, might be called a jihad.[14]

Florus and his Treverans were quickly overcome by Roman forces in the Ardennes Forest, but Sacrovir and his Aeduans were more robust in their bid for freedom: their army had the advantage that many of their soldiers had been trained and equipped in the Roman fashion. Sacrovir occupied the Roman *civitas* capital of the Aedui at Augustodunum (Autun) and won over a group of young Gallic noblemen who were there learning to become Romans, first by taking them hostage for their parents' good behaviour and then winning their hearts and minds. But they, too, were defeated by Tiberius's forces and, like Florus before him, Sacrovir committed suicide. Despite their victories, the activities of Florus and Sacrovir had given the Romans a bad fright, undermining their confidence about the security of the western Empire, sending shock-waves through the city's population, and threatening to destabilise the imperial regime itself. Indeed, Tacitus comments that:

> At Rome it was said that not the Treveri and the Aedui alone but all the sixty-four peoples of Gaul had revolted, that the Germans had joined them, and the Spanish provinces were wavering. As usual, rumour magnified everything. Every respectable Roman deplored his country's difficulties. But

many disliked the existing regime and hoped for change so greatly that they even welcomed danger for themselves.

Tacitus *Annals*[15]

The second, perhaps more significant revolt took place soon after Nero's death and the chaos of the 'Year of the Four Emperors' (AD 69). This was the rebellion of Julius Civilis, who belonged to the Batavian tribe which, according to Tacitus, had been a sub-group within the Germanic federation of the Chatti, who lived on the east bank of the Rhine. Tacitus recounts how – at the time of the events he was chronicling – the Batavians had broken away from their master polity, driven out because of 'domestic dissensions'. They then 'occupied the uninhabited fringe of Gaul on the lower reaches of the river, together with the neighbouring 'Island' which is washed by the North Sea on the west, and on the other three sides by the Rhine'.[16] Despite his royal descent and the loyalty the Batavians had shown to Rome, Civilis was seized on a 'trumped-up charge of rebellion' and sent in chains to the Emperor Nero. He was released but got into further trouble under one of the short-lived AD 69 emperors, Vitellius, and so decided to foment rebellion. On the face of it, this is another example of Roman blundering analogous to what happened to Boudica and her daughters in AD 60.

During the battles that had raged between the would-be successors to Nero in 69, the Capitol at Rome had been burned. The Capitoline Hill was the religious heart of the city and the empire, so its destruction symbolised something very fundamental both to Romans and to the populations of the western provinces. The Gauls and Germans, some of whom sat uneasily under the Roman yoke, as we have seen, were especially interested in these cataclysmic events, predicting the imminent collapse of the empire, and it is here that the Druids emerged as whippers-up of sedition.

But it was above all the burning of the Capitol that had driven men to the belief that the empire's days were numbered. They reflected that Rome had been captured by the Gauls in the past, but as the house of Jupiter remained inviolate, the empire had survived. Now, however, fate had ordained this fire as a sign of the gods' anger and of the passing of world dominion to the nations north of the Alps. Such at any rate was the message proclaimed by the idle superstition of Druidism.

Tacitus *Histories*[17]

Jane Webster has interpreted this kind of prediction as part of a wider revitalisation movement taking place within the Roman Empire as a whole, a sense of the opportunity to rise up in active protest against colonial oppression.[18] In presenting this argument, Webster cites such scholars as MacMullen[19] and Adas,[20] both of whom suggest that the 'accelerated change' experienced by freshly colonised people, such as the Gauls and the Britons, was likely to have led to their loss of spiritual and personal identities and so provided a vacuum that could be filled by indigenous prophets. In this way, the Druids – by predicting disaster for the colonising powers – sought to regain the influence they had lost through conquest and the imposition of the new order. It is well known, too, that prophets are particularly vocal at times of crisis, and prophecies about the weakness of enemies, for instance, serve to comfort, to reassure and to exhort.[21]

The link between Civilis and religious practitioners, such as the Druids, was crystallised by ensuing events that unfolded as the rebellion progressed, for Tacitus described Civilis's liaison with the priestess Veleda who, though not named as a Druid, nonetheless shared much of their power, as prophetess and adviser of rulers (see also Chapter 4). She had rightly predicted the defeat of Roman forces at the hands of Civilis and had thus gained a great deal of 'street cred' as a successful seer.[22] Although Tacitus (as a republican) had shown some sympathy with Civilis (as with Florus and Sacrovir before him), we can detect a distinct change in the writer's attitude once the Batavian began to destroy Roman forces in the field. Now the German rebel leader is described as being a savage barbarian, a 'primitive savage', who had dyed his hair red (to symbolise the business of shedding blood) and grown his beard as part of a sworn oath to leave it uncut until the legions had been smashed: he had now shaved it off in honour of his victories. Tacitus blackens his character further by recounting an allegation that Civilis had handed over some Roman prisoners of war to his little son 'to serve as targets for the child's arrows and spears'. Civilis was ultimately defeated by Petillius Cerialis, but the Romans had learned a hard lesson, namely not to underestimate the potential for revolt in the west, a lesson they had already experienced in Britain with Boudica.

Britain and the Druids

> But why should I speak of these things when the craft [of Druidism] has even crossed the Ocean and reached the empty voids of nature? Even today Britain

practises magic in awe, with such grand ritual that it might seem that she gave it to the Persians.

Pliny *Natural History*[23]

Thus wrote Pliny the Elder more than a hundred years later than Caesar's comment about the British origins of Druidism. Indeed, the younger author appears to contradict him. But this discrepancy matters less than what Pliny is saying about Roman attitudes to both Britain and the Druids: both were beyond the pale, outside the boundaries of civilisation; each belonged to 'the empty voids of nature'. While Caesar speaks of the Druids with considerable respect, Pliny was writing within the context of serious Roman engagement with Britain, as an annexed Roman province within which the weird practices of Druids were perceived to have no place. Pliny comments with scorn on British magic, comparing ritual behaviour on the outer rim of the known world in the West with that of the Persians, who lived beyond the eastern edge of 'civilisation'.

It is time to revisit the passage from Tacitus's *Annals* with which this chapter opened, for we now have a context in which to situate both the event it records, its *dramatis personae* and the attitude of the author. On the face of it none of this is concerned with Boudica but the timing of the Anglesey campaign is highly significant, for it took place at almost exactly the same time as the Icenian rebel leader's push for British freedom. So, is it possible to establish connections between what was going on in the far north-west of Britain and the south-east, where Boudica was whipping up sedition, gathering military forces and preparing to sack the three Roman towns of Colchester, Verulamium and London? The answer is yes, not least because while the Roman governor and most of his army was away fighting Druids on a remote island, the fledgling province of Britain was left unprotected. Suetonius Paulinus's action was extraordinary: it seems to us utter folly to turn his back on a very recently pacified Britain in order to crush a few religious fanatics guarding a sacred grove. So we need to unpick this and see what exactly was going on. I think that the destruction of the Druids on Mona created an enormous psychological impact that far outweighed strictly military or political consequences. If this were the case, then Druidism must still have presented a very real threat to the stability of Britain as a conquered province and establishment of the *pax romana* there. Not only must the continued – and disaffected – presence of the Druids in Britain have been cause for serious concern to the Roman administration, but their potential for acting as foci for rebellion in continental Gaul (by providing a rallying point and refuge for Gaulish dissidents) was almost certainly in Nero's thoughts when he sanctioned Suetonius Paulinus's activities in North Wales. Indeed, a close reading of Tacitus's text shows that this was exactly what was in Paulinus's mind: 'So Suetonius planned to attack the Island of Mona, which although thickly populated had also given sanctuary to many refugees'.[24]

We need to consider critically Tacitus's message in the above-quoted passage. Here, despite his republican and thus anti-imperial political persuasion, the writer gives the Druids – and the Britons generally – a bad press. So, although elsewhere in his work he appears to side with the 'noble savage' model of the Britons, yet in recording this particular episode, he presents the occupants of the holy island as given to wild disorder, immoderacy and barbarism. In describing the nature of the enemy faced by Paulinus's men, Tacitus specifically mentions three distinct groups of opponents: warriors, women (whom he describes scornfully and misogynistically as a ' horde of fanatical women') and Druids (see Plate 16). If Caesar's words (a hundred years earlier) still held good for AD 60, the Druids themselves, exempt from bearing arms, were unlikely to have formed the 'dense armed mass' alluded to by Tacitus. So we should assume the presence of a strong British garrison, either stationed permanently on the island to protect the shrine or, more likely, hastily assembled to deal with this particular crisis. We may even imagine that the island's defenders were gathered from a wide area in order to make up numbers.

The presence of the women as part of the British defence corps on Anglesey is interesting: they were clearly not Druids themselves, for Tacitus makes a definite distinction between the 'Furies' and the Druids, but were probably religious officials of some sort. Other writers, such as the Greek geographer Strabo and the Roman Pomponius Mela, tell us that women were heavily involved in ritual, particularly sacrificial practice that sometimes involved religious murder. Mela speaks of nine virgin priestesses on one of the Scilly Isles.[25] Strabo gives us a chilling account of auto-sacrifice among a group of priestesses, whom he called the Samnitae, inhabiting a women-only island community, this time in the estuary of the river Loire.[26] Speaking about an annual temple-ceremony, he says:

> *It is their custom once a year to remove the roof from their temple and to roof it again by the same day before sunset, each woman carrying part of the burden; but the woman whose load falls from her is torn to bits by the others, and they carry the pieces around the temple crying out 'euoi', and do not cease until their madness passes away; and it always happens that someone pushes against the woman who is destined to suffer this fate.*

Both Mela's and Strabo's accounts are interesting for they record female ritualists on sacred islands, thus presenting a broadly analogous situation to Anglesey. Islands may have been considered special because they consisted of isolated pieces of land surrounded by water. Certainly in early Irish mythology, islands were regarded as entrances to the Otherworld or even as part of the Otherworld itself. Early Christian Welsh saints, like Dwynwen, on Llanddwyn Island, off Anglesey,[27] might occupy holy islands and the Irish hero Bran undertook a voyage to the 'Isles of the Blest', inhabited by women.[28] Strabo's description of the bloodthirsty Samnitae also resonates with the British situation on Mona because of Tacitus's reference to 'the blood of prisoners' and the consultation of the gods 'by means of human entrails'. Elsewhere in his *Geography* (as we saw in Chapter 4) Strabo makes reference to elderly priestesses among the Cimbri (who inhabited northern Germany and southern Denmark) associated with human sacrifice of war-captives, the purpose of which, as on Mona, was to predict the future by examining the guts of the victims.[29] This kind of prognosticatory activity is precisely the same as the ritual practices of the Romans themselves, except that they used the innards of animals rather than people. Indeed, one of the most prominent religious practitioners in the Roman religious system was the *Haruspex*, the 'gut-gazer', who enthusiastically studied livers and other 'delectable' animal viscerae and proclaimed the will of the gods. We know of one Memor from Britain, who lived at Bath and who dedicated a statue to the presiding goddess Sulis.[30] The presence of female ritualists in Britain is relevant to our study of Boudica, for Dio Cassius records that she was involved in religious activity, both in her release of a hare in the sacred grove of Andraste before battle and in her shocking 'sacrifice' of the women of London.[31]

Tacitus provides information on two other aspects of Mona's holy women: the state of their hair and their possession of torches, whirled about like weapons. Their dishevelled locks reminded Tacitus of the classical Furies, ghastly creatures of myth that delighted in the gory disasters of the battlefield. But the hair also has further significance in that its dishevelled state was the classic symbol of mourning. Anglesey's religious women were not only defending the holy of holies, but were, in a sense, presaging its failure, bemoaning the potential loss of political and religious freedom and the downfall of sacred autonomy for Britain. The torches are interesting, too, for their presence suggests the murky gloom of the sacred grove, and one wonders, too, whether the attack might have taken place in the dim light of dawn, like so many historically recorded battles.[32] Second, it may be that the torches symbolised fire, not simply as a destructive force but as a symbol of the sacred: we know from both literary and archaeological evidence that the Gauls and Britons worshipped a god of thunder and lightning, called Taranis.[33]

The final, and most important group of Britons confronting Suetonius Paulinus and his army on the shore of Anglesey consisted of the Druids themselves, whose one contribution to the event seems to have been the screeching of imprecations on the sacrilegious Roman army. This is itself significant, in terms of what the Druids were about, since cursing was an important part of their function and 'word power' would have been considered extremely potent, just as it has been in many traditional shamanistic societies.[34] Indeed, we have numerous examples of curse tablets, *defixiones*, from such Gallo-Roman and Romano-British sanctuaries, as Bath and Uley in the west of England.[35] These were presumably written, or at least overseen, by religious practitioners, even Druids; and we have Caesar's statement about the potency of Druidic displeasure, cursing, excommunication and spiritual exile.[36] In early historical Irish mythic texts, Druids and Bards, such as Amairgin (his very name means 'Wonderful Mouth') had the power literally to scorch people with satirical speech.[37] For classical chroniclers, the Druids were inextricably bound up with sacred groves. Indeed, Jane Webster has suggested that the association between holy groves and the Druids was a dynamic phenomenon relating to the secrecy within which the priesthood was forced to operate, once successive Roman emperors tried to eradicate it from Gaul and Britain.[38] She argues that in earlier periods their religious practices were undertaken in open-air sanctuaries, in the full public gaze, whereas later Druids had recourse to hidden forest shrines. I am not sure about this: my view is that secrecy and exclusivity were part and parcel of what

Druidism was all about. After all, Caesar remarks that the Gaulish Druids were keen to avoid writing down their doctrines:

> They do not think it right to commit their teachings to writing ... I suppose this practice began originally for two reasons: they did not want their doctrines to be accessible to the ordinary people, and they did not want their pupils to rely on the written word and so neglect to train their memories.[39]

Knowledge is power, and there is plenty of evidence from the classical world that priests jealously guarded that knowledge. For example, we know that both Athenian and Roman priests were in charge of the sacred calendars that recorded the correct day for conducting ceremonies and sacrificial rites and that these were kept secret.[40] The use of sacred groves by the Druids is not simply because they provided secluded, hidden spaces but that the very trees themselves were charged with spirit-force. In describing the sacred grove outside the city of Massilia, encountered by Caesar's army in 48 BC on their way to confront Pompey's forces, Lucan recounts the fear with which Caesar's legionaries regarded the holy forest and the rotting wooden images of the gods carved from the trees.[41] Lucan says that even the priest of the grove was frightened of the supernatural power lurking in the wood.

Mona's sacred grove and its Druids has direct relevance to Boudica herself in so far as Dio specifically refers to a similar *locus sanctus* in south-east England, where the Icenian ruler conducted prognosticatory rites and human sacrifice. Boudica's grove was dedicated to Andraste, goddess of victory and, in a sense, she may have been seen as the divine aspect of Boudica herself, for the queen's name incorporates the epithet 'bouda' meaning victory. Dio does not tell us whether Druids were present here; his account suggests that Boudica herself took charge of the rituals. She may even, like the Aeduan chieftain Diviciacus, Caesar's ally and Cicero's acquaintance, have been a Druid herself.

Archaeology and the British Druids

In seeking to establish linkages between Mona's Druids, whose clash with the Romans in AD 60 was virtually simultaneous with the events led by Boudica, the evidence of material culture is of vital importance. I shall argue that the proximity of the two episodes, in time – the destruction of the island sanctuary and the Boudican Rebellion – were by no means coincidental, but that the fulcrum upon which both events pivoted was the influence of the Druids. Archaeology can tell us a great deal that classical writers, like Tacitus, omit, usually because they were interested in broad political and military manoeuvres rather than the detail of provincial life. We need to scrutinise the material remains of the period in question to ascertain the nature of evidence for Druidical or cognate activity, both in North Wales and in Boudica's territory.

Two pieces of archaeological evidence may be especially relevant to the sanctity of Anglesey in the late Iron Age and early Roman periods: the ritual deposit from Llyn Cerrig Bach, on Mona itself, and the bog body from Lindow Moss in Cheshire. In 1943, during Second World War work on the airfield at RAF Valley in the west of Anglesey, workmen discovered a large group of metalwork – bronze and iron – including two massive iron chains in a marsh pool known as Llyn Cerrig Bach.[42] (see Plate 15). Having no notion of the assemblage's antiquity, they proceeded to use one of the chains to haul out a lorry stuck in the mud: the chain held and pulled the vehicle clear. The two chains turned out to be slave gang-chains, each fitted with five collars, for transporting felons or other prisoners across country. With them was a range of chariot fittings, including iron wheel tyres, blacksmithing tools, military equipment and sacred regalia. Some of the bronzework was exquisitely decorated with complex, swirling, semi-abstract designs that belong to a style known as La Tène,[43] that was circulating all over non-Mediterranean Europe in the later first millennium BC, though with considerable regional variation. The date range for the manufacture of these objects is second century BC to first century AD. The deposit was cast into the bog from a low but sheer cliff, and there is debate as to whether the material was placed here in one episode or, as the uncorroded condition of the metal makes more likely, was the result of repeated acts of votive offering. Importantly, most of the Llyn Cerrig Bach assemblage consists of high-status objects, suggesting that the appeasement of the gods was ensured by appropriately valuable items, and that the devotees were themselves of high rank. Metalwork was not the only material deposited here: when the site was excavated, little cognisance was taken of a group of animal bones from the site, but the remains of some domestic species were found, perhaps representing the sacrifice of beasts. In recent new research on the Llyn Cerrig material and the National Museum of Wales archive, Phil

Macdonald suggests that human remains were also recovered from the marsh but that, in the context of Second World War patriotism, the knowledge of their discovery was suppressed lest Britain be seen as less than highly civilised![44]

The nature of the offerings and the richness of the deposit at Llyn Cerrig Bach are unique in Britain and argue for very special and formalised ritual behaviour, probably orchestrated by local 'clergy'. Its location, on a remote island off the edge of North Wales, suggests that it may have been a place of pilgrimage, of visitations, perhaps from a wide area over a long period of time. The high status represented by the metalwork is enhanced by the specifically ceremonial character of objects, such as a fragmentary trumpet and part of what was probably a sceptre. The horse and chariot gear and the martial equipment evoke the presence of knights, the noble elite of Britain, and the smithing tools speak of the ironworker's skill – skill that could produce superb wrought-iron tyres that could be shrunk on to the wooden wheel-rim to create a perfect fit, and chains that, 2000 years after they were made, could be used for heavy haulage (see Plate 17). Two bronze cauldrons were deposited with the hoard and they, too, reflect high-status feasting and collective ritual.[45] The gang-chains represent a society with an underclass of slaves, prisoners of war or criminals. It has been suggested that slave chains like these may not have been purely utilitarian objects but were, perhaps, used for the transport of human sacrificial prisoners, the remains of some of whom might have been found in 1943.[46] All this means that there was certainly an important natural sanctuary at a spiritually charged bog pool on Mona before and during the time of the Roman threat to the island chronicled by Tacitus. We cannot locate a shrine for Tacitus within Anglesey but, given the small size of the island, it is not impossible that Llyn Cerrig and the Tacitean Druidic sanctuary are connected.

In August 1984 workers for a commercial peat-extraction company at Lindow Moss in Cheshire discovered a long object they thought was a piece of wood. It turned out to be a human foot and part of a lower leg; the next day more of the body was found: it was Lindow Man (Lindow II).[47] Thought at first to have been the victim of a modern murder, the body was dated by radiocarbon in the British Museum and was found to be ancient, probably of the period of the Roman conquest in the middle of the first century AD. The bogs of north-west Europe have revealed many ancient bodies, their exceptional state of preservation arising from a combination of bog acids and of the airless conditions, which inhibit the development of bacteria and therefore of decay. So, skin, flesh, internal organs and hair thousands of years old will often survive, even though the acidic environment sometimes eats away the bones. The Cheshire body was that of a young man, about 25 years old, naked but for an armlet made of fox fur. He had not died by wandering into the marsh and drowning, for multiple signs of violence were identifiable from the well-preserved soft tissue: he had been beaten about the head so severely that his skull was fractured, garrotted with a leather rope and his throat had been cut. Indeed, the strangulation and bloodletting may well have occurred as part of a single act, thereby causing the arterial blood to spurt up in a fountain as he choked and died.

So who was Lindow Man? Why was he killed? Was the location of his burial significant? It is thought that the young man was someone of high status, despite the absence of grave-goods and clothing, for his body was well-nourished, his finger nails were carefully manicured and his hair and beard neatly trimmed with shears (expensive toilet instruments that appeared for the first time in the late Iron Age and seem to have contributed to a new concern for the presentation of the body among high-ranking Britons).[48] Like another, later, Lindow victim, who died in about AD 100,[49] his body seems to have been painted with a greenish-blue paint. In his mid-twenties, he was of prime fighting age, yet he appears not to have died an honourable death in battle but rather to have been subjected to a humiliating death. The multiple modes of dispatch suggest something other than murder, but instead indicate either that he was executed or that he was the victim of a ritual, sacrificial killing. The precise location of his deposition may have been meaningful from more than one perspective: first, his were not the only human remains to have been found here: another man had been consigned to the same piece of bog minus his head; and the head of a woman was also interred here. The headless man (Lindow III) could have died about a half a century later than Lindow Man himself, and the woman perhaps 50 years later again.[50] So we are dealing with a small burial ground in which three people, who all arguably died violently, were placed. Second, this was no normal cemetery: those who placed them there were probably their killers, they would have been well aware of the preservative qualities of the bog and would have known that the bodies would therefore not perish but remain fresh and unchanged for some time.[51]

Lindow Man may have been a criminal, someone who transgressed social or religious taboos, a hostage or a human sacrificial victim. Whoever he was, ritual crept into the act of killing him, for there was no need to kill him three times (the blows to the head, strangulation and throat-cutting). And why was he naked except for a fur armlet? My contention is that he may well have died as a sacrifice to the gods, the ultimate gift made only in times of crisis. Classical authors make many allusions to human sacrificial killing among the Britons, Gauls and Germans[52] and, indeed, the Greeks and Romans themselves conducted such ritual on occasions, though it was made illegal in Rome in 97 BC. Tim Taylor has suggested that strangulation was a particularly significant form of ritual killing since it literally cuts off the dying breath and was perhaps meaningful, therefore, in terms of what happened to the person's soul or spirit after death.[53] Many bog bodies in northern Europe – in Ireland, Britain, Denmark, North Germany and the Netherlands – were hanged or garrotted, and so this kind of death seems to have been special and carefully selected. Not only was suffocation recurrent, but also many of the victims appear to have undergone significant levels of ante-mortem violence and there is often evidence for binding. The nakedness of several Iron Age bog people, too, may be indicative of ritual practice. So Lindow Man fits into a broader context of habitual cult-killing, and we should appreciate that the deaths of these people would have been conducted in public, as performance, an act perhaps witnessed by the entire community, with the Druids or other priests acting like public hangmen. Tim Taylor has reconstructed Lindow Man's last moments:

> *First he was knocked to the ground by a heavy blow from behind, causing a rib to fracture. He was probably already on his knees when he was hit again, this time by an axe blow to the head. This was done violently enough to stun him and send shards of skull into his brain, but not violently enough to kill him outright ... Next, a carefully knotted animal-sinew garrotte was placed around his neck, and with this in place, his throat was cut with a knife. The garrotte was then tightened, fracturing his neck and causing the blood to spurt from the severed arteries with great force. He then fell or was thrust forward into the bog. Fragments of sphagnum moss in his stomach suggest that he may have made one last gasp for air as he lay face down in the mire.*[54]

If Lindow Man was a human sacrifice, why was he killed there and then? The answer may lie in the combination of Suetonius Paulinus's attack on Anglesey and the Boudican Rebellion. In order to make the march from south-east England (where the seat of Roman government in Britain lay) to the north-west, where the Druidic stronghold was situated, the Roman army would have needed to pass quite close by the Lindow area. If we believe the testimony of Caesar and his peers, the Druids were in charge of all private and public sacrificial rituals, including human sacrifice. It would seem certain, then, if Lindow II (and the other Lindow bodies) were victims of ritual murder, that the Druids were almost inevitably involved. Geographically, Lindow and Anglesey are not far from each other – at the most 100 miles (160 kilometres) – and we know that at Llyn Cerrig Bach religious practices were going on in the first century AD. Although it has to remain speculative, it could be that the Druids on Anglesey, knowing that a Roman attack on their holiest shrine was imminent, tried to avert catastrophe by means of a desperate act of propitiation, calling upon the gods for help by means of human sacrifice. The apparently high status of the victim would have enhanced the value of the offering even more. One piece of evidence that supports this model of interpretation is the presence of a few grains of mistletoe in the stomach contents of Lindow Man. We learn from Pliny that the Gaulish Druids engaged in ceremonies that involved the cutting of mistletoe from a sacred tree for use in healing and the cure of infertility.[55] So there is a tangible link between the Druids, mistletoe and Lindow Man's death.

But what is all this to do with Boudica and the rebellion in south-east England? First, the destruction of Mona and the sacking of the three Roman towns, at the other end of Britain, were momentous events that are not only closely linked chronologically but likely to be in some way connected. If that is the case, the inference is that the Druids were involved in the Boudican Rebellion. Caesar tells us that the Druids had a finger in every political and religious pie and that nothing of moment happened without their say-so. It is almost inconceivable, therefore, that the cataclysmic occurrences in the lands of the Trinovantes and Catuvellauni were unfolding without the connivance of the Druids, if not with their full support. It is even possible that the whole rebellion was orchestrated by the Druids themselves, perhaps because of their fear that their power was on the wane under the stifling hand of Rome. The

Boudican Rebellion could, indeed, be part of a British revitalisation movement,[56] a last-ditch attempt to regain control over Britain, after the Roman conquest of Gaul and its reabsorption into the Roman empire and when even Britain was slipping from their control. We have seen that Boudica was engaged in ritual activities, involving both divining (telling the future) and human sacrifice. She was probably closely connected with the Druidic movement. There is no clear evidence – beyond the strongly circumstantial – to link Boudica, the Druids, Anglesey and Lindow, but a key linking factor may be provided by Suetonius Paulinus and his legions. The Druids might have considered that the attack on Anglesey could be averted both by the sacrifice of a high-ranking individual (whether he was a local nobleman or a foreign hostage) and by ensuring that Boudica made the continued tenure of Britain by the Romans impossible. If so, then they nearly succeeded, for the Emperor Nero nearly decided to abandon Britain after the rebellion of AD 60 (although the ancient sources do not make it clear whether Nero's uncertainty about the viability of retaining Britain was a direct result of Boudica's uprising).

Boudica, the Iceni and cult practices

In AD 47, more than a decade before Boudica's Rebellion, the Iceni rose in revolt against Rome and its British governor Ostorius Scapula. This appears to have happened because the new governor, in quelling a rebellion that was taking place among the Welsh border tribes, issued an edict that all the tribes he suspected as being susceptible to sedition should have their weapons confiscated.[57] It has been suggested that this first Icenian revolt may have had as its focal point Stonea Camp, an Iron Age fortified site on an island in the Cambridgeshire Fens that archaeological investigation has shown to have been abandoned at around this time.[58] While the narrative concerning Icenian rebellion and its reasons is properly the theme of another chapter, it is worth pausing for a moment to consider the site of Stonea, because of the symbolism of its island location. The choice of site may simply have been defensive, but islands were resonant with ritual significance, and it is possible that Stonea, like many other defended sites in Iron Age Britain, may have had sacred as well as secular prominence. The settlement at Saham Toney in Norfolk, with its concentration of high-status late Iron Age finds (including beau-

6 ◆ The role of the Druids in Boudica's Rebellion

tifully crafted and ornamented horse gear) was almost certainly another such site: right next to it, at Ashill, was a ritual shaft containing highly structured depositions that included sets of more than a hundred pots, more than half of which were complete, together with other objects and carefully selected animal parts.[59] (See Map 3.)

By far the most important late Iron Age ritual site in Icenian territory was at Fison Way, Thetford: a huge ceremonial enclosure that was refurbished on a massive scale in the 50s AD (see Figure 6.1). This was a significant period, between the first Icenian revolt when Ostorius Scapula was governor, and the second uprising, when Suetonius Paulinus was in charge of the province. At this time, an enormous rectangular space

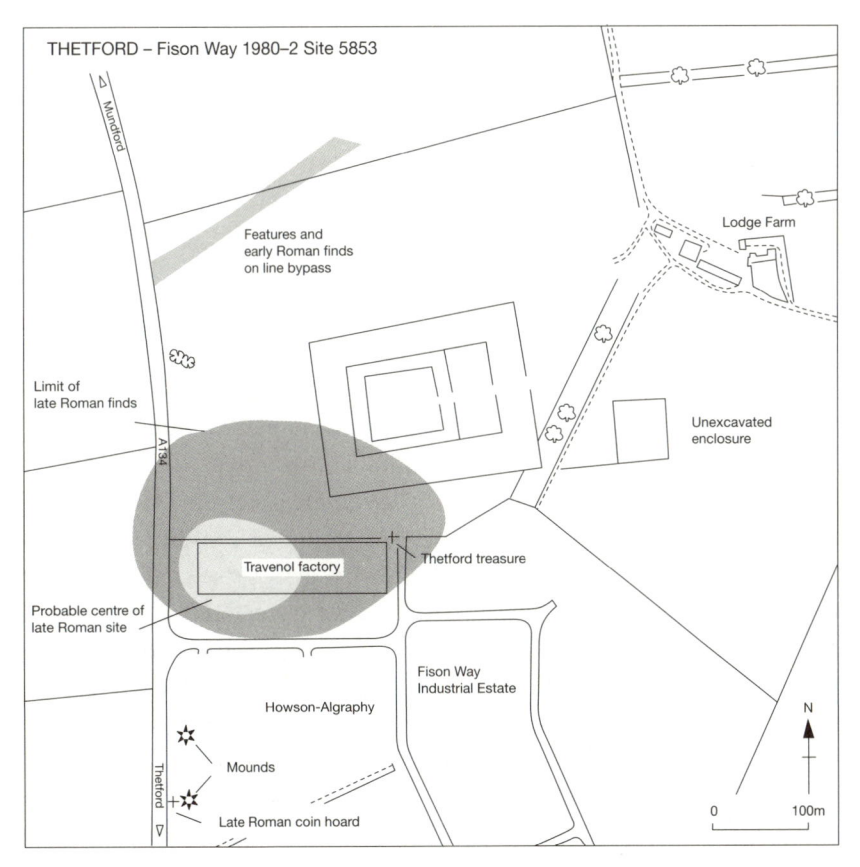

FIGURE 6.1 ◆ *The great ritual enclosure at Fison Way, Thetford.*

Source: Aldhouse-Green 2004d.

(38,000 square yards/32,000 square metres) was demarcated by a bank-and-ditch earthwork and, inside it, lay another. In between these two earthworks, a series of nine parallel palisades was erected, their great timber uprights flanking an east-facing entrance where a massive wooden gateway gave way to an inner precinct consisting largely of empty space but with a two-storey building at the back, belonging to an earlier Iron Age phase.[60] The size and layout of this imposing structure, rearing up, on the relatively steep-sided Gallows Hill, out of the gently undulating, low-lying lands of Norfolk, suggests its importance as a public space – its palisades, perhaps, even acting as a kind of artificial sacred grove. This may have functioned as a centre of assembly where matters of state were conducted; where business and matrimonial contracts were made; where priests mediated between tribesfolk and the gods. We know from analogies in early historical Ireland that such gathering places were charged with symbolic force and that major religious festivals, as well as political debate, took place. Tara,[61] for instance , was where the early Irish kings were inaugurated, and we can imagine that sites like this had similar purposes to Westminster Abbey in London (a place of Christian worship but with a highly politicised profile as well).

The Thetford enclosure is extremely significant for our understanding of the Iceni and their mood during this crucial period between the two rebellions. Paul Sealey has suggested that 'Thetford may well have been the scene of a tribal meeting that decided to follow Boudica in her crusade against the Romans in AD 60'.[62] The 47 brooches found here presumably represent accidental loss, and if that is a correct assumption, we can imagine, too, that on occasions of this magnitude the Druids would have been heavily involved. Thus, Caesar writes of Druidic councils in Gaul, mentioning that the order met once a year at a designated place in the territory of the Carnutes (a tribe living around Chartres).[63] This annual meeting was a pan-Druidic affair, but it is possible that Thetford and other central foci, such as Saham Toney and Sedgeford, fulfilled an analogous purpose within the tribal territory of the Iceni, and that both secular and religious authorities were involved in such gatherings.

The involvement of Thetford as a symbolic statement about independence, and even contra-Roman sedition, is strongly indicated by its fate after the rebellion had been crushed. For archaeological testimony points to the abandonment of the site for over 200 years. The massive timber structure was not razed to the ground by fire but was systematically dismantled; the wooden uprights were deliberately removed and the ditches filled in. The perpetrators show themselves in pieces of discarded Roman military equipment. In Sealey's words 'after the revolt, a detachment of Roman soldiers had descended on Thetford and obliterated it'.[64] Despite the presence of great timber fences, Thetford is less likely to have been defensive than a political and ceremonial structure: if the ideology, symbolism and religious identity of the rebels was bound up in its erection by British Icenians, then its destruction by opponents of its builders makes sense in symbolic as well as practical terms. Systematic clearance would have been more effective than fire, less dramatic and more thorough. It would have been as though it had never existed, and it was probably done in order to erase ancestral memory. It may even be that Thetford was destroyed in an apt act of vengeance for the burning of the temple of Claudius at Colchester.[65]

But, despite the dismantling of the Thetford enclosure, over 300 years later, someone or some community came to almost exactly the same spot and deposited a hoard of rich treasure at Thetford.[66] The cache was deposited in about AD 390 but it was buried so close to the ancient Icenian enclosure that its location was purposely chosen to reflect a continued sanctity for the place, a sense of lasting spiritual presence and – perhaps – commemorative recognition of ancestral power that might extend right back to the independent Icenian rulership of Prasutagus and Boudica. The contents of the late hoard are interesting: they consist of 81 gold and silver objects, including gold finger-rings and other precious jewellery and a set of 33 silver spoons, almost certainly the property of a religious *collegium* (guild). Kenneth Painter has suggested that the spoons might represent a particular kind of votive offering, perhaps a specific measure of wine, oil or water.[67] The religious character of the assemblage is indicated by the inscribed dedication on many of the spoons, several of which mention Faunus, an obscure Italian nature deity. So far, then, the Thetford hoard appears to reflect deposition within an entirely Roman context. But Faunus's name is often twinned with local spirits that have British names, and one of these was Medugenus' ('Mead-Begotten'). The latter was the British equivalent of the Roman god Bacchus, whose devotees consumed liquor in order to enter an ecstatic, out-of-body experience and so realise the deity. The cult of Faunus may here have included the consumption of alcohol, for liquor-strainers formed part of the treasure found here. So, first-century Thetford may have been removed from the landscape by Romans, seeking to wipe out Boudica's memory but, even so, the site continued to live on first in first-hand remembrance and later in folk memory and ancestral myth. The outward appearance of the late Roman treasure hoard was entirely Italian but lurking beneath was a strong British presence, with the worship of local deities. Thetford remained a place of religious resonance and may, indeed, have become a place of pilgrimage over the centuries.

New religious movements in early Roman Britain: protest and resistance

Archaeological material like the Thetford enclosure, the ritual site of Llyn Cerrig Bach and the ritual killing of Lindow Man, provide possible clues to a religious protest in response to the coming of Rome to Britain and, specifically, to the actions of freedom fighters and British clergy in resistance to the new order. It is, perhaps, possible to point to other archaeological evidence relating to an upsurge of British ritual activity at about the time of the Roman conquest, maybe as a direct reaction to the political, ideological and religious upheaval that such a cataclysmic event must have represented. Studies of the practice of human sacrifice in late Iron Age and Roman Europe reveal a flurry of extreme ritual behaviour in the decades immediately following the initial Claudian conquest.[68] These include the ritual murder of three women near the entrance to a funerary enclosure in which a local man of supremely high status was cremated in about AD 55, at Folly Lane (St Albans) in Hertfordshire;[69] and the ritual violence that took place at Alveston, near Bristol, some time in the early–mid first century AD, when a young girl was bludgeoned to death and the femur of another person was broken open as if to extract the marrow, in an act of cannibalism.[70] These extreme forms of cult behaviour are the kinds of things that occur when societies are under great stress and crisis, when all the rules are broken and people seek desperate measures to avert catastrophe.

Martin Henig,[71] John Creighton[72] and Richard Hingley[73] have all expressed the view that south-east Britain was already in close relations with Rome during the hundred years between Caesar's visits and the

Claudian invasion. Creighton, indeed, speaks of the British court as being 'riddled with Romans' long before Claudius and his elephants paraded through Colchester. The reality of *romanitas* was undoubtedly a dislocative process to British tribal society, its politics and religion. That being so, one would expect the Britons to have reacted – positively or negatively – to a new and different ideological presence in their midst. We know that religious inscriptions, for the first time in the Roman period, served to codify and pin down the names and identities of the gods[74] and that iconography on a large scale was introduced for the first time after the conquest.[75] It is also quite possible that the Druids were involved in the selection of motifs and images on late Iron Age gold and silver coins[76], many of which have an undoubtedly symbolic and religious dimension.

What we need to ask ourselves is whether we can trace some elements of new, resistive, religious movements as expressed in iconography of early Roman times in Britain. One way in which this can happen is by subtle appropriation of foreign, colonial religious systems, including their material manifestations, so that indigenous, colonised populations take ownership of them, sometimes in a deliberately subversive manner. In this way, coercion by a dominating power can be inverted and resisted, and 'subjugated knowledge' can be expressed without fear of reprisals.[77] It is possible to identify traces of such actions in early Roman Britain, whether or not these were being played out according to a Boudican framework. Old cosmologies were apparently re-emerging and ancient memories revived. It is sufficient here to point to two good illustrations of this revival of religious memory, which may have operated within a framework of conscious protest.

High-status late Iron Age burials in south-east England, particularly north of the Thames, frequently contained the paraphernalia of British drinking ceremonies, most notably in the form of metal-clad wooden stave-buckets. According to Bettina Arnold, consumption of alcohol in late Iron Age Europe was associated with empowerment, hospitality and expressions of wealth.[78] The buckets are especially significant for they refer not to wine drinking, an essentially Mediterranean custom (albeit one enthusiastically embraced by Gallo-Britons), but to indigenous alcoholic substances, such as mead, fermented berry juice and ale. What is interesting, in terms of early Romano-British cult-iconography, is that this same bucket-motif appears in stone imagery in the Cotswold region[79] in depictions of native goddesses, who are sometimes associated with the Roman god Mercury.

The second illustration is contained within the iconographic repertoire of Roman Bath, an early spa town centred on the great healing shrine to Sulis Minerva and its hot springs. While the gilded bronze head from the cult-statue of the presiding deity depicts a totally classical Minerva, almost all the inscriptions dedicated by pilgrim visitors allude either to Sulis alone or to Sulis Minerva (with the native name coming first). This in itself is not necessarily a sign of anti-Roman feeling, but rather an example of the undoubted synergies that took place between British and Roman panthea. But, bearing in mind the early (Flavian) date of the monumentalisation of the shrine by the Romans, it is interesting that at least two pieces of iconography express ideas that were contrary to Roman religious perspectives. One is a little schist plaque of three women, carved in deceptively simple, schematic form, with overlarge heads and undeveloped anatomical detail. Perhaps they represent the British alternative to the Roman version of Sulis Minerva.[80] The second is the glorious statement of Britishness that is the carved male head on the pediment of the temple,[81] who resembles a river god, with his swirling hair, moustache and beard, and eels in his hair, but with the wings and staring eyes of a male Gorgon (see Figure 6.2). One particular feature of this sculpture brings to mind the idea of past and memory, like the bucket-motifs just mentioned: that is the curious lotus-flower pattern on the 'Gorgon's' forehead, which is highly reminiscent of early relief carvings of human heads from central Europe. The idea of a connection between such heads and the one from Bath is not as fanciful as it may seem, for many of the sculptors at Bath were from Gaul, a region that included the Rhineland, the area where these earlier carvings were made. The precise meaning of this strange tri-lobed symbol remains hidden, but the Iron Age heads come from funerary monuments and, in antiquity, the lotus was associated with longevity and rebirth. Such a theme would not be out of place at Bath, a sanctuary dedicated to healing bodies, restoring minds and, perhaps, reaffirming identities.

If, alongside the influx of Roman religious cults to Britain in the mid–late first century AD, we can identify what might be termed resistant cult behaviour among the Britons of the south, it is valid to suppose that

6 ♦ The role of the Druids in Boudica's Rebellion

FIGURE 6.2 ♦ *The male head from the temple pediment at Bath.*

Source: © Anne Leaver.

organised clergy were behind such protest movements, as well as human sacrificial activity and other 'unroman' ritual practices. The Druids' web of influence may still have been strong, albeit less direct, in the decades after conquest, and Boudica herself may have felt the more confident of victory if she knew she had their support. It may even be that the ability of the Iceni and the neighbouring Trinovantes to join forces – in a manner very rare for Gallic or British tribes – was effected under the auspices of this formidable priesthood.

Notes and references

1 Tacitus *Annals* XIV, 30–1; trans. Grant 1956, 317.
2 Caesar *de Bello Gallico* VI, 13.
3 For those readers interested in the Druids *per se*, a body of accessible literature on the subject is readily available; for example Chadwick 1966; Piggott 1968; Green 1997a.

4 Caesar *de Bello Gallico* VI, 13.

5 Op. cit. VI, 14.

6 For instance, the fanatical pursuance of Islamic jihads that may result in suicide bombings in the West and the Middle East.

7 Lucan *Pharsalia* I, 422–65; trans. Graves 1956.

8 Pliny *Natural History* XXX, 4; trans. Jones 1956.

9 Some scholars would interpret the concept as being that of *humanitas* rather than *romanitas*, arguing that the Romans perceived themselves as spreading the culture of being human to a barbarian world (a concept even more arrogant than the imposition of *romanitas*).

10 Webster 1998; 1999.

11 Tacitus *Annals* III, 39–46; trans. Grant 1956, 135–8.

12 Op. cit. III, 35–6.

13 Op. cit. XXIX–XXXIX; Dio Cassius *Roman History* 62, 2.

14 Although the Arabic term jihad is frequently so translated in the West, its correct meaning is 'struggle'. A jihad is more likely to take the form of verbal engagement than of armed struggle: Armstrong 2000, 37.

15 Tacitus *Annals* III, 43; trans. Grant 1956, 137.

16 Tacitus *Histories* IV, 12; trans. Wellesley 1964, 211.

17 Op. cit. IV, 54; trans. Wellesley 1964, 242.

18 Webster 1999, 14.

19 MacMullen 1992, 152–62.

20 Adas 1979, 183.

21 Owen Davies makes this point in the BBC Radio 4 programme *Making History* (7 June, 2005).

22 Tacitus *Histories* IV, 61.

23 Pliny *Natural History* XXX, 4; trans. Jones 1956/63.

24 Tacitus *Annals* XIV, 29.

25 Pomponius Mela *De Chorographis* III, 6; Green 1997a, 103.

26 Strabo *Geography* IV, 4, 6.

27 Bartram 1974, 27; Henken 1987, 227–32.

28 Mac Cana 1976.

29 Strabo *Geography* VII, 2, 3.

30 Green 1997a, 114.

31 Dio Cassius *Roman History* LXII, 6–7.
32 The Battle of Agincourt is a good example, as narrated in Shakespeare's *Henry V*.
33 Lucan *Pharsalia* I, 444–6; Green 1984, 251–64; 1991, 86–106.
34 'In commands, prayers, curses and spells, words make things happen. They create reality by declaring the speaker's intention': Vitebsky 1995, 78.
35 Tomlin 1988, 58–277; 1993, 113–30. Gager 1992.
36 'Any individual or community not abiding by their verdict is banned from the sacrifices, and this is regarded among the Gauls as the most severe punishment': Caesar *de Bello Gallico* VI, 13; trans. Wiseman & Wiseman 1980, 121.
37 The tale of Amairgin is told in the *Mythological Cycle* of medieval prose tales: Green 1997a, 124; O'Rahilly 1946, 326.
38 Webster 1998.
39 Caesar *de Bello Gallico* VI, 14.
40 Green 1998a
41 Lucan *Pharsalia* III, 399–453.
42 Fox 1946; Lynch 1991, 285–315; 2000, 189–196; Macdonald 1996, 32–3; Parker Pearson 2000, 8–11; Savory 1976, 84, 93.
43 After the so-called 'type site' of La Tène in Switzerland, where a great deal of Iron Age metalwork, including prestige goods, was discovered buried in the mud, alongside a series of upright timbers, on the shores of Lake Neuchâtel in November 1857, when the level of the lake fell, revealing the archaeology: Dunning 1991, 366–71.
44 Macdonald 1996 (fn 36) and pers. com.
45 Green 1998b.
46 Aldhouse-Green 2001a, 27; Vincent Guichard pers. com.; Aldhouse-Green 2004c.
47 Turner in Stead *et al.* 1984, 10–13.
48 Aldhouse-Green 2004b; Hill 1997, 96–107; Carr 2000.
49 Housley *et al.* 1995, 39–46.
50 Tim Taylor, however, suggests that Lindow II and III may have been killed at the same time: 2002, 147, and certainly the radiocarbon dates may allow for such ambiguity in dating. In any case, it seems as though Lindow Moss was a recurrent spot for the deposition of ritually murdered victims and may therefore have been perceived as a special place, perhaps a gateway to the spirit world.

51 Powerful relevant imagery is present in the second of the *Lord of the Rings* trilogy, 'The Two Towers', in which Frodo, Sam and Gollum cross the dead marshes in their approach to Mordor. Clearly visible beneath the bog surface are the bodies of people who died long ago in battle.

52 Aldhouse-Green 2001a.

53 Lecture delivered at the University of Manchester, September 2002; Taylor 2002a, 146–7.

54 Taylor 2002a, 147.

55 Pliny *Natural History* XVI, 95.

56 Webster 1999.

57 Tacitus *Annals* XII, 31–2.

58 Jackson & Potter 1996; Todd 2004, 50.

59 Ross 1968, 258–9.

60 Gregory 1991; Sealey 1997, 12; Aldhouse-Green 2004d, 199, fig. 11.4.

61 O'Rahilly 1946, 176–7; Mac Cana 1970

62 Sealey 1997, 12.

63 Caesar *de Bello Gallico* VI

64 Sealey 1997, 42.

65 Paul Sealey (pers. com.), after a comment by an anonymous sixth-form college student. Sealey has drawn my attention to the fact that, according to ancient battle etiquette, to destroy enemy temples was considered a war crime.

66 Aldhouse-Green 2004d, 199–200, 216 Fig. 11.4; Johns & Potter 1983; Painter 1997, 93–110.

67 Painter 1997.

68 Aldhouse-Green 2001a.

69 Niblett 1999, 17–21.

70 Aldhouse-Green 2001a, 59; Mick Aston pers. com. *Time Team* September 2000.

71 Henig 1998, 8–9.

72 Creighton 2000, xi.

73 Hingley 2000.

74 Webster 1995.

75 Green 1998c.

76 Creighton 1995.

77 Aldhouse-Green 2004a, 222.
78 Arnold 1999; 2001.
79 Aldhouse-Green 2004a, 224–5.
80 Aldhouse-Green 2004a, 213–14, fig. 7.20; Cunliffe & Fulford 1982, no. 26, pl. 7.
81 Cunliffe & Fulford 1982, nos 32–7, pl. 10; Aldhouse-Green 2004a, fig. 8.3.

CHAPTER 7

Rape, rebellion and slaughter

Neither before nor since has Britain ever been in a more uneasy or dangerous state. Veterans were butchered, colonies burnt to the ground, armies isolated. We had to fight for life before we could think of victory. The campaign, of course, was conducted under the strategy and leadership of another, and the decisive success and the credit for recovering Britain fell to the general [Suetonius Paulinus]. Yet everything combined to give the young Agricola fresh skill, fresh experience and fresh ambition, and his spirit was invaded by the passion for military glory – a thankless passion in an age in which distinction was misconstrued and a great reputation was as dangerous as a bad one

Tacitus *Agricola*[1]

Early on in his eulogy of his father-in-law, Agricola, Tacitus describes the dire situation obtaining in the newly established province of Britannia, where Agricola first served as a military tribune on Suetonius Paulinus's staff in AD 60/1. This chapter represents the climax of the Boudican story, and deals with the evidence for events immediately preceding and leading up to the rebellion and during the course of the revolt itself. The ancient texts that describe the Boudican uprising consist of Tacitus's *Annals*, his *Agricola* and a later source, Dio Cassius's *Roman History*. These we will analyse in some detail but, before doing so, it is worth standing back to consider the nature and tone of their accounts because they have a bearing on how we should read them. Both authors record dramatic events and one of the ways they do this is by putting words into the mouths of the main *dramatis personae* (Boudica and Suetonius Paulinus). Such reported speech is evocative in written form, but we should appreciate that such texts were written to be read aloud and so anything that can heighten the drama of the spoken word, whether feigned speech, hyperbole, word-painting or sonority of language, would have been employed.

We need now to examine the events that led to the disaster, to the sacking of three Roman cities, a huge loss of life and the near-demise of Roman Britain, and to bear in mind the involvement of at least two tribes, the Iceni and the neighbouring Trinovantes.

Trinovantian grievances

> With them [the Iceni] rose the Trinobantes and others. Servitude had not broken them and they had secretly plotted together to become free again. They particularly hated the ex-soldiers who had recently established a settlement at Camulodunum. The settlers drove the Trinobantes from their homes and land, and called them prisoners and slaves. The troops encouraged the settlers' outrages, since their own way of behaving was the same – and they looked forward to similar licence for themselves. Moreover, the temple erected to the divine Claudius was a blatant stronghold of alien rule, and its observances were a pretext to make the natives appointed as its priests drain the whole country dry
>
> Tacitus *Annals*.[2]

This passage in Tacitus's *Annals* is the only account to mention the Trinovantes by name, although other sources allude to 'Britons' in general. According to Tacitus then, the people of this tribe, whose capital was Camulodunum (Colchester), were systematically dispossessed of their ancestral lands, together with their political centre. Thus, at one fell swoop, the Romans took away the identity of this community; its past, enshrined in ancestral memory; the very gods perceived to reside in their landscapes. When they annexed a province, the Roman army had a custom of allocating to retired soldiers a parcel of land to farm in occupied territory, resonant of Israeli settlements in Gaza or on the West Bank. Moreover, very often, legionaries and auxiliary troops had formed permanent common-law relationships with local women, and had no wish to depart from the country in which they had spent most of their fighting lives. Thus legionary veterans were frequently settled in newly created Roman townships called *coloniae*, which had a triple function: to act as beacons of *romanitas* within alien lands; to house retired soldiers; and to add to the security of a province (a particularly valuable asset for recently conquered territory).

The takeover of Camulodunum for the new *colonia* was a quite deliberate act of provocation but one taken in confidence that the locals had no teeth and would simply have to accept the consequences of conquest. Arrogant symbols of Roman military superiority, such as the tombstone of the cavalry officer, Longinus, with its depiction of a Roman horseman trampling down a defeated British (Trinovantian) adversary, can hardly have helped win local hearts and minds (see Plate 19).[3] Found by workmen in 1928, the image had lost its face and it was long considered that this had been a deliberate act of defacement by angry Britons. But in 1988 the missing face was discovered,[4] and the complete figure of Longinus now sits proudly on his horse on display in the Castle Museum in Colchester. But the Romans' complacency about the Trinovantes was to prove grossly mistaken, for the tribe was soon to join Boudica. Archaeological evidence suggests that this people had a military capability, as objects such as the warrior burial and the potsherd depicting an armed horseman, both from Kelvedon, serve to demonstrate, and the very name of the Trinovantian tribal capital means 'the fortress of Camulos' (see Chapter 1).

The dispossession of the Trinovantes was bad enough, but the insensitivity of the colonial power did not end there. Right in the centre of their old tribal capital work began on a huge new edifice, a classical-style temple[5] (see also Chapter 2: Figure 2.7) which was to be dedicated to the spirit of Emperor Claudius, the one in whose name the Britons were being enslaved. The erection of this alien structure was itself a trumpet-blast of colonial arrogance and, to add insult to injury, the local people were expected to pay for the temple and its upkeep via newly appointed priests, called *Severi Augustales*: special clergy associated with the imperial cult. This financial burden was just one of many forms of taxation the new province had to bear. Outside the temple there almost certainly stood a great bronze equestrian statue of the emperor himself, in full military gear (see Figure 2.1). As we shall see later in this chapter, parts of just such an image were violently broken and placed in watery contexts, probably by Trinovantians or Icenians in dual acts of destruction and ritual deposition.[6]

7 ◆ Rape, rebellion and slaughter

One of the reasons why the Trinovantes chose to strike now, and to throw in their lot with Boudica and the Iceni, can be found in a passage of Dio's *Roman History,* an account that does not name the Trinovantes but speaks of 'the leading Britons' to whom Claudius had apparently given money, presumably to build the temple and otherwise convert to *romanitas*.[7] Suddenly, this funding ceased to be a gift and became a loan, which the Romans demanded to be repaid. Added to this was a further debt: money loaned to them at high interest by the upper-class Roman usurer Seneca. Dio comments: 'The ostensible cause of the war was the confiscation of money which Claudius had given to the leading Britons, but which now had to be repaid – so at least the Procurator of the island Decianus Catus claimed'.[8]

The Britons, probably mainly the Trinovantes, were desperate: anything was better than penury, confiscation of remaining assets and eventual mass enslavement. There is a passage in the *Agricola* in which Tacitus, using the customary reported speech,[9] puts into the mouths of the aggrieved Britons the reasons for their unrest in AD 60, namely the oppressive presence not only of the Roman governor but the procurator or finance officer (perhaps to be seen as the equivalent of the prime minister and the chancellor of the Exchequer), at the same time, there was also the opportunity to act given by the absence of the governor and his forces, who had departed for Anglesey. Indirectly, the author also hints at the function of the storyteller, whose role it was to fan the flames of sedition, enhance the truth and act as go-between to spread news among neighbouring communities.

> *For the Britons, freed from their repressions by the absence of the dreaded legate, began to discuss the woes of slavery, to compare their wrongs and sharpen their sting in the telling. 'We gain nothing by submission except heavier burdens for willing shoulders. Once each tribe had one king, now two are clamped on us – the legate to wreak his fury on our lives, the procurator on our property. We subjects are damned in either case, whether our masters quarrel or agree. Their gangs of centurions or slaves, as the case may be, mingle violence and insult. Nothing is any longer safe from their greed and lust. In war it is the braver who takes the spoil; as things stands with us, it is mostly cowards and shirkers that rob our homes, kidnap our children and conscript our men. Any cause is good enough for us to die for – any but our country's.'*[10]

The emperors of Rome in the first century AD lived with the memory of the war-lords of the later Republic: Marius, Sulla, Pompey and – most famously – Julius Caesar. The last-named, as governor of Gaul, had marched on Rome at the head of his legions, holding the Senate to ransom and threatening the whole fabric of imperial government. After the inception of the Principate, the first emperor, Augustus, and his successors, put in place a provincial administrative structure that made it much more difficult for governors of provinces to use their armies as power weapons and, at the same time, ensured that governors were unable to fleece their provinces to line their own pockets, as had frequently happened in the first century BC, hence Cicero's legal attacks on bad governors, notably on Verres in 70 BC, for his corrupt practices in Sicily:

> *Among all the treasures that so richly adorn this beautiful city of ours, is there one statue, one picture, that has not been captured and brought hither from the enemies we have defeated in war? And the country houses of our wealthy men are furnished to overflowing with the countless beautiful things stripped from our most loyal allies.*[11]

To stop the recurrence of such extortion, the emperor allocated each imperial province two high officials: a governor and a procurator.[12] Although the former would always outrank the latter, both in terms of class and status, the procurator was answerable not to the governor but directly to the emperor. Thus, not only was the job of governing a province split between military (the governor) and fiscal (the procurator) duties, but the emperor could also use each man in effect to keep a watch on the other and to report to him if things got out of hand. This was particularly important in far-flung provinces and those provinces with a massive army presence. The reported speech of British grievances before the Boudican Rebellion (see above), refers directly to these two masters and to the unhappiness of the conquered at having to cope with the double burden. The impact of such dual responsibility for the fledgling province of Britannia was to make itself felt in the tragic sequence of events that unfolded in AD 60. While Suetonius Paulinus, the governor, was away on campaign in the north-west, the *procurator Britanniae*, Decianus Catus, was at work in East Anglia. As chief finance officer, Catus was responsible for all matters associated with money and revenue, particularly taxation; it was his job to make sure that Britain paid its way and represented as little a drain as possible on the central purse. Army pay, land taxes and poll taxes were within his remit,[13] and he would thus have levied as much tax as he could get away with, for therein lay the measure of his success and his chance of promotion, away from a godforsaken, fog-girt island in the middle of nowhere. Clearly, Catus's role within the province was crucial to its well-being and its success in terms of being part of the Roman empire, and it was Catus – above all – who blundered and whose crass rapacity[14] caused the Icenian war to erupt in the absence of the governor and most of the Roman fighting power allocated for the conquest and policing of Britain.

Roman blunders and Icenian fury

It is time to turn to the main protagonists in the story of the Boudican Rebellion, Boudica and the Iceni, and to the shocking events that sparked off the British war, as recorded by Tacitus. The trigger for the debacle was the death of the Icenian client-king Prasutagus.

> *While Suetonius was thus occupied, he learnt of a sudden rebellion in the province. Prasutagus, king of the Iceni, after a life of long and renowned prosperity, had made the emperor co-heir with his own two daughters. Prasutagus hoped by this submissiveness to preserve his kingdom and household from attack. But it turned out otherwise. Kingdom and household alike were plundered like prizes of war, the one by Roman officers, the other by Roman slaves. As a beginning, his widow Boudica was flogged and their daughters raped. The Icenian chiefs were deprived of their hereditary estates as if the Romans had been given the whole country. The king's own relatives were treated like slaves.*
> *And the humiliated Iceni feared still worse, now that they had been reduced to provincial status'. So they rebelled.*[15]

Let us see what Tacitus is telling us in this typically terse account. First, we learn that Suetonius Paulinus, believing the Druids to be a real focus of resistance, had marched off with his legions to smash the priesthood on their sacred island of Anglesey (see Chapter 6), thus leaving the province to his rear exposed and vulnerable. We can only assume that the governor had misjudged the apparent quiescence of the south-east, perhaps having over-relied on the steady loyalty of the fiercely loyal southern client-king Togidubnus and so having no cause to be concerned about the lands north of the Thames.[16] The word 'sudden' expresses surprise at the rebellion and the lack of perceived context for such an event.

As discussed in Chapter 3, the relationship between a client-king and the Roman state was personal, not dynastic, and, therefore, when such a monarch died, the terms of the alliance would have to be reconsidered. We also know that, for Rome, the creation of a buffer-state was often regarded as a temporary measure, designed to relieve pressure on Rome to provide massive occupation forces in regions about to be annexed or otherwise 'associated' with the empire. We can only surmise that Decianus Catus wished to make Britain pay its way and, although Togidubnus was alive and useful and his kingdom thus inviolable, the same was not true of the Icenian monarchy. The death of King Prasutagus, then, provided Catus with ample opportunities to make money and, perhaps, to acquire glory at the same time as adding to the territory of the province, in the absence of the governor, particularly if – as can be surmised both by analogy and by hints in the texts – the two officers were at odds with each other and the procurator wished to make capital out of Suetonius Paulinus's preoccupation on the other side of Britain.

According to Roman law, under which treaties with client-kings were automatically broken at their deaths, Icenian assets would, indeed, have become Roman property after Prasutagus died. To this extent, Catus was acting within his rights as procurator and imperial agent, in his confiscation of Icenian public assets. If Boudica had been closely associated with rulership of her tribe when her husband was alive and if, as has been suggested (above, Chapter 3), she was herself a Roman citizen, she may have had a precise comprehension of her legal situation as widow of the king. What was not legal was the treatment of free Icenians, and in particular the nobility, as if they were slaves, nor the wholesale seizure of private property.

Most of all, the treatment of Boudica and her daughters was a gross war crime, even by Roman standards.[17] Some scholars have doubted whether these acts of violence actually took place, but I see no reason to doubt Tacitus on this issue, even if he was using the events in Britain to highlight the decadence inherent in imperialism. Flogging was a punishment inflicted on free individuals only for heinous offences such as murder: in imperial Roman law, beating to death was a method of punishing those found guilty of *parricidium* (murder of a parent).[18] But in army contexts, both centurions and *optiones* carried disciplinary staves with which they could inflict severe injuries without fear of reprisals.[19] Indeed, it may have been just such military personnel who, under the direction of the procurator, flogged Boudica; individuals like Favonius Facilis, a centurion of Legion XX, whose tombstone was erected at Colchester and who could have been seconded to policing duties in Icenian territory prior to the Boudican Rebellion.[20]

The act of beating was designed, above all, as an act of public humiliation,[21] as a gesture of contempt and a message of power and subjugation, a method of telling the world that Icenian territory and all its inhabitants were Roman property. Such extreme behaviour might be explicable in terms of Boudica's attitude to the Romans before her husband's death, the idea that the Iceni were divided into pro- and anti-Roman factions, and revenge for a protest movement perhaps led by the Icenian woman (see Chapter 3). Rape was (and is) also a war crime, an act that, unhappily, is still part of military behaviour in some parts of the world. Again, it is an act both of violence and of gross shaming, where the victim is despised, either because of gender or discrepant status. Decianus Catus was in charge of the Icenian situation and, at best, the behaviour of his men represents crass stupidity, incompetence and an inability to control; at worst, it was actively condoned in order to humiliate the Britons. What is especially significant in this Tacitean account is that what is being described is the sort of behaviour that occurs as part of war, while there is no question that formal hostilities between the Romans and the Iceni had yet taken place.

In his *Enemies of Rome* Iain Ferris has explored Roman attitudes to 'barbarians' and, in particular, to female barbarians which, he claims, combined contempt with expressions of 'otherness'.[22] Roman soldiers and civil servants would not have been used to dealing with women according to any notions of gender equality, and the extreme treatment of the female members of the Icenian royal house perhaps reflects a certain outrage at being confronted with women who held themselves to be on a par with Catus's men. I suggest, also, that the dual acts of flogging and raping – whether or not they actually took place or are simply part of Tacitean 'narrative' – were elements in what Ferris, in the context of describing imagery, has termed 'the colonial gaze': 'Its use related to the gendered nature of Roman imperial power, and almost certainly also testified to a fear of female transgression and unsuitable behaviour, both by barbarian women and by the women of Rome and the empire'.²³ In Roman eyes, Boudica's role was not suitable for a woman; hence she and her daughters could be treated as less than human. It is worth referring here again (see also Chapter 2) to the image of Claudius in the act of raping Britannia at Aphrodisias (see Figure 2.4), because there is a close parallel between this piece of imperial propaganda iconography and the treatment of Boudica and her daughters. The rape of the children is especially significant, for they were not only female, and thus vulnerable to sexual attack, but also, as children, they represented the future existence of the Iceni. By raping Boudica's daughters, Rome was symbolically compromising that future and potentially contaminating it with Roman genes. Furthermore, we can – probably – assume that the girls were pubescent virgins and their violation was thus even more shocking and humiliating to them, their mother, the royal house of Prasutagus and the entire tribe.

The final issue to be explored in Tacitus's account is that of slavery. We have already seen that the Britons were extremely sensitive to this subject, jeering at Claudius's imperial freedman, Narcissus, and marvelling that a person of such low status could hold the Roman army in thrall (see Chapter 5). It is clear from this passage that the Icenians considered that Catus and his men (of whom some of the civil servants were undoubtedly of freedman status) were of inferior rank: so there was a double shaming in that slaves (the nuances of ex-slave status would not have been significant to the Britons) were treating free Britons as unfree and therefore as inferior to genuine slaves.²⁴ In this respect it is interesting to note the presence of Roman slave-shackles from the Sheepen site at Colchester, now on display in the Colchester Castle Museum as exemplars of the fetters used on Trinovantians in the early years of Roman domination.²⁵

Omens of disaster

Indeed the gods gave them advance warning of the disaster: during the night a clamour of foreign voices mingled with laughter had been heard in the council chamber and in the theatre uproar and lamentation, but it was no mortal who uttered these words and groans; houses were seen underwater in the river Thames, and the Ocean between the island of Britain and Gaul on one occasion turned blood-red at high tide.

Dio Cassius *Roman History*²⁶

7 ♦ Rape, rebellion and slaughter

The Boudican Rebellion represented a cataclysm in the history of Roman provincial administration that caused ripples of horror throughout the settled empire. It was on a scale similar to other catastrophes that had become legends because of the horror associated with them, notably the Varian disaster of AD 9, when three of Augustus's legions were lost to the German Arminius in the Teutoberg Forest, and the Battles of Cannae and Carrhae, when the Carthaginians and the Parthians respectively successfully challenged the power of the Roman army. At Cannae in Apulia, Hannibal cut to pieces a huge Roman force in 216 BC;[27] Crassus was badly defeated at Carrhae in Mesopotamia in 53 BC.[28] This being so, it is not surprising that, according to both Tacitus and Dio, the revolt in Britain merited magical predictions, omens that indicated the presence (and sometimes the intervention) of the spirits. Portents and prodigies were experienced at Colchester and London, two of the three Roman cities to be sacked by Boudica's forces, and the English Channel ran with blood, reflecting the massacres that were to come. Dio's account is very similar to that of Tacitus, though there are differences in detail. It has been suggested that both Tacitus and Dio were drawing on a common earlier source but, while 'Dio is probably transmitting his material in much the same form as he found it, Tacitus has transformed it to suit his own emphasis on the destruction of Colchester'.[29] This is what Tacitus says about divine prophecy of the event, at the time of the attack upon Colchester:

> *At this juncture, for no visible reason, the statue of Victory at Camulodunum fell down – with its back turned as though it were fleeing the enemy. Delirious women chanted of destruction at hand. They cried that in the local senate-house outlandish yells had been heard; at the mouth of the Thames a phantom settlement had been seen in ruins. A blood-red colour in the sea, too, and shapes like human corpses left by the ebb tide, were interpreted hopefully by the Britons – and with terror by the settlers.*[30]

The appearance of unnatural phenomena is well-known in classical literature (and, of course, is chronicled in many other ancient and modern contexts). Known as 'prodigies', their occurrence heralds momentous events, often associated with crisis and danger. The felling of a Roman statue of Victory in an unstable British province is especially significant, for it conveys a stark message of defeat for the conquerors. In terms of an iconic event (in two senses of the word), the phenomenon that took place at Camulodunum is analogous to the toppling (this time by human agency) of Saddam Hussein's statue in Baghdad in 2003. Following a suggestion by Simpson, Giles Standing draws attention to the, not uncommon, literary habit of using statues of Victory as a device to express predictions of triumph or defeat for the Romans against barbarians.[31] In a Roman context, prodigies consisted of

> any unusual occurrence in society which is reported to the senate and accepted by that body as a *prodigium publicum* requiring ritual expiation. Examples of such prodigies may be cult-statues dripping with sweat, weeping or bleeding, cows speaking, mules giving birth, the discovery of hermaphrodites, the raining of stones or blood, earthquakes, solar eclipses, etc.[32]

In observing Tacitus's account of such odd happenings at the beginning of the Boudican Rebellion, it is important to realise that Tacitus's work makes many references to omens and divine prophecies. This being the case, we cannot come to any understanding of what such phenomena meant to the author without being aware of his own religious standpoint.[33] It is a matter of debate as to how much of a sceptic or a believer Tacitus was, but his interest in omens is strictly contextualised within the events he is describing at the time they are said to occur. In his essay on Tacitus and omens, Gwyn Morgan argues for the presence of at least a degree of sarcasm in his accounts of such supernatural events, basing his arguments upon the author's discussion of Vespasian's accession to the imperial purple in AD 69.[34] But Morgan suggests that Tacitus's attitude may be more complex than derision at the emperor himself, arguing that the author may also have been challenging 'too narrow a belief in the official state religion' and that omens and portents might carry significance outside such a narrow focus.

What is particularly interesting, in terms of the particular portents described by Tacitus, in the context of the Boudican Rebellion, is that he mentions very similar phenomena elsewhere, notably in his discussion of Otho (one of the contenders for the throne in the Year of the Four Emperors in AD 68/9). Otho left Rome in March AD 69 and this was apparently accompanied by a range of prodigies and portents that took place on the Capitol, including odd behaviour on the part of the statue of Victory, the rotation of the statue of the divine Julius Caesar and the sudden flooding of the river Tiber.[35] This suggests that, in part at least,

7 ◆ Rape, rebellion and slaughter

Tacitus was using supernatural phenomena as a literary device, something to add emotion and *gravitas* to important or critical episodes in Roman history. He is employing the *leitmotif* of portents in order to anticipate and draw attention to an oncoming disaster: in the case of Otho, the mention of prodigies flags up the fact that he will fail;[36] in alluding to supernatural happenings before Boudica's destructive onslaught on the Roman cities of Britain, he is sounding the horn of doom for the Roman settlers living there.

'Romans go home':[37] death of three cities

> The whole island rose under the leadership of Boudicca, a lady of royal descent ... They hunted down the Roman troops in their scattered posts, stormed the forts and assaulted the colony itself, in which they saw their slavery focused; nor did the angry victors deny themselves any form of savage cruelty.
>
> Tacitus *Agricola*[38]

> For this reason, she sacked and plundered two Roman cities and inflicted untold slaughter, as I have said.
>
> Dio Cassius *Roman History*[39]

It was the Roman *colonia* of Colchester that received the first brunt of Boudica's savage revenge, an opportunity Boudica seized while the governor and his army were far away in north Wales. British vengeance was fuelled not only by the boiling over of bitter Icenian resentment but also of Trinovantian hatred at the way their homes, lands and tribal capital had been commandeered by the conquerors, the crippling burden of British taxation and perceptions of enslavement. Colchester was a smug, over-confident settlement of veteran Roman soldiers and their families; so sure were its inhabitants of their inviolability that they had not bothered to protect themselves by constructing any form of town wall or other physical defence system. Tacitus aims a side-swipe at the provincial administrators, in commenting 'That was a matter which Roman commanders, thinking of amenities rather than needs, had neglected'.[40] In other words, the governor, Suetonius Paulinus, made a huge error of judgement in failing to secure and consolidate the 'conquered' British territory in the east or to leave anyone capable in charge before moving the focus of his campaign to the north-west. What followed in Colchester was a massacre, compounded by the ineptitude and lack of ability of the procurator who, after all, was not a military man though he, above all, perhaps, was responsible for the insurgence by his fiscal blundering. According to Tacitus, more than 70,000 Romans and loyal Romanised Britons were slaughtered, by burning, hanging or crucifixion, in Boudica's ferocious attack on the three cities.[41]

One point of interest is the divergence between the historical and archaeological accounts of Boudican destruction. It is clear from the material remains of the three cities targeted by the Icenian freedom fighter that only parts of these urban settlements were destroyed. Equally striking is the lack of evidence for systematic burning or slighting of rural sites in East Anglia or in the vicinity of the three cities, suggesting that – as one might expect – the fury of the Boudican army was directed on centres of *romanitas*. It is noteworthy, too, that there is little evidence for Suetonius Paulinus's destruction of Icenian rural settlements, although a roundhouse at Sedgeford was burnt,[42] probably by the Roman general's army, perhaps at about the same time that Fison Way, Thetford, was systematically dismantled.

Camulodunum delenda est

Marcus Porcius Cato repeatedly spoke the famous words '*Carthago delenda est*' in the Senate about the need for Rome to destroy Carthage utterly, so that it could never again rise to challenge Roman power in the Mediterranean after the Second Punic War, and this came about in 146 BC.[43] We can surmise that the Iceni and the Trinovantes made a similar vow about the hated *colonia* at Camulodunum. It is Tacitus who gives us the fullest account of the Colchester cataclysm, following desperate calls for aid from its inhabitants:

> *Suetonius, however, was far away. So they appealed for help to the imperial agent Catus Decianus. He sent them barely two hundred men, incompletely armed. There was also a small garrison on the spot. Reliance was placed on the temple's protection. Misled by secret pro-rebels, who hampered their plans, they dispensed with rampart or trench. They omitted also to evacuate old people and women and thus leave only fighting men behind. Their precautions were appropriate to a time of unbroken peace.*
> *Then a native horde surrounded them. When all else had been ravaged or burnt, the garrison concentrated itself in the temple. After two days' siege, it fell by storm. A Roman division, attempting relief, was stopped by the*

7 ◆ Rape, rebellion and slaughter

victorious Britons and routed; such infantry as it possessed was massacred, while the commander escaped to the camp with his cavalry and sheltered behind its defences. The imperial agent Catus Decianus, horrified by the catastrophe and by his unpopularity, withdrew to Gaul. It was his rapacity which had driven the province to war.[44]

Even at a distance of 2000 years, Tacitus's laconic account has the power to chill its readers. Suetonius Paulinus was more than 100 miles (160 kilometres) away, with most of the troops that had been protecting the south-east, exposing Britain's underbelly to attack; despite his high office, Decianus Catus had already demonstrated his stupidity in his treatment of the Iceni, and now compounded it by his totally inadequate response to the needs of the beleaguered colonials and his cowardice in deserting the province. The people of Colchester, the vast majority non-combatants, had no defences and precious few weapons; indeed, Tacitus makes the telling statement that the settlers' pitiful lack of defence was totally inappropriate for a frontier region that was anywhere near a war zone: they were sitting ducks for Boudica's army. The situation was made worse by British infiltrators, 'moles',[45] who deliberately dismissed the need even to erect basic ramparts or dig ditches, the kind of basic precautionary manoeuvre that was undertaken by any army as it pitched camp while on the march. The only structure of any solidity was the temple of Claudius and it was here that the tiny garrison and as many people as could cram themselves in for shelter, holed up, seeking deliverance from slaughter or starvation but waiting in vain. Boudica's troops howled around them, setting fire to everything that would burn. More than 30,000 people are said to have been killed in the Trinovantian capital, an indirect revenge for the death of Britons at Colchester, whose broken and decapitated heads[46] bear witness to the execution of local people by the Romans about five years or so before rebellion erupted.

A modicum of military help did attempt to reach the besieged Roman settlers. As soon as news of the disaster unfolding to the south reached Petillius Cerialis,[47] commander of the Legio IX Hispana, stationed in the East Midlands (possibly at Lincoln, where three tombstones commemorating soldiers of the legion were erected no later than AD 55,[48] but more likely at Longthorpe, Peterborough[49]), he immediately despatched some infantry and cavalry units to relieve Colchester. This was the 'Roman division' to which Tacitus refers in the above-quoted passage. But, in the midst of their sack of Colchester, the Boudican forces wheeled about and attacked Cerialis's troops with such fury that his infantry was annihilated, and the commander and his cavalry fled back to the camp whence he had come. This was a catastrophe indeed: it was one thing for a horde of well-armed British fighters to destroy a town full of veteran soldiers, women, children and other non-combatants, but quite another for a non-professional 'rabble' army to rout a Roman legion, then the best-trained forces in the world. 'The loss of even a part of the legion was a terrifying disaster'.[50] The memory of the destruction of three legions under the command of general Varus by the Germans in AD 9 haunted the Roman government, who saw history repeating itself and the empire to be not quite as invincible as had been perceived. Rome must also have been worried that the eyes of the western empire would be looking interestedly at Britain at this moment, wondering whether it might be possible for others, too, to throw off the yoke of *romanitas*.

According to the ancient literature, Colchester was completely destroyed by Boudica. In the Colchester Castle Museum, there is an evocative painting by Peter Froste (see Plate 20) showing the drama played out in the Roman *colonia* when it was attacked: the focus of fury was concentrated on the hated symbol of Roman oppression, the arrogant statement represented by the temple of Claudius. Froste's picture is dominated by the great classical façade of the sanctuary, wreathed in flames, surrounded by jubilant Icenian and Trinovantian fighters. In its massive stone presence, the temple symbolised foreign domination, alien religion and the veneration of an authoritarian ruler whose whimsical desire to add to his empire had caused the Britons to lose their freedom.

There are, indeed, abundant archaeological signs of a Boudican 'destruction layer', particularly associated with the early Roman legionary fortress,[51] although – as seems true of the two other cities that were victims of Boudica's wrath – it may be that the sacking of the city was less wholesale than has previously been thought. On display in the Castle Museum is a section of burnt daub wall from Lion Walk with the holes left by timber and wattles consumed in the flames clearly visible. The evidence from one Colchester site, St Mary's, situated just outside the city walls,[52] is particularly significant, for a building here exhibits not just signs of burning but of deliberate fire-setting, presumably by Boudica's army. In addition to the presence of burnt daub, archaeologists here discovered traces of brushwood and small kindling, and a charred mattress, a rare example of soft furnishings surviving from the Roman period.[53] The burning uncovered by archaeologists at the Head Street site also shows signs of thorough and systematic fire-setting; indeed it has been pointed out that much of the burning that took place here must have been deliberate, for early Roman buildings would not have caught fire easily 'because the floors and walls were of mud brick and few of the timbers in the walls were exposed' and 'furniture and combustible fittings would have been fairly sparse in those days'.[54] Excavations at the Gilberd School site uncovered a remarkable object, a burnt iron gridiron, semi-circular in shape, with an ornate 'flammiform' design,[55] which appears to be of local rather than of Roman type, perhaps the property of one of the Romanised Britons who fell victim to Boudica's fury.

In addition to the burning of the hated *colonia*, the attacking Trinovantians and Iceni almost certainly tore down the great statue of Claudius that stood in front of his reviled temple. The head was tossed (or ritually deposited) in a nearby river and, more interestingly, one of the horse's legs, looted from Colchester, was taken all the way to Ashill, near Saham Toney in north-west Norfolk, where it was again placed in a sacred context. John Davies has suggested that the leg might have been carried around in the Icenian equivalent of a back-pack into battle and then deposited.[56] If this is right, then it exhibits quite complex issues concerning insult, destruction and the need to neutralise alien force by appropriating parts of the statue and subjecting them to local cult-practice.

Atrocities at Londinium

> But Suetonius, undismayed, marched through disaffected territory to Londinium. This town did not rank as a Roman settlement, but was an important centre for business-men and merchandise. At first, he hesitated whether to stand and fight there. Eventually, his numerical inferiority – and the price only too dearly paid by the divisional commander's rashness – decided him to sacrifice the single city of Londinium to save the province as a whole. Unmoved by lamentations and appeals, Suetonius gave the signal for departure. The inhabitants were allowed to accompany him. But those who stayed because they were women, or old, or attached to the place, were slaughtered by the enemy. Verulamium suffered the same fate
>
> Tacitus *Annals*[57]

London was a 'prime site',[58] established as a new town less than five years after the Claudian invasion of AD 43. Initially, the Roman army identified and fortified a crossing point over the river; then the entrepreneurs moved in: merchants, artisans, shop keepers and others attracted to the prospect of starting anew in a virgin province with limitless opportunities for business. Archaeological evidence demonstrates that these mid–first-century prospectors were already engaged in importing Mediterranean goods, including fine tablewares in ceramics and glass, great amphorae of wine and olive oil,[59] the accoutrements of 'civilised' living in the Roman empire. In the words of Ralph Merrifield London was a place of 'teeming activity and commercial eagerness' in the mid-first century AD.[60] The Thames-side settlement had great natural advantages for development as a city: the largest ocean-going vessels could reach it via the Thames Estuary; moreover, its two hills with the Walbrook running between made the north bank of the Thames ideal for building, free from flooding and with a copious and constant water supply. So even a decade or so after its establishment, London was a flourishing port and trading centre (and, despite its unofficial beginnings, by AD 100 it would replace Colchester as the capital of Britannia). At the time of its threat from Boudica's army, London consisted of a dense huddle of wooden shops and houses, many of them rectangular 'strip-houses', with workshops or retail shops fronting the streets and living quarters behind, together with the hub of any Roman town, its market-place or *forum*.

Archaeological discoveries at Gresham Street have revealed the kind of early Roman communities that occupied London at about the time of the rebellion. A group of roundhouses, built *c.* AD 50, was inhabited by people involved with the production of glass beads (see Plate 21). Curiously, the ornaments were fashioned according to local styles but using glass recycled from Roman vessels and gaming counters. It may be that the glassworkers were working as artisans, even, perhaps enslaved labour for Roman masters, but they may equally have been pragmatic and entrepreneurial Britons exploiting a niche in the market and appropriating Roman discarded goods to make a livelihood out of new, exotic materials.[61] The roundhouses are of Iron Age form, quite distinct from the Roman-introduced long rectangular strip-houses built by Romans or the adopters of Roman ways, so they clearly belonged to Londoners whose affiliations were with their indigenous roots and who used Roman

7 ♦ Rape, rebellion and slaughter

material to fashion jewellery to their own local taste. Significantly, their houses were not burned down by Boudica.[62]

Like Colchester, London was undefended but, unlike the Trinovantian capital, it did not even have the benefit of a great stone temple to shelter in or any kind of garrison to lead its defence. Tacitus paints a bleak picture of the cataclysm that overtook London. It was an event made the more poignant by the arrival of Suetonius Paulinus's army: a sight that must have brought such relief to the Londoners, only to change to horrified dismay as they realised that the general was not stopping to defend them but was going to march away, leaving the old, infirm and vulnerable to their fate. The townsfolk were given a stark choice: to abandon their homes and all their possessions (and the weaker members of their families) and keep up with a highly trained and mobile military machine, or to be left behind to their fate – inevitable massacre. It may be that many inhabitants of the threatened town took to the road, with what they could carry, and that London was fairly empty by the time Boudica's rebel army reached it.

The full horrors of what happened to London can be found in the account of Dio, which is much fuller and less clinical than the testimony of Tacitus. The later historian describes unspeakable atrocities inflicted upon the inhabitants:

> Those who were taken prisoner by the Britons underwent every possible outrage; the most atrocious and bestial committed was this: they hung up naked the noblest and most beautiful women, cut off their breasts and sewed them to their mouths so that they seemed to be eating them. Then they impaled them on sharp stakes which ran the length of their bodies. All this they did to the accompaniment of sacrifices, feasting and orgies in their various sacred places, but especially in the grove of Andate. This is the name they gave to Victory, and they regarded her with particular reverence.[63]

Dio does not specifically mention that it was London that received such a vicious attack but it is usually accepted that it was this city to which he referred in this horrendous account, so reminiscent of examples of recent and present-day ethnic violence, like those perpetrated on the Tutsis by the Hutus (and *vice versa*) in Ruanda.[64] Taking into consideration Dio's undoubted gift for dramatising historical events, together with the embellishments associated with stock Graeco-Roman descriptions of perceived 'barbarism' north of the classical world, this passage has considerable significance, either as a true account or as a fictionalised reconstruction of a war atrocity. Boudica's Britons are portrayed by the Greek historian as merciless savages, wreaking pitiless vengeance on unarmed civilians simply because they were Roman settlers, but there is more to it than that. I suggest that particular cruelty might have been reserved for some of the women as deliberate reprisals for the treatment meted out to Boudica and her daughters. In particular, the mutilation of their breasts and their impalement on spikes seems to represent the symbolic rape of London's Roman women, in direct retaliation for the violation of Boudica's children.

The torture and slaughter of the Roman noblewomen, happening as it did within a sacred grove, has all the hallmarks of human sacrificial killing (see Chapter 6). What is more, cutting off breasts and stuffing them into mouths 'so that they seemed to be eating them' is highly suggestive of vicarious ritual cannibalism. If this is the correct interpretation of Dio's testimony, we can read it in one of two ways: either it is just a further example of barbaric stereotyping, of making out the Britons to be so savage as to be outside humanity, or – if it has any veracity as reportage – such behaviour might constitute a kind of double-insult cannibalism, whereby the enemies of the Britons were made to appear to be eating themselves, in a gross act of humiliation. Although Dio does not say so, lurking behind his words is a particular horror that a woman would do this to other women and that Boudica thus presented herself in even more stark denial of her own gender than that indicated by her position as a battle commander.

Archaeological testimony endorses the violence of Boudica's onslaught on London although, as at Colchester, the destruction horizon here is by no means total. Fire debris is represented, for instance, by burnt clay layers, sometimes containing charred pottery, grain (see Plate 22) and coins as well as fired daub from house-walls.[65] A jeweller hastily buried his or her precious belongings to protect them from the Boudican looters: a pot made at Lugdunum (Lyon) in south-central Gaul was found in Eastcheap; it contained four finger-ring intaglios (gems) of early Neronian date, all decorated with Graeco-Roman motifs, including depictions of Roma, Pegasus and a discus thrower (see Plate 23).[66] Such images would have been meaningless to anyone not clued-in to at least the outward trappings of Roman culture, and these intaglios were surely commissioned for a 'Roman' clientele. Whoever the owner was, he or she never came back to recover them: perhaps he or she fled before Boudica's savagery, or maybe they died as a result of it.

7 ◆ Rape, rebellion and slaughter

A curious occurrence, reported in *British Archaeology* in 2003, was discovered during excavations in the City of London of an early Roman cemetery: it seems that some graves may have been interfered with during Boudica's sack of the town.[67] Two bodies contemporary with the cemetery appear to have been deliberately disturbed and 'desecrated'; an overlying coin confirms that this happened before the 70s AD. An elderly man, minus his lower legs, was thrown into a drainage ditch and the head of a young woman, her jaw missing, placed between his legs. The excavators interpreted the treatment of these bodies as the result of their deliberate removal, as body parts, from graves soon after burial in acts of contemptuous desecration by members of Boudica's forces. While this might well be the correct interpretation, an alternative explanation could have more ritualised overtones. Chris Fowler has explored the symbolism of separating and redepositing parts of human bodies in after-death ceremonies that may be charged with meanings that may have little or nothing to do with dishonouring the dead, but may rather be associated with a need to use human bodies in ritual acts that serve to reaffirm the community's identity or otherwise present notions of personhood.[68] Therefore, it could be that, in the context of the violent upheavals of AD 60, this was a localised act on the part of the kin of the deceased, designed to help rebuild a sense of place and belonging, perhaps by removing certain body parts from their graves and taking them back to their dwellings, or even disposing of them in holy ground in order that the ancestors might help in the re-establishment of the community.

Trial and retribution: the empire strikes back

The natives enjoyed plundering and thought of nothing else. By-passing forts and garrisons, they made for where loot was richest and protection weakest. Roman and provincial deaths at the places mentioned [Colchester, London and Verulamium] are estimated at seventy thousand. For the British did not take or sell prisoners, or practise other war-time exchanges. They could not wait to cut throats, hang, burn, and crucify – as though avenging, in advance, the retribution that was on its way.

Tacitus *Annals*[69]

Hearing of the disaster unfolding behind him, Suetonius Paulinus withdrew from Anglesey and began the long march back to the south-east. Once back on the mainland, his army would have been put on forced march and would have been able to cover perhaps as many as 35 miles (56 kilometres) per day for a short period (his cavalry would have been swifter still).[70] We should appreciate, though, that Suetonius Paulinus's legionaries were heavily armed infantry, whereas the auxiliaries, whose function was to support the legions, were furnished with lighter equipment and could therefore have moved faster than the citizen army.[71] Perhaps as part of his strategy to ensure that Boudica would be unable to call on support from Welsh tribes, the general may have established a chain of forts of this period in south-west Wales, in the territory of the Demetae.[72]

It is useful here to indulge in a brief digression to look at the nature and character of the man who was to defeat Boudica in such a spectacular and final fashion. Tacitus tells us a little about him. In describing Suetonius Paulinus's appointment to the governorship of Britain by Nero, the author refers to him as 'Corbulo's rival in military science',[73] a man of intensely competitive ambition who wished to cover himself with glory through his military campaigns in Britain, just as the famous general Corbulo had done in Armenia two years before, in AD 58,[74] and, indeed, to outdo his rival's achievements in the east. Nero's appointment of such an aggressive imperialist as Suetonius Paulinus indicates very clearly how seriously he took the subjugation of Britain and how formidable a task this was perceived to be. A backwards glance at Suetonius Paulinus's earlier career shows how carefully Nero picked him, for Suetonius Paulinus had a reputation for gaining results in difficult provinces. In AD 41 he had led campaigns against the Mauretanians of North Africa, and was the first general to lead an army across the Atlas mountains.[75] The terrain there was fearsomely rugged, encouraging native guerrilla warfare against the Roman forces, and this valuable experience may well have influenced Nero's choice of commander for Britain, for the Welsh tribes, in particular, took advantage of just such hilly landscapes to set traps and ambushes for the foreign enemy.

Suetonius Paulinus proved to be a worthy opponent of Boudica. His decision to abandon London to its fate is an illustration of his single-mindedess. But in his initial action of moving the main army to Anglesey, leaving the province exposed, he had exhibited gross negligence and an impetuosity that has to be set against his undoubted prowess on the battlefield. Once 'on the case', as it were, the general moved swiftly in pur-

7 ♦ Rape, rebellion and slaughter

suit of Boudica's destructive hordes. Tacitus and Dio both provide detailed accounts, the latter certainly drawing upon the former. According to Tacitus:

> Suetonius collected a brigade and detachments of another, together with the nearest available auxiliaries – amounting to nearly ten thousand armed men – and decided to attack without further delay ... Suetonius drew up his regular troops in close order, with the light-armed auxiliaries at their flanks, and the cavalry massed on the wings. On the British side, cavalry and infantry bands seethed over a wide area. Their numbers were unprecedented, and they had confidently brought their wives to see the victory, installing them in carts stationed at the edge of the battlefield.[76]

Dio says:

> On learning of the disaster in Britain he immediately sailed back from the island [of Mona]. However, fear of the natives' numbers and their mad fury dissuaded him from risking everything against them. Rather, he was inclined to put off battle till a more suitable occasion, but since he was short of food and there was no let-up in the native onslaught, he was forced to engage them, even against his better judgement.[77]

In the later first century AD, Sextus Julius Frontinus wrote a treatise on Roman warfare, entitled *The Art of War*. The only portion of this work to survive in its original form is an appendix (the *Strategemata*). Fortunately, the later military writer Flavius Vegetius included a great deal of Frontinus's material in his own manual of Roman army institutions, the *Epitoma rei militaris*, probably written in the later fourth century AD.[78] Vegetius (probably following Frontinus) stresses how important it was for the soldiers to be rested and well fed before pitched battles, and also, how crucial was the choice of the army's position on the ground. Clearly, as Tacitus relates,[79] Suetonius Paulinus was able to select the best terrain for his stand against Boudica's forces. Even so, following his dash down from Anglesey to his encounter with the rebels (somewhere in the Midlands: see below), his troops would have been neither rested nor well nourished, and Dio makes this very point. Not only did Suetonius Paulinus have to cope with tired and hungry soldiers (and if forced marches were involved, then the heavily encumbered infantry[80] would probably have had to jettison some of their equipment before the dash south) but also he could muster only 10,000 men,[81] whereas, if Dio is to be believed,[82] Boudica commanded a force of 230,000. Suetonius

Paulinus had most, if not all, of Legion XX, some units of Legion XIV and 'those auxiliaries he was able to summon from nearby bases'.[83] Legion IX was in a bad way after its earlier mauling by Boudican forces, and its commander, Cerialis, had retired back to his fortress (at Lincoln?) to lick his wounds and to try and restore morale in the legionaries who were left. Suetonius Paulinus's desperate shortage of manpower was exacerbated by the absence of Legion II, stationed at Exeter. For some reason, it was under the command of the *praefectus castrorum*, the third-ranking officer, a man named Poenius Postumus who failed to answer Paulinus's summons to battle.[84] The odds, it seemed, were stacked against the Romans. There was fallout, too, when the final reckoning came. Thus, after recounting the final battle between the Romans and Boudica's Britons, Tacitus refers to the disgrace felt by Poenius's legion in not participating in the fighting, and to Poenius's suicide: Poenius was humiliated by his soldiers' opprobrium at his cowardice and his cheating them of their share of battle-spoils; he also knew that he had disobeyed orders[85].

Discipline and disorder: carnage and defeat

Boudicca drove around all the tribes in a chariot with her daughters in front of her. 'We British are used to women commanders in war', she cried. 'I am descended from mighty men! But I am not fighting for my kingdom and wealth now. I am fighting as an ordinary person for my lost freedom, my bruised body, and my outraged daughters. Nowadays Roman rapacity does not even spare our bodies. Old people are killed, virgins raped. But the gods will grant us the vengeance we deserve! The Roman division which dared to fight is annihilated. The others cower in their camps, or watch for a chance to escape. They will never face even the din and roar of all our thousands, much less the shock of our onslaught. Consider how many of you are fighting – and why! Then you will win this battle, or perish. That is what I, a woman, plan to do! – let the men live in slavery if they will.'[86]

In this harangue, Tacitus puts into the mouth of Boudica all the outpouring of resentment felt by the Britons against Roman domination. Boudica refers to the need for reparation following the dishonour done to the Icenian royal house; she jeers at the rout of Cerialis's relief force from Legion IX and is probably also making scornful allusion to the cowardice she reads into the non-appearance of Legion II from Exeter. What is especially interesting is her double reference to her role as a female com-

7 ◆ Rape, rebellion and slaughter

mander; in particular, she hints that some of her male warriors are showing a reluctance in following her into open war with Suetonius Paulinus preferring, perhaps, to continue their plundering way through the Roman settlements of the province rather than risk all on the battlefield in a pitched fight (which they may – rightly – have perceived as perilous, given the Roman army's reputation as a highly efficient fighting machine). Boudica also alludes to the noise the Britons made in battle; this consisted not only of blood-curdling yells and the clash of weapons against shields, but also of the heart-stopping blare of the *carnyx*, the famous Gallo-British war-trumpet, sometimes as large as a warrior, mentioned in the ancient literature, depicted in iconography and surviving as fragments in the archaeological record (see Plate 10).[87]

Both Tacitus and Dio describe how Suetonius Paulinus gives a pre battle pep-talk to his army. Dio is quite long-winded, presenting the general as making separate, though similar, speeches to three divisions. Tacitus, as usual, is briefer and more terse and precedes his exhortation with the statement that 'Suetonius trusted his men's bravery' (unlike Boudica). Suetonius Paulinus, like the Icenian war commander, makes reference to gender and he reassures his troops that the Britons' superior numbers should not cause them undue anxiety:

> *Disregard the clamours and empty threats of the natives ... In their ranks, there are more women than fighting men. Unwarlike, unarmed, when they see the arms and courage of the conquerors who have routed them so often, they will break immediately. Even when a force contains many divisions, few among them win the battles – what special glory for your small numbers to win the renown of a whole army! Just keep in close order. Throw your javelins, and then carry one: use shield-bosses to fell them, swords to kill them. Do not think of plunder. When you have won, you will have everything.*[88]

Tacitus makes Suetonius Paulinus encourage the Roman troops in a stock fashion, jeering at the enemy's weakness, and extolling the virtues of small numbers because the honour is the greater and so is the spoil. The detail of fighting methods is interesting: reference is made to the carrying of two javelins, the use of shields not only to protect but also to batter, and the employment of the *gladius* or short sword for close combat. The allusion to plunder is, perhaps, a contrast to how the pillaging behaviour of the Britons is perceived. There is macho blustering here, too, and a display of the self-confidence emanating from the apparent ease of initial conquest.

The longer speech presented in Dio's text gives similar but more detailed messages.[89] Suetonius Paulinus refers to the Britons as 'murdering savages' and 'accursed creatures'; he comforts the troops by telling them that the gods are on their side and that the Britons' torching of the Roman towns was achieved through treachery, and because one of the towns (London) was abandoned before the rebels arrived, rather than by superior battle technique. In Dio's account the tone of Suetonius Paulinus's harangue indicates that his army is frightened, and he seeks to encourage them by promising glorious victory and the riches that accrue from such an outcome. He also refers to the alternative to fighting the enemy: the total loss of the province. The arrogance of the Roman attitude is embedded in the phrase 'it is not our adversaries we are about to engage but our slaves whom we have conquered even when they were free and independent'. Dio makes the general end his speech on a sinister note:

> If, however, something unexpected happens – I will not shrink from mentioning even this possibility – it is better for us to fall fighting manfully than to be captured and impaled, to see our own entrails cut from us, to be skewered on red-hot spits, and to perish by being rendered down in boiling water, to perish as though we had been thrown to lawless and godless wild beasts. Let us therefore conquer them or die here. Britain will be a fine monument for us even if all other Romans are driven out of it, since at all events we shall possess it with our bodies.[90]

Nobody knows exactly where the denouement of the drama took place. Tacitus describes the terrain selected by Suetonius Paulinus but, maddeningly, does not pinpoint its location: 'He chose a position in a defile with a wood behind him. There could be no enemy, he knew, except at his front, where there was open country without cover for ambushes'.[91]

There has been considerable speculation as to the precise location of this final and decisive pitched battle. It is usually placed somewhere in the Midlands (see Map 5), and Mancetter has long been a favoured choice.[92] But recent suggestions include Paulerspury near Towcester in Northamptonshire, a place that fits Tacitus's brief description of the battlefield and which would accord with the Roman army's march down

7 ◆ Rape, rebellion and slaughter

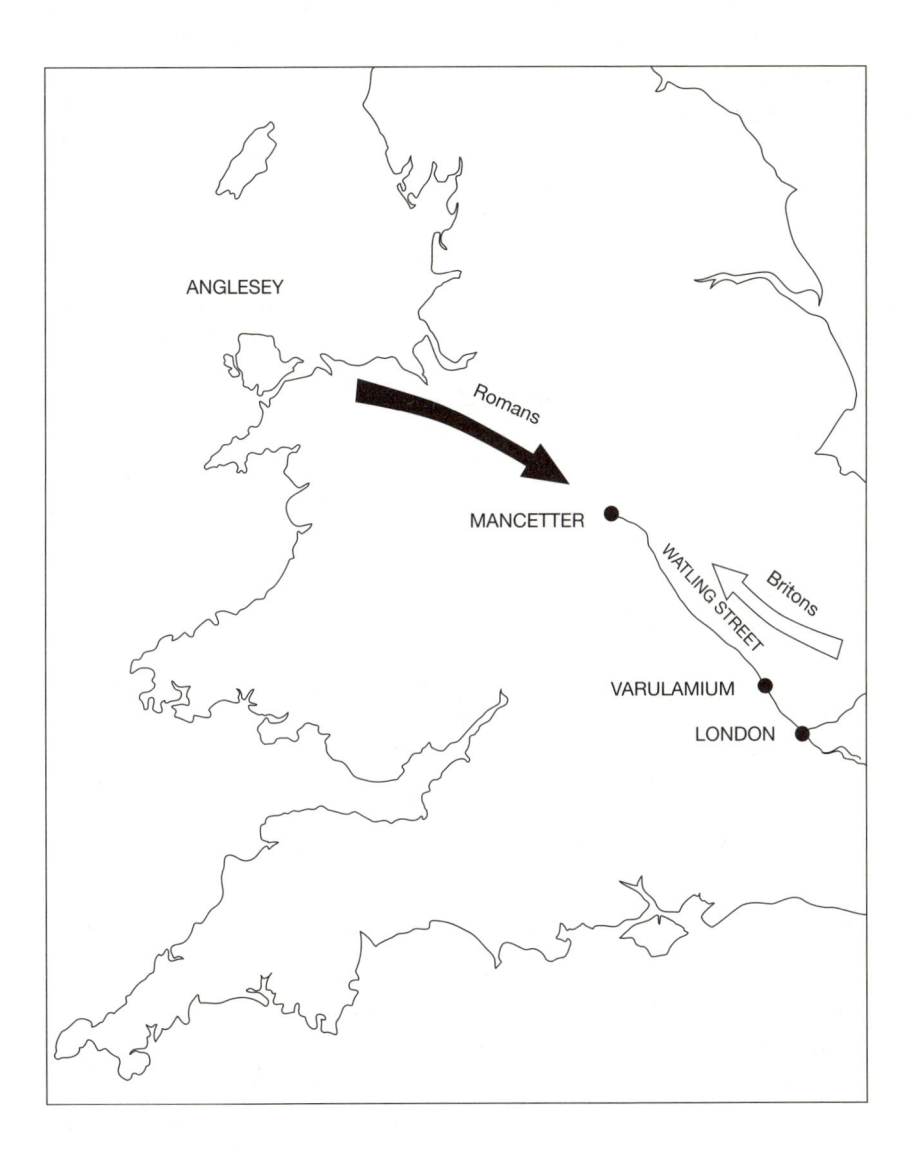

MAP 5 ◆ *British and Roman forces before the final pitched battle between Boudica and Suetonius Paulinus.*

Source: Sealey 1997.

Watling Street from the north-west to intercept Boudica's forces surging towards them from St Alban's, the last urban victim of their annihilation campaign;[93] and a location between Godmanchester in Cambridgeshire and Great Chesterford, Essex.[94] The simple fact is we will never know. Importantly, though, we do have some detailed documentation about the battle itself from our two classical commentators, Tacitus and Dio. Let us listen to the latter historian first:

> *The two sides closed on one another: the natives with much shouting and threatening warsongs, the Romans in silence and order until they came within javelin range. Then, when the enemy was still advancing against them at walking pace, the Romans rushed forward in a mass at a given signal, and charged them for all they were worth. In the onslaught they easily broke through the opposing ranks of the Britons, though they were surrounded by the great numbers (of the enemy) and engaged in fighting on all sides at once. The struggle took many forms: light-armed troops exchanged missiles with other light-armed forces; heavy-armed were matched against heavy-armed; cavalry engaged cavalry, and Roman archers clashed with the native chariots. The natives would swoop upon the Romans with their chariots, throwing them into confusion, and then be themselves repulsed by the arrows, since they fought without breastplates. Horsemen would ride down infantrymen, and infantrymen would strike down cavalrymen. One group of Romans in close formation would advance on the chariots; another would be scattered by them. Some of the Britons would close with the archers and put them to flight; others kept out of their way at a distance, and all this was going on not just in one spot but in three places at once. Both sides fought for a long time, spurred by equal spirit and daring, but finally, late in the day, the Romans prevailed. Many Britons were cut down in the battle and before the wagons and the woods. Many too were taken alive.*[95]

In their recent book *Battlefield Britain* Peter and Dan Snow have analysed the battle techniques of the Romans and the Britons in this great culmination of the Boudican war.[96] The small, tightly disciplined Roman force proved more than a match for the huge numbers of British combatants. Boudica made some fatal errors, not least an overweening self-confidence based entirely upon her superior numbers and the grouping of wagons full of supporters that, in the event, restricted the Britons' ability to manoeuvre and to escape. This custom of battle-watching from the vantage point of baggage vehicles was apparently quite common in Britain and Gaul. In his account of his war with the Germans in 58 BC, Julius Caesar mentions how their women lined up around the battlefield on a

7 ♦ Rape, rebellion and slaughter

barrier made of wagons,[97] and Tacitus's description of the rebellion of the Batavian leader Civilis in AD 69 includes reference to the way in which the freedom fighter's female relatives were positioned behind the army to shriek encouragement or imprecations so that the rebels would fight all the harder.[98]

While the Britons appeared to lack cohesion and real leadership, the Roman army relied on its discipline and long history of tried and tested battle tactics, built upon tight formation and the reliance placed by each soldier upon his fellows, led by a superb veteran commander. Suetonius Paulinus's soldiers first each hurled one of their two javelins at the enemy: this would produce a deadly volley of fire that could travel about 100 feet (30 metres), and would have the further effect that the soft iron shafts bent on impact, so that if they stuck in warriors' shields, they could not be pulled out and thrown back. What is more, the shields themselves became useless and had to be discarded. Once the Romans had discharged their javelins, close combat was initiated, but here again the Britons were at a disadvantage, for their swords and spears were long and cumbersome, unsuitable for hand-to-hand combat, while the short sword of the Roman legionary was eminently appropriate for this kind of fighting. The British chariots[99] might be thought of as capable of giving them an advantage over the Romans, who had no such 'battle-taxis'.[100] But recent consultation with equestrian experts has revealed indications – arising from experimental archaeology[101] – that chariots, used in battle, would have been no match for well-drilled and experienced cavalry.

Tacitus gives us further information on the final battle between Boudica and Suetonius Paulinus, following the Roman commander's exhortation to his troops:

> *The general's words were enthusiastically received: the old battle-experienced soldiers longed to hurl their javelins. So Suetonius confidently gave the signal for battle. At first, the regular troops stood their ground. Keeping to the defile as a natural defence, they launched their javelins accurately at the approaching enemy. Then, in wedge formation, they burst forward. So did the auxiliary infantry. The cavalry, too, with lances extended, demolished all serious resistance. The remaining Britons fled with difficulty since their ring of wagons blocked the outlets. The Romans did not spare even the women. Baggage animals too, transfixed with weapons, added to the heaps of the dead.*[102]

Tacitus goes on to stress the glorious victory achieved by the Romans, making the (undoubtedly exaggerated) claim that only about 400 of Suetonius Paulinus's soldiers fell in the battle, while he alleges (again, the numbers are almost certainly grossly distorted) that the Britons lost nearly 80,000 of their fighters. Paul Sealey suggests that many Icenian casualties were likely to have been caused by crushing and trampling as they were squeezed between Roman troops and their own baggage trains.[103] One interesting point is Tacitus's mention of the 'wedge formation' used by the Roman troops: a time-honoured method (employed by the Greeks and Macedonians before them) of deploying soldiers massed in a repeated double-arrowhead/wedge formation to smash their way through a mass of enemy warriors.[104] This proved irresistible: each man's flank was protected by the soldier fighting next to him, while the *gladius* could be used to good effect. The Britons were hopelessly out-manoeuvred and were cut down in their thousands. The blood-bath that ensued, and the berserk behaviour of the Roman forces, in sparing neither non-combatants nor even the baggage-animals (both of which it would have been economically useful to preserve, as slaves or pack-beasts) exhibits the pent-up anger felt by Suetonius Paulinus and his men at the destruction of Colchester, London and Verulamium and the ruthless massacre of their Roman or Roman-friendly inhabitants.

The extreme aggression shown by Britain's Roman governor in his treatment of the rebels (both at the time of the final confrontation and afterwards: see Chapter 8) led ultimately to his disgrace and recall from the province. But in his punitive actions, which amounted to war crimes in themselves, Suetonius was not alone among Roman generals. Julius Caesar, who had a certain reputation for clemency, could (and, perhaps, should) have been indicted for his treatment of the Nervii, a Belgic tribe who inhabited territory in northern Gaul, to the east of the river Scheldt. Caesar admired the courage and indomitable spirit of this tribe, yet after fighting them, virtually the entire people – and even the name of the Nervii – were obliterated. 'In describing the disaster their tribe had suffered, they said that from their council of 600 only three men had survived, and barely 500 from their fighting force of 60,000'.[105] But, unlike Suetonius Paulinus, Caesar did display compassion to the pitiful few that were left and took measures to ensure they were left unmolested either by the Romans or fellow Gauls from neighbouring tribes.

The death of Boudica: an ignominious or noble end

Boudicca vitam veneno finivit: *'Boudicca killed herself with poison'*.

Tacitus *Annals*[106]

Thus Tacitus, always an economical wordsmith, dismisses the death of Boudica and, by implication, the end of the British war, in a brief sentence. Dio tells a slightly different and fuller story, saying that:

> Many Britons were cut down in the battle and before the wagons and the woods. Many too were taken alive. Some, however, escaped and made preparations to fight again, but when in the meantime Boudouica fell ill and died the Britons mourned her deeply and gave her a lavish funeral, and then they disbanded in the belief that now they really were defeated.[107]

Dio, then, says something that departs radically from Tacitus's narrative, both in the recording of Boudica's end and in his account of the collection of war prisoners. The divergence between the two authors in the description of the Icenian leader's death need not concern us over much except that, if poison was used, Tacitus's comment suggests that it was a fast-acting toxin that killed her on the battlefield before she could be captured (doubtless in order to avoid the same humiliation meted out to Caratacus some ten years earlier: see above, Chapter 5), while Dio suggests that Boudica lingered for a time before dying. Of course, it is not known what kind of poison Boudica may have taken, but we can speculate about the sorts of narcotic available in Britain at the time: alkaloids, such as *datura* and *belladonna* and other plant drugs, such as mandrake or hemlock,[108] might have been used; it might be that Boudica was accustomed to ingest psychotropic substances[109] in order to attain a trance-state and predict the future, and so she may have been familiar with what constituted a 'safe' amount and how much extra to take to induce a fatal overdose. What we should appreciate, though, is that the *topos* (or theme) of suicide by a defeated commander is a common literary device designed to project an image of honour and courage. Thus Boudica's noble end is paralleled by Diodorus Siculus's account of the Gaulish chieftain Brennus' suicide after defeat by the Greeks in the campaign at Delphi in 279 BC. According to Diodorus, the Gallic warrior-chief killed himself by a combination of neglecting a battle injury and alcohol abuse.[110]

Dio's final words are highly significant: according to his testimony the rebellion died with Boudica. While she was alive, the tattered remnants of the British army could regroup within a focused and relatively unified context; at her death, the Britons fell back into their tribes, clans and factions. Even when the revolt was at its height, Boudica was unable to hold her army together with the single goal of defeating the Romans; instead, many of them were more interested in plunder than in a fight for freedom. So when Boudica was no longer among them, even the tenuous links that bound the British forces together were broken: the fragments of her army, no longer even bound to her, were easy for Suetonius Paulinus's legionaries to hunt down and pick off without risk. The flames of resistance were quenched as quickly as they had been ignited. But we should not forget the 'lavish funeral' that Dio reports the Britons give their fallen freedom leader: perhaps, like the earlier ladies from Vix, Wetwang and elsewhere in Iron Age Europe (see Chapter 4), her burial was conducted with great ceremony. We do not know where her remains were interred, but we can imagine that her funeral rites would have been conducted with a view to embedding memory of who she was and what she represented. But also – perhaps – this was an act of closure, a way of saying farewell. There is no reason why (*contra* Sealey[111]) her funeral should not have been a spectacular event, even though her grave, like those of other Icenians, has left no archaeological trace.

Finally, it is worth posing the question as to how Boudica might have perceived and explained her defeat, against all the odds and the auguries.[112] I suggest that the answer may well have been that she interpreted the event in terms of a contest between British and Roman divine forces, in which the gods of the colonial intruders were deemed to be the stronger. As Dio makes Suetonius say,[113] the Britons were accursed and the gods were on his side.

Notes and references

1 Tacitus *Agricola* 5; trans. Mattingly 1948, 55.
2 Op. cit. 14.31; trans. Grant 1956, 318.
3 Castle Museum, Colchester: de la Bédoyère 2003b, 216.
4 Hingley 2005.

5 Fishwick 1972; 1995.

6 The head of a statue of Claudius, hacked from the body, was found in the river Alde in Suffolk (British Museum); part of the leg of his horse was deposited near the ceremonial and high-status site of Saham Toney in Norfolk: Sealey 1997, 29, fig. 17; Norwich Castle Museum, John Davies pers. com.

7 Dio Cassius *Roman History* 62.2.

8 Op. cit. 62.2; trans. Ireland 1996, 63–70. It may be that the large numbers of Roman coins turning up in East Anglian coin-hoards of pre-Boudican and Boudican date can be explained in terms of Seneca's loan money. Paul Sealey (pers. com.) has drawn my attention to the dearth of Roman forts in the area of pre-Boudican vintage, so these coins cannot be the result of military activity in the region at this period.

9 A literary device designed to bring historical accounts to life and give them the stamp of authenticity.

10 Tacitus *Agricola* 15; trans. Mattingly 1948, 65.

11 Cicero *In Verrem (Against Verres)* 2.5.48.127; after Chisholm & Ferguson 1981, 406.

12 The governor would have been of senatorial rank, the procurator the class below, known as the equestrian class. 'Augustus had made a sharp distinction between these two social orders, providing both with an opportunity for a progressive career in public service within the framework of an ordered pattern of promotion. The senatorial order filled military posts, while the equestrians were mainly civil servants': Scullard 1979, 88.

13 Scullard 1979, 88.

14 Mellor 1993, 127.

15 Tacitus *Annals* 14.30.

16 Undoubtedly a serious error of judgement: in putting conquest and a greed for glory before consolidation, Suetonius left the province dangerously vulnerable: Shotter 1998, 18–20.

17 Flogging was almost unheard of in the treatment of free women, and rape was undoubtedly a capital offence: Allason-Jones 1989, 16–20.

18 Bauman 1996, 24, 72.

19 Alston 1998, 219.

20 De la Bédoyère 2003b, 216.

21 Witness the public scourging of Christ before his crucifixion by Roman soldiers: Mark 15:15; John 19:1, an act of public degradation along with stripping, spitting (by the Jews) and the mocking crown of thorns.

22 Ferris 2000, especially 57–61.
23 Op. cit. 104. In the book *Erotic Ambiguities* (2001), McDonald alludes to nakedness as associated with the availability of the body for a sexual encounter. On the Aphrodisias monument, Britannia has an exposed breast and Claudius is also virtually nude.
24 Rankin 1996, 220–2.
25 Children visiting the Colchester Castle Museum can 'try on' a Roman slave-chain: Berridge & Hodgson 1997, 9. For skeletal evidence of shackle wearing in Roman Britain *see* Watts 2005, 101.
26 Dio Cassius *Roman History* 62.1.
27 Polybius *Histories* 3.107–18; Livy *History of Rome* 22.43–9.
28 Plutarch *Life of Crassus* 19ff; Pliny *Natural History* 5.85.
29 Black 2001, 416.
30 Tacitus *Annals* 14.32.
31 Simpson 1996, 386; Standing 2005, 373.
32 Rasmussen 2000, 11; as, for instance, discussed by Cicero in speeches such as *de doma sua* and *de haruspicum responso*.
33 Morgan 2000, 26–7.
34 Op. cit. 29.
35 Tacitus *Histories* 1.86.
36 Morgan 2000, 35.
37 A fictional graffito in the Museum of London's Roman Gallery (see Figure 5.1), next to the Boudican display.
38 Tacitus *Agricola* 16; trans. Mattingly 1948, 66.
39 Dio Cassius *Roman History* 62.7.
40 Tacitus *Annals* 14.32. This is a good example of Tacitus's expression of Roman decadence and slipshod governance presented – at least in part – in order to make a contrast between the performance of governors like Paulinus and his paragon of a father-in-law, Agricola: Mellor 1993, 128.
41 Tacitus *Annals* 14.33.
42 Farrar 2005, 18.
43 Scullard 1959, 5; Polybius *Histories* 36.9. For the phrase '*Carthago delenda est*' see Plutarch, *Life of Cato* 27; trans. Scott-Kilvert 1965, 150.
44 Tacitus *Annals* 14.32; trans. Grant 1956, 318–19.

45 In later twentieth-century Cold-War parlance: *see*, for example John Le Carré's *Tinker, Tailor, Soldier, Spy*, 1974.

46 Sealey 1997, 18.

47 Cerialis was later to become the governor of Britain, his major military success being the subjugation of the Brigantes: 'But when Vespasian, in the course of his general triumph, recovered Britain, there came a succession of great generals and splendid armies, and the hopes of our enemies dwindled. Petillius Cerialis at once struck terror into their hearts by attacking the state of the Brigantes, which is said to be the most populous in the whole province': Tacitus *Agricola* 17; trans. Mattingly 1948, 67.

48 Todd 2004, 52.

49 Frere & St Joseph 1974, 38–9.

50 De la Bédoyère 2003a, 65.

51 Colchester Archaeological Trust 2003a, 22–3.

52 These walls were not in place at the time of Boudica's attack but were built later on in the Roman history of the city.

53 Paul Sealey, Philip Crummy pers. com.; Colchester Archaeological Trust 2003b, 10–15.

54 Colchester Archaeological Trust 2001, 10.

55 Crummy 1992, 217–18, fig. 6.13.

56 Pers. com. (Norwich Castle Museum).

57 Tacitus *Annals* 14. 33.

58 The heading for one of the display boards on the establishment of London in the Museum of London's Roman Gallery (9 April 2005).

59 Marsden 1980, 25.

60 Merrifield 1983, 52.

61 Museum of London display board 17 May 2005; Bateman 1998, 213.

62 Hingley 2005, 40.

63 Dio Cassius *Roman History* 62.7.

64 Paul Theroux's biography of V.S. Naipaul (*Sir Vidia's Shadow*, 1998, 91) gives a horrific account of Hutu atrocities on the Tutsi people in Ruanda.

65 Verulamium similarly had evidence of burning in a Boudican layer of ash beneath part of the city: Verulamium Museum; Niblett 2001, 67.

66 Museum of London 17 May 2005; Schofield & Maloney 1998, 192.

67 Denison 2003, 4.

68 Fowler 2004, 79–100.
69 Tacitus *Annals* 14.33; trans. Grant 1956, 310.
70 I am indebted to Dr Kate Gilliver, of the School of History and Archaeology, Cardiff University, for information about forced marches. Julius Caesar was a notoriously quick-moving general: in his *de Bello Gallico* 5.47, for example, he refers to marching 20 miles (32 kilometres) a day; but his forced marches (5. 48) were faster still, and involved legionaries' shedding a great deal of their heavy gear. Kate Gilliver (pers. com. 13 April 2005) has made the point that a forced march could be sustained only for a short period of time and that an army would be in no fit state to fight at the end of it. But Caesar is reported to have force-marched his legions at 35 miles (56 kilometres) a day with a two-hour rest-break during times of crisis: Benario 1986, 360 and his fn 146.
71 Anderson 1987, 104.
72 For instance at Llandeilo: Jones & Cook 2005.
73 Tacitus *Annals* 14.29.
74 Gnaeus Domitius Corbulo was a superb military commander who conducted a successful campaign against the Parthians, Rome's most formidable enemy, for the possession of Armenia: Tacitus *Annals* 13.32–9; trans. Grant 1956, 289–93. Corbulo had the reputation for being a severe disciplinarian, remorseless in hunting down and executing deserters, and not flinching from the infliction of any necessary hardship on his army.
75 Pliny *Natural History* 3.14. 'In pursuit of the Moors retreating to the desert, C. Suetonius Paulinus ... led his troops into the typical *reg* of the Sahara, all bare rock, and black gravel': Raven 1969, 45. Bearing in mind comparisons between Paulinus and the famously harsh command of his rival Corbulo, it is worth mentioning that on the African campaign Paulinus had to abandon the pursuit of the Mauretanian resistance fighters after ten days because his army suffered so badly from thirst and the effects of the desert sun (Raven *op. cit.*).
76 Tacitus *Annals* 14. 34; trans. Grant 1956, 319–20.
77 Dio Cassius *Roman History* 62.8; trans. Ireland 1996, 63–70.
78 Some time between AD 383 and 450.
79 Tacitus *Annals* 14.34, and see below.
80 Speidel 1992, fig. 6.
81 Tacitus *Annals* 14.34.
82 Dio Cassius *Roman History* 62.8.
83 Sealey 1997, 38.

84 After the legionary commander and senior tribune. The *praefectus castrorum* was a kind of non-commissioned officer (or chief of staff), a career soldier of middle years who had risen through the ranks and gained seniority as a chief centurion or *primus pilus*: Webster 1969, 117 and fn2.

85 Tacitus *Annals* 14.37.

86 Op. cit. 14.35.

87 Hunter 2001; Maniquet 2005, 29–31: Christophe Maniquet reports on new finds of bronze *carnyces* at a temple-complex at Arènes near Tintignac, Corrèze, Central France. Four of the five had boars' heads, the fifth that of a snake. They were ritually deposited in the shrine, probably in the first century BC, as offerings to the gods of victory.

88 Tacitus *Annals* 14.36.

89 Dio Cassius *Roman History* 62.9–11.

90 Op. cit. 62.11.

91 Tacitus *Annals* 14.34; trans. Grant 1956, 319–20.

92 See, for example, the map in Sealey 1997, fig. 24; Hingley & Unwin 2004, 102.

93 Snow & Snow 2004, 23.

94 Gould 2004, 300.

95 Dio Cassius *Roman History* 62.12; trans. Ireland 1996, 63–70.

96 A publication arising from a BBC Television series of the same name: Snow & Snow 2004, 12–37.

97 Caesar *De Bello Gallico* 1.51.

98 Tacitus *Histories* 4.18. I have suggested elsewhere (Green 1995, 29–30) that this audience might be seen as the ancient equivalent of cheer-leaders at an American football or baseball game.

99 The Romans would have been unused to dealing with chariot warfare: Caesar (*de Bello Gallico* IV, 24, 32; V, 15–17) speaks of British chariots encountered by his army in 55 and 54 BC, but such war vehicles had long been obsolete in Gaul.

100 James 1993, 78 According to Caesar (*de Bello Gallico* 4.33), British war-chariots were employed mainly to convey warriors into battle and out of it into safety.

101 Chris Winstanley, pers. com. 'Archaic pursuits and events: horses through history' June 2004.

102 Tacitus *Annals* 14. 36–7; trans. Grant 1956, 320.

103 Paul Sealey pers. com.

104 Snow & Snow 2004, 32–4. Incidentally a version of this tactic was – until made illegal – used in rugby games (Ray Howell pers. com.).

105 Caesar *de Bello Gallico* 2.27–28; trans. Wiseman & Wiseman 1980, 54.

106 Tacitus *Annals* 14.37; trans. Grant 1956, 321.

107 Dio Cassius *Roman History* 62.12; trans. Ireland 1996, 63–70.

108 Rudgley 1999, 76.

109 Substances such as ergot, henbane and artimesia have been found in Iron Age contexts: Aldhouse-Green & Aldhouse-Green 2005, especially ch. 5. *See* also this volume Chapter 6; Schultes *et al.* 2001, 86–7; Rudgley 1993, 94–5. There is evidence for the presence of hemlock on Romano-British sites, including those in Norfolk, south-east England and South Wales: Godwin 1975, 223.

110 Diodorus Siculus *Library of History* 22.92; Rankin 1996, 95–6.

111 Paul Sealey, pers. com.

112 Nigel Bryant (Marlborough College) pers. com.

113 Dio Cassius *Roman History* 62, 9–11.

CHAPTER 8

Aftermath: retribution and reconciliation

The whole army was now united. Suetonius kept it under canvas to finish the war. The emperor raised its numbers by transferring from Germany two thousand regular troops, also eight auxiliary infantry battalions and a thousand cavalry. These were stationed together in new winter quarters, and hostile or wavering tribes were ravaged with fire and sword. But the enemy's worst affliction was famine. For they had neglected sowing their fields and brought everyone available into the army, intending to seize our supplies.

Tacitus *Annals*[1]

At the end of Chapter 7 we left the defeated Boudica dead from poisoning or illness, either on the battlefield or soon after having left it to the victorious Roman enemy, and being laid to rest with elaborate ceremony, in a richly furnished tomb. This chapter is concerned with what happened next. The province of Roman Britain had suffered a major setback in its progress towards full integration into the empire. According to Derek Allen the Boudican rebellion and its consequences put the territories most fully engaged with the uprising back into the dark ages, and 'delayed the Romanisation of East Anglia by at least a generation'.[2] But this is to get ahead of the immediate aftermath of the great war, and we need first to examine the direct results both of the revolt itself and the means taken to quell the remaining flickers of resistance and to punish the rebels. While Boudica had, through her death, deprived Suetonius Paulinus of a triumphal spectacle in Rome with her display in chains before the Roman people – a fate that would undoubtedly have come her way, as it had to Caratacus before her – the governor nonetheless wreaked his vengeance with uncontrolled savagery on the survivors. Not only did the Britons have to endure 'fire and sword' but also extreme hunger, brought about partly by the destruction of land and livestock by Paulinus's avenging troops. But the decision not to plant crops, mentioned by Tacitus (above), may be accounted for by a decision the Iceni may have taken to emigrate from East Anglia, a suggestion made by Sheppard Frere.[3] We can imagine here the kind of 'scorched earth' policy that unhappily still takes place in present-day war areas: the devastation of the Darfur region of Sudan, a once beautiful land where strawberries grew on the slopes of Jebel Marra, is a case in point.[4]

Britannia in chains

One feature of the Boudican war cannot be overestimated: the peril in which the British revolt placed the integrity of Rome's empire. In a typical throwaway phrase, Tacitus summed up the situation, saying that 'had not Paulinus, on hearing of the revolt, made speed to help, Britain would have been lost'.[5] In his *Life of Nero*, the imperial biographer, (another) Suetonius, wrote what amounts to the same thing:

> Nero probably felt no ambition to extend the Roman Empire, and even considered withdrawing his forces from Britain; yet kept them there because such a decision might have reflected on the glory won by his adoptive father Claudius.[6]

Such a reaction to the ruin engendered in the province by the rebellion and consonant punitive measures was almost unheard of for a Roman emperor, even one who did not follow an aggressively expansionist policy, for, without doubt, withdrawal from a province – and because of a native revolt – would have severely dented his reputation, both at home and abroad and would, furthermore, have served to lower army morale very considerably. Most dangerous of all, however, would have been the green light such a move would have shown to any other unhappy provincials anywhere in the empire, potentially giving rise to a domino-cascade of uprisings and anarchy.

It is difficult to judge what posed the greater threat to the survival of Britannia as a Roman province: the rebellion itself or the retribution meted out by Suetonius Paulinus. In his *Agricola*, Tacitus comments that 'many guilty rebels refused to lay down their arms out of a peculiar dread of the legate',[7] suggesting a vicious spiral of resistance, punishment, further insurgence and so on until the province was drained of resources and morale. The writer makes further reference to the part played by the character of the governor, describing his behaviour as unduly harsh, even to the Britons who surrendered to him, saying that Suetonius Paulinus behaved as though the wrongs done to the Romans in Britain (whether soldiers or civilians) had been inflicted on him personally and he thus punished the Britons in a particularly personal manner, allowing his rage to get the better of his judgement. Suetonius Paulinus was clearly a brilliant general but he seems to have been a less than competent governor; the mistake perhaps made by central administration had been to equate the two jobs and to assume that a good field commander would be equally adroit at managing an emergent province: a task that required the specialist administrative skills of a senior civil servant that were by no means identical to those needed for an army leader.

In Chapter 7 a comparison was made between the actions of the Roman governor at the battle that ended the Boudican rebellion and those of Julius Caesar in his conflict with the Gallic Nervii some hundred years earlier. But there is a vital difference, in so far as Caesar was acting in the context of a front-line war situation, whereas Suetonius Paulinus was continuing to behave as though this were the case even when the Britons had been utterly defeated. The inference has to be that Suetonius Paulinus was being driven by vindictiveness and a desire to annihilate those who had had the temerity to rise against his administration. But there are certain similarities between Caesar and Suetonius Paulinus: both were driven by desire for glory through conquest; and both had been thwarted by heavy defeats, the one at the hands of Vercingetorix at Gergovia, in the Auvergne, the other in the form of Boudica's destruction of Roman cities in Britain and the trouncing of Legion IX led by Cerialis. So each Roman commander had scores to settle with an unruly and presumptuous barbarian enemy. After the final battle with Boudica, Suetonius Paulinus continued the slaughter; after the battle of Alesia in 52 BC, Caesar pursued the Gallic fugitives, and 'killed or captured great numbers of them'. He tells us that he employed some of the prisoners as bargaining counters, 'hoping to use them to regain the loyalty of their tribes'. The remainder of them 'I distributed as booty among the entire army, giving one prisoner to each of my men'.[8] We can only assume that the war captives that fell into the hands of Suetonius Paulinus's soldiers suffered a similar fate and were dispersed as slaves.

Derek Allen has drawn attention to archaeological evidence for the non-reoccupation of old Icenian settlements after AD 60, something that may well indicate that their inhabitants did not survive to return home.[9] It has been suggested[10] that Caesar's actions, both at Alesia and (see above) and in the aftermath of other battles in Gaul, like those against the Nervii, were tantamount to genocide. It is an accusation that we may fairly apply to Suetonius Paulinus's behaviour after the Boudican battle. The high-status 'city' settlement at Sedgeford in north-west Norfolk was abandoned within at most a decade of the Boudican Rebellion: the archaeological record here simply stops. Such total population shift begs questions as to whether the Icenian inhabitants fled, were massacred or were forcibly dispossessed of their ancestral territory. The burnt roundhouse would fit with theories of Roman military violence.[11] An alternative explanation might be that such a politically (and sacrally) charged site was deliberately cleared and left in a systematic and controlled manner by its people. Some of the archaeology lends itself to such an idea and, if this were to have been so, it could – perhaps – reflect a reaction by the population to the crisis of Roman vengeance that ensured the retention of some measure of control over the land and ancestral identity.

Another site that adds to the picture of East Anglia in the immediate post-Boudican phase is the Neronian military installation at the Lunt, Baginton,[12] just outside Coventry, a fort built just after the Boudican uprising probably as a campaign headquarters and supply base for the Roman army. The Lunt was only occupied for about 20 years (AD 60–80), and was constructed of timber, earth and turf. Its numerous granaries suggest its use as a food depot not only for its own troops but also for others stationed nearby. One interesting feature of the fort is the presence of a large circular structure, about 36 metres in diameter, which has been interpreted as a cavalry training ring (see Figure 8.1), used specifically for the training of horses confiscated from the Iceni. The large amount of horse-harness from such Icenian sites, as Saham Toney; the copious coin-issues decorated with horse-images;[13] and the ritually interred horse burials from Sedgeford[14] all indicate the military and symbolic importance of this animal to the Iceni: the confiscation and redeployment of

8 ◆ Aftermath: retribution and reconciliation

FIGURE 8.1 ◆ *The cavalry training ring at the Lunt, Baginton, outside Coventry.*
Source: © Miranda Aldhouse-Green.

such precious commodities by the enemy must have been especially galling to the defeated.

The attitude to the defeated Britons shown by Suetonius Paulinus and his troops is demonstrated with reference to some Roman 'conquest iconography' that, although later in date than the mid-first century AD, has a strong resonance with this troubled period. Two second-century examples of monumental imagery serve to explore the degrading and humiliating treatment of subjugated enemies: one from the Antonine Wall in Scotland, the other on Trajan's Column in Rome, a pillar erected to celebrate and commemorate that emperor's victorious campaigns in Dacia (present-day Romania) in the early second century. The first comprises a distance slab from Bridgeness, West Lothian (see Figure 8.2), which portrays a powerful victory scene dominated by a Roman cavalryman riding down a group of defeated Caledonians: a depiction of *romanitas* triumphing over the barbarian 'other'.[15] The horseman is in parade armour, with a flying cloak, long-crested helmet and riding breeches, and he holds a spear, to threaten the naked, unarmed enemies who sit, lie or kneel beneath the hooves of his mount: one of them is on his back, his

FIGURE 8.2 ◆ *Conquered Britons, on a distance slab at Bridgeness, on the Antonine Wall, Scotland.*

Source: © Anne Leaver.

face trampled by the animal's hind legs; another half kneels, half crawls away, a dagger or sword buried in his back; a third sits facing the viewer, one hand pressed to his mouth (to stop himself from screaming?), the other hand protecting his genitals; the fourth sits with his back to the spectator's gaze, his decapitated head beside him and a torc around the severed neck. This is powerful imagery, redolent of boastful victory and gloating contempt; the Britons are presented without dignity or identity: anonymous barbarian opponents, presented in positions of utter defeat. The imagery of the defeated Dacians on Trajan's Column is likewise a cogent illustration of imperialism at its most triumphant: once again,

8 ◆ Aftermath: retribution and reconciliation

there is a striking discrepancy between the way the bodies of Roman soldiers and those of the Dacians are treated. The Romans are short-haired, immaculately clothed, disciplined and in control; the Dacians, on the other hand, represent a wholly displaced, conquered people: old men, women and children are portrayed alongside men of fighting age; their hair is long and unkempt; they sometimes wear the soft pointed 'Phrygian cap', which denotes their otherness; their clothes are long and sometimes ragged; and they appear in abject positions: kneeling, seated or thrown to the ground, some with their heads pulled back by the hair.[16] If Boudica's Britons were regarded in this kind of contemptuous light by their Roman adversaries, it is little wonder that the province was on its knees.

The Roman governor's fall from grace

The result of the general's extreme behaviour in Britain in the immediate post-conquest period was a rapid and abrupt 'cabinet reshuffle', in which both the governor, Suetonius Paulinus, and the procurator, Decianus Catus (the real villain of the piece) were recalled and replaced. It is always interesting to learn (either from ancient literature or from epigraphy) about imperial appointments to the provinces, for the people chosen aptly reflect an emperor's attitude to a particular annexed region and the state of the territory concerned. The testimony of Tacitus makes it clear that Nero realised at once what kind of crisis was unfolding in Britain, and he acted. The first thing he did was to appoint a new procurator, a man called Gaius Julius Alpinus Classicianus. Tacitus is not very charitable about him, saying that he 'was on bad terms with Suetonius, and allowed his personal animosities to damage the national interests'.[17] It is clear that Tacitus did not approve of the new finance officer, but Nero had his reasons. Chapter 7 noted that emperors shrewdly appointed not one but two senior ministers to provincial government office. These two, the governor/army commander and the procurator/fiscal officer, were each independent of the other and each reported straight to the emperor. Nero and his advisers knew full well what was going on in Britain immediately post-Boudica, and were aware that the governor's vengeful behaviour would ruin Britain if not checked. By appointing a new procurator, Nero was doing three things at once: ridding the province of the shameful

Decianus Catus; providing an opportunity for up-to-date news on Suetonius Paulinus's excesses from his new appointee; and, above all, in appointing Classicianus in the new post, he was sending an important message of conciliation to the Britons.

Classicianus: the man of Gaul

> *To the spirits of the departed (and) of Gaius Julius Alpinus Classicianus, son of Gaius, of the Fabian voting tribe ... procurator of the province of Britain; Julia I[ndiana] Pacata, daughter of Indus, his wife, had this built.*
> Collingwood & Wright *The Roman Inscriptions of Britain*[18]

This is the surviving lettering from an inscription that adorned the tombstone of Classicianus, part of which was found in 1852, reused at the base of a bastion that reinforced the city wall of Roman London.[19] The tombstone tells us that the deceased died in office and, given that he was appointed soon after the Boudican rebellion, in AD 61, and that *procuratores augusti* generally held office for no more than four years, the inference is that he died sometime around AD 65. Classicianus proved to be a very different procurator from his predecessor, Catus. For one thing, the affiliation described in the funerary dedication informs us that he came not from the ranks of the Roman aristocracy but from provincial Gallic stock. Yet, while his name is indicative of a northern Gaulish tribal origin, perhaps from the Helvetii or the Treveri,[20] his *tria nomina* (three names) demonstrate his Roman citizenship. Furthermore, we learn from Tacitus[21] that Classicianus's father-in-law, Julius Indus, was of the Treveran ruling class, a loyal Romanising local nobleman who had stood fast against the Gallic rebels Florus and Sacrovir in AD 21 when the Treveri of the Moselle Valley and the Burgundian Aedui together rose against Rome in protest both against debt and high taxation (resentments familiar to us from the context of the later Boudican uprising). Tacitus states that the Romans used this Indus to help quell the revolt among the Treveri, although the Aedui, under Julius Sacrovir, proved more difficult to overcome. Indus's role as a peacemaker may have given rise to the bestowal on his daughter of the *cognomen* (third name) of Pacata ('the Peaceful One'). Incidentally, the London inscription refers to this woman by three names and so she, as well as her husband, clearly enjoyed Roman citizenship.

8 ♦ Aftermath: retribution and reconciliation

The tombstone of Classicianus itself (see Figure 8.3) reveals a personal biography and a set of meanings that help us get closer to the man it commemorated. In its original position, it would have been set up by his widow over his cremated remains. Three pieces of the stone have been found in Trinity Place, Tower Hill, first in excavations of 1852, and later during further investigations in 1935. Together, they enable a reconstruction of what must have been a handsome burial monument, with elegant 'bolster' ornament at the top and the inscription set out in highly skilled lettering,[22] betraying the presence of a remarkably accomplished craftsman. The tombstone was finished to such a high standard that it was almost certainly carved not by Britons or even Gauls but by Roman stonemasons. The monument, though, was not imported but was carved from finest Cotswold stone. Some three centuries after it was set up in the heart of Roman London, the great stone was broken up and the pieces reused as building material for massive defences protecting Londinium.[23] The irony is that, given Classicianus's own role as peacemaker and negotiator at one of the most perilous periods in the history of Roman Britain, one could argue that in the contribution to the city's walls made by his tombstone hundreds of years later, his spirit still continued to protect Britannia from destruction.

FIGURE 8.3 ♦ *The tombstone of Julius Classicianus, found in London.*

Source: Millett 1995.

The burial of Classicianus in London, together with that city's undoubted role as the financial centre of the province, must mean that the new procurator had his headquarters there. Tentative attempts have been made to identify the exact site of his offices and dwelling, and it may be that it is to be connected with the remains of one of the earliest stone buildings known from Londinium, a structure in Lombard Street that is certainly pre-AD 80 and that was demolished to make way for the city's forum.[24] Although its function cannot be identified with any certainty, 'it represents a degree of wealth and permanence that was probably exceptional in London at that time, and so it could have been an official building'.[25]

While the identity of Classicianus's house and workplace remains a matter for speculation, there is doubt also of his exact resting place after death, though we can be confident that his remains were laid in a cemetery probably not far away from his putative HQ. But recent research on the tombstone itself has led to debate about its original interpretation as a relatively modest, though lavishly ornamented monument,[26] suggesting, instead, that it may have been a much grander affair than exhibited by its current restoration. In this new study, it has been argued that the size and method of carving of the 'bolsters' adorning each end of the top, the large font of the lettering and other clues in the positioning of words in the inscription all contribute to an indication that the tomb was meant to make a visual impact from a distance.[27] If this interpretation is right, then Classicianus's monument was 'substantially larger and more impressive than the present reconstruction',[28] taller, with an elevated inscription that viewers would cast their eyes upwards to read, and probably raised on a plinth or podium so that it would tower above other burial monuments in the cemetery. If Classicianus's tombstone, then, was as lavish as it might now appear, it follows that he made a success of his last job and that his family benefited from his emperor's approval, in terms of money and favours. This is not surprising, for he may have been the catalyst that turned a ruined, about-to-be-abandoned province into a viable and valuable part of the Roman Empire. Classicianus may even have been responsible for converting much of Icenian territory into an imperial estate, thus creating a large tract of land under direct Roman military control (see below).[29] As Tacitus wrote:

> [Classicianus] passed round advice to wait for a new governor who would be kind to those who surrendered, without an enemy's bitterness or a conqueror's arrogance. Classicianus also reported to Rome that there was no prospect of ending the war unless a successor was appointed to Suetonius, whose failures he attributed to perversity – and his successes to luck.[30]

Crime and punishment

The recent prosecution of the American soldier, Linndie England, for war atrocities at Abu Graib prison in Iraq serves to remind us that, in modern western society, there is – in theory anyway – zero tolerance for abuses of human rights, even in the context of war. It is invalid to make direct comparisons between the present day and the Roman empire because notions of *humanitas* and its rights were accorded different perspectives and, more importantly still, slavery was endemic in Roman society, and slaves, as owned people, had far fewer rights than the free. Strictly speaking, a valuable, highly educated slave teacher in a high-born Roman's house would have less protection from abuse than a free man living in utter poverty outside the gates. In the context of warfare, the accepted fate for captured enemies was either execution or slavery, no matter what status the prisoner had enjoyed before his captivity. However, that is not to say that generals who broke the rules of conduct in warfare could not be impeached or otherwise brought to justice. There is a telling comment in Plutarch's *Life* of Julius Caesar, in the context of one of the Gallic campaigns, in which Caesar broke a ceasefire treaty with two German tribes, the Usipites and Tencteritae. The senator Cato denounced Caesar in Rome, saying that 'in his opinion, Caesar ought to be surrendered to the natives; that action, he said, would clear Rome of the guilt of breaking a truce and would bring the curse which must follow such an action home to the man who was responsible for it'.[31] This is important for it highlights the fact that generals engaged in foreign conquest campaigns were accountable to Roman authority and to the rule of law.

Two issues concerning criminal prosecution for atrocities during the Boudican Rebellion arise from the accounts in the ancient literature. The first is associated with Suetonius Paulinus's own actions and, as we have seen, there is a case for suggesting that he, like Caesar in Gaul, laid himself open to prosecution at home for his extreme brutality after the war was over. The new procurator, Classicianus, clearly considered that

Suetonius Paulinus had a case to answer, and sent urgent messages to the emperor to request that the governor be recalled immediately. What happened next indicates a massive cover-up on the part of the authorities who – indeed – took measures to replace Suetonius Paulinus but without his overt disgrace. Nero listened to Classicianus and apparently trusted his judgement, but decided to gain further evidence before making a decision. Like Claudius during the initial invasion of Britannia, Nero used one of his imperial staff, a freedman, named Polyclitus (almost certainly a Greek), to investigate the situation on the ground.

> So a former imperial slave, Polyclitus, was sent to investigate the British situation. Nero was very hopeful that Polyclitus's influence would both reconcile the governor and agent and pacify native rebelliousness. With his enormous escort, Polyclitus was a trial to Italy and Gaul. Then he crossed the Channel and succeeded in intimidating even the Roman army. But the enemy laughed at him. For them, freedom still lived, and the power of ex-slaves was still unfamiliar. The British marvelled that a general and an army who had completed such a mighty war should obey a slave.[32]

Tacitus paints a vivid picture of Polyclitus's stately journey from Italy to Britain, his huge retinue trailing behind and causing a tremendous burden of food provision, accommodation and protection to all the communities through whose territory he passed. His arrival in Britain would have caused an enormous stir, and he and his entourage must have looked as out of place in the war-torn province as exotic flowers on a dung heap, or as the beautiful storks foraging on domestic rubbish heaps in the Spanish Extramadura. Tacitus projects a fine image of contrast between this sleek, bejewelled and beautifully dressed civil servant and the soldier, Suetonius, on campaign, who probably received Polyclitus in the stark austerity of his camp. The Roman historian is here giving us a glimpse of his deeply ingrained class prejudice and his sense of outrage that a mere ex-slave (however exalted) be sent to judge a man of senatorial rank.[33]

But despite his own experience as a visitor to the ravaged province, and what he must have gleaned from conversations with Classicianus and others, Polyclitus seems to have massaged the truth in his report back to Nero. Tacitus says: 'But all this was toned down in Polyclitus's reports to the emperor. Retained as governor, Suetonius lost a few ships and their crews on the shore, and was then superseded for not terminating the war'.[34]

8 ◆ Aftermath: retribution and reconciliation

So Nero ensured that neither Rome nor its legate, Suetonius Paulinus, lost face. An 'honourable' excuse for the latter's removal was found, one that neither ended his career nor caused any opprobrium to adhere to the emperor. We know that the British governor continued to play a prominent role in Roman politics: Tacitus alludes to his holding of the consulship (the highest magistracy) in the capital in AD 66,[35] though there is no mention of any further active role as an army commander.

But what of the soldiers who committed atrocities in the days leading to the full-blown rebellion, and especially those who acted under Decianus Catus's leadership, when the assets of the Iceni were seized immediately following king Prasutagus's death? Boudica (and presumably her daughters) were free Roman citizens and members of the Icenian royal family and the flogging of the mother and the rape of her children were illegal and criminal acts, the more so because they were not carried out in the context of officially declared warfare. We turn first to the greater crime, the rape of Boudica's daughters. In terms of Roman law, there were severe penalties for sex crimes: in the case of incest the penalty was death, in Tiberius's reign, by being thrown from the top of the Tarpeian Rock; in later periods the penalty was deportation.[36] There is also literary evidence, for example from the late empire, that rape was considered a heinous offence, punishable by *poena capitalis* (capital punishment, including beheading).[37] In the time of Nero, particular attention was paid to crime and punishment, and theories relating to the appropriateness of the penalty to the offence. But in the later years of his reign, Nero himself committed a number of atrocities, not least on his own family[38].

Rape was (and is) a lamentable but all too common act within the context of hostilities; it is associated less with sex than with violence and with the related issues of abuse, insult, dishonour, control and the creation of victims.[39] Rape is loaded with all sorts of other connotations and messages: the peculiar contempt shown by men for the female victims of sexual violence; something perhaps, in this context, associated with the equation of women with the barbarous, especially if those women were perceived as challenging male power. Rape, with its risk of pregnancy, is also linked with the violation and potential interruption of lineage. Here, we think of the Arab 'pride of race', which is so strong a feature of Wilfrid Thesiger's classic travel story *Arabian Sands*.[40] What is of particular note, in this instance, is the absolute control of a colonial power over the colonised, even to infiltrate and alter bloodlines and to own the bodies of others.[41] However, it is the status of the victims that makes the deed simultaneously more shocking and more comprehensible. Catus's men may have acted in the heat of the moment, but we may see this particular act of rape as reflective of a deeper meaning that fits into a conquering and all-powerful arrogance of Rome/warriors/males/victors in opposition to Britain/non-combatants (children)/females/conquered. The rape of the girls may, perhaps, be perceived in parallel with the rape of Icenian lands, the stripping of material assets and looting.

The violation of her daughters leads to consideration of the flogging of Boudica herself, a Roman citizen and therefore – in theory – protected against the excesses meted out to other foreigners. We have an example of the way Roman citizens expected to be treated in the New Testament *Acts of the Apostles* when Paul of Tarsus is flogged and imprisoned by the Roman authorities, and protests that his citizen rank, and that of his companion Silas, made such treatment unlawful.[42] Flogging or scourging was designed not just to punish but as a gross act of humiliation, as a means of showing utter contempt; it was used in this symbolic manner, in the treatment of Christ by Pilate's soldiers before his crucifixion.[43] There is no record of retribution for either the rape of the royal Icenian children or the illegal flogging of Boudica, and it is almost certain than none was meted out to the perpetrators, though at least Decianus Catus was stripped of office for his part in the bungled attempt to annex Prasutagus's kingdom.

Britain after Boudica

His successor Publius Petronius Turpilianus, neither provoking the enemy nor provoked, called this ignoble activity peace with honour.

Tacitus *Annals*[44]

The government therefore replaced him by Petronius Turpilianus. They hoped that he would be more merciful and readier to forgive offences to which he was a stranger. He composed the existing troubles, but risked no further move before handing over his province to Trebellius Maximus. Trebellius was deficient in energy and without military experience, but he governed the province like a gentleman. The barbarians now learned, like any Romans, to condone seductive vices, while the intervention of our Civil

8 ♦ Aftermath: retribution and reconciliation

> *Wars gave a reasonable excuse for inactivity. There was, however, a serious outbreak of mutiny, for the troops, accustomed to campaigns, ran riot in peace. Trebellius fled and hid to escape his angry army. His self-respect and dignity compromised, he now commanded merely on sufferance. By a kind of tacit bargain the troops kept their licence, the general his life, and the mutiny stopped short of bloodshed.*
>
> Tacitus *Agricola*[45]

Thus, both in the *Annals* and the *Agricola*, Tacitus presents a scathing account of the governors appointed by Nero in the immediate aftermath of the Boudican debacle, each of whom he describes in terms of their ineptitude as successors to Suetonius Paulinus. Tacitus is being deliberately disingenuous here: his agenda is twofold in so far as, on the one hand, he admired Suetonius Paulinus as an 'action hero', and an active war commander; on the other, he was concerned to show off his father-in-law, Agricola, in a preferential light, and how better to do this than by denigrating his predecessors?

It is very clear that Nero had been badly rattled by both the British insurgence (and its near success) and by the jeopardy in which Suetonius Paulinus's angry vengeance placed the province. Realising that the only way to salvage the situation was to adopt a policy of consolidation, rather than aggressive conquest, the emperor put in a series of governors who would be 'safe pairs of hands': who would not be seeking to make mileage out of Britain in terms of career or personal glory but who might give the province a chance to begin the healing process. We know that Turpilianus, Suetonius Paulinus's immediate successor, was one of the two consuls in Rome at the time the rebellion broke out.[46] He was clearly regarded by Nero as a close ally, for Tacitus tells us that the emperor granted him an honorary triumph in AD 65, following the burning of Rome, a major contributory factor in a serious conspiracy against Nero by 'senators and other gentry, officers, even women'.[47] Triumphs, involving processions to the temple of Jupiter Capitolinus, were originally granted to victorious Roman generals but, by the imperial period, they were almost entirely confined to the emperor or his immediate family, though victorious generals could be granted triumphal regalia. An 'honorary' triumph, stripped of its military connotations, would merely have been a conspicuous honour designed, in this instance, to make a public statement of gratitude for Turpilianus's support during the plot to overthrow

Nero and, indeed, probably consisted of no more than the bestowal of 'triumphal insignia'.[48] But it may be that Turpilianus's time in Britain was not quite as inglorious as Tacitus makes out: after his sojourn in the province, he held a senior military post in Italy, and 'was one of the very few men of high rank executed by Galba',[49] Nero's successor, albeit only for a few brief months. Galba's grounds for removing Turpilianus were that Turpilianus had been appointed a commander by Nero. Tacitus tells us that Turpilianus was killed 'without trial or defence'.[50] In his challenge to Galba, Otho (another contender for the imperial purple, and once a staunch supporter of Galba) is said to have publicly accused Galba of atrocities to those he considered his opponents, including Turpilianus.[51] So perhaps this governor was not quite such a negligible force in Britain as Tacitus would have us believe.

Trebellius Maximus took over the governorship of Britain in AD 63 and continued in office until 69 when, according to Tacitus, his tenure came to an abrupt and ignominious end. In his *Histories*[52] Tacitus fleshes out the drama hinted at (above) in his account, in the *Agricola*, of Trebellius's administration in Britain, commenting on a serious quarrel that broke out between the governor and the commander of Legion XX, Roscius Coelius. Trebellius accused Coelius of insubordination, while Coelius retaliated by drawing attention to the poor morale of the army. Trebellius was deserted by legions and auxiliaries alike, and the only course open to him was to flee for protection to Vitellius who, like Galba and Otho, was laying claim to Nero's throne in AD 69. Vitellius responded by depriving him of his office and replacing him with another governor of Britain, Vettius Bolanus.[53] The appointment of Trebellius Maximus to Britain may well have been an error of judgement on the part of Nero, for the province was highly militarised, with one of the greatest concentrations of soldiers anywhere on the imperial frontiers, and Trebellius had had no previous military experience,[54] although he had served in Gaul in AD 61, where he had undertaken a census and a review of taxation. Nero may have promoted him to the governorship of Britain because of his experience at dealing with provincial problems.[55] But, in the aftermath of the Boudican Rebellion, the Roman army in Britain was restless and volatile, and certainly was in no mood to remain idle, without prospect of excitement or booty, after all it had been through in the Boudican and post-Boudican campaigns. There is no record of whether or not the

8 ♦ Aftermath: retribution and reconciliation

mutineering soldiers were punished for their sedition; traditionally military crimes such as cowardice or mutiny would incur harsh penalties such as decimation (the execution of every tenth man[56]) but, if such punitive action was taken, Tacitus did not see fit to mention it.

Consequences: the Iceni

The revolt against Rome was an unqualified disaster for the Iceni. Such was the scale of casualties inflicted on the tribe that it may have taken centuries for the population to return to its former levels.

Sealey *The Boudican Revolt against Rome*[57]

We have already discussed the virtual genocide inflicted on the Iceni by Suetonius Paulinus's forces during and after the pitched battle with Boudica. What we need to do now is to study the economic, political and social effect of the war on the inhabitants of East Anglia. This is not easy to determine from the key literary sources, the writings of Tacitus and Dio, since they were not overly concerned with events in provinces following wars. So we need to rely on archaeological evidence for Roman destruction or development in the areas affected by the Boudican war. Many hoards of coins and metalwork were buried by the Iceni at the time of the uprising, presumably in attempts to safeguard possessions or amass wealth to fund the war effort. Another significant indicator of conflict should be the presence of burnt daub on Icenian sites, attesting to the laying waste of enemy settlements by the Roman army. Such 'daub' was mud plastered on to the walls of timber-framed buildings. Paradoxically, it needed the action of fire to ensure its preservation on archaeological sites.

While this kind of evidence has been collected from sites in Essex, it seems to have been neglected by archaeologists working on sites in Norfolk and Suffolk.[58] Perhaps more telling is the rate of development of the new Roman town of Caistor-by-Norwich (Caistor St Edmund). This tribal capital was called *Venta Icenorum* (the Market of the Iceni). There may have been a Roman fort at Caistor in the late 40s AD, established at the time of the first Icenian revolt.[59] But the Roman town, centre of the *civitas* (state/tribe) of the Iceni, was not established until relatively late, in the Flavian period, whereas other cognate cities were beginning to flourish rather earlier in the first century. For instance, Chichester

(*Noviomagus Regnorum*), Winchester (*Venta Belgarum*) and Silchester (*Calleva Atrebatum*) were all developing and exploiting their commercial potential before AD 60, their communities enjoying the benefits of going along with *romanitas*.[60] But the Iceni were held back from full participation in the 'Roman Dream' by their hostile attitude to Rome and partly because their population was relatively low,[61] itself due – in no small measure – to the loss of life sustained in the Boudican Rebellion. This tardiness in the adoption of *romanitas* by the Iceni (whether deliberate or not) is reflected in the slow development of their tribal capital at Caistor. (Interestingly, the same is true of Caerwent, the *civitas* capital of the Silures, the unruly tribe of south-east Wales who resolutely opposed Roman forces for most of the first century AD.[62])

It may be (but is not necessarily) significant that Caistor was not apparently built on the site of a previous Icenian focal settlement. By no means all Romano-British tribal centres were direct descendants of earlier Iron Age sites, but – given the troubled history of the area in the mid-first century – it was perhaps expedient for the Roman administration to develop *Venta Icenorum* well away from settlements that were ridden with ancestral memories of heroic resistance and independence movements, like those of Fison Way (Thetford), Saham Toney or Sedgeford,[63] which stand out from the many small and scattered dwelling sites in the region for their large, agglomerated *oppidum*-like (political-centre) status with a concentration of finds. We know from Tony Gregory's work that Fison Way, Thetford was systematically dismantled by the Roman army at about the time of the Boudican Rebellion.[64] The important site of Sedgeford near King's Lynn in the far north of Norfolk, currently under investigation, is a prime candidate for an Icenian *oppidum*. Indeed, the richness of its finds confirms that it was a place of high status.[65] The burning there of at least one roundhouse, and the dramatically sudden abandonment of the site (see above), is suggestive of Roman attempts to obliterate the site and its memory.

We have to be careful not to assume that the effect of the Boudican Rebellion and Roman retaliation were cataclysmic throughout Icenian territory. We have already seen (Chapter 7) that the three cities, recorded by ancient literature as having been destroyed, were only partially damaged. Archaeological evidence from some rural settlements indicates no hiatus in occupation. One such site is Hacheston in Suffolk, excavated in the early 1970s, where 'the evidence from the excavation does not suggest any dramatic changes which might correspond with the known historical events of the 1st century, namely the Conquest of 43 and the Boudican Revolt of 60'.[66] Similarly, the fortified ring-work on Wardy Hill, Coveney (Cambridgeshire)[67] exhibits some interesting information on continuity and change during the Boudican years and afterwards for, despite its evident high status and defended nature, Wardy Hill remained in use for at least 20 years after AD 60, and there are no signs that Roman armies ever attacked or sought to slight the ramparts. What is more, the material culture of the site indicates that its inhabitants chose to adopt some trappings of Romanisation, such as pottery, but not others: notably absent is the personal grooming equipment (tweezers, ear scoops, nail cleaners) that occurs on other sites in the region and in the south-east. The evidence from Wardy Hill is highly significant for it suggests that, here at least, local elites were not always removed or destroyed by a vengeful Roman administration. The Tacitean account has to be leavened with the archaeological indicators that, on the one hand, Roman retaliation was patchy and, on the other, that the Icenians and their neighbours were by no means eschewing all things Roman during and after Boudica's uprising. The extreme measures taken by the Romans at Fison Way, Thetford serve to illustrate that this particular site had a special symbolic and political resonance: a pulse of Icenian power that had to be obliterated.[68]

The situation of the Iceni was certainly compromised by the Boudican Rebellion and its aftermath, in terms of the region's florescence within the Roman Empire. Caistor always remained relatively modest, in its size and prosperity, and the region is not renowned for its Romanised country estates, unlike those of the Cotswold Dobunni and other territories in lowland Britain. The house excavated at Feltwell in south-west Norfolk represents an Icenian villa, but it is late in date, belonging to the fourth century AD, and it was never other than a modest, unpretentious country dwelling.[69] It is suggested that, after the Boudican Rebellion, part of Icenian territory was taken over by the Roman administration to be run as imperial estates.[70] There is archaeological evidence that at this period large swathes of Icenian territory were divided up in a grid pattern of substantial rectangular parcels in a Roman system of land management known as *limitatio*. This exercise was designed to prepare confiscated territory for repopulation by new communities. The system was reversed by Agricola (governor of Britain from AD 77 to 84), whose legal expert, Liberalis, was given the appointment of *Iuridicus* in Britain and who may have had responsibility for giving back this land to the Iceni.

The slow development of Caistor must reflect not only, perhaps, a reluctance, on the part of the Roman administration, to make an early investment in a tribal area that had exhibited such hostility and instability, but also – again a consequence of the turbulence in the region – a dearth of 'local *equites*, capable of assuming novel municipal responsibilities'.[71] It is possible, too, that the paucity of Roman villas and the modest progress of Caistor (together with the scarcity of smaller Roman towns) means that the Iceni never wholly embraced *romanitas*, and its commercial and cultural opportunities, with the enthusiasm of their southern and western neighbours.[72] Indications of this counter-culture may be cited in the prevalence of British-made tankards for ale, mead or berry juice over wine-drinking equipment. But against that argument must be set the striking evidence for early engagement with Roman material culture and ideas in Norfolk, as represented – for instance – by the Crownthorpe Hoard, a cache of bronze drinking paraphernalia made in Prasutagus's time, and by items such as the Roman silver wine cups from Hockwold.[73] But even this is not as straightforward as it might appear: the deliberate damage inflicted on the fine silverware from the latter site suggests an adhesion to old cult practices enacted during the late Iron Age;[74] however, the act might equally be interpretable as a gesture of contempt for the soft and decadent Roman way of life represented by wine drinking, and maybe – then – a material fingerprint of tension between pro- and anti-Roman factions within the Icenian power base.[75]

Despite the suffering, economic deprivation and loss of identity undoubtedly suffered by many of the Iceni at and immediately after the Boudican uprising, some sense of being Icenian must have been maintained. After all, Caistor was called *Venta Icenorum*, which is itself a marker of continuing identity. What is more striking is the evidence for a richness, in terms both of prosperity and ancestral memory, that is represented by the archaeological record for the late Roman period. This is best illustrated with reference to the outstanding find of gold and silver treasure from Thetford,[76] a few metres away from the great Boudican enclosure at Fison Way that was flattened by the Roman army in AD 60.

8 ♦ Aftermath: retribution and reconciliation

The fabulously valuable hoard was deposited by a religious guild probably in the very late fourth century AD, and included a set of 33 silver spoons, many of them inscribed with the names of Roman and British deities: one of the latter was called Medugenus (mead-begotten), and I have suggested elsewhere that such a title might have referred to a shaman, his trance-experience and connection with the spirit world enabled by his ingestion of mind-altering alcoholic drink;[77] another was named Ausecus (prick-eared),[78] perhaps a reference to a divinity perceived as half-human, half-animal which, once again, could refer to shamanic experience.[79] The main god of Roman origin, to whom dedications were inscribed, was Faunus – a somewhat obscure Italian deity of the wild. In spite of the discrepancy in dates, the positioning of this late treasure is highly significant: in the later Iron Age Fison Way was a ritual/political focus of high status, perhaps even the location of a Boudican 'palace' or public place of assembly, 'clearly the result of a major investment of resources'.[80] The siting of the hoard of religious material cannot be dismissed as coincidental.

Other late Roman precious metal finds serve to confirm that the region did not remain in a state of permanent decline after the Neronian period: here we may cite the late Roman jeweller's hoard from Snettisham (see Plate 18),[81] buried at the same location as the fabulously rich Iron Age deposits of torcs and other metalwork made in about 70 BC and almost certainly representing an offering to the gods of enormous worth. What is particularly fascinating is that the goldsmith responsible for the Roman hoard buried at Snettisham was working with gold wire 'reminiscent of torcs' and with gold ingots whose gold content was far closer to that of the Iron Age jewellery from the site than 'normal' Roman gold.[82] It is difficult not to deduce from this and from the siting of the late Roman cache that folk memory was being invoked in the preservation of knowledge both of techniques and of ritual behaviour over some 300 years. The wealth of the Iceni in late Roman times is confirmed, too, by the recently discovered treasure from Hoxne in Suffolk, which includes some sophisticated Italianate material, as well as a quantity of gold and silver coins.[83] The coins indicate that the owners of the Hoxne fortune were undoubtedly important and influential landowners, and items such as the wooden and ivory caskets in which the treasure was stowed for safe-keeping, the gold jewellery, and the tiger-handled silver vessel[84] demonstrate that their possessors enjoyed the luxury elements of Roman imperial material culture, despite their (probable) local Icenian identity.

The ripple effect of the rebellion: reconciliation and renewal

By AD 67 safer conditions prevailed and it was deemed possible to withdraw Legion XIV from the province.[85] Southern Britain, at least, must thus have been regarded as relatively safe and peaceful only seven years after its near-destruction, although some new garrisons were undoubtedly added in newly built forts in central and southern England in the immediate aftermath of the rebellion. But it is noteworthy that Nero did not celebrate Boudica's defeat on his coinage,[86] perhaps because of the shame associated with the slaughter of so many Roman soldiers and civilians by a female ruler of a subjugated people.[87]

It is interesting to look at the subsequent development of the three Roman towns sacked by Boudica, when reconciliation, physical renewal and the rebuilding of confidence were all of paramount importance to the health of Britannia. The Roman exhibition in the Museum of London features a display board headed 'Capital Growth', signifying the rebirth of one of these three Roman cities. Before AD 60 Londinium had grown up somewhat haphazardly. Established four or five years after the Claudian invasion of AD 43, it had been developed primarily because of its position on the Thames and its accessibility by even the largest ocean-going ships.[88] Initally the army may have established a defended crossing point, and then the prospects for trade caused the merchants and the entrepreneurs to move in, so that the town evolved according to need. But in the aftermath of Boudican destruction, London totally re-invented itself, being rebuilt as a major, planned Roman town, with ambitious new administrative centres and residential quarters. Its reincarnation was sufficiently successful for it to replace Colchester as Britain's capital.[89] In a sense then, London owed its new prosperity to Boudica: the town's wholesale destruction by fire meant that the slate could be wiped clean and Roman planners, architects and builders could work on a prime, virgin site to establish what would become the economic hub of the province.

What of Colchester and Verulamium? It would have been politically unacceptable not to re-establish the *colonia* on the site of the old

8 ♦ Aftermath: retribution and reconciliation

Trinovantian capital Camulodunum as quickly as possible; archaeological evidence indicates that the new Roman city was indeed founded very soon, probably under Trebellius Maximus (AD 63–9). Significantly, the new *colonia* was given the highly emotive name of *Colonia Victricensis* (the Victorious *Colonia*) and, heeding the bitter harvest reaped from complacency, the new town was given stout stone defences. 'These town walls are the most striking field monument of the Boudican revolt and testify to the impact the destruction of Colchester made on the Roman administration'.[90] Archaeological testimony contains some poignant reminders of the city's suffering at the hands of the maurauding Britons: when the Romans reoccupied Colchester, the helmets of Roman soldiers killed in action were collected and ceremonially buried in a pit.[91] The Romans also lost no time in restoring and completing the temple of Claudius, such a source of hatred to the Trinovantes in the lead-up to the uprising; like London, the town was laid out in a typical grid of planned streets and new shops and houses sprang up on the ashes of the old. Theatres and temples attested to *romanitas*, and Colchester's industry flourished, particularly the production of ceramics, both fine tableware and coarser vessels for cooking and storage.[92]

While evidence of Boudican destruction by fire is clear from the excavation of many early buildings in London and Colchester, the archaeological testimony from Verulamium is less overt and the destruction appears to have been less wholesale.[93] Some deliberate burning did take place, but on nothing like the scale of evidence from its two sister-towns. Ros Niblett is of the view that 'at the time of the revolt Verulamium was still very much an emerging town where there was, as yet, comparatively little to destroy in terms of "Roman buildings".[94] The paucity of investigation in the archaeology of the rural periphery of St Albans (Verulamium) makes it impossible to make a realistic assessment of how farms in the vicinity were affected. Certainly, in those that have been excavated,[95] the identification of a definite Boudican destruction horizon has been problematical. Despite the poverty of evidence from Verulamium itself, what there is suggests, nonetheless, that the events of AD 60 had a profound and sometimes chasmic effect upon its population. One of the complex of wooden workshops that developed in the pre-Boudican phase was burned out and 15 years elapsed before rebuilding took place, indicating that confidence in working here took a considerable time to be restored.

Not only this, but there are signs that those of the tribal aristocracy that emerged from the massacre unscathed, and with surviving wealth, hesitated before investing once more in property that could be destroyed in other uprisings but, instead, chose to put their disposable income in less risky commodities, like coin.[96] However, once confidence was restored, and it became clear that there were unlikely to be further revolts in southeast England, the city's building programme surged ahead; a new city-centre complex of forum, basilica (marketplace and town hall) – the economic and administrative pulse of any Roman city – sprang up, together with temples, industrial zones and private houses.[97] Roman St Albans never looked back.

The other town – albeit that it played no direct part in the Boudican episode – that is worth noting in this post-revolt period is Bath, *Aquae Sulis*, (the Waters of Sulis) built beside the Bristol Avon at the site of hot medicinal springs and centred around a great temple and bathing complex dedicated to the composite Britto-Roman goddess Sulis Minerva. The Roman city lies buried several metres below the present ground surface. A late pre-Roman Iron Age presence at *Aquae Sulis* is implied by the deposition of 17 coins minted by the Dobunni and Durotriges[98] and, although these could have been deposited in the Roman period,[99] 'the fact that the majority of them were fresh and unworn strongly suggests pre-Roman deposition'.[100] Already in the pre-Roman Iron Age, local communities were probably visiting the springs and offering gifts to the presiding spirit, presumably Sulis (see also Chapter 6). The earliest Roman presence here may have been a Claudian military establishment at nearby Bathwick.[101] Then, in the Neronian or early Flavian period (late 60s or early 70s AD),[102] the main hot spring was monumentalised, with the spring-water contained within a polygonal reservoir. At this time, the temple and baths were established in the grand Roman manner. At first glance the evidence indicates that a totally Roman socio-religious complex was imposed on the local Britons: the temple's architectural form is classical and the baths likewise owe nothing to the ancestral use of the site. It may be that some of those building the first Roman structures were Roman soldiers.[103] But there is clear indication that the construction of the sanctuary and accompanying edifices was not as straightforward as that, and there may even be an indirect connection with Boudica and her rebels.

8 ♦ Aftermath: retribution and reconciliation

Tom Blagg's dating evidence indicates that the building explosion at Bath was broadly contemporary with the Boudican or immediately post-Boudican period:[104] the timing may well be significant in terms of the renaissance of Roman Britain. There is another interesting link between Bath and the turbulence of the Icenian revolt: Nero's newly appointed finance officer, brought in to replace the disgraced Decianus Catus, was Classicianus, whose tombstone – found in London – suggests that he was a Treveran, from the Moselle Valley. We have already discussed how the appointment of a man from Gaul to the procuratorship of Britain, was an act of reconciliation, designed to placate and to heal wounds. It is all the more striking, then, that architectural elements (including decorative stonework), with their best parallels in the same Treveran region of north-east Gaul, have been identified in Bath.[105] Early Roman Bath, and particularly its temple, serves to make a highly charged statement about the new persona of Britannia. If the architecture shows signs of Gaulishness, the religious material shows distinct and determined elements of Britishness. The name of the presiding goddess, given in several inscriptions, was Sulis Minerva, a hybrid spirit with a local and a Roman name: an example of typical syncretistic pairing between native and foreign cults. The fact that, at Bath, the British name is almost always mentioned first in the epigraphy indicates that it is the indigenous element that was driving the cult. Sulis was not simply the goddess of the healing spring waters; she was the personification of the water and the site itself.[106]

More significant still may be the famous head carved on the temple pediment that is generally interpreted as a male Gorgon, with its swirling, serpent-girt hair (see Figure 6.2).[107] The identification of the head as a Gorgon, despite its masculinity, rests almost entirely upon the fact that traditional representations of Minerva depict a Gorgon's head[108] on her breastplate. But the mature bearded head with its heavy moustache and beard resembles a river god rather than Medusa, perhaps even Oceanus himself (Chapter 1), and this may represent a deliberate appropriation of a classical theme to a British temple context. Even more significant, perhaps, is the curious tri-lobed mark on the forehead of the pediment image: a motif that appears to resonate with much earlier Iron Age funerary sculpture from the Rhineland, and which I have interpreted elsewhere as a purposeful signature of 'retro-ideology', a harking back to a pre-Roman past by Gallo-British craftspeople, tapping into a symbolic reservoir of continental sculpture that may still have been visible in the Rhenish landscape at the time the temple of Bath was constructed. [109] The adoption of such a symbol would make all the more sense if the masons and sculptors came from north-eastern Gaul, not far from the homeland of these early monumental carvings.

However we may interpret the detail, it is likely that the early sanctuary at Bath had a political as well as a religious message. In the words of Barry Cunliffe 'To lavish such care and expense on one of the great shrines of the western Celtic fringe might have been designed to be an act of reconciliation, the careful conflation of the native deity with the Roman Minerva representing the new spirit of partnership'[110] in the aftermath of the Boudican Rebellion.

Templa, fora, domos

> Agricola gave private encouragement and official assistance to the building of temples, public squares and private mansions. He praised the keen and scolded the slack, and competition to gain honour from him was as effective as compulsion. Furthermore, he trained the sons of the chiefs in the liberal arts and expressed a preference for the British natural ability over the trained skills of the Gauls. The result was that in place of distaste for the Latin language came a passion to command it. In the same way, our national dress came into favour and the toga was everywhere to be seen. And so the Britons were gradually led on to the amenities that make vice agreeable – arcades, baths and sumptuous banquets. They spoke of such novelties as 'civilization', when really they were only a feature of enslavement.
>
> Tacitus Agricola[111]

The use of architecture and religion as tools of cultural reconciliation and conflation, as has been suggested in the context of Roman Bath and at other towns, such as Verulamium, is reflected in Tacitus's scornful description of the British aping of Roman ways. Tacitus was writing about Britain in AD 78/9, Agricola's second year as governor of the province, in the somewhat sycophantic manner he adopted for his biography of his father-in-law Agricola. The writer is sending mixed messages: on the one hand, he commends Agricola's proselytising zeal in making Romans out of Britons; on the other, he sneers at the Britons for being so quick to engage with the trappings of civilisation, their corrupting influence and the resultant loss of innocence: in other words, he laments the conversion of the noble savage to the decadent luxury of the Roman gentleman. Of the various governors appointed to rule Britain in the years after the Boudican uprising, some – like Trebellius and Turpilianus – were caretakers rather than conquerors, but others, like Agricola's immediate predecessors, Petillius Cerialis and Julius Frontinus, showed vigour in expanding the frontiers of Britannia: Cerialis in the north and Frontinus in Wales. Agricola continued Frontinus's work in subduing North Wales and Anglesey (the latter unfinished business since Suetonius's disastrous attempt at destroying the sacred island).

Tacitus's account of the Britons' seduction by the effeteness of Roman living shows a dramatic turnaround between AD 60 and 78, even if he is only referring to regions outside the north and west. The writer paints a picture of a province full of Roman towns, villas and Latin-speaking toga-clad Britons, a far cry from the Britain-beyond-the-edge attitude of Caesar and Claudius. Clearly Tacitus is using hyperbole as a means of getting his point across, and we should take a critical look at the detail of his testimony. For instance, it is considered that, by the time of Nero, the toga was largely obsolete for everyday wear and that its wearing, in any case, signified a particular and formal attire associated with oratory and public office. But the toga is highly symbolic in so far as it marked Roman citizenship, and embracing the toga meant engaging with the leisurely, physically inactive way of life of the upper-class Roman.[112] Tacitus is thus describing a province that, though on the edge of the world and despite the catastrophe of the Boudican rebellion, was fast becoming more Roman than Rome itself. Certainly the burgeoning of *templa, fora, domos* (temples, marketplaces, houses) to which he refers is manifest in the three Roman cities that had borne the brunt of Boudica's fury only a decade or so earlier. Indeed, it is even possible that it was this very setback in 'Romanisation' that acted as a spur for accelerated *romanitas* in the years after the catastrophic events associated with the life and death of Boudica.

Notes and references

1 Tacitus *Annals* 14.38; trans. Grant 1956, 321.
2 Allen 1970, 2.

3 Frere 2000, 350 (citing Brian Hartley) compares the Icenian situation with the planned mass migration of the Helvetii recounted by Caesar a hundred years before the Boudican Rebellion (Caesar *de Bello Gallico* 1, 3–5).

4 BBC Television News 3 July 2005.

5 Tacitus *Agricola* 16; trans. Mattingly 1948, 66.

6 Suetonius *Life of Nero* 18; trans. Graves 1962, 195.

7 Tacitus *Agricola* 16; trans. Mattingly 1948, 66.

8 Caesar *de Bello Gallico* 7.88–9.

9 Allen 1970, 2

10 BBC *Timewatch* 'The Battle of Alesia': UK TV History 9 May 2005.

11 Farrar 2005; Neil Faulkner pers. com.; David Thorpe pers. com.

12 Rylatt undated.

13 Norwich Castle Museum; Davies 1999, 20–9.

14 Neil Faulkner pers. com.

15 Aldhouse-Green 2004c, 328 and fig. 5; Keppie & Arnold 1984, no. 68, pl. 21.

16 Le Bohec 1994; Settis *et al.* 1988; Ferris 2003.

17 Tacitus *Annals* 14.38; trans. Grant 1956, 321.

18 Collingwood & Wright 1965, 12.

19 Grasby & Tomlin 2002, 46.

20 Wightman 1985, 64.

21 Tacitus *Annals* 3. 42–7.

22 Grasby & Tomlin 2002, 43, and fig. 2.

23 Marsden 1980, 36–7.

24 Op. cit. 37, and fig. at top of page.

25 Op. cit. 37; Marsden 1963, 75.

26 As displayed in the British Museum, with a replica in the Museum of London.

27 Grasby & Tomlin 2002, 71–3 and fig. 21.

28 Op. cit. 72.

29 Frere 2000, 350.

30 Tacitus *Annals* 14.38; trans. Grant 1956, 321.

31 Plutarch *Life* of Julius Caesar; trans. Warner 1958, 236.

32 Tacitus *Annals* 14.39; trans. Grant 1956, 321.

33 Paul Sealey pers. com.
34 Tacitus *Annals* 14.39; trans. Grant 1956, 322.
35 Op. cit. 16.11; trans. Grant 1956, 375.
36 Bauman 1996, 60.
37 Op. cit., 157.
38 Op. cit. 76–91.
39 Watt 2002, 29–31.
40 Thesiger 1959.
41 Walters 2002, 78.
42 Acts 16: 35–9. 'But Paul said to the officers "They gave us a public flogging, though we are Roman citizens and have not been found guilty; they threw us into prison" ... The magistrates were alarmed to hear that they were Roman citizens, and came and apologized to them.'
43 John 19: 1–2.
44 Tacitus *Annals* 14.39; trans. Grant 1956, 322.
45 *Agricola* 16; trans. Mattingly 1948, 67.
46 Tacitus *Annals* 14.29.
47 Op. cit. 15; trans. Grant 1956, 357, 368.
48 Warmington 1969, 139.
49 Tacitus *Annals* 78; *Histories* 1.6
50 Tacitus *Histories*; trans. Wellesley 1964, 24.
51 Tacitus *Histories* 1.34.
52 Op. cit. 1.60.
53 Op. cit. 2.65.
54 Warmington 1969, 78.
55 Tacitus *Annals* 14.45; Sealey 1997, 52.
56 Tacitus *Annals* 14.44; Bauman 1996, 82.
57 Sealey 1997, 56.
58 Paul Sealey pers. com. March 2005.
59 Todd 2004, 51, 53. Claudian coins have been found here.
60 Jones 2004, 171–5.
61 Tyers 1996, 84, fig. 49 – a map of Roman pottery sites in Britain.
62 Green & Howell 2000, 44–55.

63 Davies 1999; Gregory 1991; Hill 1999; Neil Faulkner pers. com.
64 Gregory 1991.
65 Neil Faulkner, pers. com. 25 May 2005. A gold torc has come from this site.
66 Blagg *et al.* 2004, 197.
67 Evans 2003, 270–1.
68 Gregory 1992.
69 Painter 1997, 95–6.
70 Owned by the reigning emperor and managed by tenants who might be free or unfree: Sealey 1997, 57; Paul Sealey pers. com.; Frere 2000.
71 Potter & Johns 1992, 84.
72 Op. cit. 94.
73 Norwich Castle Museum: the Hockwold material consists of a silver hoard that included the deliberately damaged remains of seven silver cups of early Roman form; they date from the mid–later first century AD. Silverware was high-status material, and this cache demonstrates the presence, at the time of, or shortly after, the Boudican Rebellion, of Icenian nobility who, perhaps, wished to adopt Roman social manners: Potter & Johns 1992, 128–9.
74 Bradley 1990; a good example of such practice is in the late Iron Age ritual water deposit at Llyn Cerrig Bach, Anglesey: Macdonald 1996, 32–3; Parker Pearson 2000, 8–11.
75 In the context of an attitude essentially analogous to present-day acts of protest against unpopular regimes: good examples of recent circumstances include boycotting of South African produce because of apartheid, or the deliberate refusal by Australians and New Zealanders to buy or drink French wine, in protest against French nuclear test sites in New Zealand.
76 Johns & Potter 1983.
77 Aldhouse-Green & Aldhouse-Green 2005, 152.
78 Painter 1997, 99.
79 Aldhouse-Green & Aldhouse-Green 2005, 172–5.
80 Gregory 1992, 189.
81 Potter 1986.
82 Paul Sealey pers. com,
83 Bland & Johns 1993; Johns & Bland 1994; Guest 2005.
84 Johns & Bland 1994, 165, 169.
85 Potter 1997, 11.

86 De la Bédoyère 2003b, 142.

87 Analogous, perhaps, to the attitude displayed at the defeat of the rebelling slave army of Spartacus by Crassus in 70 BC: Cicero *Against Verres* 1; trans. Grant 1969, 53, fn. 2.

88 Sealey 2004, 30.

89 Museum of London May 2005; Marsden 1980, 16–30.

90 Sealey 1997, 53. Paul Sealey informs me (pers. com.) that waterlogged ground beneath a stretch of town wall excavated by Colchester Archaeological Trust has produced timbers that are currently in process of being dated by dendrochronology.

91 One of these helmets is on display in the Castle Museum, Colchester.

92 Berridge & Hodgson 1997, 10–11.

93 Niblett 2001, 67–8.

94 Op. cit., 67.

95 Such as Gorhambury, Park Street and Prae Wood: Niblett 2001, 67.

96 Niblett (2001, 68) refers to a coin-hoard of gold and silver issues of Flavian date (i.e. between AD 70 and 96) found at Shillington, 17 miles (27 kilometres) to the north of the city: the coin-hoard may represent either an offering to the gods or burial of money for safekeeping.

97 A building dedication from the governorship of Agricola found in the forum-basilica dates its construction to the Flavian period: Niblett 2001, 73–8.

98 British tribes occupying territory in southern England: the Dobunni's focal territory was Gloucestershire and Oxfordshire, the Durotriges in Dorset.

99 A feature of deliberate archaism argued for some Iron Age coin-deposits occurring in Romano-British temples: Haselgrove 1989.

100 Cunliffe & Davenport 1985, 9.

101 Op. cit. 10.

102 Blagg 1979.

103 Perhaps those belonging to Legion II Augusta stationed at Exeter: Cunliffe & Davenport 1985, 179.

104 Blagg 1979.

105 Cunliffe & Davenport 1985, 28–9.

106 Green 1995, 73–9.

107 Cunliffe & Fulford 1982, pl.10, nos. 32–7; Aldhouse-Green 2004a, fig. 8.3.

108 An apotropaic or protective symbol designed to avert the evil eye.

109 Aldhouse-Green 2004a, 223–4.
110 Cunliffe & Davenport 1905, 179.
111 Tacitus *Agricola* 21; trans. Mattingly 1948, 72.
112 Davies 2005.

CHAPTER 9

The Icenian wolf: legend and legacy

What Hollywood will make of the life and times of the flame-haired, 1940-year-old rebuffer of Romans is anyone's guess. A Celtic Madonna, perhaps, with great muscle tone and a weirdo religion? A proto-feminist as ballsy as Germaine Greer but handier with spears? A skimpily-clad anti-slavery Xena, Warrior Princess, with cross-demographic appeal to rad-fems and FHM soft-porn fetishists? The legend can flourish so richly because we know so little about the real-life warrior-queen. We're not even sure how to spell her name: is it Boadicea, Boudicca or Boudica?

Jeffries 'Return of the queen'[1]

So wrote Stuart Jeffries in an article for *The Guardian* in 2004, in which he explores the plans for production of a series of blockbuster films about Boudica. Despite the racy, somewhat over-contemporary tone, Jeffries gets to the heart of how Boudica is and has been presented through time, in a few pithy sentences. Boudica/Boadicea is a romantic figure, about whom copious legends have been woven. The name Boadicea is probably a derivation from an inaccurate transcription of Tacitus, but Jeffries is right: we cannot be certain of the precise form of her name, nor how it would have been pronounced. She has always fascinated historians and literary figures, and she continues to exercise a magnetism out of all proportion to her treatment in the ancient Graeco-Roman texts, partly because of her defiance of gender conventions, but above all because she, as self-appointed ruler of part of a small island on the edge of the world, took on the Roman empire and very nearly won.

A wander down the lane called Priory Walk, in the centre of Colchester, leads to an encounter with a striking concrete mural, mounted on the external wall of Sainsbury's supermarket.[2] The frieze presents a visual history of Colchester in a series of schematised frames, whose images leap out at the viewer. One panel depicts the confrontation between Boudica's Britons and the Roman army of Suetonius Paulinus (see Figure 9.1); to the right, the conquerors are represented by a Roman imperial coin surmounted by the helmet-crest of an army officer (the coin is used as an ambivalent image: the head of a soldier and a unit of Roman currency); to the left, a phalanx of British spears faces the enemy and, among the weapons (almost blending with them) is the image of a rearing wolf, a symbol of Boudica's ferocious fight for freedom. The whole frieze is emblematic of a civic pride in which Britain's oldest city remembers both its Roman foundations and the woman who challenged *romanitas* and so nearly drove it out of the island altogether. The mural is of particular interest in so far as the wolf image picks up on an ancient theme, that of the 'Norfolk wolf', a motif present on an Icenian coin-series

FIGURE 9.1 ◆ *Modern concrete frieze, by Henry and Joyce Collins, depicting schematised confrontation between the Romans and Boudica's Britons; outside Sainsbury's in Priory Walk, Colchester.*

Source: © Miranda Aldhouse-Green.

that predates Boudica but is idiosyncratic to the tribe from *c.* 65 to 40 BC.[3] Given that Dio makes Boudica say of Suetonius Paulinus's army 'let us show them that they are hares and foxes attempting to rule over dogs and wolves',[4] it is perhaps fitting to refer to the British freedom fighter as the 'Icenian wolf': a fierce creature, symbolic of the untamed wilderness, in opposition to what have often been seen as cowardly and hunted lesser animals.

After visiting Priory Walk, the wanderer may visit the splendid Moot Hall in Colchester Town Hall, wherein three Edwardian stained-glass windows, ranged along one wall, display portraits of historical characters who have influenced the development of the town since pre-Roman times. The great middle window, the Ladies Window, commemorates the queens of England, and was presented by the Ladies of the Borough under the leadership of the President of the Committee, Emily Sandars, who was Colchester's Mayoress 1898–9. The central place in the window is occupied by Queen Victoria and around the edges are smaller roundels, each bearing the portrait of other noble ladies (all – incidentally – depicted as young and beautiful), including Helena, the mother of Constantine and Eleanor of Aquitaine. At the bottom right is the image of a young fair-haired girl (see Plate 25), wearing a triple-roundel diadem around her brow and a great golden, triple-stranded bead necklace around her neck; she carries a large spear, apparently in her left hand, since – from the viewer's angle – the weapon runs diagonally from bottom right to top left. Beneath the portrait is the word 'BOADICEA'. The window to the left depicts English kings: the central figure this time is Edward the Elder (AD 922) and the earliest king present here is 'CARACTACUS' (see Plate 7).[5] Both the Priory Walk mural and the town hall windows reflect a similar sense of national and civic pride – albeit on a much more modest scale than the bolder and more overtly nostalgic statements about a remote and noble past in France, for instance by Napoleon III, who set up magnificent (if anachronistic) statues of the Gallic resistance leader Vercingetorix at Alesia and Clermont-Ferrand.[6]

This final chapter concerns the presentation of Boudica and the Boudica myth as it has travelled through time from the period of her life until the present. I do not intend, however, to go into great detail of her treatment by historians, literary figures and antiquarians, for the very good reason that this path has been thoroughly and well-trodden by

Hingley and Unwin,[7] and it is pointless for me to repeat this well-researched aspect of their book. In any case, that theme is not the focus of this present volume, which is concerned almost exclusively with Boudica and her immediate historical and archaeological context. Nonetheless, in the course of my own search for Boudica, I have become interested in one or two elements of her iconicity, not least in the way the Boudica brand has been appropriated in the present, by the media, in museum presentation, and even in such unlikely locations as the fashion industry. I am also concerned to draw some parallels between Boudica and other powerful women, past and present and, in particular, the way in which their gender, in common with that of Boudica, has often been treated as abnormal, as 'other', in order that society may cope with the female that does not conform to the persisting social conventions of how women should conduct themselves.

Abnormal women and iron ladies: icons and symbols

> *Our society is very odd. There's a sense that if women come to power, the only way we can cope with that is to make them superhuman figures. That's certainly what happened with Elizabeth I, Mrs Thatcher and Boadicea.*
>
> Jeffries 'Return of the queen'[8]

This quotation comes from an interview held between the author and Stuart Jeffries in *The Guardian* on 30 June, 2004. We can take such a view further and argue not only that women in power are superhuman but supra-gender beings as well. Indeed, the dust jacket of Brenda Maddox's biography[9] quotes a question posed in the *Sun* newspaper in 1972: 'Is Mrs Thatcher human?' Norman St John Stevas characterised her as 'Attila the Hen' and 'the Blessed Margaret', and lost his Cabinet post in consequence. In Alan Clark's *Diaries*,[10] for example, Margaret Thatcher is constantly referred to as 'the Lady', a term that, though arguably just a mark of respect, contains undertones of specialness that would simply not be found in referrals to male prime ministers.[11] In all his descriptions of Thatcher, Clark's words about her suggest someone who is, at one and the same time, very feminine (and, indeed, very attractive to some parliamentarians, including Clark himself) and beyond gender. Clark's attitude to women in general, within the *Diaries* and its prequel,[12] exhibits a degree of chauvinism, but never towards the Lady. Parallels between Boudica and Thatcher (particularly during and after the Falklands campaign) are very obvious. John Sergeant's biographical bestseller, *Maggie*,[13] includes a chapter entitled 'The assassin with the golden hair', an epithet (albeit applied, in this context, to Thatcher's political killings) that could just as easily have applied to Boudica. During her time as British Prime Minister, Thatcher was repeatedly referred to as 'the Iron Lady',[14] a term that, at the same time, inverted conventions of 'soft' femininity and projected an image of steely ruthlessness. In the 'Britain and the Revolt against Rome' display at Norwich Castle Museum the visitor enters past a video showing a succession of female faces, including various antiquarian images of Boudica together with that of Margaret Thatcher.[15] It is a powerful visual image that requires no words to make the link. Indeed, cartoonists of the Thatcher era made great play of perceived synergies between the two 'warrior' women: see Antonia Fraser's book, *The Warrior Queens*, published in 1988.[16]

A glance at some other modern and historical women, of charisma and iconic status, who might be compared with Boudica, reveals a range of parallels. Staying with current (or recent) British politics, it is pertinent to look briefly at the persona of Cherie Blair who, though a consort of the prime minister Tony Blair, nonetheless exercises a great deal of power and influence in her own right, although her image struggles between the roles of top QC (with salary to match), premier's wife (with all the concomitant duties attached) and mother. Mary Ann Sieghart portrayed Cherie Blair, in *The Times* in September 2004, as not only a woman who had achieved a successful combination of career, independence and motherhood, but also as consort to the British 'president'.[17] This analysis was supported by carefully chosen pictures that served to present a woman who, in some ways, mirrored Boudica's own ambivalence: Boudica, too, took the stage initially as consort, as mother and 'career' woman, but she was eventually catapulted into prominence by her husband's death. Sieghart makes the point that 'in any other marriage, Cherie would have been the star', and there is little doubt that she possesses all the ingredients for a formidable political career, were she to have chosen that pathway.

Another charismatic woman on the current political stage – this one more overtly like Boudica – is the Palestinian freedom fighter and suicide bomber Reem Saleh Al-Riyashi, a mother of two children who blew herself up and, in this process, she killed four Israelis at the Erez crossing between Israel and Gaza. The first female suicide bomber recruited from Hamas, she is depicted on a website posted on 27 January 2004, when the female Lebanese spokesperson for Hezbollah – Ghada Musawi – spoke at her memorial service in Beirut.[18] The website picture shows the bomber dressed as a devout Muslim woman but with a copy of the *Qu'ran* in her left hand and guns in her right. Al-Riyashi's brand of self-destruct terrorism was not so very different from Boudica's, although the Iron Age freedom fighter had no wish to conquer by dying.

English and European history is not without its Boudicas. A clear linkage between the Icenian and Queen Victoria is apparent in their very names: Boudica's name means 'victory'. So the Victorians felt an especial affinity with the Iron Age queen. Shortly after Victoria became queen of England, the artist Selous painted a portrait of a bare-breasted, gesticulating 'Boadicea' in full battle-rig, addressing her forces before battle.[19] In similar genre is the great bronze statue of *Boadicea and her Daughters* on the Thames Embankment, outside Westminster tube station, which was produced by Thomas Thornycroft in the later part of Victoria's reign and put in its present place by the London County Council in 1902 (see Plate 24). The Icenian ruler is depicted in a long flowing robe, a diadem around her head, arms upraised, a spear brandished in her right hand; she rides a chariot, with scythed wheels, like a Victorian version of the film Ben Hur,[20] and behind her are her two daughters. Inscriptions in gold letters on the pediment read (south side) 'Boadicea / Boudicca / Queen of the Iceni / Who died AD 61 / After leading her people / against the Roman invader'. On the east side are two lines from the poem *Boadicea* by William Cowper: 'Regions Caesar never knew / Thy posterity shall sway'.[21] The allusion to Queen Victoria is very obvious, both from the statue and the poem.

A very different portrayal of Boudica and her daughters is on display at the City Hall in Cardiff (see Plate 9): sculpted from Serravesa Marble by J. Havard Thomas, the statue was installed in the Marble Hall' along with other 'Heroes of Wales', in October 1916, when they were all unveiled by David Lloyd George, having been donated to the city by Lord Rhondda of Llanwern.[22] Unlike the belligerent chariot driver of the London Embankment, this Cardiff Boudica and her children present a distinctly unwarlike demeanour, unarmed and almost in the manner of refugees. The queen is a buxom middle-aged woman (seemingly too old to have adolescent daughters), her long hair bound by a fillet, wearing a long belted robe and cloak and thonged sandals. Her maternal arms encircle the two traumatised girls, each of whom wears a knee-length tunic and is barefoot. Beneath the statue is the inscription 'Buddug, Boadicea, Died AD 61': Buddug is the Welsh translation of Boudica. Despite her location in the 'Heroes of Wales' gallery, Havard Thomas's Boudica is depicted as a protective mother, but she is certainly not presented as a virago but rather as a dignified, defeated barbarian.

A 'gold-haired assassin'[23] can be found in the persona of Elizabeth I, whose powerful, beyond-gendered persona is projected by descriptions and imagery alike. This is no place to dwell in detail on Elizabeth and her treatment, as an all-powerful supra-human, by her peers. But the discrepant portraits of her and her half-sister Mary are significant. While Mary is portrayed as sombre and intense, she is still presented as an austere female, with no gender ambiguity. In contrast, some of Elizabeth's iconography shows a distinctly masculine woman who, even when a young princess, shows implacability and obsessive power-hunger so similar to that of her father: her face, shape and clothing project the image of a youthful and essentially male princeling.[24]

Of greater interest, perhaps, is the persona of Jean d'Arc (Joan of Arc), the maiden warrior who so nearly defeated the English in France in the early fifteenth century and whose atypical gender behaviour led to such vilification of her and to jibes at her 'male womanhood' not dissimilar to those levelled against Boudica by her ancient biographers. Joan of Arc was born in 1412 in the village of Domremy, on the river Meuse near Lorraine in north-east France. Brought up as a simple peasant girl, she became convinced that God was calling her to oppose the English/Burgundian alliance against the French royalists. In April 1429, at the head of an army, she rode into Orléans on a white horse, relieving the city in three days from its seven-month siege. After winning many battles, Joan was captured at Compiègne, having been betrayed to the English.[25] In 1429, the year of Orléans, a clerk of the Parisian Parliament drew a sketch of Joan (the only extant contemporary image of her): the drawing shows a young girl, with long flowing hair, female dress, and carrying a banner and a sword.[26] This is interesting because accounts of

Joan's meeting with the Dauphin, Charles, at which she persuaded him to let her ride at the head of an army of resistance, indicate her adoption of male dress: 'The contrast between the confident, inspired young peasant girl in simple male dress and the anxious, uncertain Dauphin Charles smothered in velvet and ermine was indeed dramatic'.[27] Observant readers will appreciate the essential similarity between this inverted comparison between the girl and the prince and between the female Icenian war-leader and the effete emperor Nero, as recounted by Dio Cassius.[28] The scorn with which the Romans regarded Boudica, a female warrior, and as therefore an unnatural creature who behaved outside proper gender conventions,[29] resonates closely with the English attitude to Joan of Arc who, in her captivity, was subjected to particular harassment because she was a woman: she was constantly examined for proof of her virginity, accused of prostitution and witchcraft, and berated for sinning against the Church and the Bible for dressing as a man.[30] It is as though this 'unnatural' cross-dressing behaviour caused the greatest opprobrium to be heaped upon her – greater even than her successful campaigns against the English.

The Boudica brand: perception and presentation, past and present

> But the truth is, that in this Battel and whole business the Britains never more plainly manifested themselves to be right Barbarians; no rule, no Foresight, no Forecast, Experience or Estimation, either of themselves or of their Enemies; Such Confusion, such Impotence, as seem'd likest not to a war, but to the wild Hurry of a distracted Woman, with as mad a Crew at her heels.
>
> John Milton The History of Britain[31]

'Every age invented their own version'[32] of Boudica. Milton clearly had no time for her, perceiving her as an inappropriately masculine woman in a man's world, 'as if in Britain Women were Men and Men Women'.[33] According to him, Gildas (a sixth-century monk) 'calls her a crafty Lioness, and leaves an ill fame on all her doings'.[34] Legends of Boudica, amassed since earliest historical times, particularly in the context of renewed interest by antiquarians in Britain's remote past, from the early seventeenth century onwards, accord her a presence not only in south-

9 ♦ The Icenian wolf: legend and legacy

east England and East Anglia but throughout Britain. Good examples of her widespread mythology may be found in the various claims as to her burial site and the stories of her ghostly visitations. In 1624 Edmund Bolton proposed Stonehenge as the location of the warrior queen's tomb, reasoning that such a monument would have been a fitting site for the lavish funeral mentioned by Dio (see Chapter 7). The link between Boudica and Stonehenge was maintained at least until the late eighteenth century, when it was included in Edward Barnard's *New, Comprehensive, Impartial and Complete History of England*.[35] Other legendary locations of her burial site range from North Wales to London: a nineteenth-century story places her grave on Gop Hill in Flintshire; London's Parliament Hill Fields also lays claim to her tomb.[36] But the most bizarre fantasy is that the Icenian queen is interred beneath platform 8 at King's Cross Station.[37] Wherever Boudica's remains are to be found – in reality or myth – there is a strong vein of fantasy concerning sightings of her restless and wandering ghost. She has been seen by inhabitants of the rural environs of Epping, where one legend has it that she committed suicide; and as late as the 1950s the somewhat disconcerting apparition of the warrior queen appeared 'driving a chariot out of the mists, near the Lincolnshire village of Cammeringham',[38] presumably her spirit searching for the equally ghostly Legion IX and its commander Cerialis.

The presentation of Boudica's Rebellion as part of Britain's cultural heritage today is at its best in the museums that lie in Icenian territory (such as Norwich Castle Museum) or whose ancestral cities were the targets of Boudica's 'terrorist' activities: The Castle Museum, Colchester, the Museum of London and Verulamium Museum, St Albans. Apart from the archaeology of the war and, in particular, the material remains of the attack on these Roman towns, these museums have presented the drama of Boudica in a variety of ways. A comparison between treatments of the event in the museum displays at Norwich, Colchester and London reveals discrepant coverage and, more marked still, is the way in which these asymmetries keep pace with the narratives in the classical literature.[39] Thus, while the destruction of Colchester and London receive considerable attention in these texts, the presumably equally savage assault upon Verulamium merits only a perfunctory statement, to the effect that it suffered the same fate as the other two Roman towns. The museum displays echo this differential treatment so, while those at

Colchester and London (as well as Norwich) make much of Boudica, the splendid and newly designed Roman museum at St Albans makes little of the Roman city's annihilation: a single modest panel describes its fate at the British queen's hands, albeit including quite a dramatic reconstruction drawing of the event.[40] It appears, then, that the Classical literature has a strong influence on how this episode of early British history is interpreted.

At Colchester, the visitor can see (and touch) the very chariot that was reconstructed for the 2002 'teleplay' about the queen made by Andrew Davies for ITV and starring Alex Kingston as Boudica (see Plate 10). Davies is quoted as saying about the film: 'I wrote a mixture of *Braveheart*, *I Claudius* and *Carry On Somebody*'.[41] After seeing the chariot, bristling with weapons and war-trumpets,[42] the visitor's appetite is whetted still further by the enticing display text: Now go upstairs and find out more about how Boudica destroyed Colchester. Once upstairs, an excellent five-minute film, *The Revenge*, relives the town's destruction in a dramatised reconstruction of the Romans' attempt to protect themselves in the great temple while desperately and vainly awaiting relief by the legions. Additionally, a powerful reconstruction painting[43] depicts the holocaust at the temple. At the Norwich Castle Museum, it is possible to go one better and take a ride on another Boudican chariot which is set up in front of a simulation video, so that the modern 'charioteer' can relive the action.[44] This museum recreates Boudican Britain in a successfully atmospheric manner: the display entitled 'Boudica and the Revolt against Rome' is approached through an Iron Age roundhouse and, at the entrance to the gallery, there is a video illustrating the several faces of Boudica and her peers, as depicted in historical literature; the most modern 'Boudica' being represented by the face of Margaret Thatcher (see above). An inventive way of presenting archaeological evidence is by the use of clear glass as a real and metaphorical window between the Iron Age and Roman period, which – of course – can be viewed from both directions, as though the Britons were looking to a Roman future while the Romans gazed at a British past. Finally, the story of Boudica's attack on London is graphically told in the Museum of London's Roman Gallery. Eye-catching display headers make an immediate impact: the exhibitions entitled 'Chariots of Fire' and 'Romans Go Home!' give the ancient story a compelling contemporary resonance, as do others describing London's commercial prosperity, such as 'Prime Site' and 'Capital Growth', both of which are such common buzz-phrases in current economic jargon.

On 16 April 2005 the *Independent Magazine* carried a feature entitled 'Show and Tell' which was sub-titled 'Boudicca is famous as Britain's most uncompromising fashion label ...'.[45] Just before its first New York fashion show, the preparation work of the label's creators, Zowie Broach and Brian Kirkby, was described in the article: 'They are quietly putting the finishing touches to Boudicca's sabre-sharp, tarmac-black collections'.[46] So, in the twenty-first century, the 'Boudica brand' lives on in a fashion collection designed to make statements about empowerment, independence, bucking trends and going against the grain. We are a very long way from the first Boudica, with her multi-coloured garments and showy gold necklet, but she, too, stood for ideals of independence, defiance of tradition and freedom, albeit the infinitely serious ideologies of freedom from oppression and the right to self-determination for which people all over the world still strive. Boudica is the embodiment of the 'Rule Britannia' image that graced the old pennies some of us can still remember.

Notes and references

1 Jeffries 2004, 2.
2 The frieze is by Henry and Joyce Collins.
3 Davies 1999, 22.
4 Dio Cassius *Roman History* 62,5; trans. Ireland 1996, 63–70.
5 The Kings Window was dedicated in 1901 and presented by the Corporation of the Borough led by Thomas Hetherington of Berechurch Hall.
6 These images can be seen today at the great hillfort of Alesia in Burgundy and in the main square of Clermont-Ferrand, Auvergne.
7 In their recent book *Boudica. Iron Age Warrior Queen*, Hingley & Unwin 2005. More than half of their study is taken up with the legend of Boudica in historical and modern times. In the words of a recent reviewer of their book 'Hingley and Unwin capture some of the more extraordinary modern histories of Boadicea with considerable verve': Beard 2005, 5.
8 Miranda Aldhouse-Green in Jeffries 2004, 2.

9   Maddox 2003, inner front flap of book jacket.
10 Clark 1993, 83 and *passim*.
11 For biographies and autobiographies of Thatcher, see e.g. Young 1989; Maddox 2003; Sergeant 2005; Thatcher 1993, 1995, 2002.
12 Clark 2001.
13 Sergeant 2005, 39.
14 Witness, for instance, Campbell's biography of Thatcher, vol. 2, which is entitled *The Iron Lady*: Campbell 2004
15 As at 23 March 2005.
16 *The Warrior Queens. Boadicea's Chariot*, Fraser 1988, pls between pp. 336 and 337: cartoons by Griffin in *The Daily Express*, 24 June 1982 and Gale in *The Telegraph* 11 June 1987 (polling day).
17 Sieghart 2004, 4–5.
18 http://editorial.gettyimages.com.
19 Jeffries 2004, 2.
20 There is no archaeological evidence for Iron Age chariots with scythes on their wheels; indeed, such a feature would have been deadly not only to the enemy but to other chariots and horses moving alongside and thus would be totally impractical. For a fuller account of the statue's construction see Hingley & Unwin 2005, 162–3.
21 Wilkinson & Wilkinson eds 1954, 25–6; Hingley & Unwin 2005, 166: Cowper's dates are 1731–1800.
22 Cardiff City Council 2003, 24.
23 A paraphrase of Sergeant's chapter title: Sergeant 2005, 39 as applied to the political deadliness of Margaret Thatcher in her prime.
24 Weir 1996. Pl. 12 shows Mary as a young woman; pl. 18 the princess Elizabeth.
25 Schoyer Brooks 1990.
26 Op. cit. 14–15.
27 Op. cit. 41.
28 Dio Cassius *Roman History* 62.5–6. Dio puts words into the mouth of Boudica before battle against Suetonius Paulinus to the effect that Boudica and her followers are better men than the man-woman Nero and the soft-living Roman army.
29 Tacitus *Annals* 14.36.
30 Schoyer Brooks 1990, 115, 117, 123, 149.

31 *The History of Britain. That part especially, now call'd England. From the First Traditional Beginnings, continu'd to the Norman Conquest* 1670; http://humanities.ualberta.ca/emls/iemls/work/etexts/histbrit.txt, 51.

32 Display panel in the Roman Gallery in the Castle Museum, Colchester.

33 Op. cit. (fn 24).

34 Op. cit. (fn 24), 53.

35 Hingley & Unwin 2005, 135.

36 Op. cit. 163, 200.

37 Apparently a favourite tale told to tourists by London taxi-drivers: *op. cit.* 214.

38 Kightly 1982, 52.

39 Tacitus *Annals* and Dio Cassius's *Roman History* (see preceding chapters, particularly 2, 7 and 8)

40 The panel reconstruction painting is by John Pearson and is displayed in the Verulamium Museum.

41 Jeffries 2004, 2.

42 These trumpets, with their distinctive animal (usually boar-) heads are known as *carnyces* (singular *carnyx*) and are often mentioned by classical writers as being effective at frightening the Romans when employed on the Gallic or British battlefield.

43 By the artist Peter Froste.

44 The author tried this in March 2005, and very effective it was too, but gave her innards a decidedly unsettled feeling as the world lurched and swayed from the chariot on its way through the trees into battle.

45 Callendar 2005, 32.

46 The website for the 'Boudicca' fashion designers is www.lerage.com/designers/BOUDICCA

47 From W.H. Auden's poem *September 1, 1939*: Mendelson ed. 1979, 86.

Epitaph

I and the public know
What all schoolchildren learn,
Those to whom evil is done
Do evil in return.

W.H. Auden *September 1, 1939*[47]

The Preface to this book ends with a quote from W.H. Auden. It is equally fitting to use Auden to end the book itself for, in these few lines, well known to many, Auden states a simple, yet universal truth about wrongdoing and revenge. Had not the Romans behaved with crass cruelty and insensitivity, would the Boudican Rebellion ever have happened? Was Boudica simply a fanatical terrorist, or was she 'more sinned against than sinning'? Was it inevitable that 'barbarians' should be defeated by 'civilisation'? Did Boudica expect to win, or was she the world's first suicide bomber? These are legitimate questions for students of Boudica's extraordinary career as a freedom fighter to ponder.

Bibliography

Abbaye de Daoulas 1986. *Au Temps des Celtes. Ve–1er Siècle avant J.C.* Quimper: Association Abbaye de Daoulas/Musée Departemental Breton de Quimper.

Adas, M. 1979. *Prophets of Rebellion. Millenarian Protest Movements against the European Colonial Order.* Carolina: Carolina Academic Press.

Adkins, L. & Adkins, R. 1996. *Dictionary of Roman Religion.* New York: Facts on File.

Alberge, D. 2000. 'Woman gladiator found buried in London', *The Times.* 13 September 2000.

Aldhouse-Green, M.J. 2000. *Seeing the Wood for the Trees: The Symbolism of Trees and Wood in Ancient Gaul and Britain.* Aberystwyth: Centre for Advanced Welsh and Celtic Studies, University of Wales, Aberystwyth Research Paper No. 17.

Aldhouse-Green, M.J. 2001a. *Dying for the Gods. Human Sacrifice in Iron Age and Roman Europe.* Stroud: Tempus.

Aldhouse-Green, M.J. 2001b. 'Gender-bending images: permeating boundaries in Ancient European iconography', in R.J. Wallis & K. Lymer eds *A Permeability of Boundaries: New Approaches to the Archaeology of Art, Religion and Folklore.* Oxford: British Archaeological Reports (International Series) No. 936, 19–30.

Aldhouse-Green, M.J. 2003. 'Poles apart? Perceptions of gender in Gallo-British cult-iconography', in S. Scott & J. Webster eds *Roman Imperialism and Provincial Art.* Cambridge: Cambridge University Press, 95–118.

Aldhouse-Green, M.J. 2004a. *An Archaeology of Images. Iconology and Cosmology in Iron Age and Roman Europe.* London: Routledge.

Aldhouse-Green, M.J. 2004b. 'Crowning glories: languages of hair in later prehistoric Europe', *Proceedings of the Prehistoric Society* 70, 299–325.

Aldhouse-Green, M.J. 2004c 'Chaining and shaming: images of defeat, from Llyn Cerrig Bach to Sarmitzegetusa', *Oxford Journal of Archaeology* 23, No. 3, August 2004, 319–40.

Aldhouse-Green, M.J. 2004d. 'Gallo-British deities and their shrines', in M. Todd ed. *A Companion to Roman Britain*. Oxford: Blackwell, 193–219.

Aldhouse-Green, M.J. & Aldhouse-Green, S. 2005. *The Quest for the Shaman: Shape-Shifters, Sorcerers and Spirit-Healers of Ancient Europe*. London: Thames & Hudson.

Allason-Jones, L. 1989 *Women in Roman Britain* London: British Museum Press.

Allason-Jones, L. 2004. 'The family in Roman Britain', in M. Todd ed. *A Companion to Roman Britain*. Oxford: Blackwell, 273–87.

Allen, D.F. 1970. 'The coins of the Iceni', *Britannia* 1, 1–33.

Allen, D.F. 1975. 'Cunobelin's gold', *Britannia* 6, 1–19.

Allen, D.F. & Haselgrove, C. 1979. 'The gold coinage of Verica', *Britannia* 10, 1–18.

Alston, R. 1998. 'Arms and the man: soldiers, masculinity and power in republican and imperial Rome', in L. Foxhall & J. Salmon eds *When Men were Men: Masculinity, Power and Identity in Classical Antiquity*. London: Routledge, 205–23.

Anderson, Scott, A. 1987. 'The imperial army', in J. Wacher ed. *The Roman World*. London: Routledge, 89–106.

Armstrong, K. 2000. *The Battle for God. Fundamentalism in Judaism, Christianity and Islam*. London: HarperCollins.

Arnold, B. 1991. 'The deposed princess of Vix: the need for an engendered European prehistory', in D. Walde & N.D. Willows eds *The Archaeology of Gender*. Calgary: University of Calgary Archaeological Association, 366–74.

Arnold, B. 1995. ' "Honorary males" or women of substance? Gender, status and power in iron age Europe', *Journal of European Archaeology* 3 (2), 153–68.

Arnold, B. 1999. 'Drinking the feast: alcohol and the legitimation of power in Celtic Europe', *Cambridge Archaeological Journal* 9 (1), 71–93.

Arnold, B. 2001. 'Power drinking in Iron Age Europe', *British Archaeology* 57, February 2001, 14–19.

Barrett, A. 1979. 'The career of Tiberius Claudius Cogidubnus', *Britannia* 10, 227–42.

Barrett, A. 1991. 'Claudius' British victory arch in Rome', *Britannia* 22, 1–19.

Bartman, E. 1999. *Portraits of Livia. Imaging the Imperial Woman in Augustan Rome.* Cambridge: Cambridge University Press.

Bartram, P.C. 1974. *Welsh Genealogies: AD 300–1400* Vol. 1. Cardiff: University of Wales Press.

Bateman, N. 1998. 'Guildhall House, 81–87 Gresham Street', in J. Schofield & C. Maloney eds *Archaeology in the City of London 1907–91: A Guide to Records of Excavations by the Museum of London.* London: Museum of London. The Archaeological Gazetteer Series, Vol. 1, 213.

Bauman, R.A. 1996. *Crime and Punishment in Ancient Rome.* London: Routledge.

Beard, M. 2005. 'Rebel in spirit', *Times Higher Education Supplement* 24 June 2005.

Benario, H.W. 1986. 'Legionary speed of march before the battle with Boudicca', *Britannia* 17, 358–62.

Berridge, P. & Hodgson, T. 1997. *Colchester Castle Museum Souvenir Guide.* Colchester: Jarrold/Colchester Borough Council.

Black, E.W. 2000. 'Sentius Saturninus and the Roman invasion of Britain', *Britannia* 31, 1–10.

Black, E.W. 2001. 'The first century historians of Roman Britain', *Oxford Journal of Archaeology* 20, No. 4, November 2001, 415–28.

Blagg, T.F.C. 1979. 'The date of the temple at Bath', *Britannia* 10, 101–7.

Blagg, T.F.C., Plouviez, J. & Tester, A. 2004. *Excavations at a Large Romano-British Settlement at Hacheston, Suffolk in 1973–4.* East Anglian Archaeology 106. Ipswich: Archaeology Service Suffolk County Council.

Bland, R. & Johns, C.M. 1993. *The Hoxne Treasure. An Illustrated Introduction.* London: British Museum Press.

Bogaers, J.E. 1979. 'King Cogidubnus in Chichester: another reading of *RIB* 91', *Britannia* 10, 243–54.

Bonenfant, P.-B. & Guillaumet, J.-P. 1998. *La Statuaire Anthropomorphe du Premier Âge du Fer.* Besançon: Annales Littéraires de l'Université de Franche-Comté, No. 667.

Boyle, A. 2004. 'Riding into history', *British Archaeology* May 2004, 22–6.

Bradley, R. 1990. *The Passage of Arms.* Cambridge: Cambridge University Press.

Braund, D. 1993. 'Fronto and the Iberians: language and diplomacy at the Antonine court', *Ostraka* 2, 53–5.

Braund, D. 1996. *Ruling Roman Britain. Kings, Queens, Governors and Emperors from Julius Caesar to Agricola.* London: Routledge.

Briggs, D., Haselgrove, C. & King, C. 1992. 'Iron Age and Roman coins from Hayling Island temple', *British Numismatic Journal* 62, 1–62.

Brunaux, J.-L. 1988. *The Celtic Gauls. Gods, Rites and Sanctuaries.* Paris: Éditions Errance.

Brunaux, J.-L. 1996. *Les Religions Gaulois. Rituels Celtiques de la Gaule Indépendente.* Paris: Errance.

Caldecott, M. 1988. *Women in Celtic Myth.* London: Arrow/Hutchinson.

Calder, A. 2004. *Disasters and Heroes. On War, Memory and Representation.* Cardiff: University of Wales Press.

Callender, C. 2005. 'Show and tell', *The Independent Magazine.* 16 April 2005.

Cameron, A. & Kuhrt, A. eds 1993. *Images of Women in Antiquity.* London: Routledge.

Campbell, J. 2004. *The Iron Lady*. London: Pimlico.

Campbell, R. 1969. 'Introduction', in Campbell, R. trans. *Seneca. Letters from a Stoic*. Harmondsworth: Penguin, 7–28.

Cardiff City Council 2003. *Cardiff City Hall*. Cardiff: Cardiff City Council.

Carey, J. 2004. *Mind Reading*. BBC Radio 4, 4 September 2004.

Carr, G. 2001. '"Romanisation" and the body', in G. Davies, A. Gardner & K. Lockyear eds. *TRAC 2000. Proceedings of the Tenth Annual Theoretical Archaeology Conference London 2000*. Oxford: Oxbow, 112–24.

Carr, G. 2005. 'Woad, tattooing and identity in later Iron Age and early Roman Britain', *Oxford Journal of Archaeology* 24, 273–92.

Cary, M. 1965. *A History of Rome*. London: Macmillan.

Chadwick, N. 1966. *The Druids*. Cardiff: University of Wales Press.

Champlin, E. 1991. *Final Judgments: Deity and Emotion in Roman Wills, 200 BC–AD 250*. Berkeley: University of California Press.

Cheesman, C.E.A. 1998. 'Tincomarus Commi filius', *Britannia* 29, 309–15.

Cherry, J. ed. 1995. *Mythical Beasts*. London: British Museum Press.

Chisholm, K. & Ferguson, J. eds 1981. *Rome The Augustan Age*. Oxford: Oxford University Press.

CIL (*Corpus Inscriptionum Latinarum*). 1861–1973 Berlin: Georgium Reimerum.

Clark, A. 1993. *Diaries*. London: Weidenfeld & Nicolson/Phoenix.

Clark, A. 2001. *Diaries. Into Politics*. London: Weidenfeld & Nicolson/Phoenix.

Cleland, L., Harlow, M. & Llewellyn-Jones, L. eds 2005. *The Clothed Body in the Ancient World*. Oxford: Oxbow.

Coates, R. 2005. 'Cogidubnus revisited', *Antiquaries Journal* 85, 359–66.

Cohen, B. 1997. 'Divesting the female breast of clothes in classical sculpture', in A.O. Koloski-Ostrow & C.L. Lyons eds *Naked Truths:*

Women, Sexuality and Gender in Classical Art and Archaeology. London: Routledge, 66–92.

Colchester Archaeological Trust 2001. 'Roman Colchester uncovered', *The Colchester Archaeologist* No. 14, 9–17.

Colchester Archaeological Trust 2003a. 'Harpers – Roman floors under your feet', *The Colchester Archaeologist* No. 16, 22–3.

Colchester Archaeological Trust 2003b. 'The western suburb', *The Colchester Archaeologist* No. 16, 10–15.

Collingwood, R.G. & Wright, R.P. 1965. *The Roman Inscriptions of Britain.* Oxford: Oxford University Press.

Cool, H. 2005. 'Pyromania', *British Archaeology* January/February 2005, 31–5.

Creekmore, H. trans. 1963. *The Satires of Juvenal.* London/New York: Mentor Books.

Creighton, J. 1995. 'Visions of power: imagery and symbols in late Iron Age Britain', *Britannia* 26, 285–301.

Creighton, J. 2000. *Coins and Power in Late Iron Age Britain.* Cambridge: Cambridge University Press.

Creighton, J. 2006. *Britannia: the Creation of a Roman Province.* London: Routledge.

Crummy, P. 1992. *Excavations at Culver Street, The Gilberd School, and Other Sites in Colchester 1971–85.* Colchester: Colchester Archaeological Report No. 6, Colchester Archaeological Trust.

Crummy, P. 1993. 'Aristocratic graves at Colchester', *Current Archaeology* 132, 492–7.

Crummy, P. 1995. 'Late Iron Age burials at Stanway, Colchester', in J. Swaddling, S. Walker & P. Roberts eds *Italy in Europe: Economic Relations 700 BC–AD 50.* London: British Museum Occasional Paper No. 97, 263–5.

Crummy, P. 1997. 'Colchester: the Stanway burials', *Current Archaeology* 153, 2, No. 9, 337–41.

Crummy, P. 2002. 'Des tombes aristocratiques à Stanway, Colchester, Grande-Bretagne', in V. Guichard & F. Perrin eds *L'Aristocratie Celte* à la Fin de l'Âge du Fer (IIe s. avant J.-C.-Ier après J.-C.). Glux-en-Glenne: Collection Bibracte No. 5, 145–52.

Cunliffe, B. 1995. *Roman Bath*. London: English Heritage.

Cunliffe, B. 1998. *Fishbourne Roman Palace*. Stroud: Tempus.

Cunliffe, B. & Davenport, P. 1985. *The Temple of Sulis Minerva at Bath*. Vol. 1 (1), *The Site*. Oxford: Oxford University Committee for Archaeology Monograph 7.

Cunliffe, B. & Fulford, M.G. 1982. *Corpus Signorum Imperii Romani. Corpus of Sculpture of the Roman World. Great Britain*. Vol. 1, Fasc. 2. *Bath and the Rest of Wessex*. Oxford/London: Oxford University Press/British Academy.

Daniels, C. 1987. 'Africa', in J. Wacher ed. *The Roman World*. London: Routledge, 223–65.

Davies, G. 2005. 'What made the Roman toga *virilis*?', in L. Cleland, M. Harlow & L. Llewellyn-Jones eds *The Clothed Body in the Ancient World*. Oxford: Oxbow, 121–30.

Davies, J.L. & Lynch, F. 2000. 'The late Bronze Age and Iron Age', in F. Lynch, S. Aldhouse-Green & J.L. Davies eds *Prehistoric Wales*. Stroud: Sutton, 139–219.

Davies, J. 1999. 'Patterns, power and political progress in Iron Age Norfolk', in J. Davies & J. Williamson eds *Land of the Iceni. The Iron Age in Northern East Anglia*. Norwich: Centre of East Anglian Studies, University of East Anglia, 14–43.

Davies, J. & Williamson, T. eds 1999. *Land of the Iceni. The Iron Age in Northern East Anglia*. Norwich: Centre of East Anglian Studies, University of East Anglia.

Davies, O. 2005. *Making History*, BBC Radio 4 (presenter Sue Cook), 7 June, 2005.

Davies, S. 1997. 'Horses in the *Mabinogion*', in S. Davies & N.A. Jones eds, *The Horse in Celtic Culture. Medieval Welsh Perspectives*. Cardiff: University of Wales Press, 121–40.

Davies, S. & Jones, N.A. eds. 1997. *The Horse in Celtic Culture. Medieval Welsh Perspectives*. Cardiff: University of Wales Press.

De Jersey, P. 2001. 'Cunobelin's silver', *Britannia* 32, 1–44.

De la Bédoyère, G. 1993. *Roman Villas and the Countryside*. London: Batsford/English Heritage.

De la Bédoyère, G. 2003a. *Defying Rome. The Rebels of Roman Britain*. Stroud: Tempus.

De la Bédoyère, G. 2003b. *Eagles over Britannia*. Stroud: Tempus.

Denison, S. 2003. 'London graves desecrated by Boudica's army', *British Archaeology* May 2003, No. 10, 4.

Dent, J. 1985. 'Three cart burials from Wetwang, Yorkshire', *Antiquity* 59, 85–92.

Deyts, S. 1992. *Images de Dieux de la Gaule*. Paris: Éditions Errance.

Drinkwater, J. 1983. *Roman Gaul*. London: Croom Helm.

Dunning, C. 1991. 'La Tène', in S. Moscati, O.H. Frey, V. Kruta, B. Raftery & M. Szabó eds *The Celts*. London: Thames & Hudson, 366–71.

Duval, P.-M. 1987. *Monnaies Gauloises et mythes celtiques*. Paris: Hermann, Éditeurs des Sciences et des Arts.

Eckardt, H. 1999. 'The Colchester "child's grave"', *Britannia* 30, 57–90.

Evans, C. 2003. *Power and Island Communities. Excavations at the Wardy Hill Ringwork, Coveney, Ely*. East Anglian Archaeology 103. Cambridge: Cambridge Archaeological Unit.

Farrar, S. 2005. 'The last stand of Boudicca and the Celtic good guys', *Times Higher Education Supplement* 8 July 2005, 18–19.

Ferguson, J. 1970. *The Religions of the Roman Empire*. London: Thames & Hudson.

Ferguson, J. 1980. *Greek and Roman Religion. A Source Book*. Park Ridge, New Jersey: Noyes Press.

Ferguson, J. 1987. 'Ruler-worship, in J. Wacher ed. *The Roman World*. London: Routledge, 766–84.

Ferris, I. 1994. 'Insignificant others: images of barbarians on military art from Roman Britain', in S. Cottam, D. Dungworth, S. Scott, & J. Taylor eds *TRAC 94. Proceedings of the Fourth Annual Theoretical Roman Archaeology Conference Durham 1994*. Oxford: Oxbow, 24–31.

Ferris, I. 2000. *Enemies of Rome. Barbarians Through Roman Eyes.* Stroud: Alan Sutton.

Ferris, I. 2003. 'The hanged men dance: barbarians in Trajanic art', in S. Scott & J. Webster eds. *Roman Imperialism and Provincial Art.* Cambridge: Cambridge University Press, 53–68.

Fincham, C. 2004. Review of J. Davies & T. Williamson eds *Land of the Iceni: The Iron Age in Northern East Anglia. Proceedings of the Prehistoric Society* Vol. 70.

Fishwick, D. 1972. 'Templum Divo Claudio Constitutum', *Britannia* 3, 164–81.

Fishwick, D. 1973. 'Tacitean usage and the temple of *Divus Claudius*', *Britannia* 4, 264–5.

Fishwick, D. 1991. 'Seneca and the temple of *Divus Claudius*', *Britannia* 22, 137–42.

Fishwick, D. 1995. 'The temple of *Divus Claudius* at Camulodunum', *Britannia* 26, 11–28.

Fishwick, D. 1997. 'The provincial centre at Camulodunum: towards an historical context', *Britannia* 28, 31–50.

Fitts, R., Haselgrove, C., Lowther, P.C. & Willis, S.H. 1999. 'Melsonby reconsidered: survey and excavations 1992–5 at the site of the discovery of the "Stanwick" North Yorkshire hoard of 1843', *Durham Archaeological Journal* 14–15, 1–52.

Flitcroft, M. 2001. *Excavation of a Romano-British Settlement on the A149 Snettisham Bypass, 1989.* East Anglian Archaeology 93. Dereham: Norfolk Museum Services.

Foster, J. 1986. *The Lexden Tumulus: A Re-appraisal of an Iron Age Burial from Colchester, Essex.* Oxford: British Archaeological Reports No. 156.

Fowler, C. 2004. *The Archaeology of Personhood.* London: Routledge.

Fox, C. 1946. *A Find of the Early Iron Age from Llyn Cerrig Bach, Anglesey.* Cardiff: National Museum of Wales.

Foxhall, L. 1994. 'Pandora unbound: a feminist critique of Foucault's

History of Sexuality', in A. Cornwall & N. Lindisfarne eds *Dislocating Masculinity*. London: Routledge, 133–46.

Foxhall, L. & Salmon, J. eds. 1998. *When Men were Men: Masculine Power and Identity in Classical Antiquity*. London: Routledge.

Fraser, A. 1988. *The Warrior Queens. Boadicea's Chariot*. London: Phoenix Press.

Freeman, C. 1996. *Egypt, Greece and Rome. Civilizations of the Ancient Mediterranean*. Oxford: Oxford University Press.

Frere, S. 2000. 'A *Limitatio* of Icenian territory?', *Britannia* 31, 350–5.

Frere, S. & Fulford, M. 2001. 'The Roman invasion of AD 43', *Britannia* 32, 45–55.

Frere, S. & St Joseph, J.K. 1974. 'The Roman fortress at Longthorpe', *Britannia* 5, 1–129.

Fuentes, N. 1983. 'Boudicca re-visited', *London Archaeologist* 4, No. 12, 311–17.

Gager, J.G. ed. 1992. *Curse Tablets and Binding Spells from the Ancient World*. Oxford: Oxford University Press.

Godwin, H. 1975 (2nd edition). *History of the British Flora. A Factual Basis for Phytogeography*. Cambridge: Cambridge University Press.

Gould, J. 2004. 'Boudica – yet again', *London Archaeologist* 10, No. 11, 300.

Grant, M. trans. 1956. *Tacitus. The Annals of Imperial Rome*. Harmondsworth: Penguin.

Grant, M. trans. 1969. *Cicero. Selected Works*. Harmondsworth: Penguin.

Grasby, R.D. & Tomlin, R.S.O. 2002. 'The sepulchral monument of C. Julius Classicianus', *Britannia* 33, 43–76.

Graves, R. 1941a *I Claudius*. Harmondsworth: Penguin.

Graves, R. 1941b *Claudius The God*. Harmondsworth: Penguin.

Graves, R. trans. 1956. *Lucan Pharsalia*. Harmondsworth: Penguin.

Graves, R. trans. 1962. *Suetonius. The Twelve Caesars*. London: Cassell.

Green, M.J. 1976. *The Religions of Civilian Roman Britain*. Oxford: British Archaeological Reports No. 24.

Green, M.J. 1984. *The Wheel as a Cult-Symbol in the Romano-Celtic World*. Brussels: Latomus.

Green, M.J. 1989. *Symbol and Image in Celtic Religious Art*. London: Routledge.

Green, M.J. 1991. *The Sun-Gods of Ancient Europe*. London: Batsford.

Green, M.J. 1995. *Celtic Goddesses. Warriors, Virgins and Mothers*. London: British Museum Press.

Green, M.J. 1996. *Celtic Art. Reading the Messages*. London: Weidenfeld & Nicolson.

Green, M.J. 1997a. *Exploring the World of the Druids*. London: Thames & Hudson.

Green, M.J. 1997b. 'Images in opposition: polarity, ambivalence and liminality in cult representation', *Antiquity* 71, 898–911.

Green, M.J. 1997c. 'The Symbolic Horse in Pagan Celtic Europe', in S. Davies & N.A. Jones eds *The Horse in Celtic Culture Medieval Welsh Perspectives*. Cardiff: University of Wales Press, 1–22.

Green, M.J. 1998a. 'The time lords: ritual calendars, druids and the sacred year, in A. Gibson & D.D.A. Simpson eds *Prehistoric Ritual and Religion*. Stroud: Sutton, 190–202.

Green, M.J. 1998b 'Vessels of death: sacred cauldrons in archaeology and myth', *Antiquaries Journal* 78, 63–84.

Green, M.J. 1998c. 'God in man's image: thoughts on the genesis and affiliations of some Romano-British cult-imagery', *Britannia* 29, 17–30.

Green, M.J. 1998d. 'Crossing the boundaries: triple horns and emblematic transference', *European Journal of Archaeology* 1(2), 219–40.

Green, M.J. & Howell, R. 2000. *Celtic Wales*. Cardiff: University of Wales Press.

Gregory, A.K. 1992. *Excavations at Thetford, 1980–82, Fison Way*. Norwich: East Anglian Archaeological Report 53.

Guest, P. 2005. *The Late Roman Gold and Silver Coins from the Hoxne Treasure.* London: British Museum Press.

Hammond, N. 2005. 'Celtic find trumpets the spoils of war', *The Times* 29 August, 2005.

Haselgrove, C. 1989. 'Iron Age coin deposition at Harlow temple, Essex', *Oxford Journal of Archaeology* 8 (1), 73–88.

Haselgrove, C. 2002. 'The later Bronze Age and the Iron Age in the Lowlands', in C. Brooks, R. Daniels & A. Harding eds *Past, Present and Future: The Archaeology of Northern England.* Durham: Architectural and Archaeological Society of Durham and Northumberland Research Report 5, 49–69.

Haselgrove, C. 2004. 'Society and polity in late Iron Age Britain', in M. Todd ed. *A Companion to Roman Britain.* Oxford: Blackwell, 12–29.

Henig, M. 1998. 'Togidubnus and the Roman Liberation' *British Archaeology* 38, September 1998, 8–9.

Henig, M. 2002. *The Heirs of King Verica. Culture and Politics in Roman Britain.* Stroud: Tempus.

Henig, M. 2004. 'Roman religion and Roman culture in Britain', in M. Todd ed. *A Companion to Roman Britain.* Oxford: Blackwell, 220–41.

Henken, E.R. 1987. *Traditions of the Welsh Saints.* Cambridge: Boydell & Brewer.

Hill, J.D. 1997. 'The end of one kind of body and the beginning of another kind of body? Toilet instruments and "Romanization" in southern England during the first century AD', in A. Gwilt & C. Haselgrove eds. *Reconstructing Iron Age Societies.* Oxford: Oxbow, 96–107.

Hill, J.D. 1999. 'Settlement, landscape and regionality: Norfolk and Suffolk in the pre-Roman Iron Age of Britain and beyond', in J. Davies & T. Williamson eds *Land of the Iceni: The Iron Age in Northern East Anglia.* Norwich: Centre of East Anglian Studies, University of East Anglia, 185–207.

Hill, J.D. 2001. 'A new cart/chariot burial from Wetwang, East Yorkshire', *PAST* No. 38, August 2001, 2–3.

Hill, J.D., Spence, A.J., La Niece, S. & Worrell, S. 2004. 'The Winchester Hoard: a find of unique Iron Age gold jewellery from Southern England', *Antiquaries Journal* 84, 1–22.

Hingley, R. 2000. *Roman Officers and English Gentlemen*. London: Routledge.

Hingley, R. 2005. 'Freedom fighter or tale of the Romans', *British Archaeology* July/August 2005, 40–1.

Hingley, R. & Unwin, C. 2005. *Boudica: Iron age warrior queen*. London: Hambledon & London.

Housley, R.A., Walker, A.J., Otlet, R.L. & Hedges, R.E.M. 1995. 'Radiocarbon dating of the Lindow III bog body, in R.C. Turner & R.G. Scaife eds *Bog Bodies. New Discoveries and New Perspectives*. London: British Museum Press, 39–46.

Howard, P. 2000. 'Spice Girls with serious attitude', *The Times* 13 September 2000, 3.

Hunter, F. 2001. 'The carnyx in Iron Age Europe', *Antiquaries Journal* 81, 77–108.

Hurley, D.W. 2001. *Suetonius: Divus Claudius*. Cambridge: Cambridge University Press.

Hutcheson, N.C.G. 2004. *Later Iron Age Norfolk: Metalwork, Landscape and Society*. Oxford: British Archaeological Reports BS 361.

Ireland, S. 1996 (2nd edition). *Roman Britain. A Sourcebook*. London: Routledge.

Jackson, K.H. 1979. 'Queen Boudicca?', *Britannia* 10, 255.

Jackson, R.P.J. & Potter, T.W. 1996. *Excavations at Stonea, Cambridgeshire, 1980–85*. London: British Museum Press.

James, S. 1993. *Exploring the World of the Celts*. London: Thames & Hudson.

Jeffries, S. 2004. 'Return of the queen', *The Guardian G2*. 30 June 2004, 2–3.

Johns, C.W. & Bland, R. 1994. 'The Hoxne late Roman treasure', *Britannia* 25, 165–73.

Johns, C.M. & Potter, T. 1983. *The Thetford Treasure*. London: British Museum Publications.

Jones, G. & Jones, G. trans. 1976. *The Mabinogion*. London: Dent.

Jones, M.J. 2004. 'Cities and urban life', in M. Todd ed. *A Companion to Roman Britain*. Oxford: Blackwell, 162–92.

Jones, R. & Cook, N. 2005. 'Llandeilo Roman fort, Dinefwr Park.' *Cambria Archaeology Excavation 2005. Newsletter No. 1*, 27 May 2005. Llandeilo: Cambria Archaeology/National Trust.

Jones, W.H.S. trans. 1956/1963. *Pliny Natural History*. Macmillan: Loeb Classical Library.

Kampen, N. 1994. 'Material girl: feminist confrontations with Roman art', *Arethusa* 27, 111–49.

Kampen, N. 1996. 'Gender theory in Roman art', in D. Kleiner & S. Matheson eds *I Claudia: Women in Ancient Rome*. Austin: University of Texas Press.

Kaul, F. 1991. *Gundestrupkedlen*. Copenhagen: National Museet/Nyt Nordisk Forlag Arnold Busck.

Kaul, F., Marazov, I., Best, J. & de Vries, N. 1991. *Thracian Tales on the Gundestrup Cauldron*. Amsterdam: Najade Press.

Kavenna, J. 2005. *The Ice Museum. In Search of the Lost Land of Thule*. London: Viking.

Kelly, P. 1997. 'The earliest words for "horse" in the Celtic languages', in S. Davies & N.A. Jones eds *The Horse in Celtic Culture. Medieval Welsh Perspectives*. Cardiff: University of Wales Press, 43–63.

Kendall, R. 1997. *Kerma and the Kingdom of Kush 2500–1500 BC. The Archaeological Discovery of an Ancient Nubian Empire*. Washington DC: The Smithsonian Institution/National Museum of African Art.

Kennedy, D. 1987. 'The East', in J. Wacher ed. *The Roman World*. London: Routledge, 266–308.

Keppie, L. J.F. and Arnold, B.J. 1984. *Corpus Signorum Imperii Romani. Corpus of Sculpture of the Roman World*. Vol. 1, Fasc. 4. *Scotland*. Oxford: London: Oxford: Oxford University Press British Academy.

Kightly, C. 1982. *Folk Heroes of Britain*. London: Thames & Hudson.

King, A. & Soffe, G. 1991. 'Hayling Island', in M. Jones ed. *Roman Britain: Recent Trends*. Sheffield: J.R. Collis Publications, 111–13.

King, A. & Soffe, G. 1999. 'L'Organisation interne et l'enfouissement des objets au temple de l'Age du Fer à Hayling Island (Hampshire)', in J. Collis ed. *Society and Settlement in Iron Age Europe, L'habitat et l'occupation su Sol en Europe. Actes du XVIIIe colloque de l'AFEAF, Winchester – Avril 1994*. Sheffield: J.R. Collis Publications, 113–26.

King, H. 1993. 'Bound to bleed: Artemis and Greek women', in A. Cameron & A. Kuhrt eds *Images of Women in Antiquity*. London: Routledge, 109–27.

King, H. 1995. 'Half-human creatures', in J. Cherry ed. *Mythical Beasts*. London: British Museum Press, 138–67.

Kleiner, D. 2005. *Cleopatra and Rome*. Harvard: Harvard University Press.

Knight, J. 2003 (3rd edition). *Caerleon Roman Fortress*. Cardiff: Cadw.

Le Bohec, Y. 1994. *The Imperial Roman Army* (trans. Raphael Bate). London: Routledge.

Le Carré, J. 1974. *Tinker, Tailor, Soldier, Spy*. London: Pan Books.

Lewis, N. & Reinhold, M. 1966. *Roman Civilization. Sourcebook II. The Empire*. New York: Harper & Row (Harper Torchbooks).

Lynch, F. 1991 (2nd edition). *Prehistoric Anglesey*. Llangefni: Anglesey Antiquarian Society.

Lynn, C. 1992. 'The Iron Age mound in Navan Fort: a physical realisation of Celtic religious beliefs?', *Emania* 10, 33–57.

Lyons, A. 2004. *Romano-British Industrial Activity at Snettisham, Norfolk. Archaeological Investigations at Strickland Avenue and Station Road*. Dereham: East Anglian Archaeology Occasional Paper 18. Archaeology & Environment. Norfolk Museums and Archaeology Service.

Lyons, C. & A. Koloski-Ostrow eds 1997. *Naked Truths. Women, Sexuality and Gender in Classical art and Archaeology*. London: Routledge.

Mac Cana, P. 1970. *Celtic Mythology*. London: Newnes.

Mac Cana, P. 1976. 'The sinless other world of "Immram Brain"', *Ériu* 27, 95–115.

Macdonald, P. 1996. 'Llyn Cerrig Bach; an Iron Age votive assemblage', in S. Aldhouse-Green ed. *Art, Ritual and Death in Prehistory*. Cardiff: National Museum of Wales, 32–3.

MacMullen, R. 1992. *Enemies of the Roman Order*. London: Routledge.

Maddox, B. 2003. *Maggie. The First Lady*. London: Hodder & Stoughton.

Maniquet, C. 2005. 'The Tintignac Celtic warrior hoard', *Minerva* 16, No. 4, July/August 2005, 29–31.

Manley, J. 2002. *AD 43. The Roman Invasion of Britain. A Reassessment*. Stroud: Tempus.

Manning, W.H. 2001. *Roman Wales*. Cardiff: University of Wales Press.

Marsden, P. 1963. 'Archaeological finds in the city of London, 1960', *Transactions of the London and Middlesex Archaeological Society* 21, part 1, 70–77.

Marsden, P. 1980. *Roman London*. London: Thames & Hudson.

Mason, J. 2005. *The Hare*. London: Merlin Unwin Books.

Mattingly, H. trans. 1948. *Tacitus on Britain and Germany*. West Drayton: Penguin.

McAvoy, L.H. & Walters, T. eds 2002. *Consuming Narratives: Gender and Monstrous Appetite in the Middle Ages and the Renaissance*. Cardiff: University of Wales Press.

McClintock, A. 1995. *Imperial Leather: Race, Gender and Sexuality in the Colonial Contest*. London: Routledge.

McDonald, H. 2001. *Erotic Ambiguities: The Female Nude in Art*. London: Routledge.

Megaw, R. & Megaw, V. 1989. *Celtic Art from its Beginnings to the Book of Kells*. London: Thames & Hudson.

Megaw, V. 1970. *Art of the European Iron Age*. New York: Harper & Row.

Mellor, R. 1993. *Tacitus*. London: Routledge.

Mendelson, E. ed. 1979. *W.H. Auden. Selected Poems*. London: Faber & Faber.

Merrifield, R. 1983. *London City of the Romans*. London: Batsford.

Michie, J. trans. 1964. *The Odes of Horace*. Harmondsworth: Penguin.

Millar, F. 1964. *A Study of Cassius Dio*. Oxford: Clarendon Press.

Millett, M. 1995. *Roman Britain*. London: English Heritage.

Milton, J. *The History of Britain. That Part Especially, Now Call'd England. From the First Traditional Beginnings, Continu'd to the Norman Conquest.*
www.humanities.ualberta.ca/emls/ieml/work/etexts/histbrit.txt

Mohen, J.-P. 1991. 'The princely tombs of Burgundy', in S. Moscati, O.H. Frey, V. Kruta, B. Raftery & M. Szabó eds *The Celts*. London: Thames & Hudson, 102–7.

Mohen, J.-P., Duval, A. & Eluère, C. 1987. *Trésors des Princes Celtes*. Paris: Éditions de la Réunion des Musées Nationaux.

Moore, R.W. 1954. *The Romans in Britain. A Selection of Latin Texts*. London: Methuen.

Morelli, A. 2005. The Representation of Gender and Sexuality in Roman Art (With Particular Reference to that of Roman Britain). Newport: University of Wales, Newport, unpublished PhD thesis.

Morgan, G. 2000. 'Omens in Tacitus' *Histories* I-III', in R. Lorsch Wildfang & J. Isager eds *Divinations and Portents in the Roman World*. Odense: Odense University Press, 25–42.

Naipaul, V.S. 1980. *The Return of Eva Peron*. London: André Deutsch.

Niblett, R. 1999. *The Excavation of a Ceremonial Site at Folly Lane, Verulamium*. Britannia Monograph Series No. 14. London: Society for the Promotion of Roman Studies.

Niblett, R. 2001. *Verulamium. The Roman City of St Albans*. Stroud: Tempus.

Niblett, R. 2003. 'The chair of the man who became a Roman', *British Archaeology* No. 70, May 2003.

Niblett, R. 2004. 'The native elite and their funerary practices', in M. Todd ed. *A Companion to Roman Britain*. Oxford: Blackwell, 30–41.

Nunn, P.G. 1995. *Problem Pictures: Women and Men in Victorian Painting*. Aldershot: Scolar Press.

O'Connor, D. 1993. *Ancient Nubia: Egypt's Rival in Africa*. Philadelphia: University Museum.

Ogilvie, R.M. 1970. *A Commentary on Livy Books 1-5*. Oxford: Oxford University Press.

O'Gorman, E. 2000. *Irony and Misreading in the Annals of Tacitus*. Cambridge: Cambridge University Press.

Olivier, L. 2003. 'Des Hommes aux Femmes', *Les Chars des Princes et Princesses Celtes. L'Archéologue: Archéologie Nouvelle*. No. 65, Avril-Mai 2003, 12–14.

Olmsted, G.S. 1979. *The Gundestrup Cauldron*. Brussels: Latomus.

O'Rahilly, T.P. 1946. *Early Irish History and Mythology*. Dublin: Institute for Advanced Studies.

Orna-Ornstein, J. 1997. 'Early hoards of denarii from Britain', in R.F. Bland & J. Orna-Ornstein eds *Coin Hoards from Roman Britain*. Vol. 10. London: Routledge, 23–9.

Padel, R. 1993. 'Women: model for possession by Greek daemons', in A. Cameron & A. Kuhrt eds *Images of Women in Antiquity*. London: Routledge.

Page, R. 2005. 'The mad March world of the real Easter bunny', (review of Mason 2005), *Daily Mail* 25 May 2005.

Painter, K.S. 1997. 'Silver hoards from Britain in their late Roman context', *Antiquité Tardive* 5, 93–110.

Parker Pearson, M. 2000. 'Great sites: Llyn Cerrig Bach', *British Archaeology* 53, June 2000, 8–11.

Pascal, C.B. 1964. *The Cults of Cisalpine Gaul*. Brussels: Collection Latomus Vol. LXXV.

Pelletier, A. 1984. *La Femme dans la société gallo-romaine*. Paris: Picard.

Phillips. E.J. 1975. 'The gravestone of M. Favonius Facilis', *Britannia* 6, 102–5.

Piggott, S. 1968. *The Druids*. London: Thames & Hudson.

Portillo, M. 2005. *Things we Forgot to Remember: Events Following the Spanish Armada*, BBC Radio 4, 23 May 2005.

Potter, T. 1986. 'A Roman jeweller's hoard from Snettisham', *Antiquity* 60, 137–9.

Potter, T. 1997. *Roman Britain*. London: British Museum Press.

Potter, T.W. and Johns, C.M. 1992. *Roman Britain*. London: British Museum Press.

Raftery, B. 1991. 'The island Celts', in S. Moscati, O.H. Frey, V. Kruta, B. Raftery & M. Szabó eds *The Celts*. London: Thames & Hudson, 555–72.

Rankin, D. 1996. *Celts and the Classical World*. London: Routledge.

Rasmussen, S.W. 2000. 'Cicero's stand on prodigies. A non-existent dilemma?', in R. Lorsch Wildfang & J. Iseger eds *Divination and Portents in the Roman World*. Odense: Odense University Press, 9–24.

Raven, S. 1969. *Rome in Africa*. London: Evans Brothers.

Riggs, C. 2006. 'Woman of influence, whose mystique reveals a great chink in the historian's armour'. (review of Kleiner 2005), *Times Higher Education Supplement* 6 January 2006, 24–5.

Rivet, A.L.F. 1988. *Gallia Narbonensis. Southern Gaul in Roman Times*. London: Batsford.

Rivet, A.L.F. & Smith, C. 1979. *The Place-Names of Roman Britain*. London: Batsford.

Rodgers, R. 2003. 'Female representation in Roman art: feminising the provincial "Other"', in S. Scott & J. Webster eds *Roman Imperialism and Provincial Art*. Cambridge: Cambridge University Press, 69–93.

Rolley, C. 2003. *La Tombe Princière de Vix*. Paris: Picard.

Ross, A. 1967. *Pagan Celtic Britain*. London: Routledge & Kegan Paul.

Ross, A. 1968. 'Shafts, pits, wells. Sanctuaries of the Belgic Britons?', in J.M. Coles & D.D.A. Simpson eds *Studies in Ancient Europe. Essays Presented to Stuart Piggott*. Leicester: Leicester University Press, 255–85.

Ross, A. 1986. *The Pagan Celts*. London: Batsford.

Rudgley, R. 1993. *The Alchemy of Culture: Intoxicants in Society*. London: British Museum Press.

Rudgley, R. 1999. *The Encyclopaedia of Psychoactive Substances.* London: Abacus.

Rylatt, N. undated. *Lunt Roman Fort.* Coventry: Coventry City Council.

Savory, H.N. 1976. *Guide Catalogue of the Early Iron Age Collections.* Cardiff: National Museum of Wales.

Schofield, J. & Maloney, C. eds 1998. *Archaeology in the City of London 1907–91: A Guide to Records of Excavations by the Museum of London.* London: Museum of London. The Archaeological Gazetteer Series, Vol. 1.

Schoyer Brooks, P. 1990. *Beyond the Myth. The Story of Joan of Arc.* Boston: Houghton Mifflin Company.

Schultes, R.E. , Hofmann, A. & Rätsch, C. 2001. *Plants of the Gods. Their Sacred, Healing and Hallucinogenic Powers.* Rochester, Vermont: Healing Arts Press.

Scott-Kilvert, I. trans. 1965. *Plutarch. Makers of Rome.* Harmondsworth: Penguin.

Scullard, H.H. 1959. *From the Gracchi to Nero. A History of Rome 133 BC–AD 68.* London: Methuen University Paperbacks.

Scullard, H.H. 1979. *Roman Britain. Outpost of the Empire.* London: Thames & Hudson.

Sealey, P.R. 1979. 'The later history of Icenian electrum torcs', *Proceedings of the Prehistoric Society* 45, 165–78.

Sealey, P.R. 1997. *The Boudican Revolt against Rome.* Princes Risborough: Shire Archaeology No. 74.

Sealey, P.R. 2004 (2nd edition). *The Boudican Revolt against Rome.* Princes Risborough: Shire Archaeology No. 74.

Sergeant, J. 2005. *Maggie. Her Fatal Legacy.* London: Macmillan/Pan.

Settis, S., La Regina, A., Agosti, G. & Farinella, V. 1988. *La Colona Traiana.* Turin: Giuilio Einaudi Editore.

Shotter, D. 1998. *Roman Britain.* London: Routledge.

Shotter, D. 2004. 'Vespasian, *auctoritas* and Britain', *Britannia* 35, 1–8.

Sieghart, M.A. 2004. 'Great with children but bad with money', *The Times T2* 6 September 2004, 4.

Simpson, C.J. 1993. 'Once again Claudius and the Temple at Colchester', *Britannia* 24, 1–6.

Simpson, C.J. 1996. 'The statue of Victory at Colchester', *Britannia* 27, 386–7.

Smallwood, M. 1982. *Rome The Augustan Age. Units 15 and 16. Provincial Case Studies II: Judaea.* Milton Keynes: The Open University Press.

Smith, R.R.R. 1987. 'The imperial reliefs from the Sebasteion at Aphrodisias', *Journal of Roman Studies* 77, 88–138.

Snow, P. & Snow, D. 2004. *Battlefield Britain. From Boudicca to the Battle of Britain.* London: BBC Books.

Southern, P. 1999. *Cleopatra.* Stroud: Tempus.

Speidel, M. 1992. *The Framework of an Imperial Legion.* Caerleon: Roman Legionary Museum: The Fifth Annual Caerleon Lecture, 23 September 1992.

Stacey, R. 2004. 'Evidence for the use of birch-bark tar from Iron Age Britain', *PAST* No. 47, July 2004, 1–2.

Standing, G. 2005. 'The Varian disaster and the Boudiccan Revolt: fabled victories', *Britannia* 36, 373–5.

Stead, I.M. 1991. 'The Snettisham Treasure: excavations in 1990', *Antiquity* 65, 447–65.

Stead, I.M., Bourke, J.B. & Brothwell, D. eds 1984. *Lindow Man. The Body in the Bog.* London: British Museum Press.

Stewart, P.C.N. 1995. 'Inventing Britain: the Roman creation and adaptation of an image', *Britannia* 26, 1–10.

Syme, R. 1986. *The Augustan Aristocracy.* Oxford: Oxford University Press/Clarendon Press.

Taylor, L.R. 1931. *The Divinity of the Roman Emperor.* Middletown, Connecticut: American Philological Association.

Taylor, T. 1992. 'The eastern origins of the Gundestrup cauldron', *Scientific American* 266 (3), 66–71.

Taylor, T. 2002 *The Buried Soul. How Humans invented Death.* London: Fourth Estates.

Thatcher, M. 1993. *The Downing Street Years.* London: HarperCollins.

Thatcher, M. 1995. *The Path to Power.* London: HarperCollins.

Thatcher, M. 2002. *Statecraft. Strategies for a Changing World.* London: HarperCollins.

Theroux, P. 1998. *Sir Vidia's Shadow. A Friendship Across Five Continents.* Harmondsworth: Penguin.

Thesiger, W. 1959. *Arabian Sands.* London: Longman Green.

Thomas, C. ed. 2003. *London's Archaeological Secrets. A World City Revealed.* New Haven/London: Yale University Press/Museum of London Archaeology Service.

Thompson, L. & Ferguson, J. 1969. *Africa in Classical Antiquity.* Ibadan: Ibadan University Press.

Todd, M. 2004. 'The Claudian conquest and its consequences', in M. Todd ed. *A Companion to Roman Britain.* Oxford: Blackwell, 42–59.

Todd, M. ed. 2004. *A Companion to Roman Britain.* Oxford: Blackwell.

Tomlin, R.S.O. 1988. 'The curse tablets', in B.W. Cunliffe ed. *The Temple of Sulis Minerva at Bath.* Vol. 2. *The Finds from the Sacred Spring.* Oxford: Oxford University Committee for Archaeology No. 16, 58–277.

Tomlin, R.S.O. 1993. 'The inscribed lead tablets: an interim report', in A. Woodward & P. Leach eds *The Uley Shrines. Excavation of a Ritual Complex on West Hill, Uley, Gloucestershire: 1977-9.* London: English Heritage, 113–30.

Turner, R.C. 1984. 'Discovery and excavation of the Lindow bodies', in I.M. Stead, J.B. Bourke & D. Brothwell eds *Lindow Man. The Body in the Bog.* London: British Museum.

Tyers, P. 1996. *Roman Pottery in Britain.* London: Batsford.

Van Arsdell, R.D. 1989. *Celtic Coinage of Britain.* London: Spink.

Vellacott, P. trans. 1973. *Euripides The Bacchae and Other Plays.* Harmondsworth: Penguin.

Vitebsky, P. 1995. *The Shaman. Voyages of the Soul. Trance, Ecstasy and Healing from Siberia to the Amazon.* London: Macmillan.

Wacher, J. 1987a. *The Roman Empire.* London: Dent.

Wacher, J. ed. 1987b. *The Roman World.* London: Routledge.

Walters, T. 2002. 'Such stowage as these trinkets', in L.H. McAvoy & T. Walters eds *Consuming Narratives: Gender and Monstrous Appetite in the Middle Ages and the Renaissance.* Cardiff: University of Wales Press, 67–80.

Warmington, B.H. 1969. *Nero: Reality and Legend.* London: Chatto & Windus.

Warner, R. trans. 1958. *Plutarch. The Fall of the Republic.* Harmondsworth: Penguin.

Watt, D. 2002. 'Consuming passions in Book VIII of John Gower's *Confessio Amantis*', in L.H. McAvoy & T. Walters eds *Consuming Narratives: Gender and Monstrous Appetite in the Middle Ages and the Renaissance.* Cardiff: University of Wales Press, 28–41.

Watts, D. 2005. *Boudicca's Heirs. Women in Early Britain.* London: Routledge.

Webster, G. 1969. *The Roman Imperial Army.* London: Adam & Charles Black.

Webster, G. 1978. *Boudica.* London: Batsford.

Webster, G. 1980. *The Roman Invasion of Britain.* London: Batsford.

Webster, G. 1981. *Rome Against Caratacus. The Roman Campaigns in Britain AD 48–58.* London: Batsford.

Webster, G. & Dudley, D.R. 1966. *The Roman Conquest of Britain.* London: Batsford.

Webster, J. 1995. 'Roman word-power and the Celtic gods', *Britannia* 26, 153–61.

Webster, J. 1998. 'Druids under a mystic cloak', *British Archaeology* 39, November 1998, 18.

Webster, J. 1999. 'At the end of the world: druidic and other revitalization movements in post-conquest Gaul and Britain', *Britannia* 30, 1–20.

Weir, A. 1996. *Children of England. The Heirs of King Henry VIII.* London: Jonathan Cape.

Wells, P.S. 1995. 'Resources and industry', in M.J. Green ed. 1995. *The Celtic World.* London: Routledge, 213–309.

Wellesley, K. trans. 1964. *Tacitus The Histories.* Harmondsworth: Penguin.

Whiston, W. trans. 1886. *The Works of Flavius Josephus.* London: Nelson.

Whittaker, C.R. trans. 1969. *Herodian.* London: Heineman (Loeb Edition).

Wightman, E.M. 1985. *Gallia Belgica.* London: Batsford.

Wildfang, R. Lorsch & Isager, J. eds 2000. *Divination and Portents in the Roman World.* Odense: Odense University Press.

Wilkinson, W.A.C. & Wilkinson, N.H. eds 1954. *The Dragon Book of Verse.* Oxford: Clarendon Press.

Williams, J.H.C. 2000. 'The silver coins from East Anglia attributed to king Prasutagus of the Iceni – a new reading of the obverse inscription', *Numismatic Chronicle* 160, 276–81.

Winder, R. 2004. *Bloody Foreigners.* London: Abacus.

Wiseman, A. & Wiseman, P. trans. 1980. *The Battle for Gaul. A New Illustrated Translation.* London: Chatto & Windus.

Wood, J. 1997. 'The horse in Welsh folklore: A boundary image in custom and narrative', in S. Davies & N.A Jones eds *The Horse in Celtic Culture. Medieval Welsh Perspectives.* Cardiff: University of Wales Press, 162–82.

Worthington, I. 2004. *Alexander The Great: Man and God.* London: Pearson Longman.

Young, H. 1989. *One of Us. A Biography of Margaret Thatcher.* London: Macmillan.

Index

Abu Graib (or Ghraib) 219
Actium, Battle of 76
Addedomarus 19
Adminius 20, 41, 52, 84
Aedui 4, 84–6, 147, 154, 216
Aeneas 116
Aeneid 12
Africa 74, 75, 76
afterlife (*see* Otherworld)
Agincourt, Battle of 55
Agricola, Gnaeus 48, 130, 134, 172, 223, 228, 234–5
Agrippina 87, 94, 122, 139
Al-Riyashi, Reem Saleh 246
alcohol (*see* ale; beer; wine)
Alde, river 37
ale 65, 228 (*see also* beer)
Alesia, Battle of 6, 211, 212, 243
Alexander the Great 4, 74, 77, 80
Alexandra Salome 80–81
Alexandria 78
Algeria 75
Allen, Derek 23, 71, 72, 209, 212
Almondsbury 129
altar 44, 61, 144
Alveston 164
Amairgin 153
Amazons 46, 95, 116
amber 99
American Dream 134
Ammianus Marcellinus 102
ancestors 16, 25, 27, 58, 59, 146, 164, 173, 191, 212, 228, 232
Ancyra 11
Andate (*see* Andraste)
Andraste 106, 132, 138–9, 152, 154, 189
Anglesey 124, 144, 150–56, 159–60, 175, 177, 191–3, 235
animals xiv, 3, 122, 152, 158, 161, 199–200, 229 (*see also* under individual species)
Antedios 22
Antiochus 73, 74, 82
Antonine Wall 213–14

Antony, Mark (Marcus Antonius) 75–6, 78, 81
Anubis 113
Aphrodisias 45, 47–8, 180
Aphrodite 45
Aquae Sulis (*see* Bath)
Arabia 12
Arch of Claudius 44, 45, 46, 54
Archelaus 77
Ardennes Forest 147
Argentina 46
Århus, University of 95–6
Aristobulus 80, 81
Aristotle 93
Armenia 74, 78–9, 192
Arminius 86–7, 181
Ariovistus 83, 84–6
Artabazus 78
Artaxes 78
Arverni 56, 84
Ashill 24, 161, 187
Asia 74
Athene 104
Athens 122, 154
Atrebates 5–10, 15, 51, 53
atrocities (*see* war-crimes)
Attalus III 74
Auden, W.H. xvi, 254
Augustodunum (*see* Autun)
Augustus 11–14, 17, 20, 27, 36–7, 41, 61–2, 67–8, 70–71, 76–8, 81–2, 86, 122, 137, 176, 181
Priests of (*see* Severi Augustales)
Aulerci Cenomani 23
Ausecus 229
Autun 147

Baghdad (*see* Iraq)
Bard 153
Barnard, Edward 249
Barrett, Anthony 49
Batavians 108, 148–9, 199
Bath 51, 153, 166–7, 232–4
Bédoyère, Guy de la 53
beer 69

Beirut 246
Belgae 9
Bellovaci 4, 10
Ben Hur 246
Berenice 77
Berikos (*see* Verica)
birds 100
Bithynia 74, 131
Blagg, Tom 233
Blair, Cherie 245
Blair, Tony 245
Boadicea xiv, 139, 241, 243–4, 246–7 (*see also* Boudica; Boudican Rebellion)
Bocchus 75
body-paint 123, 157 (*see also* tattoo; woad)
bog, bog-bodies xiv, 95–7, 138, 155–9
Bolton, Edmund 249
Bond, James 93
Bosporus 73
Boudica xiv–xv, 1, 10, 18, 23–4, 27–30, 45, 48, 51–2, 54, 57, 59, 62, 67, 70, 73, 80–1, 87–8, 93–4, 97–9, 104–6, 111–12, 115–16, 120–23, 125, 130–35, 137–40, 145–9, 152, 154–5, 159–60, 162–5, 167, 174, 177–202, 209–12, 215, 221, 225, 228–30, 232–3, 235, 241–6, 248, 250–2
Boudican Rebellion 28, 37, 43, 48, 58, 60–1, 63, 68, 70, 72, 76, 88, 97, 104, 121–2, 127, 131, 134–5, 144, 154, 159–60, 162, 172, 176–202, 209, 211–12, 216, 219, 221, 223–8, 230–1, 234–5, 249, 254
boundaries 28
Bran 152
Braund, David 4, 10, 11, 17, 21, 72, 123
Brennus 201
Bridgeness 213–14
Brigantes 9, 40, 55, 87, 120, 122–4, 126–30, 138
Briggs, Daphne 16
Britannicus 39
Broach, Zowie 251
Brough-under-Stainmore 136
Brougham 94
buckets 104, 165–6
Bucy-le-Long 99
Buddug 247
buggery 46
bull 121
  three-horned 63
burials 19, 21, 22, 25, 28–9, 62–3, 94, 97–9, 100, 113, 129, 156–7, 164–5, 191, 201–2, 209, 217–18, 231
  chariot 97–8, 105, 127

Burnham Market 23
burning 184, 186–7, 191, 196, 209–10, 212, 225, 230–1

Caerleon 51
Caerwent 226
Caesar, Julius xv, 2–11, 20–1, 24, 29–30, 41–2, 55–7, 61, 75, 77–8, 81, 83–5, 97, 106, 127, 135, 137, 144–6, 150, 154, 159–60, 164, 182, 198, 200, 211–12, 219, 235
Caistor St Edmund 24, 225–8
Caledonians 108, 130, 134, 213
calendars, sacred 154
Calgacus 108, 130, 134
Caligula (*see* Gaius)
Cammeringham 249
Camulodunum 19, 25, 29, 40, 42–3, 58–60, 62, 125, 173–4, 181–2, 184, 231 (*see also* Colchester)
Camulos 29, 174
Cannae, Battle of 181
cannibalism 164, 190
Cantii/Cantiaci 5, 9, 13
Caracalla, Emperor 131
Caratacus 21, 41, 52–7, 86, 108, 124–6, 128–30, 140, 210, 243
Cardiff 246–7
Carmarthen 54
Carnutes 162
carnyx 195, 250
Carrhae, Battle of 181
Carthage 181, 184 (*see also* Hannibal)
cart 99–100, 193, 198–9
Cartimandua 55–6, 87–8, 120–30, 133, 138, 140
Carvetii 9
Cassiterides 109, 151
Cassivellaunus 6, 8–10, 13, 18
Catherine of Aragon 100
Cato, Marcus Porcius 184, 219
Catuarus 50–1
Catuvellauni 5, 8–10, 18, 20, 21, 25, 29, 41, 53–8, 159
cauldrons 25, 101, 105, 109, 156
Cenomagni 23
Cerialis, Petillius 149, 185–6, 194, 211, 235, 249
chain-mail 19
chair, curule 19, 21
chariots 8, 93, 97–8, 102, 105, 106, 155–6, 194, 198–9, 246, 250
  burials (*see* burials)
Chartres 162
Chatti 148
Chedworth 104
Cherusci 86

Chichester 49–50, 52, 71, 225–6
Christ 222
Christians 61, 95, 152, 162
Cicero 4, 106, 154, 176
Cilicia 73, 75
Cimbri 109, 152
Civilis, Julius 108, 110–11, 148–9, 199
Clark, Alan 244
Classicianus, Julius Alpinus 215–20, 233
Claudian Invasion 2, 17–18, 20, 22, 29, 38–43, 49, 71, 135, 146, 164–5, 188, 227, 230
Claudius, Emperor xv, 5, 21, 29, 36–9, 41–9, 51, 53–4, 56–62, 73–4, 80, 82, 84, 86, 122–5, 128–9, 137, 163, 165, 173–5, 180, 185–7, 210, 231, 235
Cleopatra 75–8, 87
  Selene 75
Clermont-Ferrand 243
client-kingship 7, 8, 10, 13, 17–20, 23, 48, 50, 53, 67–92, 120, 124–6, 133, 177–8
Cogidubnus (*see* Togidubnus)
coins xv, 7, 13–23, 25–6, 29, 44–5, 53, 71–2, 102, 104, 121, 165, 212, 229–30, 232, 242
  hoards 26, 28, 72, 225
Colchester 29, 37, 40, 42, 51, 58–63, 122, 132, 137, 139–40, 147, 150, 163, 165, 173–4, 179–81, 183, 185–91, 200, 230–1, 242–3, 249–50
  Gilberd School site 187
  Head Street site 187
  Lion Walk site 186
  St Mary's site 186
Collins, Henry and Joyce 242
Cologne 110–11
colonialism xiv, 29, 57, 88, 108, 138, 149, 165, 174, 179, 202, 222
Commagene 73, 74, 82
Commius 5–8, 10, 14–16, 18–19, 41
Communism 25
Compiègne 247
conspiracy 122
Cool, Hilary 95
coral 97–99
Corbulo 192
Corieltavi 5, 9, 23, 73
Cornovii 9
Correus 6
Corsica 60
cosmetic grinders 121
Cottius, Julius 82–3
Coudrot, Jean-Louis 99
Cowper, William 246

Crassus 75, 77, 181
Creighton, John 1, 8, 11, 15–16, 18–19, 164–5
crimes (*see* war-crimes)
cross-dressing 248
Crownthorpe 69
crucifixion 184, 191, 222
Cunliffe, Barry 51, 234
Cunobelinus 1, 2, 18–22, 29, 41–2, 52–3
curation 27
curses (*see defixiones*)
Cymbeline (see Cunobelinus)
Cyzicus 125

Dacia 213–5
Danube, river 12, 74, 83, 95
Davies, Andrew 250
Davies, John 187
decapitation 157, 214, 221
Deceangli 9, 55, 124
Decianus Catus 26, 175–80, 184–5, 215–16, 221–2, 233
decimation 225
defixiones 152
Delphi 110–11, 201
Demetae 9, 54, 192
Dench, Dame Judi 93
Dendera 77
Denmark 158
deposition (see ritual deposition)
Dinéault 103
Dio Cassius xiv–xv, 12–13, 20–1, 27, 38–9, 41–4, 52–3, 73–4, 79, 88, 97, 105–6, 112, 115, 120–2, 130–32, 134–5, 137–40, 152, 172, 175, 180–81, 183, 189–90, 195–6, 198, 201–2, 225, 248–9
Diodorus Siculus 29, 135, 201
Dionysus 115
disability 98
disfigurement (*see* disability)
Diviciacus 84, 86, 106, 154
divination (*see* prophecy)
Dobunni 5, 9, 53, 227, 232
dogs 135, 138, 243
drowning 157
Druids 71, 106, 124, 127, 144–67, 177
Dubnovellaunus 11, 13
Dumnonii 9
Dumnorix 86, 106–7
Durotriges 5, 9, 232
Dwynwen 152

Eceni (*see* Iceni)
Edward the Elder 243
Egypt 61, 71, 76–8, 87, 106, 139

England, Linndie 219
Eleanor of Aquitaine 139, 243
elephants 42, 105, 165
Elizabeth I, Queen 139, 244, 247
Epicharis 123
Epping 249
Esico 72
Esuprastus 71–2
Ethiopia 78
Euphrates, river 74
Euripides 115, 122
Eutropius 38, 41
Eva Perón 46
Exeter 194
exogamy 100

Facilis, Favonius 179
fashion 244, 251
Faunus 163, 229
feasting 156, 189
Feltwell 227
Ferris, Iain 45, 179
film 241, 246
fire (*see* burning)
Fishbourne 50, 51–2
Fishwick, Duncan 60
Florus, Julius 146–7, 149, 216
Folly Lane, Saint Albans 21, 164
Fowler, Chris 191
Fraser, Lady Antonia 245
Frere, Sheppard 210
Frontinus, Sextus Julius 193, 235
Froste, Peter 186

Gaius, Emperor 11, 16, 20, 21, 36–9, 41, 53, 60, 62, 73, 76, 78, 84, 137
Galba 224
Gallus, Cornelius 78
Gaul 1–2, 4–8, 11, 15, 23, 26–7, 39, 42, 56–7, 81, 83–4, 97, 101–2, 104, 107–8, 127, 133, 135–7, 146–7, 151, 153, 158–60, 166–7, 176, 180, 198, 200–1, 211–12, 216–17, 219–20, 224, 233, 234
Gaza 173, 246
genocide 212
Gergovia 211
Germanicus 17–18, 39, 86–7
Germans 6, 20, 44, 84–7, 107, 109–11, 147–9, 158, 181, 198, 209, 219
Gildas 248
gladiators 42, 113
  female 112–15
goddess 101, 104, 110
Godmanchester 198
Goewin 109
goose 103
Gop Hill 248

Gorgon (*see* Medusa)
Gournay-sur-Aronde 15
Graves, Robert 38
Great Chesterford 198
Greer, Germaine 241
Gregory, Tony 226
grove, sacred 132, 140, 144, 150–54, 162, 189–90
gryphons 105
guerrilla warfare 8, 87, 192
Gundestrup 104–6
Gunhild, Queen 95

Hacheston 226
Hadrian, Emperor 38
Hamas 246
Hanging (*see* strangulation)
Hannibal 42, 181
Haraldskaer 95–7
hare 106, 138, 152, 243
Harpy 116
Harudes 84
Haruspex 152
Hasmoneans 80
Hayling Island temple 14–16
healing 109, 159, 166, 232–3
Helena, Queen 243
Helvetii 216
Henig, Martin 49–51, 164
Henry V 55
Henry VIII 100
Hermundurians 84
Herod 50, 67, 70, 73, 80–2
Herodian xiv, 3
Hezbollah 246
Hill, J.D. 14–15
Hingley, Richard 3, 164, 244
Hirschlanden 102
Hirtius, Aulus 6–8
hoards 26, 28, 163, 225, 228–9
Hockwold 25–6, 69, 228
Hollywood 241
Horace 11–12
horse 22–3, 28–9, 72, 94–5, 123, 127, 140, 174, 187, 212
horse-harness 25, 29, 97, 155–6, 161, 212
horsemen 29–30, 101, 174, 198–9, 212–3
horsewomen 95
hostages 84–5, 96, 107, 111, 147, 158 (*see also* obsides)
Hoxne 229
Hungary 100
Hvass, Lone 95
Hyrcanus 80–1

Iachimo 1
Iceni xv, 2, 5, 8–9, 18, 22–29, 48, 68,

70–3, 81, 83, 88, 97, 115, 120, 130, 137–8, 150, 161–3, 173–4, 177–9, 183–7, 195, 200, 212, 221–2, 225–8, 230, 233, 241, 246, 248–9
Imperial Cult 44, 49, 58–62, 147, 173–5 (*see also* Severi Augustales)
imperial estates 218, 227
imperialism 214 (*see also* colonialism)
incest 221
India 3
Indus, Julius 216
Ipswich 27
Iraq 74, 182, 219
Ireland 158, 162
Islam 147, 246
Israel 246

Jason 116
Jeffries, Stuart 241, 244
jihad 147
Joan of Arc 247–8
Josephus, Flavius 80–2
Jove (*see* Jupiter)
Juba 75–6
Judaea 50, 61, 67, 70, 80–2
Julia Domna 131
Jupiter 12, 148, 223
Juvenal 112, 114

Kelvedon 29–30, 174
Kingston, Alex 250
Kipling, Rudyard 3
Kirkby, Brian 251

La Tène 98, 155
Labienus 6
Latin language 7, 18, 60, 125, 234–5
Lefthandedness 104
Lemington 100, 104
Lesenho 102
Lexden 19
lignite 99
limitatio 227
Lincoln 185, 194
Lindow Moss 155–60
Livia 36, 122
Llandeilo 54
Lloyd George, David 246
Llyn Cerrig Bach 155–6, 159, 164
Loire, river 151
London 51,115, 122, 131–4, 137, 150, 162, 181, 187–92, 196, 200, 216–17, 230–1, 233
  City of 191
  Eastcheap 190
  Gresham Street 188
  King's Cross 249

Lombard Street 218
Parliament Hill Fields 249
Southwark 113, 115
Tower Hill 217
Longinus 174
Longthorpe 185
Lucan 146, 154
Lugdunum 190
Lunt 212–13

Mabinogi 109
Macdonald, Philip 155–6
Maddox, Brenda 244
Madonna 241
magic 127, 150, 181
manacles 25–6
Mancetter 196–7
Mandubracius 8, 10, 16, 20, 24, 41, 84
Manley, John 7, 14–15
March, Cambs., 26
Marius 176
Mars 36, 43
marsh (*see* bog)
Martial 3
Mary, Queen 247
Massilia 154
Mauretania 75–6, 192
Medugenus 163, 229
Medusa 114–16, 166–7, 233
Mela, Pomponius 38–9, 109, 151–2
Melsonby 129
Memor, Lucius 152
Mercury 113, 166
Merrifield, Ralph 188
Messalina 39, 122, 128, 139
Millar, Fergus 131
Milton, John 248
Minerva 49, 50, 104, 166, 233–4 (*see also* Sulis Minerva)
mirrors 97–8
mistletoe 159
Mithras 79
Mithridates 73, 74
Mona (*see* Anglesey)
monsters 17–19, 116
Mont Lassois 98–9
Morgan, Gwyn 182
Morocco 75
Mount Bures 63
mutiny 225

Naipaul, V.S. 46
nakedness 96, 157, 158, 213
Napoleon III 243
Narbonne 61
Narcissus 136, 180
Nasica, Caesius 127

Navan 15
Near East 73, 74
Needham 71
Neptune 49–50
Nero, Emperor xv, 26, 30, 38, 50, 51, 57,
     60, 62, 68, 70, 72, 78–9, 81, 115–16,
     122–4, 126, 135, 139, 148, 151, 160,
     190, 192, 210, 212, 215, 220–21,
     223–4, 229–30, 232–3, 235, 248
Nervii 200, 211–12
Netherlands 158
New Testament 222
New York 251
Niblett, Rosalind 231
Nicaea 131
Nicomedes IV 74
Nile, river 12, 78
Norfolk Wolf (see wolf)
Norwich 245, 249–50
numerus 94–5
Numidia 75
nuncupatio 44

O'Gorman, Ellen 48, 93–4, 108
obsides 19, 41, 67
Oceanus 2, 4, 19, 21, 39, 44, 123–4, 133,
     137, 149, 180, 233
Octavian (see Augustus)
Odysseus 116
omens (see prophecy)
Oracle, Delphic 110–11
oratio obliqua 57, 133, 172, 175, 195
Ordovices 9, 55
Orléans 247
Osmanthorpe 129
Otherworld 19, 21, 109, 152
Otho 182–3, 224
Ovid 3, 10

Painter, Kenneth 161
Palestine 73, 80–1, 245
Pamphylia 74
Parisii 9
Parthia 12, 74, 79, 181
Paulerspury 196
Pegasus 19, 190
Pelletier, André 99
Pergamum 74
Persians 150
personhood 191
Pharos 21
Philodemus 4
Pilate, Pontius 222
pilgrimage 15, 164
Piso, Calpurnius 122
Plautius, Aulus 38, 40–1, 48, 52–3, 55,
     125, 136

Pliny 146, 150, 159
Plutarch 2–3, 56–7, 219
Poenius Postumus 194
poison 201
Polemo 73, 82
Polyclitus 135, 220
Pompey 74, 75, 77, 80–1, 154, 176
Pontus 74, 77, 82
pork 98
Portillo, Michael 43
Prado, Madrid 114
Praetorian Guard 36, 56
Prasutagus 23, 26, 40, 67–72, 77, 80–1, 83,
     87–8, 115, 137, 177–8, 180, 221, 228
Preiddeu Annwfn 109
priests 51, 62, 96, 99, 144–67, 173 (see
     also Druids; Severi Augustales)
priestesses 96, 99–101, 109, 111
Proculus, Aulus Vicirius 43–4
procurators 26, 175–6, 184, 215–16,
     218–19
Propertius 3
prophecy 99, 106–7, 109–11, 132–3,
     148–9, 152, 160, 180–83, 201
prostitution 248
Ptolemy 76–7, 80
pyre, funeral 21–2

Quintillian 27

rape 45–7, 115, 172, 177, 179–80, 190,
     194, 221–2
Raven, Susan 75
Ravenna 86
rebirth (see reincarnation)
Receptus, Calpurnius 51
Redones 102
Regni 9
reincarnation 145–6
Reinheim 100, 102, 105
religion 58, 122, 127, 145–6, 150, 158–9,
     162–5, 234 (see also ritual;
     sanctuaries)
Remi 6, 102
Rennes 102–3
Res Gestae 11, 13, 76
Rex, title 15, 18, 50, 71, 88
Rheims 6, 102
Rhine, river 74, 84, 86, 148
Ribera, Jusepe de 114
Richborough 40
Riigina, Dea 104
ritual 127, 140, 145, 150, 152, 159–61
  curation 27
  damage 15, 28, 174, 228
  deposits 15, 25–6, 28, 155–7, 161, 174,
     187, 191

Roma 62, 190
Rossington Bridge 129
Ruanda 189
Rusellae, Etruria 44

sacrifice, human 21–2, 95–7, 109–10,
    144–5, 151–2, 156–60, 164, 189–90
Sacrovir, Julius 146–7, 149, 216
Saddam Hussein 182
Saham Toney 24, 160–2, 187, 212, 226
St Albans (*see* Verulamium)
St Clare's Drive 63
St John Stevas, Norman 244
St Paul 222
Salassi 13
salt 73
Sambre, river 6
Samnitae 151–2
sanctuaries 14–16, 22, 25, 49–50, 58–62,
    111, 137, 144, 147, 151, 153–5,
    159–64, 166–7, 173–5, 177, 185–6,
    189, 212, 231–5, 250
Sanders, Emily 139, 243
Saturn 136
Saturnalia 136
Scapula, Ostorius 48–9, 55, 70, 88,
    124–5, 160–1
Scheldt, river 200
Scilly Isles (*see* Cassiterides)
Scythia 12
Sealey, Paul 24, 72, 162–3, 200, 202, 225
Segestes 86
Sedgeford 24, 27–8, 73, 162, 184, 212,
    226
seer (*see* prophecy)
Segusio 83
Seleucid dynasty 80
Seleucus 74
Selous 246
Semiramis 139
Seneca, Lucius Annaeus 60, 71, 73, 88,
    123–4, 137, 147, 175
Sentius, Gnaeus 38
Sequani 84–5
Sergeant, John 245
Severi Augustales 43–4, 173–4
sexual violence 45–7, 180, 221 (*see also*
    buggery; rape)
shackles 25, 180 (*see also* manacles;
    slaves)
Shakespeare, William 1–2, 55
shamans 98, 100, 127, 153, 229 (*see also*
    priests)
shape-shifting 100, 109, 127, 229
Sheepen 25–6, 180
Sicily 176
Sieghart, Mary Ann 245

Silchester 52, 226
Silures 9, 54–5, 125, 138, 226
Simpson, C.J. 60, 182
Sirens 116
slaves/slavery 26, 57, 75, 111, 123,
    135–7, 155–6, 173, 175, 178, 180,
    183, 194, 196, 200, 212, 219–20
smithing 26, 155–6
Snettisham 26–7, 229
Snow, Peter and Dan 198
solutio 44
Somme, river 6
soothsayer (*see* prophecy)
Soviet Union 25
Spain 12, 60, 147, 220
Spanish Armada 43
stags 101
Standing, Giles 182
Stanway 25, 29, 62–3
Stanwick 129
Stonea 24, 73, 160
Stonehenge 249
Strabo 11–13, 26, 75, 77, 109, 110, 135,
    151–2
strangulation 95–6, 123, 157–8, 184, 191
Strettweg 100–1
Sudan 210
Suessiones 4, 6
Suetonius (the writer), 20, 36, 38–9,
    42–3, 67, 112–13, 210
Suetonius Paulinus 28, 71, 76, 97, 106,
    133–5, 144, 150–1, 153, 159–61,
    172, 178, 183–5, 187, 189, 191–7,
    199, 200, 202, 209–13, 215, 219–21,
    223, 225, 235, 242–3
suicide bombers 245–6, 254
Sulis (Minerva), 51, 152, 166, 232–3
Sulla 176
Sybil, Cumaean 110
Syme, Ronald 106
Syria 80

Tacitus xiv, 17, 22, 43, 48–9, 53, 55–60,
    62, 68, 70–1, 86–8, 93–4, 97, 107–9,
    110–11, 112–13, 120–35, 138, 140,
    144–52, 155–6, 172–3, 175, 177,
    179, 181–5, 187, 189, 191–6, 198–9,
    200, 201, 209–10, 215–16, 218,
    220–5, 227, 234–5, 241
Tara 162
Taranis 153
Tarpeian Rock 221
Tasciovanus 13, 18–20
tattoo xiv, 3
taxation 134–5, 137, 145, 147, 176–7,
    183, 216
Taylor, Timothy 158

temples (see sanctuaries)
Tencteri/Tencteridae 110, 219
terrets (see horse-harness)
terrorism 254
Teutoberg Forest 87, 181
Thames, river 8, 13, 18, 42, 53, 133, 177,
    180–1, 188, 230
Thatcher, Margaret 244–5, 150
Thesiger, Wilfrid 221
Thetford 24, 71, 163, 228
    Fison Way 73, 261–2, 164, 184, 226–7
Thomas, J. Havard 246–7
Thornycroft, Thomas 246
Thrace 74
Thusnelda 87
Tiber, river 182
Tiberius, Emperor 1, 11, 17, 20, 36–8, 41,
    49, 147, 221
Tigranes 78
Tigris, river 12
tin 99
Tincomarus 11, 13–16, 18–19, 41, 76
Tiridates 78–9
Togidubnus 48–53, 68, 71, 83, 86, 138,
    177–8
Togodumnus 21, 41, 52–3
tombstones 51, 174, 216–18, 233
torcs 14, 26–7, 99, 100, 102, 105, 106,
    130, 140, 214, 229
torture 123, 190
Toutatis 30
Trajan's Column 213–14
Trebellius Maximus 222–4, 231, 235
Treveri 147, 216, 233
Trinovantes xv, 2, 5, 8–10, 13, 18, 20,
    22–6, 28–9, 41, 58–9, 61–3, 137–8,
    147, 159, 167, 173–5, 180, 183–7,
    189, 231
Tunisia 75
Turpilianus, Publius Petronius 222–4,
    235

Uley 153
Ultima Thule 38
USA 74, 219 (see also American
    Dream)
Unwin, Christina 244
Usipites 219

Varus 86–7, 181, 186
Vegetius, Flavius 193
Veleda 100–11, 149
Vellocatus 129
Venutius 122, 126–30, 133, 138
Vercingetorix 6, 54, 56–7, 211, 243
Vergentorix (see Vercingetorix)
Verica 7, 16–17, 21, 41, 50, 53–4, 84
Verlamion 18, 29
Verres 176
Verulamium 18, 21, 52, 122, 137, 150,
    187, 191, 198, 200, 230–2, 234, 249
Vespasian, Emperor 111, 182
Vestal Virgins 122
Vettius Bolanus 224
Victory, goddess of 44, 132, 154, 181–2,
    189
Victoria, Queen 139, 246
Virgil 12
virginity 109, 115, 180, 194 (see also
    Vestal Virgins)
Vitellius 148, 224
Vix 98–102, 105, 202
Volcae Tectosages 26
Vologeses 79
votive offerings 15, 26, 232
vow 44

Walbrook, river 188
Waldalgesheim 99–100, 105
war crimes 178–9, 200, 219, 221
war-trumpets (see *carnyx*)
Wardy Hill 227
Webster, Graham 53, 124
Webster, Jane 148–9, 153
Wellesley, Kenneth 108
Westminster Abbey 162
Wetwang 97–8, 202
Winchester 226
    hoard 14–15
wine 69, 99, 135, 138, 163–5, 188, 201,
    228–9
witchcraft 248
woad 3
wolf 22–4, 105, 138, 241–3
    'Norfolk Wolf', 23, 242–3

Xena, Warrior Princess 241